FOUNDATIONS OF GRAMMAR

Also available from Bloomsbury

UNDERSTANDING LANGUAGE: A BASIC COURSE IN LINGUISTICS,
Elizabeth Winkler and Trini Stickle

ADVANCED ENGLISH GRAMMAR: A LINGUISTIC APPROACH,
Ilse Depraetere and Chad Langford

ENGLISH: AN ESSENTIAL GRAMMAR,
Gerald Nelson

RHETORICAL GRAMMAR: GRAMMATICAL CHOICES, RHETORICAL EFFECTS,
Martha J. Kolln & Loretta S. Gray

FOUNDATIONS OF GRAMMAR

BEYOND STANDARDIZED AMERICAN ENGLISH

Trini Stickle and Veronika Drake

BLOOMSBURY ACADEMIC
LONDON • NEW YORK • OXFORD • NEW DELHI • SYDNEY

BLOOMSBURY ACADEMIC

Bloomsbury Publishing Plc, 50 Bedford Square, London, WC1B 3DP, UK
Bloomsbury Publishing Inc, 1359 Broadway, New York, NY 10018, USA
Bloomsbury Publishing Ireland, 29 Earlsfort Terrace, Dublin 2, D02 AY28, Ireland

BLOOMSBURY, BLOOMSBURY ACADEMIC and the Diana logo are trademarks of
Bloomsbury Publishing Plc

First published in Great Britain 2026

Copyright © Trini Stickle and Veronika Drake, 2026

Trini Stickle and Veronika Drake have asserted their right under the Copyright,
Designs and Patents Act, 1988, to be identified as Authors of this work.

For legal purposes the Acknowledgments on p. xii constitute an
extension of this copyright page.

Cover design: Jade Barnett
Cover image © akinbostanci / Getty Images

All rights reserved. No part of this publication may be: i) reproduced or transmitted in any form, electronic or mechanical, including photocopying, recording or by means of any information storage or retrieval system without prior permission in writing from the publishers; or ii) used or reproduced in any way for the training, development or operation of artificial intelligence (AI) technologies, including generative AI technologies. The rights holders expressly reserve this publication from the text and data mining exception as per Article 4(3) of the Digital Single Market Directive (EU) 2019/790.

Bloomsbury Publishing Plc does not have any control over, or responsibility for, any third-party websites referred to or in this book. All internet addresses given in this book were correct at the time of going to press. The author and publisher regret any inconvenience caused if addresses have changed or sites have ceased to exist, but can accept no responsibility for any such changes.

A catalogue record for this book is available from the British Library.

A catalog record for this book is available from the Library of Congress.

ISBN: HB: 978-1-3504-6287-8
PB: 978-1-3504-6286-1
ePDF: 978-1-3504-6288-5
eBook: 978-1-3504-6289-2

Typeset by Integra Software Services Pvt. Ltd.
Printed and bound in Great Britain

For product safety related questions contact productsafety@bloomsbury.com.

To find out more about our authors and books visit www.bloomsbury.com
and sign up for our newsletters.

CONTENTS

List of Illustrations	viii
Preface	ix
Acknowledgments	xii
List of Abbreviations	xiii

1 Which Englishes Do You Speak? — 1
- 1.1 Introduction — 2
- 1.2 Grammar: What Does It Mean? — 3
- 1.3 Diversity and Equality: Language, Dialect, Variety — 3
- 1.4 Grammar and Grammar: Describing or Prescribing Language Use? — 8
- 1.5 Language Acquisition and Grammar: The Brain, Community, and Language — 13
- 1.6 Why Study Grammars of American English Dialects? Knowledge Not Just for Teachers — 14
- 1.7 An Overview of Grammatical Dialect Features — 16

2 Toward a Linguistic Foundation for Grammar — 25
- 2.1 Introduction: What's a Word? — 26
- 2.2 Fundamentals of Morphology: Derivation and Inflection — 29
- 2.3 How Words Hang Together 1: Phrases — 33
- 2.4 Constituents and How to Identify Them — 36
- 2.5 How Words Hang Together 2: Sentences — 40
- 2.6 How Words Hang Together 3: Clauses — 43
- 2.7 The Grammatical Hierarchy — 44

3 Not Just "Things:" The Noun — 49
- 3.1 Introduction — 50
- 3.2 Disassembling the Parts: Analysis of Morphological Features — 50
- 3.3 Just Playing the Role: Analysis of Syntactic Features — 58

4 Enter Modifiers for Detail: Part 1—Adjectives — 67
- 4.1 Introduction — 68
- 4.2 Disassembling the Parts: Analysis of Morphological Features — 68
- 4.3 Just Playing the Role: Analysis of Syntactic Features — 78

Contents

5	**Enter Modifiers for Detail: Part 2—Adverbs**	87
	5.1 Introduction	88
	5.2 Adverbs—Semantics	90
	5.3 Disassembling the Parts: Analysis of Morphological Features	93
	5.4 Just Playing the Role: Analysis of Syntactic Features	98
6	**(Em)Powering the Clause: The Verb**	105
	6.1 Introduction	106
	6.2 Disassembling the Parts: Analysis of Morphological Features	107
	6.3 Just Playing the Role: Analysis of Syntactic Features	117
7	**Lending a Helping Hand: The Auxiliary Verb**	129
	7.1 Introduction	130
	7.2 Primary Auxiliary Verbs	130
	7.3 Modal Auxiliary Verbs	133
	7.4 Auxiliary Verbs and Their Superpowers	138
8	**Respectfully Replacing Nouns: The Pronoun**	149
	8.1 Introduction	150
	8.2 Types of Pronouns	152
9	**Connecting Everything: Functional Word Categories**	169
	9.1 Introduction	170
	9.2 Determiners	170
	9.3 Relationship Builders: Prepositions	175
	9.4 Conjunctions and Coordinators: Equality and Inequality in Connection	177
	9.5 Numerals and Interjections	181
	9.6 Word Classes—Taking Stock	183
10	**How Words Stick Together: The Case for Phrases**	187
	10.1 Introduction	188
	10.2 Noun Phrase {NP}	189
	10.3 Adjective Phrase {AdjP}	200
	10.4 Adverb Phrase {AdvP}	203
	10.5 Prepositional Phrase {PP}	207
	10.6 An Intermezzo: A Very Long {NP}	211
	10.7 Verb Phrase {VP}	212
11	**How Phrases Stick Together: Sentence Patterns**	219
	11.1 Introduction: Revisiting Some of the Basics	220
	11.2 Sentence Patterns	223

12	**Time and Time Again: Tense, Aspect, Finiteness**	245
	12.1 Introduction	246
	12.2 Simple Tenses	247
	12.3 Progressive (aka Continuous) Aspect	248
	12.4 Perfect (aka Completive) Aspect	252
	12.5 Complex Tense and Aspect	256
	12.6 Variation in Aspect	258
13	**Are You Talkin' to Me? Mood and Voice**	271
	13.1 The Three Moods of English: Introduction	272
	13.2 What Is Grammatical Voice?	279
	13.3 Finiteness	286
14	**To Be or Not to Be: Coordination/Subordination**	295
	14.1 Introduction	296
	14.2 Coordination	297
	14.3 Subordination	299
	14.4 Non-finite Clauses	312
	14.5 When Embedded Clauses Violate Grammar	320
15	**Stop, Pause, Consider: The Role of Punctuation**	327
	15.1 Introduction	328
	15.2 End Punctuation	330
	15.3 Commas (,)	331
	15.4 Semicolons (;)	337
	15.5 Colons (:)	339
	15.6 Bonus: A Note on the Em-dash	340
Glossary		344
Bibliography		351
Index		358

ILLUSTRATIONS

Figures

1.1	Dialect Regions in the United States	5
2.1	Grammatical Hierarchy	45
10.1	{NP} Dogs	205
10.2	Grammatical Hierarchy	206
10.3	Embedded Phrases	211

Tables

1.1	Grammatical features related to nouns, adjectives, and adverbs	16
1.2	Grammatical features related to prepositions and pronouns	17
1.3	Grammatical features related to verbs	17
1.4	Grammatical features related to sentence structure/syntax	19

PREFACE

This book introduces you to the study of grammar. It does so in a linguistically grounded way that presents grammatical features of various American English dialects. It will equip you to analyze language, language that you use yourself, and the language you encounter every day. Just to be clear, this is not a usage guide telling you how you should or shouldn't use language. If you're looking for rigid rules such as "Don't start a sentence with 'and'" or "Don't end a sentence with a preposition," this is not that book. In fact, we take to task such arbitrary and, if not downright silly, very nitpicky rules! Instead, this book presents a descriptive approach to grammar that will enable you to understand and analyze language patterns.

In fact, many grammar rules are arbitrary. That is, they are not reflective of how speakers (or writers) use grammar. For example, you may have been required to memorize such proclamations as "verbs are actions and nouns are things." Such descriptions are imprecise and/or incomplete. You may have been prohibited from using the passive voice and banned from using a sentence in a form like this: "The window was broken." Such arbitrary rules are also of limited use. The study of grammar that we present is different in that you'll uncover systematic patterns that lead to descriptive rules such as "Subjects come before verbs" or "Pronouns replace entire noun phrases." Studying grammar is also a little bit like a puzzle. This book will empower you to figure out how the language pieces fit together to make a phrase, a clause, or a sentence. And, we hope you'll have fun doing it!

Naturally, since this is a grammar book, we include lots of information ranging from word classes (often called "parts of speech") and phrases to clauses and sentences. We provide you with many tests so that you may identify grammatical units such as word classes (nouns, verbs, adjectives, adverbs, and so on) and phrases (noun phrases, adverb phrases, and so on) as well as syntactic functions such units play in a sentence (subject, direct object, and so on).

From this exploration, you will discover the underlying system for the various grammatical patterns that exist in the grammars of American Englishes. And, while you'll learn those things in just about any grammar book, we provide examples taken from various American English dialects. There is not just one English grammar but many. This is why we use the plural form "Englishes"—yes, it is intentional! You'll encounter examples from both so-called standardized American English dialects and so-called non-standardized American English dialects, including Appalachian English, Southern American English, Chicano English, Midwestern English, African-American English, Pittsburghese, New England English, and others. In this way, we highlight the richness of linguistic diversity in the United States, making space for American English dialects to be understood as grammatically valid and appreciated as legitimate dialects rather than marginalized ones. Not only will you be able to see and understand grammatical patterns of these dialects, you'll also be able to discern that all American English dialects are patterned, that they are systematic.

This underscores that no dialect is "broken" (and no dialect speakers are "lazy"!). All dialects follow systematic grammatical patterns. This approach shows an appreciation for all dialect variations and, consequently, their speakers, including speakers of non-standardized dialects who have too often been ignored or, worse, devalued. Our book challenges the conventional view that there is only one "correct" way to use language, supporting a broader acceptance of linguistic diversity. We believe that an understanding of non-standardized dialects as being equally grammatical as standardized dialects is crucial because non-standardized dialects have been stigmatized. Features such as "I'm done my homework," "I ain't got no time," and "I might could do that for you" are often considered less prestigious than others, and by extension, people who use such features are often met with bias, prejudice, and discrimination. Our goal is to help dismantle such stigmatization by showing that all dialects are equally grammatical. The realization that all dialects are systematic, that non-standardized American English features are grammatical rather than mistakes, and that language (and by extension all dialects) constantly changes is a first but crucial step in gaining linguistic awareness that in turn will help reduce linguistic bias, prejudice, and discrimination. At least that is our hope!

We do not assume that you have any prior knowledge about grammar, word classes, phrase structure rules, and sentence patterns. We introduce terms and concepts slowly in small bites. We often introduce a concept in a basic way early on and then come back to that concept in later chapters, building on what you've learned while at the same time solidifying and expanding your learning step-by-step. Thus, our approach is iterative.

Each chapter features loads of examples. Many of the standardized English examples are invented by us. We did not, however, invent examples to illustrate non-standardized English dialects, simply because while we are familiar with these dialects' main features, we are by no means experts in those dialects. Examples of non-standardized dialects are taken from published work by experts as well as from corpora, which represent language usage of regular people. All of these examples—data sets, really—are super important! Don't skip over them! In fact, we invite you to work through each data set, each example, as if you were a language detective. Make any and all observations about a data set you can—no observation is ever too small. We generally *italicize* certain portions of the examples and tell you what you may want to focus on for each, assisting you in your investigation of descriptive grammar rules. We use data sets because grammar features are best illustrated by examples and because they allow you to observe patterns first-hand.

You'll also find many in-text exercises that are meant for you to solidify what you've learned. It's one thing to read through a chapter, work through the examples, and take in all the information; it's quite another to apply what you're learning! The companion website features many additional exercises, so make sure you check it often. You can also find the answer key to all exercises on the website. If an answer is different, go back to the chapter's section and re-read it. Of course, you'll want to ask your instructor in class for more explanation. If you have a question, most likely, your peers in class will have similar questions and they might be relieved that you asked it! If you find yourself drawn to a particular topic, check out the accompanying website for further recommended readings and ideas for projects. You may end up finding a great topic for a research paper!

We hope that you'll find this approach to grammar—grounded in linguistic and systematic patterns—engaging and, with all hope, fun! Taking apart a sentence from its sentence pattern all the way down to the level of word classes is an analytic feat that we hope you find rewarding. We also hope that you'll be fascinated by the features and patterns of the various American English dialects that are represented in this book. As you work through the pages of this book, we invite you to challenge preconceived notions about language. Embrace the diversity of dialects and allow their unique structures and expressions to deepen your understanding of grammar. This is not just a conventional grammar text; it is a dialect-inclusive guide to understanding language structure from a linguistic perspective.

We would be remiss not to reference the wealth of published work on a variety of dialects. Without the scholars and researchers who have published on dialects, this book would not have been possible. Examples from published work are always cited, and while we can't name all experts we draw from here, we want to acknowledge at least some of them now. The *Corpus of Regional African American Language*[1] which is housed by the University of Oregon (https://oraal.uoregon.edu/coraal) features not just corpora of African American Language but also educational and ready-to-use materials for teachers. The online resource, *Yale Grammatical Diversity Project: English in North America* (https://ygdp.yale.edu/), is like no other. Many of our examples come from this invaluable compilation of dialect features across North America. In addition, we have drawn from work by experts in their fields. For AAE, authors include Lisa Green, April Baker-Bell, Geneva Smitherman, H. Samy Alim, Teaira McMurtry, Vershawn Ashanti Young, William Labov, and others. For ChE, authors include Carmen Fought, Robert Bayley, and Otto Santa Ana. For AE, authors include Walt Wolfram and Donna Christian. This list is by no means complete but provides a glimpse into the robust research on dialects and their grammar features that are front and center in this book.

ACKNOWLEDGMENTS

We thank our own educators who have taught us from undergraduate coursework to our doctoral work. They opened the world of linguistics to us and instilled in us a love for all things language.

We also thank our students at Western Kentucky University and Saginaw Valley State University who routinely question why the study of grammar is so stuffy and why it relies on this mythical, abstract idea of Standard English. Our students often question why some language feature is considered ungrammatical when they themselves and/or the communities they belong to in fact use that very feature. Similarly, students often comment on how they were previously taught bits and pieces of a nitpicky mix of grammar rules, and from that experience, they had become quite insecure about which forms to use. Developed from our shared classroom approaches, this book is our attempt to address such questions and concerns by grounding the study of grammar in a linguistic, descriptive approach that includes examples from major dialects of American English. We hope that many of our students and readers elsewhere can see their dialects (and themselves!) represented in this book.

Of course, a book such as this would not be possible without feedback from reviewers. We thank them for their thoughtful questions and excellent suggestions, all of which helped propel this book forward. A special, two-fold, *thank you* goes to the extraordinary Dr. Teaira McMurtry! Not only did she lend her expertise to this project by thoughtfully reviewing most of the African American English examples in this book, she also served as one of the reviewers for the manuscript. Her work and her detailed suggestions were tremendously helpful as we finalized our manuscript. Thank you!

Similarly, this text would not have been possible without the help and speedy replies from Bloomsbury's editors and staff! Thank you to Sarah MacDonald, our first contact at Bloomsbury, for sharing our excitement and enthusiasm for this project. Thank you to Laura Gallon, our editor, for patiently answering the many, many questions we had for her and for guiding us through the process from drafting the manuscript all the way to publication.

Finally, we thank our husbands for all their support throughout the past few years as we've drafted, revised, reorganized, and revised—yet again—several iterations of this text.

ABBREVIATIONS

A—Adverbial
AAE—African American English
AAL—African American Language
AC—Adverbial Complement
ADJ—Adjective
AdjP—Adjective Phrase
ADV—Adverb
AdvP—Adverb Phrase
AE—Appalachian English
ASL—American Sign Language
aux—auxiliary verb
CC—Coordinating Conjunction
ChE—Chicano English
Det/DET—Determiner
DO—Direct Object
ECE—East Coast English
F—Finite
IO—Indirect Object
HPE—Hawaiian Pidgin English
LAD—Language Acquisition Device
MAE—Mainstream American English
ME—Midwest English
mod—modal verb
mv—main verb
N—Noun
NEE—North East English
NF—non-finite
non-sE—non-standardized English
NP—Noun Phrase

Abbreviations

OC—Object Complement
OE—Ozark English
OP—Object of the Preposition
PC—Prepositional Complement
POST—Postmodifier
PP—Prepositional Phrase
PRE—Premodifier
prep/PREP—Preposition
S—Subject
SAE—Southern American English
SC—Subject Complement
sE—Standardized English
SE—Standard English
SUB—Subordinator
S-V—Subject–Verb
S-V-A—Subject–Verb–Adverbial
S-V-AC—Subject–Verb–Adverbial Complement
S-V-DO—Subject–Verb–Direct Object
S-V-IO-DO—Subject–Verb–Indirect Object–Direct Object
S-V-DO-OC—Subject–Verb–Direct Object–Object Complement
S-V-SC—Subject–Verb–Subject Complement
SVO—Subject–Verb–Object
UG—Universal Grammar
V—Verb
VP—Verb Phrase
WSE—White Southern English

Note

1. Kendall and Farrington, 2023.

CHAPTER 1
WHICH ENGLISHES DO YOU SPEAK?

Overview

This chapter introduces our approach to studying the grammar of American Englishes. This approach provides you with foundational knowledge about grammar and an understanding of grammatical differences across various American English dialects. This means that so-called non-standardized and so-called standardized American English dialects are considered on equal footing. An overview of dialect features that appear throughout this book is also provided. This approach shows an appreciation for all dialect variations and, consequently, their speakers, including speakers of non-standardized dialects who have too often been ignored or, worse, devalued. Our objectives are as follows. You'll be able to

- present a linguistically grounded rationale for studying standardized and non-standardized American English dialects;
- explain what the terms *grammar*, *dialect*, *variety*, and *language* mean;
- explain the difference between prescriptive and descriptive grammar;
- outline basic concepts about language acquisition and syntactic theories;
- gauge your familiarity with key grammar features across dialects; and
- explore applications of language knowledge and analytical skills.

> **Pre-reading tasks**
>
> 1. What kinds of associations do you have with the term "grammar"? Have you studied grammar in college or K-12? What do you know about grammar?
> 2. Which dialect(s) of English do you speak?
> 3. You hear the following two statements. Describe your impressions of Speaker A and Speaker B (i.e., their ages, levels of education, professions, personalities, etc.) based on the two statements.
>
>   Speaker A: I ain't got no time.
>   Speaker B: I don't have any time.
>
> 4. Do you agree with the following statement? Why? Why not?
>
>   There is one, and only one, correct way of using the English language.

Foundations of Grammar

1.1 Introduction

You may have either encountered or you may be actively using all or some of the following examples: *The car needs washed*,[1] *I'm done my homework*,[2] and *He don't be barking at nobody*.[3] Even if you're using these grammatical constructions yourself or if you've only heard them, you probably didn't expect them as the very first examples in a book about American English grammar! These constructions are generally considered to be examples of so-called non-mainstream English dialects, and as such, tend not to be included in grammar books. The first expression, *The car needs washed*, is common in areas including Eastern Ohio, Western Pennsylvania, Central Indiana, Kentucky, and Illinois.[4] The second one, *I'm done my homework*, is somewhat common in areas including Philadelphia, Maryland, Delaware, southern New Jersey, and parts of New England (we label it ECE for "East Coast English"); it is even more common in Canadian English.[5] The last one is common in African American English across many geographic areas in the United States. If you yourself use or have encountered these constructions, they likely don't stand out to you; in fact, you may not even notice anything about them. If you are not familiar with these constructions, you may assume that they are incorrect (even though they all are grammatically correct!) because they do not conform to the grammar of the version of English you are used to. The central goals for this grammar book are twofold:

  i. gain knowledge about American English grammar fundamentals as exemplified by patterns of *both* standardized American English dialects *and* non-standardized American English dialects;
 ii. develop an understanding that while non-standardized English constructions may be different from standardized English constructions, they are just as grammatical and systematic as those found in standardized English.

For many of you, the plural in the phrase "English(es)" in this chapter's title may be strange, especially in a grammar textbook in which you are likely expecting clear-cut, right-and-wrong rules based on "standard" or academic English. Perhaps you can more easily conceptualize different English varieties such as British, Australian, or Indian Englishes. Those and other English language varieties around the world are generally called Global Englishes. In this book, however, we focus on the varieties of English within the United States of America as we lay out the fundamentals of grammar. Therefore, we will illustrate and explain grammatical concepts via a plethora of American dialects, some of which you're probably an active user of and/or at least familiar with, and some of which you may not be familiar with. We posit that understanding how any given language works is best accomplished by understanding and valuing its varieties, whether you plan to teach, travel, or work with people from across the United States or across the world.

By drawing from major American English varieties, we take to task "standard" language ideology, which privileges standardized English and, consequently, contributes to linguistic discrimination. Each example will help show the grammaticality and equality of all American English dialects, and we expect that your understanding of

English grammar and syntax will grow alongside an appreciation of the many American Englishes, including your own dialect of American English!

Before we begin our study of the grammars of American Englishes, an introduction to some terminology such as dialect, variety, and standard English as well as to some theories of language acquisition and syntax (i.e., the study of grammar) is necessary.

1.2 Grammar: What Does It Mean?

The word **grammar** is used in many ways, both in public and academic domains. For many folks, grammar means using spelling and punctuation conventions correctly. For others, statements such as "They have good grammar" mean that someone speaks "Standard English." Sometimes, the word "grammar" is used to refer to books that are about grammar (as in "Could you hand me that grammar from the shelf?"). For some, grammar refers to the entire system of a language that is acquired as children learn a language and as such includes the sound system (phonetics/phonology), the system of how to form words (morphology), the system of how to form phrases, clauses and sentences (syntax), how those words and sentences get their meanings (semantics), and how we use language to get things done (pragmatics).[6] For some, grammar exclusively refers to prescriptive rules. Harmon and Wilson's definition of grammar is a useful starting point: "the set of internalized rules that govern our unconscious use of language."[7] Since we focus on grammatical structures used in written and spoken American English dialects, we do not cover the grammar of signed language varieties such as American Sign Language (ASL) and Black ASL.

Our focus is largely on sentence structure, and thus, we use Quirk et al.'s definition of grammar: "Words must be combined into larger units, and grammar encompasses the complex set of rules specifying such combinations."[8] Following Quirk et al.'s descriptive approach to grammar, we include both **syntax** and **morphology**. Turning a statement such as *They have good grammar* into a question as in *Do they have good grammar?* is an example of syntax; turning a verb such as *walk* into past tense as in *walked* is an example of morphology.

1.3 Diversity and Equality: Language, Dialect, Variety

The goal of this book is to help you understand the fundamentals of grammar—period. Not just the grammatical features of standardized American English but also those of some of the major non-standardized American English dialects. You will then see that all are systematic and grammatical. Our approach is to emphasize the validity of non-standardized American English dialects because they are often derided as "broken English," when in fact, they are just

Dialect: a variety of a language
Language: a collection of different dialects

as grammatical as standardized English. Wolfram and Schilling-Estes, two American dialect experts, remind us that "to speak a language is to speak some dialect of that language."[9] Since we all speak some variety, some dialect of a language, our dialects are inextricably tied to our identities and the communities we belong to.

You'll learn that what is often seen as "deviations" from standardized English or even as "errors" is, in fact, systematic and grammatical. Many non-standardized English variations simply pattern differently from standardized English, and many features across non-standardized dialects pattern exactly like those of standardized English dialects. Despite differences, all dialects of English—including standardized English—are linguistically equal and valid. In fact, "research shows that dialects are complete linguistic systems and thus have structural integrity;" consequently, "no dialect is more valuable, interesting, logical, or worthy of study than another."[10] This is why, within the field of linguistics, the term *dialect* is "a neutral label to refer to any variety of a language which is shared by a group of speakers."[11] The terms *variety* and *dialect* are often used interchangeably, and any language really is a collection of different dialects. Hence, we use the terms **dialect** and **variety** as neutral terms that imply neither a positive nor a negative evaluation.

Generally, linguists distinguish two broad groups of dialects: **regional dialects** and **social dialects**. Regional dialects are generally defined by the region in which they are found, and social dialects are based on social categories shared by their speakers (often they overlap). For instance, Wolfram and Christian define Appalachian English (AE) as referring to the "variety of English most typically associated with the working-class rural population found in one particular region of the Appalachian range."[12] This definition comes with an important caveat. As Wolfram and Christian note, dialect differences of course do exist even within this dialect region and not everyone in that region uses AE features. We want to be clear about such dialect differences within regional and social dialects. Linguists often refer to such intra-dialect differences as part of the **dialect continuum**.[13] Not everyone in the Upper Midwest, for instance, will share the same features. Consider how someone from Minnesota sounds versus someone from Michigan or Wisconsin. If you think these groups sound the same, find a couple of videos online to compare! In fact, even folks in Michigan don't all sound the same. Some regional dialects have their own unique grammatical structures that differ from grammatical structures of standardized English. And even for standardized English, there's a continuum of features! This means not only that everyone (even you!) speaks a dialect of English, but also that all labels for dialects require some form of abstraction and an acknowledgment that a continuum of features exists. Examples of regional dialects that you will learn about in this book include but are not limited to Appalachian English (AE), Southern American English (SAE), and Midwest English (ME). *I'm done my homework* and *The car needs washed*, from above, are two initial examples of regional dialect features. The map below (Figure 1.1) depicts major dialect regions in the United States.

Examples of **social dialects** include, but are not limited to, African American English (AAE) and Chicano English (ChE). Smitherman describes the AAE **variety** as follows: "a style of speaking English words with Black flava—with Africanized semantic, grammatical, pronunciation, and rhetorical patterns. AAL [African American Language] comes out of the experience of US slave descendants. This shared experience has resulted in

Which Englishes Do You Speak?

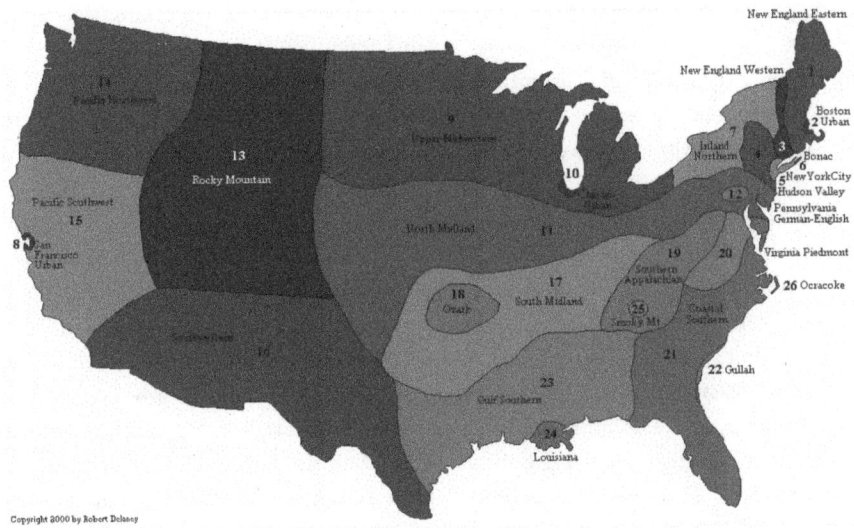

Figure 1.1 Dialect Regions in the United States.[14]

common speaking styles, systematic patterns of grammar, and common language practices in the Black community."[15] We use the label AAE to refer to this dialect, but other labels exist: African American Vernacular English, Ebonics, Black English, Black Language, and more. Another social dialect, ChE, can be defined as a "variety of English, influenced by contact with Spanish, and spoken as a native dialect by both bilingual speakers of Spanish and English, and monolingual speakers of English."[16] Like any dialect, it is acquired by children during the language acquisition process. Other terms exist, including Hispanic English, Hispanicized English, and the often pejoratively used term Spanglish. Since the example *He don't be barking at nobody* from above is common in AAE, it is an example of a social dialect construction. Again, it is crucial to remember the concept of the **dialect continuum**. These social dialects, just like regional ones, are not static, and not everyone in a given social community will use the respective dialect's features.

Dialect differences are often used to divide people. That is, they often serve as markers of social class or education level or even a person's likeability (whether warranted or not!). Understanding that we all speak a dialect is important to counter such judgments. We are hopeful this text will work toward that end; it will help you understand language differences and grammar from a linguistic perspective, which will underscore the validity of each dialect, which will—we hope—work to unify, not divide.

Often, people think of differences in sound, i.e., *accent*, when contemplating how East Coast English (e.g., New York, Boston, Providence, Bangor) differs from Midwest English (e.g., Milwaukee, Chicago, Boise, Indianapolis) or how words are pronounced differently in different regions such as the South (e.g., Memphis, Tuscaloosa, New Orleans) or the West Coast (e.g., Sacramento, L.A., Portland, Seattle). While some dialect differences are due to sound, some are due to vocabulary, such as using the word *pop* or *soda* for carbonated beverages, and some have to do with grammatical structures.[17] We focus on grammatical structures in this book.

When people refer to **Standard English (SE),** they usually have a language variety in mind that is devoid of regional/social accents, regional/social words such as *pop* or *davenport,* and regional/social grammatical features such as *y'all/youse guys*. Typically, people will think of the kind of English they see in newspapers, published books, academic papers, and so on. More importantly, there's a conception that Standard English is the one, and only, correct form of English. However, linguists repeatedly point out that such a monolithic, singular "Standard English" does not really exist. For one, it is an abstract idea rather than reality. Lippi-Green compares it to a unicorn.[18] Even though unicorns do not actually exist, our descriptions of a unicorn would likely be very similar, based on our shared background of having lived in a culture that exposes us to depictions of unicorns. When lay people, that is, people who are not linguists, are asked to describe Standard English, their descriptions will likely all be very similar, although it, too, doesn't really exist. Additionally, there are multiple versions of Standard English, including spoken and written Standard English, formal and informal Standard English, and regional versions of Standard English.[19] For example, Standard English in California will sound different from the Standard English in the Midwest or in New York, mostly because of accent differences, but also because of vocabulary differences and some grammatical structures. That means there are multiple versions of Standard English that differ in subtle ways from one another.

You are most likely more familiar with the term "Standard English" than **standardized English (sE)**. We use the term standardized English (sE) in this book as a broader term that encompasses not just edited formal written Standard English, but also informal spoken Standard English, and regional versions of Standard English. This is why we use the plural form "sE dialects" quite often over the singular "sE dialect." Both terms—SE and sE—refer to a concept that is notoriously difficult to define.[20] Who gets to decide what counts as "standard"/"standardized" and what doesn't: your teacher, a professor, a journalist, you? Standard English is generally understood to be "the dialect that most speakers assume isn't a dialect and the one they accept as authoritative, for whatever social reason."[21] Smitherman's definition makes explicit this social reason: "'Standard American English' is a form of English that gets to be considered 'standard' because it derives from the style of speaking and the language habits of the dominant race, class and gender in U.S. society."[22] In this book, you'll learn about grammatical structures of sE dialects alongside of non-sE dialects.

Various similar terms have been used to refer to what traditionally has been termed Standard English (SE), including Mainstream American English (MAE), Formal English, Edited English, School English, and Academic English. Each of these terms carries with it a set of assumptions and connotations regarding "correctness," "superiority," "appropriateness."

> **Stigmatized** means condemned, discredited, disparaged, and disapproved of. **Non-stigmatized** means *not* condemned, discredited, disparaged, or disapproved of.

MAE has been used as a more neutral term, including by the Online Resources for African American Languages, which defines MAE as referring "to varieties of English that are not characterized by a particular dialect trait under discussion."[23] Others, including Baker-Bell, argue convincingly that even terms such as MAE imply that its speakers are white.[24]

It is important to keep in mind that the term "Standard English" (and, really, all the other terms that have been used and are being used for this variety) presents this particular English dialect as a stable and objective entity when, in fact, it is actively and continually positioned and repositioned as "standard" through raciolinguistic ideologies.[25] Certain features and structures of English are *being standardized* actively rather than simply existing objectively as "the" standard. These are the other reasons why we have opted to use the term **standardized English (sE)** in this text to refer to those dialects of American English that are generally seen as non-stigmatized. We use sE in line with McMurtry's definition of standardized English as "the language patterns that those with White cultural privilege and prestige deem more desirable and appropriate, rather than what these language patterns empirically are (i.e., one of the many variations of English)."[26] We believe that the term "standardized English" helps counter the common juxtaposition of "Standard" with "good" or "correct" English and "non-Standard" with "bad" and "incorrect." We deliberately chose the lower-case *s* in the abbreviation "sE" to set it apart from the more common SE abbreviation for Standard English, and we hope that this lower-case *s* will remind you every time you see it that sE is not a stable, objective entity. Note that sE itself is just another dialect rather than the one and only correct form of English. Other dialects did not derive from sE nor are they somehow "broken" versions of sE. Instead, all dialects are equally correct and equally complex. A core tenet of sociolinguistics is that "No variety of a language is inherently better than another in terms of its logic, its systematic structure, or its ability to express creative and complex thought."[27] Hence, each dialect is grammatical, and each dialect follows different underlying structures,[28] many of which you'll learn about in subsequent chapters.

Non-standardized English (non-sE) dialects such as AAE, ChE, AE, SAE, and many others—while perfectly grammatical and linguistically correct—often come with harsh social penalties; that is, they are **stigmatized**. People have been repeatedly told by society (including by educators) that there is one correct way of using language and that this one correct way is sE. At the same time, they have learned all their lives (implicitly and explicitly) that non-sE dialects are incorrect, lazy, broken. This perspective is often referred to as **Standard Language Ideology**.[29] Put differently, the "speech of dominant groups will be viewed as superior to the speech of socially subordinate groups."[30] Adhering to Standard Language Ideology leads to judgments about people based on the dialect they speak: how intelligent, wealthy, friendly they are, and so on. These judgments often reveal other underlying views about groups of people. Someone who uses a "Southern drawl" is not inherently more or less intelligent or educated than someone who uses a Midwestern or East Coast dialect. Since even sE itself is just another variety or dialect, a person who prides themselves on perfect adherence to its rules is still simply using the rules of just one of the English dialects. A person who uses Australian English, by extension, is following the rules of Australian English; someone who uses AAE or SAE, then, is also following the rules of that variety. Each variety, each dialect, does have its own set of grammatical rules that make up that dialect's grammatical system.

> **Standard Language Ideology**: Believing that there is only one correct form of English–Standard English–which is superior to other forms of English.

Because this is a grammar book, you will learn about the syntax and morphology of American English, and because we include many dialect examples, you'll also learn about the underlying structures of some of the major American English dialects. Keep in mind that, overall, the dialects covered here share many, many grammatical rules and features. Because English dialects are so similar, when there are differences, they can quickly stand out and become the target of negative judgments. This book is not a comprehensive review of all American English dialects. For comprehensive overviews of grammatical systems for specific dialects, we refer you to the companion website, where we provide lots of suggested further reading. Instead, we include examples of some of the major American English dialects, and we focus especially on dialects, such as AAE, ChE, AE, and SAE. The discussion thus far should give you an idea for why we made the decision to especially highlight these dialects: they are the dialects that are generally (and wrongly) regarded as "least correct" or "most lazy." Plus, they are the ones whose speakers routinely face linguistic bias and linguistic discrimination. As such, they warrant, in our view, special attention. We do include examples from other non-sE dialects as well, including Midwestern dialects, Pittsburghese, and dialects in the Ozark region, because these dialects, while not as stigmatized in general, demonstrate and reinforce the rule-based nature of any dialect. People might find themselves to be more accepting of non-sE structures found in the Midwest than those found in AAE or ChE; this is an illustration of a language ideology that renders dialects associated with certain groups of people as more or less desirable.

We want to be as clear as possible about **dialect labels** in this book. We do not wish to create the impression that there is *one* AAE and *one* ChE and *one* SAE and *one* sE and so on. You yourself are a member of communities that use any one or multiple of the dialects that are represented in this book, but that doesn't mean you use all of that dialect's features all of the time or any of the time for that matter. This is because no two speakers of one of these dialect versions use the dialect in the same way or to the same degree. A speaker of SAE may use some SAE features and many sE features in the same conversation and even in the same piece of writing. A speaker of sE may also use non-sE dialect features, and speakers of non-sE dialects do use many sE features. Many sE features are not unique to sE dialects—they're also part of most or even all the non-sE dialects we cover. For our purposes here, we must make some abstractions to illustrate major features of common dialects. Practically, then, this means that if an example is labeled as "sE," that feature is likely not unique to sE. When an example is labeled something other than sE, it means that for that specific feature, a dialect difference exists. It doesn't mean every speaker of that dialect will always and in every case use it. In real life, you will use and encounter variations of these features, and you will encounter intra- and inter-dialect variations all around you.

1.4 Grammar and Grammar: Describing or Prescribing Language Use?

Standard Language Ideology, viewing one and only one form of English as correct, is intertwined with prescriptive grammar rules.[31] You may recognize several of the prescriptive rules in Chart 1.

Which Englishes Do You Speak?

Prescriptive	Descriptive

- Don't split an infinitive:
  - We want **to strongly voice** our objection.
  - "**to go boldly**" instead of "*to boldly go*."
- Don't end a sentence with a preposition: *Do you want to go **with**?*
- Use active voice: *The research group **conducted** a usability study* instead of *A usability study **was conducted** by the research group.*
- Don't use double negatives: *We **ain't** got **no** time.*
	- The subject comes before the verb: *Pat (S) laughed (V)*.
	- Adjectives come before the noun they modify: *the orange (Adj) cat (N)*.
	- The indirect object precedes the direct object in a sentence: *I bought Sam (IO) a gift (DO)*.
	- If there's a determiner, it comes before the noun *the cat* vs. **cat the*.

Chart 1 Descriptive and prescriptive grammar rules

Prescriptive rules are commands that are "dos" and "don'ts" and as such **prescribe** what you should and shouldn't do with language. In contrast, **descriptive rules** are statements that **describe** some grammatical pattern of the English language; they, crucially, do not tell you what to do. This is, in a nutshell, the difference between descriptive and prescriptive grammar: describing how language works versus prescribing how you and everyone else should use language. So, how prescriptive/descriptive are you? Rank yourself on the scale in Chart 2. Be honest. This is simply your baseline perspective, your starting point for the study of English grammars. You can see whether your ideas change when you've reached the end of the book.

```
                        How Prescriptive Are You
On the following scale, rate yourself:
|----------|----------|----------|----------|----------|----------|----------|----------|----------|
1) Notice differences in language use              Do not notice differences in language use
|----------|----------|----------|----------|----------|----------|----------|----------|----------|
2) Like hearing people's "accents"                 Do not like hearing people's "accents"
|----------|----------|----------|----------|----------|----------|----------|----------|----------|
3) Like to figure out patterns                     Do not like to figure out patterns
|----------|----------|----------|----------|----------|----------|----------|----------|----------|
4) Can imitate others' speech                      Cannot imitate others' speech
|----------|----------|----------|----------|----------|----------|----------|----------|----------|
5) Need an editor                                  Like to be an editor
|----------|----------|----------|----------|----------|----------|----------|----------|----------|
6) See yourself as descriptivist                   prescriptivist
```

Chart 2 *How prescriptive are you?*[32]

Prescriptive grammar is in line with a more traditional use of the term "grammar." Prescriptive rules are made by "self-appointed authorities who, reflecting varying judgments of acceptability and

Prescriptive grammar: prescribes the dos and don'ts
Descriptive grammar: describes the building blocks of a language

9

appropriateness, often disagree."[33] Lists of rules dominate many grammar and usage books, such as Strunk and White's *The Elements of Style*. Different usage guides will stipulate different prescriptive rules. Yet, what they have in common is that each of them *does* stipulate a clear right and wrong. They imply that if you don't follow these rules, then other people will negatively judge you. The funny thing about these kinds of rules is that, often, they are not based on actual grammar; rather, they are based on social conventions and personal tastes of grammarians.

Consider the first rule above. The full infinitive form (or base form) is marked with *to* in English (no matter which dialect!).

(1)   to go
(2)   to leave
(3)   to sleep

The infinitive contrasts with other verb forms:

(1a)   I *go*, You *go*, We *go* …
(2a)   I *leave*, You *leave*, We *leave* …
(3a)   I *sleep*, You *sleep*, We *sleep* …

Once you combine the verb with a subject, the infinitive marker *to* isn't needed anymore:

(4)   *I *to go*, You *to go*, We *to go*, …

The *to* in *to go* is, to reiterate, simply a marker that tells you that the form is the infinitive. The prescriptive rule in Chart 1 would prevent splitting the *to*-marker from the lexical/main verb *go*; that is, it does not allow another word to go in between *to* and *go*. This rule is actually based on Latin grammar. In Latin, the infinitive of the verb is one word and doesn't have anything like a *to*-marker: Latin *laudare* is the infinitive and translates as "to praise." Since the infinitive in Latin is spelled as one word, it wasn't possible to insert another word into the middle of that base form of a Latin verb.[34] Contrast that with English, where infinitives of verbs are spelled as two words [to + verb]: *to go*—with the exception of **bare infinitives** where the *to* is not required (more on that later). In English, one can thus add other words in between the *to*-marker and the verb form: *to boldly go* rather than *to go boldly*. (We won't hold it against you if you don't know this phrase. It's a Star Trek thing.) The grammar of English does allow for such additions. Grammatically speaking, then, there is nothing wrong with split infinitives. You will likely notice **split infinitives** everywhere now. Here are some examples:

(5)   *to better prepare* students
(6)   *to further explain*
(7)   *to gradually raise* rates

These split infinitives are not just common, they are grammatical!

Equally, there is nothing wrong—in any dialect—with ending a clause or sentence with a preposition:

(8) Which painting did you look *at*?

The rule "don't end a sentence with a preposition" above would have you rearrange this question as follows:

(8a) *At* which painting did you look?

Ending sentences and clauses with prepositions is something that is perfectly grammatical in English. Yet, style guides and older grammar books perpetuate the idea not just that this is somehow bad-mannered, but that it is ungrammatical. These examples illustrate that prescriptive rules are not necessarily based on English grammar, but instead are rules about style, social etiquette, individual tastes, and perceived formality.

In contrast, a **descriptive perspective** is about the underlying grammatical patterns, the structure of language. It simply describes the patterns of English via descriptive grammar rules:

- In English, subjects generally come before the verb: *My neighbor slept on the couch.*
- In English, adjectives generally come before the noun they describe: *I've seen green cards.*

Each of these rules simply describes one aspect of how English works. Since subjects generally come first in an English sentence, *My neighbor* comes before the verb. We would not produce anything like *Slept on the couch my neighbor* in English. No one must remind you to place the subject before the verb—it's simply how English works. Similarly, no one must remind you to place an adjective before the noun it describes. In fact, English users will not generate (i.e., produce) examples such as *cards green* precisely because of this general underlying rule of placing adjectives prior to nouns.

These descriptive grammar rules then simply are descriptions of how the language works, which are based on how people use that language. This doesn't mean that "anything goes." A sentence such as *Slept on the couch my neighbor* would **not** be considered grammatically correct (even by descriptivists!) as it does not follow the basic syntactic building blocks of English. Descriptive grammar rules give you a glimpse into what grammar is. **Grammar** is the collection of **patterns**—what linguistic elements you can combine and in what order—of a given language. This underlying system in each language and dialect allows us to combine words, phrases, and clauses in some ways but not in others:

(9) *cute the dog

(10) the cute dog

(11) a hungry cat

(12) *cat hungry a

In English, phrases such as *cute the dog* in (9) and *cat hungry a* in (12) are prohibited. They are ungrammatical. The * marks examples as ungrammatical. Phrases such as *the cute dog* in (10) and *a hungry cat* in (11), however, are combinations that are allowed. They are grammatical. Why is it that *the cute dog* is possible but **cute the dog* is impossible in English? The answer is that the grammar of English simply does not allow for the former phrase but does for the latter. The underlying system, the grammar, establishes what goes and what doesn't go in a language or in a dialect through an arbitrary process of selection over time by its users. To describe the underlying pattern of why (9) and (12) are ungrammatical and (10) and (11) are grammatical, we start by listing observations based on those two examples:

- words such as *the* and *a* need to be placed before words like *cute* and *hungry*
- words like *dog* and *cat* need to follow words like *hungry* and *cute*

Words like *a* and *the* are articles (or determiners), words like *cute* and *hungry* are adjectives, and words like *cat* and *dog* are nouns. Our observations from above can be rephrased as follows:

> If a phrase includes nouns, articles, and adjectives, the word order generally needs to be *article + adjective + noun* for the phrase to be grammatical.

These kinds of patterns are the grammar rules this book is about because they reveal which sentences are grammatical and which sentences are ungrammatical within a given language/dialect. These grammar rules emerge from patterns based on actual language data, that is, in how people use language.

Exercise 1

Descriptive/Prescriptive grammar rules. Decide whether the following grammar rules are descriptive (D) or prescriptive (P). Make sure to explain why. Don't worry if you're not familiar with all the grammatical terminology just yet.

a) In a series of three or more terms with a single conjunction, use a comma after each term except the last.

b) *All* occurs with plural count nouns and with noncount nouns, as in *all the books* or *all books*.

c) Place a comma before a conjunction.

d) With *who* and *whom*, the antecedent must have personal gender as in *The man who greeted me is a neighbor*; with *which*, it must have non-personal gender as in *the house which you have for sale is nice*.

e) Do not break sentences into two.

f) We distinguish three classes of determiners, set up on the basis of their positions in the noun phrase in relation to each other.

g) The definite and indefinite articles are the commonest central determiners, and their distribution is dependent upon the class of the accompanying noun.

h) Place the emphatic words of a sentence at the end.

1.5 Language Acquisition and Grammar: The Brain, Community, and Language

Grammar is all about patterns. Users of English produce structures such as *the cute cat* but do not produce structures such as **cute cat the*. Thus, what seems to guide which structures we produce and which ones we do not produce is largely based on convention and agreement. These rules develop slowly but deeply within a language community. Various syntactic theories and language acquisition theories (i.e., how we learn the structures we learn) have been posited; research in these areas is ongoing, and the debate is by no means settled. Regardless of how exactly we acquire language and its grammatical structures, we can describe grammatical patterns and structures because they are observable through language use.

We cannot provide a comprehensive overview of the various language acquisition and syntactic theories here. Instead, we present some important principles that serve as the undercurrent for first language acquisition theories about how our mental grammars are encoded in the human brain. Note that many children grow up with two or multiple languages and acquire the systems of those multiple languages. We encourage you to read more about language acquisition, but we limit ourselves here to some initial observations about language acquisition more generally.

Nativist theories posit that the encoding of one's first language is an intellectual inheritance that comes to the child with no concerted or conscious learning strategies. A child's caregiver community provides language input—either spoken language to hearing children or visual-gestural input to deaf children. Children's brains have the innate ability to parse sounds or signs, structure, and meaning from that spoken or visual-gestural language.[35] Children's linguistic ability exceeds the input received from the environment; their perception and production go beyond what they hear. Children can create acceptable and understandable utterances they have never heard. This means that as language users, we can create sentences that were *not* part of the input (the stimulus) we received. This is called poverty of stimulus. We're pretty sure that the following sentence has never been produced in this way ever before. It may not be very logical, but it is a perfectly grammatical sentence (give it a try and formulate your own unique sentence):

(13) The purple coffee was prepared by the overly cautious feline chef Mr. Kitty.

Because we can produce novel sentences, there must be something—a preordained system and/or a processor—within children's cognitive systems by which they fill in the pieces of their first language without sufficient linguistic input data. Noam Chomsky was instrumental in theorizing about these concepts within twentieth century linguistics. His theory of **universal grammar** posits a Language Acquisition Device (LAD) within the human brain that sets the parameters of the child's first language based on this (limited) input.[36] Other nativists agree that the human brain is able to take limited linguistic input (i.e., data) from the language community to encode the rules and structures of the first language (or first languages), but rather than crediting a pre-programmed set of language parameters, such as the LAD for the result, they argue that the brain is able to systematically process the input through processes akin to cognitive algorithms. This approach, then, views child language processing through a corpus-based, inductive approach to learning in which children's grammatical hypotheses are tethered to the input of primary linguistic data.[37]

Non-nativist approaches, broadly conceived, to language acquisition and grammar include **constructivist** and **usage-based approaches**,[38] which suggest that "language structure emerges from language use."[39] In constructivist approaches, language acquisition is based on "domain-general learning mechanisms such as analogy, entrenchment, and automatization"[40] rather than on an innate, language-specific learning mechanism.

Interactionists, Sociocultural, or **Constructivist theorists** focus on the human connection that is both the impetus for and the process by which first languages are attained. These theorists are less interested in the neuroprocessing of language encoding than the import of participation, collaboration, and community identity for language acquisition. Language, then, arises more from a social instinct rather than from a cognitive inheritance. They build greatly on the views of Lev Vygotsky.[41] Despite rejecting some of the nativist positions, constructivist and usage-based approaches demonstrate that linguistic input is crucial for a child's language acquisition. Based on this linguistic input, children develop function-form units and grammatical structures.[42]

One's first languages are encoded effortlessly and systematically from the linguistic input from one's social community. Understanding this fundamental fact about first language acquisition, therefore, is the first step in recognizing that a person's first language is legitimate and valid—no matter which dialect of that first language the person acquires. After all, during the language acquisition process, we acquire the grammatical rules and patterns based on the input around us. If we are surrounded by SAE speakers, we acquire the grammatical structure of SAE, including *y'all* and (likely) *ain't*. If we are surrounded by AAE, we acquire the grammatical rules of AAE, including structures like *You right about that*[43] and *She smart*.[44] Understanding this process of language acquisition is key to seeing all languages as equal, seeing all speakers as equal.

1.6 Why Study Grammars of American English Dialects? Knowledge Not Just for Teachers

This book is intended as a basic introduction to the foundations of American English grammar. While some of our students have described grammar as their favorite topic ever, comments such as "grammar is my arch nemesis" and "grammar is my Achilles heel" are more common in our classes, indicating that many of our students fear grammar. Others simply aren't very interested in studying grammar, and many believe that grammar is a collection of nitpicky, random, and obscure rules. Finally, many of our students believe that they "suffer from bad grammar."

We hope that this introduction to the grammars of American English dialects will empower you as you (re)discover your own grammatical capabilities. We hope you will see that grammar is far more than a strange collection of random, prescriptive rules: that grammar is all about the systematic and rule-governed patterns found in a language or dialect. When you master the terminology and the core concepts of grammar, you can engage in meaningful grammatical analyses of your own dialect(s) and those of others. What is more impressive is that your understanding of language and dialects will be based on empirical (data-driven) linguistic science. Some of you might find the study of grammar fascinating and, dare we say it, fun! Some of you may even find that this new-found scientific approach to language and grammar, specifically, will lead you to professional careers in publishing, editing, the law, or even one of the many areas of linguistics.

We noted our views of various dialects routinely shape our views of the communities who use those dialects; it should come as no surprise that dialects can be the cause of linguistic prejudice in the classroom.[45] This text provides a wealth of necessary information for teachers—teachers of all kinds of students and of all types of classes. Many of you may be working to become elementary, middle, or high school teachers. Many of you may be working on a degree to teach speakers of other languages. Some may be planning to teach a language other than English in any number of settings. For those of you who are **not** planning a career in education, we want to assure you, this text has great application for you as well.

Now, it is not a great stretch of anyone's imagination to see how an increased knowledge of grammar, and a skillful facility with clauses and phrases, will be beneficial to all kinds of writers (or should we call them "content creators"?), including professional, technical, and creative writers. You might not immediately connect the study of grammar to the law. And yet, it is language and the precise interpretation of phrases, clauses, and sentences that will occupy many practicing lawyers throughout their careers. Many examples of high-profile cases have hinged on the exact interpretation of single words. For instance, the meaning of *applicable* when placed in front of the phrase *attorney fees* was crucial in a decision where a quarter million dollars hung in the balance.[46] Similarly, the precise meaning of *accompany* was the crux of the issue in a case where the US Supreme Court upheld the conviction of a robber.[47] Something as tiny as a comma can mean having to pay millions to workers, as the case involving a dairy company in Maine illustrates.[48] Additionally, dialects and accents can be a major source of linguistic discrimination in the court system, with witnesses for example not seen as credible because of the dialect they speak, or court stenographers not being able to correctly transcribe testimony of non-sE speakers.[49] See the companion website for work on this fascinating topic!

Linguistic analyses have made it all the way to the US Supreme Court in the form of amicus briefs in cases involving the language of the Second Amendment of the US Constitution. The number of linguistic publications about the language and structure of that amendment is more than you'd likely expect! Check out some of Dennis Baron's work on this and other grammar-and-the-law topics.[50] Having a firm grasp of how words work together to form phrases and clauses is integral for any lawyer worth their salt. Note that we are using the singular *their* here—a practice that would have received much eyebrow raising from prescriptivists just a few years ago, but which is now considered acceptable! Additionally, reports from various occupation fields indicate that employers are unhappy with employees' writing abilities, including law school[51] and the law profession,[52] healthcare,[53] and business

Foundations of Grammar

in general.[54] Several studies show that much of the underlying cause is a lack of fundamental knowledge of the basic mechanics of writing, the basic structures of language.[55]

In short, we suggest that everyone benefits from studying grammar. Language, after all, is quintessentially human. What this text also does, perhaps unlike any other, is it does not relegate non-sE dialects to footnotes nor does it cast non-sE patterns as exceptions to some sE rule. Rather, it presents grammatical information via examples from sE and non-sE dialects alike. This knowledge should help build in us awareness of and appreciation for *all* American English dialects. Knowing even just some basics about the structure of various dialects across the United States will increase your linguistic awareness about language in general, other languages, and, more importantly, the systematicity and grammaticality of all dialects. Such increased linguistic awareness might just aid in reducing linguistic discrimination.

1.7 An Overview of Grammatical Dialect Features

We don't presume that you are familiar with all the various grammatical dialect features you'll encounter in this book. For this reason, this chapter's grand finale is an overview of these features; that way, in case you're unfamiliar with a particular feature, it won't throw you off. The point here is not for you to memorize all features, but to carefully work through Tables 1.1–1.4.

Each table provides each feature's name, a basic definition, examples, and a list of the main dialects the features are associated with. Keep in mind that both intra- and inter-dialect variation exists, and so the dialects listed for a particular feature are not the only dialects it may occur in. Use the chart in Exercise 2 below to take note about which of these features you use yourself or are familiar with. We start with features related to nouns, adjectives, and adverbs, represented in Table 1.1.

Table 1.1 Grammatical features related to nouns, adjectives, and adverbs

Grammar feature	Basic definition	Example	Dialects
Possessive -*s*	Possession is expressed via proximity; possessive -*s* is optional.	Sonya('s) sister[56] my *mom house*[57]	AAE
Plural -*s*	Plural -*s* is optional mostly for measurement words.	five *cent*[58] four *mile*[59]	AAE, ChE
Double comparatives	Adding -*er* plus *more/less* for comparatives.	Cats are *more cleverer* than humans.	SAE and others
wicked	An intensifier for adjectives, similar to *very*.	a *wicked* long time[60]	NEE
all the + comparative	Generally equivalent to *as … as* constructions.	That's all the *higher* he can jump.[61]	SAE, ME
barely	*barely* can be used to mean *just recently*.	I just *barely* checked in.[62]	ChE
Drama *so*	Unlike other degree adverbs, *so* can intensify verbs.	I am *so* not going to study tonight.[63]	sE and non-sE

Next, consider the features related to prepositions and pronouns in Table 1.2. Again, use the chart provided in Exercise 2 to check off which of these features you use and/or are familiar with.

Table 1.2 Grammatical features related to prepositions and pronouns

Grammar feature	Basic definition	Example	Dialects
Preposition variation	Preposition choice different from sE possible.	He's smiling *to* the cat.[64]	ChE
Come *with*	Some verbs can be followed by *with*; pronoun such as *us* is not required after *with*.	Do you want to come *with*?[65]	ME
Second person plural pronoun variation	Distinct forms for second person plural pronouns (*y'all, yinz, youse guys*) are possible in many dialects.	when *yinz* go outside …[66] *Y'all* come back.[67]	sE and non-sE
Possessive pronouns	Additional forms for possessive pronouns (*mines, her'n, hisn, ourn, etc.*) are possible in many dialects.	[We] generally sold *ourn* to …[68] *Her'n* on December 31.[69]	AAE, AE
Reflexive pronouns	Additional forms for reflexive pronouns (*hisself, theirself, etc.*) are possible in some dialects.	They make their juice *theirself*.[70]	AAE, ChE
Resumptive pronouns	Relative pronoun can be followed by another pronoun.	I know this lady *that she* used to live here.[71]	ChE
Personal dative	Personal pronoun forms can do the work of a reflexive pronoun.	I got *me* some candy.[72]	SAE/AE, also ChE
Alls construction	*Alls* can generally be replaced with *what*.	*Alls* I want to do is have fun.[73]	ME

Now, Table 1.3 is even longer! It summarizes major dialect variation related to verbs. The verb is a powerhouse, and different American English dialects have different grammatical structures related to verbs. Go back to the chart from Exercise 2 as you reflect on your familiarity with and use of these dialect features in Table 1.3.

Table 1.3 Grammatical features related to verbs

Grammar feature	Basic definition	Example	Dialects
Regularized agreement	Uniform verb forms for first, second, third person (*I, you, she/he/it*).	he *like*; he *know*.[74] We *was discussing* …[75]	AAE, ChE
Simple past and past participle leveling	Using simple past tense forms in place of past participle.	None of these folks have *drove* a truck …[76]	ChE, AAE, sE dialects

Foundations of Grammar

Grammar feature	Basic definition	Example	Dialects
Habitual *be*	Indicates that an action or state occurs habitually, regularly, routinely.	The news *be showing* it …[77] I *be* in my office.[78]	AAE, ChE
Past tense *-ed*	Optional past-tense *-ed* marker. Past tense is often expressed via adverbials and other context.	Then after that I *talk* English.[79]	ChE, AAE
Remote time *bin/been*	Indicates that an action was started at some point in the past and is still ongoing.	We *been* married almost twenty-six years.[80]	AAE
Completive *done*	The auxiliary *done* requires main verb in past tense; indicates that an action is *fully* complete.	You *done did* all the work.[81]	AAE; also SAE
Be absence	In progressive aspect verb phrases, the form of *be* is optional (except for *am*).	They Ø *building* these condos.[82] I Ø *been doing* dancing …[83]	AAE, ChE, SAE
could	*Could* is used in the same way as *can*.	… people that are left-handed *could* draw better than ….[84]	ChE
fixing to do / finna	Requires present progressive form of verb; indicates that something is imminent.	I'm *fixin'* to finish that budget proposal today.[85]	SAE, AAE
Double modals	More than one modal auxiliary verb (*might, could, ought, should* …) can occur in a verb phrase.	I don't think I have any grants you *might could* apply for.[86]	SAE
*a-*prefixing	Use of prefix *a-* with *-ing-* verbs (several preconditions must be met).	Fire was *a-flamin'* everything.[87]	AE, SAE
liketa	Requires past tense form of main verb; indicates that an event that was likely didn't occur.	And it *liketa* scared him to death![88]	AE, SAE, WSE, AAE
needs fed	The auxiliary *be* is replaced by *need, like, or want* to form passive voice.	The soul *needs fed* by creative, multi-dimensional teaching.[89]	ME
done my homework	A form of *be* + participle *done* or *finished*; indicates that an action has been completed.	Martin is *done* his bass tracks ….[90]	ECE
after-perfect	Form of *be* + *after* + *-ing* -form of verb; indicates an action is complete, with implications for present.	I am *after cooking* in the kitchen.[91]	Canadian English

And finally, Table 1.4 showcases features related to syntactic structures. Which of these are you familiar with, use yourself, or have never even heard before? Check your answers in the chart from Exercise 2!

Table 1.4. Grammatical features related to sentence structure/syntax

Grammar feature	Basic definition	Example	Dialects
Direct object absence	The direct object after an indirect object can be optional.	I gave him Ø to eat.[92]	ChE
Zero subject pronoun	Pronouns in subject position can be optional.	I moved the lock. Ø locks from the inside.[93]	ChE
Dative presentatives	*Here* + personal pronoun as indirect object + direct object.	Here's *you* a piece of pizza.[94]	SAE
Zero/null copula; copula absence	Copula (i.e., linking) verb is optional prior to subject complements.	You *right*.[95]	AAE, ChE
Subject contact relatives	A clause is added after a noun phrase without a relative pronoun.	That was the stormiest night *was ever in this parish*.[96]	SAE, AE
Positive *anymore*	*Anymore* is not restricted to negation; generally means *nowadays* in positive contexts.	Twitter can be a professional job *anymore*.[97]	
Multiple negation	More than one negative element can be used to form negation.	I do*n't* feel like *nobody* pets me.[98]	sE and non-sE

We hope that this initial overview gives you a taste of the rich linguistic diversity that exists across the United States! In the following chapters, you'll encounter these constructions many more times. We explain the constructions in more detail in the chapters they connect to, so don't worry: You'll build up your knowledge of grammar fundamentals in conjunction with building up your knowledge of specific dialect features throughout this book.

Exercise 2

Use this chart as you work through Tables 1.1–1.4 to indicate your familiarity with each of the grammar features. Reflect on how many you use yourself and how many you're unfamiliar with. Do you use these features in some contexts and not others? With some people but not others? Discuss your answers with at least one peer.

Foundations of Grammar

Grammar feature	I actively use this feature myself	I have heard others use this feature	I am not familiar with this feature
Possessive -s			
Plural -s			
Double comparatives			
wicked			
all the + comparative			
barely			
Drama *so*			
Preposition variation			
Come *with*			
Second person plural pronoun variation			
Possessive pronouns			
Reflexive pronouns			
Resumptive pronouns			
Personal dative			
Alls construction			
Regularized agreement			
Simple past and past participle leveling			
Habitual *be*			
Past tense -*ed*			
Remote time *bin/been*			
Completive *done*			
Be absence			
could			
fixing to do / finna			
Double modals			
a-prefixing			
liketa			
needs fed			
done my homework			
after-perfect			
Direct object absence			
Zero subject pronoun			

Grammar feature	I actively use this feature myself	I have heard others use this feature	I am not familiar with this feature
Dative presentatives			
Zero/null copula; copula absence			
Subject contact relatives			
Positive *anymore*			
Multiple negation			

Chart 3 Gauging your familiarity with grammar features across dialects

At the end of each chapter, we provide a chart with important terminology. We encourage you to write definitions of each term in your own words and, if possible, give an example or illustration. Use these charts to gauge your own learning and understanding of each chapter's content. Below is your first one!

Terminology to Know

Term	Working definition	Example/Illustration
Dialect		
Stigmatized dialect		
Non-stigmatized dialect		
Regional dialect		
Social dialect		
Dialect continuum		
Standard language ideology		
Grammar		
Syntax		
Morphology		
Prescriptive grammar		
Descriptive grammar		
Language acquisition		
Nativist approach		
Language acquisition device		

Chart 4 Key terminology Chapter 1

Notes

1. Maher and Wood, 2011.
2. Wood, 2014.
3. T. McMurtry, personal communication, March 30, 2025.
4. Maher and Wood, 2011.
5. Wood, 2014.
6. cf. Quirk et al., 1985, p. 13.
7. Harmon and Wilson, 2006, p. 4.
8. Quirk et al., 1985, p. 12.
9. Wolfram and Schilling-Estes, 2000, p. 2.
10. Reaser et al., 2017a, p. 8.
11. Wolfram and Schilling-Estes, 2000, p. 2.
12. Wolfram and Christian, 1976, p. 29.
13. Chambers and Trudgill, 2004.
14. Delaney, 2000.
15. Smitherman, 2006, p. 3.
16. ORAAL, 2021; see also Fought, 2003, 2006.
17. See Wolfram and Schilling-Estes (2000) for an overview of American dialects as such.
18. Lippi-Green, 2012.
19. Reaser et al., 2017a.
20. See, among others, Baker-Bell, 2020; McMurtry, 2023; Smitherman, 2006, pp. 1–20.
21. Curzan and Adams, 2012, p. 36.
22. Smitherman, 2006, p. 6.
23. ORAAL, 2021.
24. Baker-Bell, 2020.
25. See Alim et al., 2016; Cushing and Carter, 2022; Flores and Rosa, 2015; Rosa and Flores, 2017; among others.
26. McMurtry, 2023, p. 2.
27. Reaser et al., 2017a, p. 3.
28. Baugh, 2018; McWhorter, 2000; Reaser et al., 2017a; among others.
29. Lippi-Green, 2012; Mallinson et al., 2011; Reaser et al., 2017a; among others.
30. Reaser et al., 2017a, p. 5.
31. Lippi-Green, 2012; Mallinson et al., 2011; Reaser et al., 2017a.
32. Abrams and Stickle, 2017.
33. Quirk et al., 1985, p. 14.
34. A limited set of words can be inserted into the middle of English words. This is called *infixation*. An example would be "abso-effing-lutely" where "effing" is inserted into the middle of "absolutely" (see McMillan (1980) and Adams (2001)).
35. See Henner et al. (2019) and Henner et al. (2016) on American Sign Language acquisition.

36. See Chomsky, 1965, 1975, 1981, 1986.
37. E.g., Crain and Pietroski, 2001; MacWhinney and Bates, 1989.
38. See Bybee, 2010; Diessel, 2013; Tomasello, 2003; among others.
39. Tomasello, 2003, p. 327.
40. Diessel, 2013, p. 348.
41. Vygotsky, 1978.
42. We recommend *The Handbook of Language Emergence* (MacWhinney and O'Grady, 2015) as well as *The Oxford Handbook on Construction Grammar* (Hoffman and Trousdale, 2013) for excellent overviews of these approaches. We also recommend Figueroa and Gerken's (2019) work on verb form acquisition.
43. Baker-Bell, 2020, p. 74.
44. Kendall, Quartey et al., 2018 Transcript ID DCB_se2_ag4_f_01_1.
45. Loosen and McMurtry, 2019.
46. D'Annunzio, 2021.
47. Barnes, 2015.
48. BBC, 2018.
49. See Jones et al., 2019; Rickford & King, 2016.
50. Baron, 2022.
51. Alaka, 2010.
52. Millemann and Schwinn, 2006.
53. Mitchell, 2018.
54. College Board, 2004.
55. Mitchell, 2018.
56. Mufwene et al., 1998, p. 74.
57. Kendall, Quartey et al., 2018 Transcript ID DCB_se1_ag2_m_01_1.
58. Bayley, 2012, p. 163.
59. Reaser et al., 2017a, p. 37.
60. Wood, 2024.
61. Cassidy, 1985; cited in McCoy, 2016a.
62. Fought, 2003, p. 104.
63. Gaston, 2011.
64. Barrón and San Romón, n.d., pp. 30–1; cited in Bayley, 2012, p. 158.
65. Spartz, 2008, cited in Kaplan, 2015.
66. Johnstone, 2013, p. 189.
67. University of South Carolina (n.d.).
68. Ibid.
69. Green, 2002, p. 183.
70. Kendall, Quartey et al., 2018. Transcript ID DCB_se2_ag2_f_01_1.
71. Bayley, 2012, p. 161.
72. Christian, 1991, and Webelhuth and Dannenberg, 2006; cited in Huang and McCoy, 2015.

73. Putnam and van Koppen, 2011; cited in Wood, 2013.
74. Baker-Bell, 2020, p. 45.
75. Kendall, Quartey et al., 2018 Transcript ID DCB_se1_ag1_m_02_1.
76. Davies, 2018.
77. Fought, 2003, p. 96.
78. Green, 2002, p. 48.
79. Barrón and San Romón, n.d., pp. 30–1; cited in Bayley, 2012, p. 158.
80. Kendall, Quartey et al., 2018 Transcript ID DCB_se2_ag4_m_01_1.
81. Kendall, Fasold et al., 2018 Transcript ID DCA_se1_ag1_f_02_1.
82. Kendall, Quartey et al., 2018 Transcript ID DCB_se3_ag3_m_02_1.
83. Barrón and San Romón, n.d., pp. 30–1; cited in Bayley, 2012, p. 160.
84. Ibid.
85. Staub and Zentz, 2017.
86. Huang, 2011.
87. Wolfram and Christian, 1976, p. 69.
88. Ruffing, 2012.
89. Maher and Wood, 2011.
90. Wood, 2014.
91. Martinez, 2018.
92. Bayley and Santa Ana, 2004, p. 379.
93. Bayley, 2012, p. 157.
94. Wood, 2015.
95. Coles, 2001.
96. Doherty, 1993, p. 158; cited in McCoy, 2016b.
97. Maher and McCoy, 2011.
98. Feagin 1979; cited in Matyiku, 2011b.

CHAPTER 2
TOWARD A LINGUISTIC FOUNDATION FOR GRAMMAR

Overview

This chapter equips you with a working command of some basic, but technical, terminology necessary for the study of grammar. You'll gain an initial understanding of how the English language makes words (**morphology**) and how those words form larger units such as phrases, clauses, and sentences (**syntax**). This knowledge is fundamental to identifying **lexical categories**. Our objectives are as follows. You'll be able to

- use foundational linguistic terminology to analyze grammar;
- explain how words are formed (morphology);
- explain basic linguistic characteristics of words, phrases, clauses, and sentences; and
- identify constituents by applying constituent tests.

Pre-reading tasks

1. How would you define what a word is? A sentence?
2. Write down what you know about nouns, verbs, adjectives, and adverbs.
3. Make a list of words that you might encounter in a text message with your friends or might see almost exclusively on social media. Then, answer these questions:

   a. Which of your words do you think someone from your grandparents' generation might not understand or use?
   b. Would you expect to find these words in "the dictionary"? If not, do you consider them "real" words? Why? Why not? If not, what would make them "real"?
   c. Next, look at the forms of the words. Do they have anything in common?
   d. Can you label the words as nouns, verbs, adjectives, and adverbs?
   e. If possible, in class, share your list with your peers. Do your lists overlap at all?

Foundations of Grammar

2.1 Introduction: What's a Word?

This seems like an easy, almost silly, question. How many words are in the following sentences?

(1)   It's harder than it looks. (sE)
(2)   He bin tryna ruin Lakers.[1] (AAE)

In both (1) and (2), did you count five or six? Did you count the contraction *it's* (it is > it's) as one or two words? Conceptually, the *s* following the apostrophe is the verb, so we should count it as its own word, right? What about *tryna* (trying to > tryna) in (2): one or two words? **Orthography** (spelling) and the spaces between words, of course, are helpful clues! Remember, when children acquire their first language, they only hear the stream of spoken language or see the stream of signed language. Still, the human brain is able to parse words/gestures from that stream.[2] The *s* in *It's* in (1) and the *a* in (2), then, would be parsed as separate words.

Semantics (i.e., the meaning of words) also helps to identify words. Words usually express a semantic concept (i.e., meaning). For instance, in (3), *Luciana* refers to a person; so, the word matches neatly to one **semantic concept**. How many words are in (3) and (4)?

(3)   Luciana showed me her dog. (sE)
(4)   She a chairwoman.[3] (AAE)

Each word neatly corresponds to one semantic concept, and each word fits nicely into a grammatical slot:

(3a)	Luciana	showed	me	her	dog.
lexical category:	noun	verb	pronoun	determiner	noun
semantic concept:	person	action	person	identifier	object

(4a)	She	a		chairwoman.
lexical category:	pronoun	determiner		noun
semantic concept:	person	identifier		person

Now, what about (5):

(5)   It's raining cats and dogs. (sE)

Here, the contraction *it's* again complicates the sentence, but, more importantly, what is the semantic concept of *cats and dogs* here? Whatever that semantic concept of *cats and dogs* is, it clearly takes more than one word to express. Let's replace the semantic concept of *cats and dogs* with another word:

(5a)   It's raining <u>hard.</u> (sE)
(5b)   It's raining <u>heavily.</u> (sE)

How do we understand the phrase *cats and dogs* as a single concept that describes the manner in which it is raining and not as two separate concepts of cats ("noun, object")

1.	Orthography (spelling)	Words are separated by spaces (unless contracted)
2.	Semantics (meaning)	Words express a coherent semantic concept
3.	Phonology (sound rules)	Words have one primary stress
4.	**Morphology (formation rules)**	**Words have internal cohesion and follow a language's formation rules**
5.	**Syntax (grammar rules)**	**Words fill a syntactic slot in a sentence**

Chart 1 Linguistic features of an English word

and dogs ("noun, object")? So, once again, how many words are in *It's raining cats and dogs*? Surely, it's six words, but we understand that the phrase *cats and dogs* works as one concept, even though it consists of more than one word. While semantics can be a first clue to identify lexical categories of words, our focus here will be on morphology and syntax. See Chart 1 for an overview of linguistic features that help classify English words.

Based on morphology and syntax, a **word** is defined as the smallest **independent grammatical unit** that has meaning. So, what does that mean? We'll start with a first set of examples, i.e., a data set.[4] All examples follow the grammatical rules of their respective dialects. Most people think that non-sE examples feature grammatical mistakes, but that isn't the case. In fact, unless otherwise indicated by an asterisk, all examples in this book are grammatically correct—they *all* follow their respective dialect's grammatical rules. Don't worry; we'll explain many of these dialect patterns in later chapters. Many sE examples are *not* unique to sE, but instead are used across all American English dialects. Many of the examples labeled AAE, ChE, ME, AE, and so on are also *not* unique to just those dialects. For now, whether you're familiar with or use non-sE dialects yourself, simply try and get comfortable working with examples that don't conform to sE grammar in a grammar book!

For this first data set, pay attention to the italicized words. What observations can you make? Put differently, what do these italicized words have in common?

(6) This *cat* ran by us. (sE)

(7) He's pointing on a *cat* on a *treetop*.[5] (ChE)

(8) *People* be thinkin' *teenagers* don't know nothin'.[6] (AAE)

(9) Alls Alice brought to the *party* was *bread*.[7] (ME)

Words like *cat, treetop, people, teenagers, party*, and *bread* all fit into the same lexical category (or word class): they are all **nouns**. Each has a definable semantic meaning. For example, Merriam-Webster defines a cat as "a carnivorous mammal (Felis catus), long domesticated as a pet, largely for the purpose of catching rats and mice."[8] These words fit into a phrase or clause just as they are. Take the word *cat* for example:

(10) Our *cat* is called Mr. Kitty. (part of subject)

(11) We rescued the *cat* yesterday. (part of direct object)

(12) Rowan gave the *cat* a treat. (part of indirect object)

(13) Mr. Kitty is a *cat*. (part of subject complement)

(14) Fatima bought a bed for the *cat*. (part of object of the preposition)

Foundations of Grammar

In each sentence, the word *cat* occurs in a different slot (see parentheses after each example), which means it plays a different role in each sentence. We will come back to these functions later in this book.

How about this next set of words: *walk, write, come, bring*—what do you notice about them?

(15)   Bruce *write* fast.[9] (AAE)

(16)   I had *came* out of the hospital.[10] (ChE)

(17)   Rhys and Sam *walk* together each morning. (sE)

(18)   Alls Alice *brought* to the party was bread.[11] (ME)

The italicized words all fit into another lexical category: they are all **verbs**, and each has a definable semantic meaning. Merriam-Webster provides four definitions for the verb *walk*, one of which is "to move along on foot: advance by steps."[12] These words also fit into a particular grammar slot. When compared to nouns, this slot seems to be more fixed: verbs come after the subject. This different distribution of where in a sentence different types of words can occur (i.e., the syntactic environment) serves as evidence to determine a word's lexical category.

For these words so far, we can assign meaning fairly straightforwardly (but ask a semantician for the ins and outs of what words mean!). Some words, however, do not have an easily definable conventional meaning. Such words include *and, of, the, a/an*, and *must* (among many others). They still fit independently within a grammatical slot in a sentence, and they create the grammatical tissue holding the sentence together. We can see the individual connective work they do in the following sentences:

(19)   I picked her because she nice *and* calm.[13] (AAE)

(20)   Here's you *a* piece *of* pizza.[14] (SAE)

(21)   *The* teacher ran by us. (sE)

The italicized words above also all have specific slots that they can occur in; however, they do not all belong to the same lexical category. We have a **conjunction** (*and* in (19)), a **preposition** (*of* in (20)), as well as definite and indefinite **articles** (*the* in (21) and *a* in (20)). Nevertheless, these words all share the characteristic of providing grammatical information. This is why we call them **function words**: they have grammatical function but little semantic meaning.

While we generally don't add new words to those classes that are function words (with the exception of gender-neutral pronouns), we constantly add new nouns, verbs, adjectives, and adverbs to English (just ask a teenager for current slang terms or check out new additions to the Oxford English Dictionary!). We call the latter **open-class** words and the former **closed-class** words.

Open Class	Closed Class
Nouns	Prepositions
Verbs	Conjunctions
Adjectives	Pronouns
Adverbs	Auxiliary verbs
	Modal verbs
	Determiners
	Numerals

28

Notice that in our designation of words, we are not talking about the meaning of individual parts of words. For example, if we turn *cat* into *cats*, that final *-s* has plural meaning in sE, but we never see just an *-s* in a sentence (unless we elevate it to a noun: "How many **Ss** are there in the word Mississippi?"). In other words, such a final *-s* is not an independent grammatical unit, and as such, is excluded from "word status" based on our definition of a **word** being the smallest independent grammatical unit that has meaning.

2.2 Fundamentals of Morphology: Derivation and Inflection

While an *s* can be a part of a word and does convey important information, the *s* by itself is not a word. These individual parts of words are nevertheless important because they help make a word fit into the different syntactic slots of a sentence. Because parts of words, especially endings, reveal a lot of information about a word's lexical class, they are fundamental to understanding grammar. **Morphology** is about these parts of words, and we turn to it next.

A word can be created from smaller units. Can you break the word *teacher* into smaller units? We can split it up into *teach* and *-er*. Here, we have the word *teach* (verb, to provide instruction) and the ending *-er* (noun marker, one who does x). Notice that *teach* can stand alone in a sentence:

(22)   Latoya and Julissa *teach* syntax. (sE)

Any word that can stand alone in a syntactic slot is considered a **free root**. The *-er*, however, cannot stand alone. Items that cannot stand alone are called **morphemes**, which can be added to another part that has semantic meaning (not just grammatical meaning). These added parts are called **affixes**. A **prefix** is added to the beginning of a word; a **suffix** is added to the end of a word. The noun *teacher* is derived by adding the suffix *-er* to the verb *teach*. This kind of suffix is called a **derivational suffix**.

Adding this derivational suffix *-er* changes the lexical category of *teach* from verb to noun (i.e., one who teaches). Along with a change in semantic meaning (from doing teaching to being a teacher), adding this *-er* also involves a grammatical change that allows the new word to fit into a different grammatical slot. Compare (22) above to (23) below:

(23)   The *teacher* asked Malaika a question. (sE)

In contrast to (22), in which the free root *teach* was used as a verb and as such came after the subject, in (23), the combination of free root+*er* (*teacher*) now occurs in the subject slot. This is what we mean by *grammatical change*—the newly derived noun *teacher* fits into grammatical slots different from the slot where the verb fits.

Many different derivational suffixes exist; some can be added to free roots to form nouns (like in *teacher*), other derivational suffixes create adjectives and adverbs. We introduce you to a variety, not an exhaustive list, in what follows. Here's another example.

(24)   The *teachers* at South High is cool.[15] (AAE)

Foundations of Grammar

Here, *teacher* ends in an *-s* suffix. The word *teachers* consists of the root *teach*, plus the suffix *-er*, plus the suffix *-s*. The *-s* suffix didn't change the semantic meaning of the word: the word still means "teacher"—it's just that, now, there are at least two teachers instead of just one. This *-s* suffix is an **inflectional suffix**, and gives us grammatical information (in this case, the information is that the noun is plural). It merely inflects an existing word but doesn't derive a whole new word like a derivational suffix. A rule of thumb is this: A word created via derivational suffixes will have its own dictionary entry. The verb *to teach* and the noun *teacher* have separate dictionary entries. The word *teachers*, however, does not have its own dictionary entry; it is simply included under the entry for *teacher* as its plural form.

The types of inflectional suffixes a word can take depend on the word's lexical category, which is why suffixes provide strong evidence for a word's lexical class. Nouns, as you might expect by now, can be pluralized:

(25) one cat > *many* cats (sE)

(26) one basketball hoop > *two* basketball hoop[16] (AAE)

The plural *-s* can be added to nouns, but not to verbs or adjectives or adverbs. In some dialects, the plural *-s* is optional, not required. More on that in Chapter 3.

Verbs can, among other suffixes, add *-ing*:

(27) He's *smiling* to the cat.[17] (ChE)

(28) Fire was *a-flamin'* everything.[18] (AE)

(29) We were *dancing* last night. (sE)

And adjectives as in (30) and (30a) and adverbs as in (31)–(33) can add an *-er* and *-est* suffix (which verbs can't!):

(30) I picked her because she *nice* and *calm*.[19] (AAE)

(30a) I picked her because she *nicer* and *calmer* than Tina.[20] (AAE)

(31) My sister runs *fast*. (sE)

(32) My brother runs *faster*. (sE)

(33) My mother runs the *fastest*. (sE)

Remember that inflectional suffixes merely inflect. They change one feature of the word's overall meaning (from singular to plural, for instance) whereas derivational suffixes actually create words with entirely new semantic meaning (closely related, sure, in case of *teach* and *teacher*, but fundamentally, *teacher* (one who teaches) is an entirely different semantic meaning from *to teach* (actually doing the teaching)).

Suffixes are not the only bits we can add to words in English. Chart 2 summarizes the different **affixes** (prefixes, suffixes, infixes, and circumfixes) that contribute to the morphological processes in English. Come up with your own examples in addition to ours!

Toward a Linguistic Foundation for Grammar

Prefix (added to the beginning)	*pre-, un-, en-, a-*, etc.
• Derivational—added to a word to change the meaning; may change the lexical category	view > **pre**view happy > **un**happy close > **en**close caroling > **a**-caroling courting > **a**-courting
Suffix (added to the end)	*-s, 's, -ing, -s, -ed, -er, -est*
• Inflectional—added to a word because of its lexical category (nouns can be made plural; verbs can show tense/aspect; adjectives/adverbs can form comparatives and superlatives); never changes the lexical category	cat > cat**s** talk > talk**ed** etc. *-ness, -ful*, etc.
• Derivational—added to a word to change the meaning; may change the lexical category	happy > happi**ness** regret > regret**ful**
Infix (added in the middle) Note: English does not use this morpheme rule productively.	*-blooming-, -freaking-* abso**blooming**lutely fan**freaking**tastic
Circumfix (added to both the beginning and the end)	*en- + -en; em- + en;* **en**ligh**ten** **em**bold**en**

Chart 2 Types of affixes in English

Note that in Chart 2, all affixes are added to **free roots**—those roots that can stand on their own. English does have **bound roots** that have semantic meaning but never appear in syntactic slots without an affix:

(34) *electr* from Greek meaning "power:" *electricity, electric*

(35) *duce* comes from the Latin *ducere* meaning "to lead:" *deduce, induce*

(36) *ceive* or *cept* from the Latin *capere* which meant "to take:" *conceive; reception*

Chart 3 summarizes the features for derivation and inflection.

Derivation	Inflection
– Creates a new word by changing the semantic meaning:	– Changes existing word to fit its syntactic context
• happy (ADJ, to be pleased or content) > **un**happy (ADJ, not happy)	• **one** dog > **two** dogs
• relate (V, to show a connection) > relation**ship** (N, the way two or more people or things are connected)	• I **teach**. > Yesterday, I **taught**.
– Can change the lexical category of a word (i.e., **class-changing**)	– **Cannot** change semantic meaning or lexical category (i.e., it is always class-maintaining)
• teach (V, to provide instruction) > teach**er** (N, one who teaches)	• dog (N) > dog**s** (N, plural)

- kind (ADJ, to be friendly, generous, courteous) > kind**ness** (N, the quality of being friendly, generous, courteous)
- Can keep the lexical category of a word (i.e., **class-maintaining**):
  - happy (ADJ, experiencing pleasure or contentment) > **un**happy (ADJ, not happy)
  - view (V, to see) > **pre**view (V, to view in advance)
- teach (V) > teach**es** (V, 3rd person singular)
- realize (V) > realiz**ed** (V, past tense)
- tall (ADJ) > tall**er** (ADJ, comparative) tall**est** (ADJ, superlative)

Chart 3 Derivation and inflection

When both inflection and derivation occur, then inflection must happen after derivation. Why? If derivation changes the lexical category, then the inflectional processes change. For example, if a verb becomes a noun, then verb inflection is no longer possible. Instead, noun inflection is possible. When the verb *teach* becomes a noun via the suffix *-er* to form *teacher,* we have derived a new word. This new word is a noun, and as such, cannot endure verb inflection. You can test this yourself: We cannot add the verb suffix *-ed, -ing,* or *-s* to the noun *teacher*:

(37) *I *teachered* yesterday.

(38) *I am *teachering* today.

(39) *She *teachers* all day on Monday.

What we can do, however, to this new noun *teacher*, once we have derived it from *to teach*, is add the plural *-s* as in *two teachers*.

Exercise 1

Derivation (D) or Inflection (I). Decide if the processes below are derivational or inflectional.

a) kind > *un*kind

b) bus > bus*es*

c) drive > driv*er*

d) large > *en*large

e) nation > nation*al*

Inflectional suffixes are evidence when determining whether a word is a noun, verb, adjective, or adverb. Here are some initial basics:

- Can you make something plural as in *one cat/two cats* (sE) and *one hoop/two hoop* (AAE)? You're looking at a noun.
- Can you turn something into past tense as in *dance/danced*? You're looking at a verb.

- Can you compare something by adding an *-er* or *-est*? Then you're looking at an adjective or adverb. If the word in question tells you more about a noun, then the *-er*-word is an adjective; if it tells you more about a verb or adverb or adjective, then the *-er*-word is an adverb.

We will build on this initial, quick overview in subsequent chapters. You'll want to keep these suffixes in the back of your mind, as they are crucial in identifying lexical categories. Check out the companion website for additional morphological processes!

So far, you've learned a bit about words, components of words, and morphological processes that are helpful to identify the **lexical category** of a word. In this next section, you'll learn a little bit about how words hang together to form larger chunks. These larger chunks are phrases, and once we have **phrases**, we can form **clauses**.

2.3 How Words Hang Together 1: Phrases

2.3.1 Noun Phrases

Let's start with the word *cat*. You already know that the suffix *-s* is used to form *cats*. You also already know that in some non-sE dialects, this plural *-s* is optional. This is still within the realm of morphology since all we did is add a suffix to a word. Obviously, there must be a way to add words together to form units larger than a single word. Your turn: Combine the three words in each bullet-point list into two larger units:

- *cats, the, cute.*
- *process, mummification, the*

We're sure you came up with (40) and (41), but not with (40a) or (41a), because the word order represented in (40a) and (41a) is not grammatical (i.e., not allowed) in English:

(40) The cute cats
(41) The mummification process
(40a) *cats cute the
(41a) *mummification process the

In a whole sentence, we might encounter these three words like this:

(42) *The cute cats* are sleeping. (sE)
(43) They took part of *the mummification process*.[21] (ChE)

We know that these three words belong together because we can replace them with one single word, *they* or *it*:

(42a) *They* are sleeping. (sE)
(43a) They took part of *it*. (ChE)

Both of our three-word units are **phrases**. In both, the main word is a noun (*cat, process*). This is why they are called **noun phrases {NPs}**. Here are some more examples of {NPs}:

(44) dog (N)
(45) The dog (DET + N)
(46) The amazing dog (DET (+ADJ) + N)
(47) The amazing, tan, furry dog (DET (+ADJ⁺) + N)

{NPs} may have a determiner (articles such as *the* and *an*) prior to the noun. These determiners are required for singular count nouns. A singular count noun is something like *dog*: it is one dog and thus "singular," and dogs can be counted as in *one dog, two dogs, three dogs* ... for sE and as *one dog, two dog, three dog* ... in dialects such as AAE. Not all {NPs} will feature a determiner:

(48) *Ms. Helen* be correcting us all the time.[22] (AAE)
(49) The *dogs* over there are cute. (sE)
(50) *Dogs* are the best pets. (sE)

In (48), the noun is someone's name, so **The Ms. Helen* would not be possible. The same applies to names of cities and places such as *New York* or *Michigan*. In addition to such proper nouns, plural nouns can occur with or without a determiner ((49) and (50)). Finally, {NPs} may contain one or more adjectives. Sometimes, words that follow the noun still belong to that {NP}; you'll learn more about the {NP} structure in Chapters 3 and 10.

2.3.2 Other Phrases

Verb phrases {VPs} are those phrases that consist of one or multiple verbs:

(51) walk
(52) to walk
(53) walk/walks
(54) walked
(55) will walk
(56) is/are/was/were walking
(57) has/have/had walked

We will explore the full expressions of {VPs} and the impressive dialect variations that exist with verbs in Chapters 6, 7, 12, and 13.

Larger units around adjectives are called **adjective phrases {AdjPs}**:

(58) The *tan* dog
(59) The *amazing* dog
(60) The *extremely furry* dog
(61) The dog is *very friendly*. (sE)

An {AdjP} can consist of just one adjective ((58) and (59)). {AdjPs} can also include an adverb that comes before the adjective ((60) and (61)). We'll build on this basic structure of {AdjPs} as ((ADV) + AdjP) in Chapter 5.

Toward a Linguistic Foundation for Grammar

You'll have guessed by now that larger units around adverbs are called **adverb phrases** {AdvPs}. They have a similar basic structure to {AdjPs} in that they can consist of just one adverb (Adv) as in (62) and (64) or multiple adverbs ((Adv) + Adv) as in (63). Stay tuned for more details in Chapter 6.

Phrase types
{NP}
{AdjP}
{AdvP}
{PP}
{VP}

(62)   An *incredibly* skillful lawyer

(63)   Daya drove *very carefully*. (sE)

(64)   These were expensive when they *barely* came out.[23] (ChE)

Finally, **prepositional phrases** {PP} begin with a preposition. That preposition is then followed by the object of the preposition, which is itself generally an {NP}:

(65)   *on* the road

(66)   *toward* an acceptable solution

(67)   *by* noon

(68)   *at* the corner of Main and Third Streets

You'll learn more about what prepositions are soon. For now, remember that they tend to be "little" words like *on, about, in, at, toward, by, over*, etc. A {PP} almost always breaks down into P + {NP}. As you can see, the {NP} following the preposition can include adjectives, as in *toward an acceptable solution* in (66). More on phrase structures for {PPs} in Chapter 10.

Try to find as many phrases in the next four examples as you can. Put brackets around them and label them. Then, continue reading and see if you found all of them!

(69)   The clever students were planning their linguistic projects carefully. (sE)

(70)   The teachers at South High is cool.[24] (AAE)

(71)   The slothful students hoped for a new due date. (sE)

(72)   He's pointing on a cat on a treetop.[25] (ChE)

Do yours look like this?

(69a)   [The clever students] [were planning]
                    NP   VP

[their linguistic projects] [carefully]. (sE)
              NP   AdvP

(70a)   [The teachers at South High] [is] [cool]. (AAE)
                    NP   VP   AdjP

(71a)   [The slothful students] [hoped] [for a new due date]. (sE)
                    NP   VP   PP

(72a)   [He] ['s pointing] [on a cat on a treetop]. (ChE)
             NP   VP   PP

You'll be doing a deep dive into lexical categories very soon (wait, there's more? yes, yes, there is!), which will enable you to label each word in the phrases above.

2.4 Constituents and How to Identify Them

Constituents are groupings of words that perform a function together. Compare the following two pairs of sentences.

> **Constituent**
> A group of words that functions together in a sentence or phrase; sometimes called component

(73) *The amazing, tan, furry dog* is hiding. (sE)

(74) We found *the amazing, tan, furry dog*. (sE)

(75) Alls I want is *new shoes*.[26] (ME)

(76) *New shoes* is what I got for Christmas. (sE)

As you can see, the group of italicized words occurs in initial position in (73) but in final position in (74). The same goes for (75) and (76): the group of words *new shoes* can come before and after the verb *is*. You'll likely recognize that all four strings of words are {NPs}. Each group of words, [*the+amazing+tan+furry+dog*] and [*new+shoes*], functions as a **constituent** in each of the sentences. A constituent is a larger unit that is (often) movable as a whole. Now, what's the difference between a phrase and a constituent? Well, phrases aren't the only units that can take on functions in a sentence. Constituents, thus, is a broader label that can include phrases but also larger items such as clauses. Constituents can also function at both the sentence and phrase level. We will focus mostly on sentence-level functions in this chapter. In (73) and (76), the italicized constituents function as (i.e., play the role of) subject, in (74), they function as the direct object, and in (75), they function as the subject complement.

It is imperative to keep **function and form** separate in the study of grammar. The form (i.e., the type of thing) that the subject takes in (73) and (76) is an {NP}, not an {AdjP} or {VP}, etc. The form of the direct object in (74) and the form of the subject complement in (75) is also an {NP}. In fact, in both sentence pairs, it is the same words that make up the {NP}, and yet, these constituents perform different functions in the two sentences. We'll be returning to function/form throughout the book, so make a mental note! Because identifying constituents is crucial to understanding sentence structure, we outline three tests that will help you figure out where a constituent starts and ends as well as how many constituents are in a sentence.

2.4.1 One-Word Replacement Test

The **one-word replacement test** is also known as the **pronoun replacement test**. Pronouns are, for now, words that can stand in for (i.e., replace) nouns. The next three pairs illustrate how one word, in these cases *it*, replaces an entire constituent:

(77) [The skillful lawyer from the top firm] arrived at the courthouse. (sE)

(77a) [She/he/they] arrived at the courthouse.

(78) Yesterday, we play [another team] for the championship.[27] (AAE)

(78a) Yesterday, we play [it] for the championship.

(79)   We was discussing [the initiative that Obama curated].²⁸ (AAE)

(79a) We was discussing [it   ].

Compare those pairs to the next three:

(77b) [The skillful lawyer] from the top firm arrived at the courthouse. (sE)

(77c) [*She/he/they   ] from the top firm arrived at the courthouse.

(78b) Yesterday, we play another [team] for the championship.²⁹ (AAE)

(78c) *Yesterday, we play another [it] for the championship.

(79b) We was discussing [the initiative] that Obama curated.³⁰ (AAE)

(79c) *We was discussing [it   ] that Obama curated.

Remember that the * means that something is not grammatical. When we use pronouns such as *it*, *he/she/they* (or *something*) to replace just **some** of the words of a constituent, we end up with ungrammatical sentences! This means that you can test out exactly where a constituent starts and ends by replacing it with a pronoun. In (77), the entire constituent *the skillful lawyer from the top firm* functions as the subject, in (78), the constituent *another team* functions as the direct object, and in (79) the constituent *the initiative that Obama curated* functions as the direct object. (79) also illustrates that constituents can be larger than just a phrase: *that Obama curated* is part of the constituent and is a clause all on its own (more on clauses later!).

Note that this replacement test can also be used to identify phrase-level constituents:

(77d) The skillful lawyer from [the top firm] arrived at [the courthouse]. (sE)

(77e) The skillful lawyer from [it   ] arrived at [it   ].

The two {NPs} *the top firm* and *the courthouse* do not play a role at the sentence level; they belong within the {PPs} *from the top firm* and *at the courthouse* (and as we tested,

Exercise 2

Identifying constituents. Identify as many constituents as you can by using the one-word replacement test.

a) Some dedicated artists took extremely outstanding pictures. (sE)

b) The talented teacher wrote constructive comments on the essay. (sE)

c) My cousin think the students at South High are all mean and stuff.³¹ (AAE)

d) The nice neighbor mowed the overgrown lawn. (sE)

e) Alls Amy got from Grace was a box of chocolates.³² (ME)

f) The little kid don't have no shoes of his own.³³ (ChE)

Foundations of Grammar

from it and *at it* is possible), and these {NPs} function within those {PPs} as objects of the prepositions. More on this in Chapter 10!

2.4.2 Question Test

The **question test** boils down to turning a sentence into *who/whom/what/where/how-*questions to see which words are then left for the answer to that question—what's leftover in the answer is a constituent!

(80)   In the morning, the CEO exercised. (sE)

- Q: Who exercised in the morning?   A: *The CEO.*
- Q: When did the CEO exercise?   A: *In the morning.*

(81)   Trash *be* everywhere.[34] (AAE)

- Q: What be everywhere?   A: *Trash.*
- Q: Where the trash be?   A: *Everywhere.*

(82)   Dinner was yummy last night. (sE)

- Q: What was yummy last night?   A: *Dinner.*
- Q: When was dinner yummy?   A: *Last night.*

The Q&A pairings provide evidence that each answer is a constituent because it can stand alone as that answer and the corresponding question is grammatical. What's important to remember for this test is that you must use all non-answer words in the question, without adding additional words (except when a form of *do* is required for question creation in the first place). This is because whichever words you're unable to pack into the question are the words that are left over for the answer. Let's illustrate this with one more example:

(83)   The lawyers quickly reviewed the case at night. (sE)

- possible Q: Who reviewed the case?
- impossible A: **The lawyers quickly at night*

While *Who reviewed the case?* is a possible and grammatical question, the resulting answer is ungrammatical. Because in our Q&A pairings for this test, all words from the original sentence must be incorporated into the question or the answer, and because we have **not** incorporated *quickly* and *at night* and *the case* into the question, we are now forced to put all of those words into the answer, which results in *The lawyers quickly at night* as the answer, which we hope you agree is more than odd as an answer to the *who*-question: it's straight up ungrammatical! The following Q&A pair is how it's done grammatically:

- Q: Who quickly reviewed the case at night?
- A: *The lawyers.*

Similarly, if we wanted to test for other constituents in the same sentence, we could form these Q&A pairs:

- Q: When did the lawyers quickly review the case?   A: *At night*
- Q: How did the lawyers review the case at night?   A: *Quickly*

You can see, again, that all words need to be accounted for, either in the question or in the answer, for this test to work properly.

Exercise 3

Question test. Use the question test for at least one constituent per sentence. That is, write down the Q&A pair for the constituents you chose.

a) Some dedicated artists took extremely outstanding pictures. (sE)
b) The talented teacher wrote constructive comments on the essay. (sE)
c) My cousin think the students at South High are all mean and stuff.[35] (AAE)
d) The nice neighbor mowed the overgrown lawn. (sE)
e) The little kid don't have no shoes of his own.[36] (ChE)

2.4.3 Movement Test

The **movement test** shows which groupings of words are movable together; if a word group is movable, it forms a constituent. For this test, you need this host-phrase:

It is/was _____ *that/who* ….

If you can move words together into the blank of the host-phrase, then you know you're looking at a constituent:

(83a)   The lawyers quickly reviewed the case at night. (sE)

- It was *the lawyers* who *quickly reviewed the case at night*.
- It was *the case* that *the lawyers quickly reviewed at night*.
- It was *quickly* that *the lawyers reviewed the case at night*.
- It was *at night* that *the lawyers quickly reviewed the case*.

(84)   The baby wants cuddled by her mother.[37] (ME)

- It was *the baby* who *wants cuddled by her mother*.
- It was *by her mother* that *the baby wants cuddled*.

Both movement and question tests work for really, really long sentences, too. In fact, that is when they are most effective, since you are more likely to wonder exactly where a constituent begins and ends when you're looking at long, complicated sentences:

(85)   The day before yesterday, the incredibly talented lawyers quickly reviewed the complicated case brought by the new client at night. (sE)

- Question test:
  - Q: What did the incredibly talented lawyers quickly review at night the day before yesterday?
  - A: *the complicated case brought by the new client*
- Movement test:
  - It was <u>*the incredibly talented lawyers*</u> who *quickly reviewed the complicated case brought by the new client at night the day before yesterday.*

Each of these two tests shows us that both *the incredibly talented lawyers* and *the complicated case brought by the new client* are separate constituents. Your turn: perform additional question and movement tests to isolate the remaining constituents in (85).

Exercise 4

Movement test. Perform the movement test for at least one constituent per sentence. Write down the various host phrases with the moved portions.

a) Some dedicated artists took extremely outstanding pictures. (sE)

b) The talented teacher wrote constructive comments on the essay. (sE)

c) My cousin think the students at South High are all mean and stuff.[38] (AAE)

d) The nice neighbor mowed the overgrown lawn. (sE)

e) The little kid don't have no shoes of his own.[39] (ChE)

2.5 How Words Hang Together 2: Sentences

We've been using the term **sentence** quite a bit already, but what exactly is a sentence? Commonly encountered definitions include the following:

- A group of words that forms a complete thought.
- A group of words organized in such a way that they can stand on their own.

The concept of the written sentence is aided by punctuation: it starts with a capital letter and ends with final punctuation (e.g., period, question mark, exclamation point). This simple definition could lead to overgeneralizations for groups of words that we all probably say very often (can you come up with situations where you might say the three examples below yourselves?). Yet, we wouldn't write the sentences below in a formal document (at least not without someone marking it up, that is).

(86) *Have any?

(87) *Don't know.

(88) *Maybe.

Toward a Linguistic Foundation for Grammar

The task in Chart 4 will help you ascertain the basics of what a sentence is more systematically.

Task: Cover up the last row of the table. Take a look at the following sentences and make a list of observations. What do the sentences on the left have in common? How are they different from the sentences on the right? Hint: Try to identify the main verb in each sentence and write down observations about where in the sentence it is placed.

(89)	Mr. Kitty sleeps on the couch. (sE)	(89a)	*Sleeps Mr. Kitty on the couch.
(90)	The two turtles swim in the lake. (sE)	(90a)	*Swim the two turtles in the lake.
(91)	He's pointing from the cat.[40] (ChE)	(91a)	*'s pointing he from the cat.
(92)	They building these condos.[41] (AAE)	(92a)	* building they these condos.
(93)	She was a-goin' to the show.[42] (AE)	(93a)	* was a-goin' she to the show.
Observations:		Observations:	
– Words like *sleeps, swim, is pointing, building, was a-goin'* are in the middle of each sentence; they don't start or end any of the sentences.		– Words like *sleeps, swim, is pointing, building, was a-goin'* come at the beginning of the sentences.	
– Words like *Mr. Kitty, The two turtles, He, They,* and *She* come first in each sentence.		– Words like *Mr. Kitty, The two turtles, He, They,* and *She* come in the middle of the sentence.	

Chart 4 Basics of a sentence

Comparing the observations in each column reveals that for sentences to be grammatical, words like *sleeps* and *building* often come in the middle (not at the beginning) and words like *Mr. Kitty* and *They*—when they are the subjects—come in the beginning. Remember that we are looking **only** at the sentences provided in the chart. The pattern we are describing here only needs to hold for the data set that you are given. Words like *sleeps* and *is pointing* are verbs. You should be noticing some inflectional endings on these verbs that reveal that they are, indeed, verbs here. Words like *Mr. Kitty* and *The two turtles* function as subjects in these sentences. For now, based on our observations about the sets of sentences above, we can describe the overall pattern regarding subjects and verbs as follows:

- In English, subjects come before verbs.

We can check each of the five grammatical sentences of our data set in Chart 4 to make sure that this pattern applies to each of them, and it does. Likewise, we can apply this pattern to the four ungrammatical sentences, and we can see that each of the ungrammatical sentences *violates* that pattern: the subjects come after the verb in each case. Because these sentences violate the pattern of "Subjects come before verbs," they are ungrammatical.

The two rules that are required for a grammatically correct sentence—for all American English dialects—are as follows:

- Every sentence will contain a **subject** and a **verb**.
- The subject precedes the verb.

So, the pattern we described based on the sentences in Chart 4 is—in fact—a rule. A descriptive rule, but a rule nevertheless! Sometimes, you'll see them expressed slightly differently:

- Every sentence will contain a **subject** and a **predicate**.
- The subject precedes the predicate.

The term **predicate** refers to everything to the right of the verb, including the verb itself. The subject is what the sentence is about. More technically speaking, the subject occupies the first required position in a sentence or clause because English is a Subject–Verb–Object (SVO) language. So, the **subject** is found to the left of the verb. We've italicized the predicates in the sentences below:

(89b)   Mr. Kitty *sleeps on the couch.* (sE)

(90b)   The two turtles *swim in the lake.* (sE)

(91b)   He's *pointing from the cat.*[43] (ChE)

(92b)   They *building these condos.*[44] (AAE)

(93b)   She *was a-goin' to the show.*[45] (AE)

What about sentences such as these, you may wonder:

(94)   Sometimes, Ali *talks non-stop.* (sE)

(95)   Yesterday, we *was conversating with Mr. B. about the war.*[46] (AAE)

(96)   Hastily, the couple *fed the cats.* (sE)

(97)   For a week, he *kep' a-follerin' me around.*[47] (AE/OE)

Here, there is more than just one constituent to the left of the verb. The rule is that the subject is the first **required** constituent in the sentence; we can have **additional, optional** constituents to the left of the subject, as illustrated in (94)–(97). This is why you'll want to identify the subjects in sentences. Luckily, there are tests!

The Tag-test: Locating the Subject

For the tag question test, all you need to do is add a **tag** at the end of a sentence. Tags are little phrases such as *is it?/isn't it?, are you?/aren't you?, did she/didn't she?*, etc. This test works because the tag's pronoun will refer back to the sentence's subject. We have italicized the tags in each example, and we have bolded the pronoun in the tag and the subject it refers back to:

(98)   The guests ate the food. (sE)

(98a)   **The guests** ate the food, *didn't **they**?*

(99)   He's pointing from the cat.[48] (ChE)

(99a)   **He's** pointing from the cat, *isn't **he**?*

(100)   For a week, he kep' a-follerin' me around.[49] (AE/OE)

(100a)   For a week, **he** kep' a-follerin' me around, *didn't **he**?*

(101) Down the road, the traffic light that lost power has flickered back. (sE)

(101a) Down the road, **the traffic light that lost power** has flickered back, hasn't *it*?

Because *they* refers back to *the guests* in (98a), *the guests* is the subject in (98). Because *he* refers back to *he* in (99a) and in (100a), *he* is the subject in both (99) and (100). And in (101a), *it* refers back to *the traffic light that lost power*, which means *the traffic light that lost power* is the subject in (101). For more practice, apply this tag test to sentences (94)–(97) above to identify the subject in each.

Exercise 5

Subjects and Predicates. Identify the subject and predicate for the sentences below (punctuation marks left out on purpose).

a) The car raced down the street. (sE)

b) You be doing a class work in class.[50] (ChE)

c) A few years ago I didn't have no confidence.[51] (ChE)

d) Yesterday we was conversating with Mr. B. about the war.[52] (AAE)

e) Ms. Helen be correcting us all the time.[53] (AAE)

f) Sometimes it bes like that.[54] (SAE)

g) You stay in your office too late anymore.[55] (ME)

h) The playlist was curated by a pop music fan. (sE)

2.6 How Words Hang Together 3: Clauses

You already know one type of **clause**, the independent clause, because an independent clause is a sentence. An independent clause then is a grouping of words that consists of a subject and a predicate and can stand on its own to express a coherent thought or idea:

(102) I walk every day. (sE)

(103) We learned our grammar from our caretakers and those around us. (sE)

At the sentence level, the difference between a phrase and clause is simple: a phrase does not have a verb, and a clause does have a verb (unless the simple phrase we are looking at is itself a {VP}). Remember these phrases from Sections 2.3.1 and 2.3.2 ({NPs}, {AdjPs}, {AdvPs}, {PPs}). None of these have verbs in them. Then, look at the independent clauses (i.e., sentences) above: They all have verbs.

Words: *cat, the, dog, cute, yummy*
Phrases: *the cute dog*
Clauses: *The cute dog is cuddly because she is hungry.*
Sentences: *The cute dog is cuddly because she is hungry.*

Foundations of Grammar

Besides independent clauses, we can add complexity to our sentences by adding clauses that cannot stand on their own, which makes them **dependent clauses**. Below are some examples of such **complex sentences**, that is, sentences with dependent clauses in them (italicized).

(104) *Although we business professional,* our goal is to work with underprivileged youth.[56] (AAE)

(105) *When I get home from work,* I walk every day. (sE)

(106) Sam talks non-stop, *which can be annoying.* (sE)

(107) Alls Greg and Marsha want to do is kiss each other *when no one else is around.*[57] (ME)

(108) Aaliyah and Yegor, *who work together,* run together each morning. (sE)

(109) *When ... I'm done my homework,* I go there and skate.[58] (ECE)

(110) We learned our grammar from our caretakers and those around us, *attesting to how we learn languages through interacting with others.* (sE)

> **Independent clause**: can stand on its own
> **Dependent clause**: cannot stand on its own

We will save a complete description of the different types of clauses along with practice identifying, analyzing, and creating them for Chapter 14.

2.7 The Grammatical Hierarchy

Knowing the basics about words, phrases, clauses, and sentences allows us to bring it all together. There's a **hierarchy** when it comes to grammar: We can build structures up from the smallest unit (the word) or break them down from the largest unit (the sentence). Here's an example to illustrate the concept of grammatical hierarchy.

(111) I like all the cute cats in the world, and I also like some dogs. (sE)

This sentence consists of two clauses:

(112) I like all the cute cats in the world. (sE)

(113) I also like some dogs. (sE)

The clauses consist of various phrases:

- I
- all the cute cats
- in the world
- like
- some dogs
- also

Toward a Linguistic Foundation for Grammar

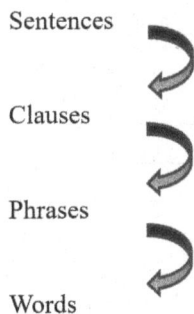

Figure 2.1 Grammatical Hierarchy.

And the phrases consist of words such as these: *I, all, cat, cute, the, some*. Figure 2.1 above illustrates this hierarchy.

Starting from the top, it breaks down as follows: sentences consist of clauses, clauses consist of phrases, phrases consist of words. Starting from the bottom, it builds up like this: words make up phrases, phrases make up clauses, clauses make up sentences.

> **Exercise 6**
>
> Practicing constituency tests. Decide if the italicized portions in the sentences are constituents or not. Apply at least one of the constituency tests (i.e., movement test, the one-word replacement test, or the question test). Complete and write out the test, then determine whether the words form a constituency.
>
> a) The nice neighbor made their yard *a wildflower paradise.* (sE)
> b) The nice *neighbor made their* yard a wildflower paradise. (sE)
> c) You could get *those big fat juicy fresh donuts.*[59] (AAE)
> d) *My friends and I* read all assigned books. (sE)
> e) My friends and I read all *assigned books.* (sE)
> f) *This thing here* I might should turn over to Ann.[60] (SAE)
> g) These gravels are *hard on your feet.*[61] (AE)

Terminology to Know

Term	Working definition	Example/Illustration
Word		
Phrase		
Clause		

Foundations of Grammar

Term	Working definition	Example/Illustration
Sentence		
Constituent		
Subject		
Predicate		
Movement test		
Question test		
One-word replacement test		
Tag test		
Grammatical hierarchy		
Derivation		
Inflection		
Prefix		
Suffix		
Form (of a word)		
Function (of a word)		

Chart 5 Key terminology Chapter 2

Notes

1. Gonzalez, 2020.
2. Crain and Pietroski, 2001.
3. Kendall, Fasold et al., 2018 Transcript ID DCA_se1_ag1_m_04_1.
4. Examples that illustrate non-sE patterns are taken from published work, including from the online resource *Yale Grammatical Diversity Project: English in North America* (https://ygdp.yale.edu/) and from the *Corpus of Regional African American Language* (Kendall and Farrington, 2023) which is housed by the University of Oregon (https://oraal.uoregon.edu/coraal). We are familiar with many features of major American English dialects, but we are not experts on all dialects. For this reason, we did not invent non-sE dialect examples ourselves and instead have relied on examples published by experts on the various dialects (see an incomplete list of experts in the preface and endnotes for sources for specific examples). Dr. Teaira McMurtry checked most (not all) AAE examples for accuracy and authenticity. We have replaced examples Dr. McMurtry flagged as inauthentic with examples she suggested. We can't thank her enough for sharing those suggestions and for sharing her expertise with us!
5. Barrón and San Romón, n.d., pp. 30–1; cited in Bayley, 2012, p. 162.
6. Baker-Bell, 2020, p. 43.
7. Wood, 2013.
8. Cat. https://www.merriam-webster.com/dictionary/cat.
9. Green, 2011, p. 206.

10. Fought, 2003, p. 94.
11. Wood, 2013.
12. Walk. https://www.merriam-webster.com/dictionary/walk.
13. Baker-Bell, 2020, p. 76.
14. Wood, 2015.
15. Baker-Bell, 2020, p. 43.
16. Reaser et al., 2017a, p. 182.
17. Barrón and San Romón, n.d., pp. 30–1; cited in Bayley, 2012, p. 162.
18. Wolfram and Christian, 1976, p. 69.
19. Baker-Bell, 2020, p. 76.
20. adapted from Baker-Bell, 2020, p. 76.
21. Bayley, 2012, p. 162.
22. Baker-Bell, 2020, p. 52.
23. Fought, 2003, p. 106.
24. Baker-Bell, 2020, p. 43.
25. Barrón and San Romón, n.d., pp. 30–1; cited in Bayley, 2012, p. 162.
26. Wood, 2013.
27. Barrón and San Romón, n.d., pp. 30–1; cited in Bayley, 2012, p. 162.
28. Kendall, Quartey et al., 2018 Transcript ID DCB_se1_ag1_m_02_1.
29. Kendall, Fasold et al., 2018 Transcript ID DCA_se1_ag1_m_05_1.
30. Kendall, Quartey et al., 2018 Transcript ID DCB_se1_ag1_m_02_1.
31. Baker-Bell, 2020, p. 43.
32. Wood, 2013.
33. Barrón and San Romón, n.d., pp. 30–1; cited in Bayley, 2012, p. 163.
34. McMurtry, 2022, p. 47.
35. Baker-Bell, 2020, p. 43.
36. Barrón and San Romón, n.d., pp. 30–1; cited in Bayley, 2012, p. 163.
37. Maher and Wood, 2011.
38. Baker-Bell, 2020, p. 43.
39. Barrón and San Romón, n.d., pp. 30–1; cited in Bayley, 2012, p. 163.
40. Ibid., p. 162.
41. Kendall, Quartey et al., 2018 Transcript ID DCB_se3_ag3_m_02_1.
42. Christian et al., 1988; cited in Matyiku, 2011a.
43. Barrón and San Romón, n.d., pp. 30–1; cited in Bayley, 2012, p. 162.
44. Kendall, Quartey et al., 2018 Transcript ID DCB_se3_ag3_m_02_1.
45. Christian et al., 1988; cited in Matyiku, 2011a.
46. Baker-Bell, 2020, p. 43.
47. Wolfram, 1976; cited in Matyiku, 2011a. Note: We fronted the adverbial to illustrate this point.

48. Barrón and San Romón, n.d., pp. 30–1; cited in Bayley, 2012, p. 162.
49. Wolfram, 1976; cited in Matyiku, 2011a. Note: We fronted the adverbial to illustrate this point.
50. Bayley, 2012, p. 158.
51. Fought, 2003, p. 97. Note: We added the adverbial for illustrative purposes.
52. Baker-Bell, 2020, p. 43.
53. Ibid., p. 52.
54. Wolfram and Schilling-Estes, 2000, p. 333.
55. Krumpelmann, 1939, p. 156; cited in Maher and McCoy, 2011.
56. Kendall, Quartey et al., 2018 Transcript ID DCB_se2_ag2_f_01_1.
57. Putnam and van Koppen, 2011; cited in Wood, 2013.
58. Wood, 2014.
59. Kendall, Quartey et al., 2018 Transcript ID DCB_se2_ag4_f_03_2.
60. Huang, 2011.
61. University of South Carolina (n.d.).

CHAPTER 3
NOT JUST "THINGS:" THE NOUN

Overview

This is the first of several chapters in which we break down **lexical categories** in detail. Building on what you know about morphology, you'll learn how to confidently identify nouns. In addition to **morphological criteria**, we also cover **syntactic** evidence for nouns. Our objectives are as follows. You'll be able to

- identify words as nouns based on morphological criteria;
- use syntactic position as well as related syntagmatic and paradigmatic evidence to identify nouns; and
- build your knowledge about the forms and functions of nouns.

Pre-reading tasks

1. Write down what you know about nouns. How is your answer different from the one you gave for question 2 in Chapter 2?
2. What do you notice about the following nouns? Can you divide them into two categories that behave similarly?

    car, water, book, milk, dog, rice, cat, sugar, chair, coffee, table, air, computer, furniture, pen, advice, bottle, information, shoe, money

3. What other words do you expect to appear close to nouns, i.e., in the vicinity of nouns?
4. If you know another language, how are the nouns and {NPs} in that language similar? Different?

Foundations of Grammar

3.1 Introduction

Many of us were taught a very simplistic way to identify nouns:

A noun is a person, place, or _____ *(or idea).*

This noun definition was made into a popular jingle and cartoon that began as a public service announcement by Schoolhouse Rock (Warburton and Dorough, 1973) on Saturday mornings and continues to run in some areas today. The practice of identifying a noun by this simple definition (a person, place, or thing) relies on semantic criteria. But is a word's meaning sufficient and reliable for determining its lexical category? Based on what you know from Chapter 2, you should at least be a bit skeptical! In the next sections, we are going to flesh out exactly how to use both derivational and inflectional morphological as well as syntactic evidence to classify words as nouns.

3.2 Disassembling the Parts: Analysis of Morphological Features

3.2.1 Derivation

As you know from Chapter 2, derivational suffixes create entirely new words by combining with a free root. For nouns, derivational suffixes include *-ment* and *-er*, which can be added to free roots as in *announcement* and *teacher*. Chart 1 illustrates a few such suffixes. Add any other derivational suffixes that are noun-markers into the empty rows in Chart 1.

Word (lexical category)	+ derivational suffix	Noun
happy (ADJ)	-ness	*happiness*
blog (N)	-er	*blogger*
govern (V)	-ment	*government*
inflect (V)	-ion	*inflection*
king (N)	-dom	*kingdom*
equal (ADJ)	-ity	*equality*

Chart 1 Some derivational suffixes for nouns

These derivational suffixes are productive, meaning a single suffix type can be added to many different words to form nouns. We can combine *-dom*, for instance, not just with *king* (*kingdom*) but also with *queen* to create *queendom*. Because of this, derivational suffixes are evidence for classifying a word's lexical category. So, if we're trying to identify the lexical category of the word *diversity* in (1), this is how it would work:

(1)　　The *diversity* of American English dialects is impressive. (sE)

Derivational evidence backs up our claim that *diversity* is a noun: *diverse* + *-ity* (derivational suffix, class changing) becomes *diversity*. We know this is a productive process because *equality* in Chart 1 works the same way, which means that the evidence for word classification is strong. Morphological analyses are helpful in figuring out the composition of a word, which in turn helps us identify lexical categories. The three questions in Chart 2 help us determine the composition of a word; we'll start with one of our previous examples, *teacher*:

1. How many morphemes?	Two (*teach* + *-er*)
2. What kind of morphemes?	*teach* (free root) + *-er* (derivational suffix)
3. What does each morpheme do?	*teach* (V, to instruct) + *-er* (one who teaches, noun marker, class changing)

Chart 2 Breakdown of the word "teacher"

3.2.2 Inflection

3.2.2.1 Plural

The word *trees* consists of two morphemes: the free root *tree* and the inflectional suffix *-s*. In sE and many other American English dialects, the *-s* inflectional suffix is used to denote plurality (i.e., more than one), and that is what the *-s* does in this example: it denotes that there is more than one tree.

Pluralization is a morphological process available to nouns:

(2)　　The *horse* is in the barn. (sE)

(2a)　　Two *horses* are in the barn. (sE)

(3)　　We had a wicked delicious *burger*.[1] (North East English (NEE))

(3a)　　We had two wicked delicious *burgers*. (NEE)

> **Derivational suffix:** creates a new word with new semantic meaning ("action of dancing" in the verb *to dance* changes to "the person who dances" in the noun *dancer*)
>
> **Inflectional suffix:** alters an aspect of a word's meaning by adding grammatical information; adding *-s* to *dancer* as in *dancers* adds grammatical information of plurality

We can determine that a word is a noun by showing it has plural morphological inflection or that it can have plural inflection in the sentence position within which it resides (the immediate context of where in the sentence the word occurs is crucial!). Because we can perform the operation of adding the suffix *-s* to go from *horse* (singular) in (2) to *horses* (plural) in (2a) and from *burger* (singular) in (3) to *burgers* (plural) in (3a), the words *horse* and *burger* are nouns.

In more technical terms: The words *horse* and *burger* are nouns because within their syntactic contexts (i.e., slots in the sentence), they can **endure** pluralization. Using an *-s* suffix is a common process to denote plurality for countable nouns (see (4), (5), and (6) below) in most dialects of English:

(4)   one professor > two *professors*

(5)   one cat > many *cats*

(6)   one dog > several *dogs*

Yet, a plural *-s* is not always required to denote "more than one"—even in sE dialects:

(7)   one deer > two *deer*

(8)   one cod > several *cod*

(9)   one sheep > many *sheep*

Sometimes, nouns take an irregular plural marking, such as an *-en* suffix or a vowel change:

(10)   one child > two *children*

(11)   one ox > two *oxen*

(12)   one mouse > three *mice*

(13)   one goose > several *geese*

A plural form that looks identical to its corresponding singular form is often described as containing a *zero-* or *null-*morpheme, commonly denoted with the symbol Ø, as in Ø-morpheme. When plural forms contain a Ø-morpheme, context including words like *all* and *twenty* often helps us understand that there is more than one, as is illustrated below for the nouns *deer* and *sheep*.

(14)   Look at all the baby *deer* in the yard. (sE)

(15)   Last night, twenty *sheep* escaped their enclosure. (sE)

Even though the nouns in (14) and (15) do not feature the inflectional suffix *-s*, English speakers have no trouble figuring out that these Ø-morpheme plural forms refer to more than one *deer* or more than one *sheep*. Even without clues such as *twenty* or *all*, these Ø-*s* plural forms exist:

(16)   The farmer released the *sheep* out into the pasture to graze. (sE)

Most likely, it would be odd for a farmer to have just one sheep on their farm. Strictly speaking, the word *sheep* in (16) could be interpreted as either singular or plural. We argue that sheep, in this context, is likely plural. Again, it would be odd, and dare we say sad, if there was just one, lonely sheep! Now, this kind of ambiguity is not all that uncommon in language, and we deal with it all the time.

Next, consider the examples below, taken from dialects other than sE. As a quick reminder, SAE stands for Southern American English, ChE for Chicano English, and AAE for African American English.

(17) I met them four *mile* down the road.² (SAE/ChE/AAE/others)

(18) The park has two basketball *hoop*.³ (SAE/ChE/AAE/others)

(19) You thirty *cent* away from having a quarter.⁴ (AAE)

(20) If you are the age of 60 or 80, you still can play many *game*.⁵ (SAE/ChE/AAE/others)

Overt plural marking via the *-s* suffix for nouns such as *mile, hoop, cent,* and *game* is optional in these dialects, which means that the examples above are perfectly grammatical the way they are. Because the *-s* plural suffix is optional—not prohibited—in some dialects, you will encounter many non-sE examples in this book where the plural *-s* suffix is present. Generally, forms such as *four mile* are restricted to examples like the ones we gave here, which include a measurement noun⁶ (*mile*) and a quantifier (*four*). In AAE and in ChE, they are most common in phrases such as *five cent* and *ten cent*.⁷

> **Nouns**
> - Can be pluralized.
> - Different ways of pluralization exist:
>   ✓ One deer > two deer
>   ✓ One game > many game/many games
>   ✓ One goose > two geese

Note that Ø-morpheme plural forms are attested in other English varieties in the United States and around the world. Conveniently, nouns such as *deer* and *sheep* that have no plural *-s* even in sE are generally considered "exceptions to the rule," while nouns such as *hoop* and *game* in the non-sE examples provided here are often derided as "mistakes" by the public. It's important to remember that none of the examples here are mistakes! They all follow a specific dialect's grammatical pattern.

What does this mean for our morphological analysis? Let's break down *deer* from (14) and *game* from (20). Within linguistics, various interpretations are provided for Ø-morphemes. For our purposes here, we count the Ø-morpheme even though it has no overt form like the *-s* suffix.

So, here is our analysis. Note that this time, we are dealing with inflectional morphemes!

1. How many morphemes?	• two (*deer* + -Ø)
	• two (*game* + -Ø)
2. What kind of morphemes?	• Free root (*deer*) + -Ø morpheme
	• Free root (*game*) + -Ø morpheme
3. What does each morpheme do?	• *deer* (N, animal) + -Ø (more than one, plural marker)
	• *game* (N, competition/contest) + -Ø (more than one, plural marker)

Chart 3 Basic morphological analysis

Foundations of Grammar

What about pluralization for the following italicized nouns?

(21) My sister studies *engineering* in college. (sE)

(22) When you start doing *research*, you find out, they ain't done nothing.[8] (AAE)

(23) Here's you some *money*.[9] (SAE)

(24) Nothin' [is] gooder than crumbled cornbread and *milk*.[10] (AE)

Turning these nouns into plural nouns by adding a final -*s*, we end up with these phrases:

(21a) *one engineering > *two engineerings

(22a) *one research > *two researches

(23a) *one money > *two moneys

(24a) *one milk > *two milks

> **Count nouns**: directly countable
> **Non-count nouns**: only indirectly countable

Even just adding the numeral *one* prior to these nouns results in an ungrammatical structure. Clearly, we cannot count these nouns! Does that mean there are nouns that cannot be pluralized? Well, not so fast. You know that there are things like *mechanical engineering* and *chemical engineering*, so there is more than one "engineering," yet we can't say that there are *two engineerings*! Can you come up with a way to express that there is more than "one engineering"? You probably came up with solutions similar to these:

(21b) many *types/fields of* engineering

(22b) four *areas of* research

(23b) some *types of* money

(24b) two *kinds of* milk

Essentially, we developed a workaround: We added a noun that we *can* count (*one type*, *two types*, etc.) and then add on the original noun as part of a {PP}. Because we cannot count individual occurrences of these nouns, we call them **non-count nouns**.

We have now covered one main characteristic of noun morphology (for countable nouns!): an inflectional suffix can be used to indicate more than one. Remember, the suffix can be -*s* or -Ø. Even if there is no plural suffix -*s*, as in *deer*, we can still count those nouns and use them with plural meaning. Other ways of pluralization such as sound change (*goose* > *geese*) exist as well. This means that one of the tests you can do to double-check that a particular word is, in fact, a noun is to try to pluralize that word. Let's imagine you're not sure if *farmer* and *graze* in (25) and *hoop* in (26) are nouns. Luckily, you remember that you can test for nouns by pluralizing the words in question:

(25) The *farmer* let the sheep out into the pasture to *graze*. (sE)

- one *farmer* > two *farmers*

- *one *graze* > *two *grazes*

(26)   The park has one basketball *hoop*.[11] (SAE/ChE/AAE/others)

- one *hoop* > two *hoop(s)* (AAE)

Let's plug the plural versions we created as our tests back into the sentences:
(25a)   The *farmers* let the sheep out into the pasture to *grazes. (sE)
(26a)   The park has two basketball *hoop(s)*. (SAE/ChE/AAE/others)

As you can see, our plural versions work for *farmers* (sE example) and *hoop* (AAE example), but not for *graze*: *to grazes is simply incorrect. In this context, *graze* does not **endure** pluralization, and so it is not a noun. In AAE, *hoop* does endure pluralization— two *hoop* is perfectly grammatical and denotes plurality. Just like sE's *sheep*, *hoop* in AAE does not have an overt plural marker in this specific example. Keep in mind that the *-s* is simply optional, not prohibited in AAE, which means that the plural *-s* test can be used across dialects.

3.2.2.2 Possessive
We're not done with S's and nouns quite yet. A second *-s* suffix is available for nouns:

(27)   the cat's paw (sE)
(28)   Sonya('s) sister[12] (AAE)
(29)   a horse's bridle (sE)
(30)   Adley's horse (sE)

We can see that nouns can express possession via a change in the noun's morphology: The *horse* belongs to *Adley* in (30), the *bridle* belongs to a *horse* in (29), the *sister* belongs to *Sonya* in (28), and the *paw* belongs to the *cat* in (27). Note that possession is used in a broad sense: a paw isn't something a cat owns, but the possessive form conveys that it is the paw of the cat, not of the horse, for instance. In sE and other dialects, this is expressed via the possessive *'s* ending. (28) highlights that the possessive *'s* is optional, not required, to indicate possession in AAE (and other non-sE dialects). Since the possessive *'s* is not forbidden in some dialects, you can use possessive marking as a test for nouns no matter the dialect!

Remember that all dialects are inherently variable. That means that not all speakers of the same dialect will use all dialect features in the same way, to the same degree, or all the time. This doesn't mean there's not a system. The examples we provide throughout this textbook are illustrative of these grammatical systems. For AAE, a grammatical rule is that possession can be marked via the "double noun sequence, with the first being the non-morphologically marked possessor and then the possessed following,"[13] that is, via proximity, which makes the possessive *'s* optional:

(31)   I moved out of my *mom house*.[14] (AAE)
(32)   I grew up going over to my *father house* maybe a couple times.[15] (AAE)
(33)   That's the street behind my *mom and dad house*.[16] (AAE)

Since our study of grammar wouldn't be fun, or complete, without some complications, here is something about possessives that you'll want to be aware of now. We'll tease it apart in later chapters, so don't worry, but here's the thing: When nouns add this possessive suffix *'s*, their function in the phrase changes (in all dialects!):

(28a) *Sonya('s)* sister[17] (AAE)

(29a) a *horse's* bridle (sE)

In (29a), *horse's* now describes another noun. In (28a), *Sonya('s)* becomes a determiner, denoting which sister we're talking about; more on all this in later chapters!

3.2.3 Putting Inflection and Derivation to Work

Morphology provides evidence for a word's lexical category within the context of a sentence. In fact, morphological rules (along with syntactic rules) prove to be much more reliable than semantics, i.e., meaning. The best way to see how morphology serves as evidence is through practice. Here is how the process works. Our focus is *swimmer* in (34).

(34) The *swimmer* took first place in the Olympics. (sE)

The lexical category of *swimmer* is a noun. How do we know? This is where both inflectional and, where applicable, derivational morphology come in handy. It's not quite as easy as A-B-C, but it builds on the three questions involved in the morphological analysis we've already used earlier, and it does involve three steps:

a) First, state the lexical category.

b) Second, provide the evidence for that class.

c) Third, provide additional evidence.

Here we go:

a) Lexical category: noun

b) Morphological evidence:

   i. derivational evidence

swim	+	-er	=	swimmer
Verb: to propel the body through water by using limbs		derivational **suffix**, noun marker: one who does the action		**Noun:** one who propels the body through the water with one's limbs

   ii. inflectional evidence: can endure pluralization

one swimmer	+	-s	=	two swimmers
singular		inflectional **suffix:** plural *-s*		plural: more than one

c) Additional evidence: this process works for words such as *drive* and *camp* as well

- drive:

drive	+	*-er*	=	*driver*
Verb: to operate a motor vehicle		derivational **suffix**, noun marker: one who does the action		**Noun:** one who operates a motor vehicle

one driver +		*-s*	=	*two drivers*
singular		inflectional **suffix**: plural *–s*		plural: more than one

- camp:

camp	+	*-er*	=	*camper*
Verb: lodge temporarily outside or in an uncomfortable environment		derivational **suffix**, noun marker: one who does the action		**Noun:** one who temporarily lodges outside or in an uncomfortable environment

one camper +		*-s*	=	*two campers*
singular		inflectional **suffix**: plural *–s*		plural: more than one

Let's walk through another example. The italicized word in (35) is once again a noun.

(35) You still can play many *game*.[18] (SAE/ChE/AAE/others)

    a. Lexical category: noun

    b. Morphological evidence:

        i. derivational evidence: Because *game* isn't a word that was created via derivation, this isn't applicable.

        ii. inflectional evidence: can endure pluralization

one game +		*-Ø*	=	*two game*
singular		inflectional **suffix**: *-Ø*		plural: more than one

    c. Additional evidence: this process works for words such as *mile* and *hoop* as well (see examples (17) and (18) from earlier)

- mile:

one mile +		*-Ø*	=	*two mile*
singular		inflectional **suffix**: *-Ø*		plural: more than one

- hoop:

one hoop +		*-Ø*	=	*two hoop*
singular		inflectional **suffix**: *-Ø*		plural: more than one

Note: We used the Ø-morpheme here because that's how it was used in the example sentences. Keep in mind that since plural *-s* is optional, not prohibited in AAE, you could still test for this plural -s as in *one game, two games*. Check out this one last AAE example before practicing this kind of analysis yourself:

(36) I ain't never seen nobody preach under *announcements*.[19] (AAE)

   a. Lexical category: noun
   b. Morphological evidence:

   i. derivational evidence

announce	+	*-ment*	=	*announcement*
Verb: to make known publicly		derivational **suffix**, noun marker: the thing via which something is made known to the public		**Noun:** a notice to the public; the act of announcing

   ii. inflectional evidence: can endure pluralization

one announcement	+	*-s*	=	*two announcements*
singular		inflectional **suffix:** plural *-s*		plural: more than one

---

Exercise 1

Use derivational evidence (if applicable), inflectional evidence, and additional evidence for why the italicized words are classified as nouns.

a) The dog chased the cat under the *table*. (sE)
b) My *parents* be correcting, too.[20] (AAE)
c) Aaliyah is faster than the other *runners*. (sE)
d) People be thinkin' *teenagers* don't know nothin'.[21] (AAE)
e) I Ø been doing dancing for a long time, for eight *years* already.[22] (ChE)
f) The *geese* are flying home. (sE)
g) Cher swims every *day*. (sE)
h) Here's me a good *pair* of jeans.[23] (SAE)

3.3 Just Playing the Role: Analysis of Syntactic Features

3.3.1 Syntactic Environment of Nouns

Syntactic environment is not a technical linguistics term, but we introduce it as a teaching tool. Think of a word's syntactic environment as its sentence "block" or "neighborhood"—where the word resides, where it might move, who it hangs out with, what it does depending on where it is and who it's with. These facets—its position (e.g., before a verb) and role (e.g., subject), along with its form (its morphology)—can reveal its lexical category.

In Chapter 2, we briefly discussed constituency. Some words in a sentence work together to function as constituents at the phrase or sentence level. Remember that we can identify *the cute cats* as a phrasal constituent by replacing it with *they*. When words join to form a constituent, the co-presence of other words within that unit can often help us identify the lexical category of a given word in that unit. That is, the linear arrangement and relationship of the words in the unit can provide **syntagmatic evidence**.

What are words that repeatedly show up prior to nouns in the following sentences? Which of those words cannot be deleted without making the sentence ungrammatical? Compare the following groupings:

(37) *The cat* jumped over *the lazy dog* lying on the shiny floor. (sE)

(37a) **Cat* jumped over **lazy dog* lying on the shiny floor. (sE)

(37b) *Cats* jumped over *lazy dogs* lying on the shiny floor. (sE)

(38) I noticed two older girls a-eating something out of *a little syrup bucket*.[24] (AE)

(38a) I noticed two older girls a-eating something out of **little syrup bucket*. (AE)

(38b) I noticed two older girls a-eating something out of *little syrup buckets*. (AE)

(39) This beat be *the beat* for *the street*.[25] (AAE)

(39a) This beat be **beat* for **street*. (AAE)

You probably noticed that sometimes adjectives (*lazy, little*) were included prior to the noun, and that sometimes the nouns had determiners (articles *the, a*) prior to them. But what makes (37a), (38a), and (39a) ungrammatical? And why are (37b) and (38b) grammatical again? It looks like it has to do with singular versus plural, right? This should be an easy difference to notice from your work earlier in this chapter! Essentially, when nouns are singular, removing the article *the* or *a* results in an ungrammatical structure.

Nearly all uses of singular count nouns in English require a **determiner**. A determiner serves to identify a noun. *The* signals that the sentence isn't about just any *dog*, but *the dog*. So, this **syntagmatic evidence**—that a determiner precedes the word *dog*—can help us classify *dog* as a noun, especially when it is a singular count noun. Plural nouns, however, do not require determiners. This doesn't mean that determiners cannot be used with plural nouns, as illustrated in (40).

(40) *The cats* on the couch tore up the pillow, not the ones on the bed. (sE)

Here, we have a determiner prior to the plural noun *cats*. The determiner helps *determine* which cats—the ones on the couch, not the ones on the bed—did something. Furthermore, adjectives can often be placed in between the determiner and noun. This means that nouns can occur in the **syntactic environments** illustrated in Chart 4.

Foundations of Grammar

Syntactic environments	Examples	Notations
alone	*Cats* are cute. *Dogs* are adorable.	N
after a determiner	The *cat* is cute. The *cats* over there are cuddly.	DET + N
after adjectives	Cuddly *cats* are cute. Fluffy *dogs* are adorable.	ADJ + N
after the combination "determiner + adjective"	The cute *cat* is cuddly. The fluffy *dog* is adorable.	DET + ADJ + N

Chart 4 Syntactic environments for nouns

We can also use **paradigmatic evidence** to establish the lexical category of a word. "Paradigm" is a word that means pattern or model. We obtain this type of evidence by substituting a word of known lexical category into the syntactic slot of the word we are assessing. What, then, could we put in place of *cat* and *dog* in (37c) and in place of *beat* in (39b)?

(37c)   The _____ jumped over the lazy _____ lying on the floor. (sE)

(39b)   This beat be the _____ for the street. (AAE)

We could fill the blanks in (37c) with words such as *cow, pig, goat, hamster,* and so on. Likewise, for (39b), we could fill the blank with words such as *tune, music, stuff*. If we have established the lexical category of our substitution word(s) as a noun, and if the sentence remains grammatical after the substitution, then this provides paradigmatic evidence that the word we substituted for is also a noun.

To spell it out, our argument would go as follows: "I have established that *cow* is a noun, and so replacing the word in question—*cat*—with this already-established noun *cow* tells me that the replaced word is also a noun." This is because we couldn't replace one lexical category with another lexical category while keeping the sentence grammatical. Let's try replacing *cat* with the verb *to write* and *beat* with the verb *to write*:

(37d)   *The <u>write</u> jumped over the lazy dog. (sE)

(39c)   *This beat be the <u>write</u> for the street. (AAE)

Similarly, we couldn't replace *cat* or *beat* with a determiner such as *a*:

(37e)   *The <u>a</u> jumped over the lazy dog. (sE)

(39d)   *This beat be the <u>a</u> for the street. (AAE)

Remember, in general, the sentence will remain grammatical only if we substitute words of the same lexical category in a given syntactic slot.

3.3.2 Functions of Nouns

The **function** of a word within a sentence can help us further identify lexical categories. Functions that nouns can perform, or syntactic slots nouns can occupy, are limited. You already know that English sentences, minimally, consist of a subject and predicate. At the sentence level, nouns, as {NPs} or as parts of {NPs}, often take on the function of subject. We will start with the three most common functions (subject, direct object (DO), indirect object (IO)) and add to our list as the chapter proceeds.

(41) The *horse* is in the barn. (sE)
(42) James bought a *horse*. (sE)
(43) Denzel bought my *horse* a new bridle. (sE)

In (41), *horse* is in the **subject** slot. The subject is often thought of as what a sentence is about: *What is in the barn? The horse.* Remember, too, the tag-test from Chapter 2 to identify subjects. It is more reliable than meaning-related explanations. The pronoun in the tag, *it*, refers back to *horse*:

(41a) The horse is in the barn, isn't it? (sE)

In (42), *horse* is in the **DO** slot. The DO is often thought of as referencing the receiver of an action: *What is being bought? A horse.* In (43), *horse* is in the **IO** slot. The IO is often thought of as conveying the beneficiary or receiver of the DO: *What is receiving a new bridle? My horse.* Note that it is important not to overlook our phrasing here: "*horse* is in the subject/IO/DO slot" rather than "*horse* **is** the subject/DO/IO." The reason for this is that in each of our examples, it is both the determiner *and* the noun that function together as the subject/DO/IO. More on that in Chapter 10. Crucially, only noun-y things can function as subjects, DOs, and IOs; because of this, the syntactic slot a word fits into can be used as evidence to support its lexical classification.

Additionally, nouns can occur in these other syntactic slots: subject complements (SCs), object complements (OCs), and objects of the preposition.

Nouns in SC slot

(44) Luciana is a *doctor*. (sE)
(45) She a *chairwoman*.[26] (AAE)

Here, *doctor* and *chairwoman* occur in the **SC** slot. An SC *complements* the subject. Note it's "complEment"—not "complIment." (The latter is a nice thing **I** say to someone: Those shoes are fabulous!) SCs are connected to the subject via a copula verb (also known as a linking verb) in sE dialects. In other dialects, this copula verb is not required; in (45), you can see the connection between the subject and SC perhaps even clearer since no verb is in between the two nouns that complete each other.

Nouns in OC slot

(46) We consider Luciana the best *doctor* in town. (sE)
(47) I've call her my *sister*.[27] (AAE)

Here, *doctor* and *sister* occur in the **OC** slot. OCs complement the DO. For (46), the DO is *Luciana*; for (47), it is *her*. The entire OC is *the best doctor in town* in (46) and *my sister* in (47), and each completes our understanding of the DO. You can see that both SCs and OCs have in common that they complete another component in the sentence.

Nouns as part of the object-of-preposition slot

(48) Tamika practices medicine in our *town*. (sE)

(49) She was a-goin' to the *show*.[28] (AE/OE)

Here, the nouns *town* and *show* occur in the slot of the **object of preposition**. *in our town* and *to the show* are the complete {PPs}. The complete {NPs} *our town* and *the show*, complete the {PP}. The preposition, in a way, then owns that {NP}. Because the {NP} is required to complete the {PP}, the object of the preposition is also sometimes called the **prepositional complement (PC)**.

It is difficult for any grammar text to discuss a single lexical category and its many forms and functions without, by necessity, bringing in other classes and lexical categories (such as that nouns can occur after adjectives or determiners). So, while you may encounter grammatical elements not yet covered in detail, these previews will help in slowly building up your understanding of grammar. So, while this can be frustrating at times, hang on because you truly know more than you think about lexical categories and their relationships. Like any complex family or organization, sometimes you simply must be introduced to members a few times in different contexts before their identities become clear. In the chapters that follow, we believe you will make those connections.

3.3.3 Semantic Evidence versus Morphological and Syntactic Evidence

At the beginning of this chapter, we asked if a word's meaning (i.e., semantics) is sufficient and reliable for determining its lexical category within a sentence (or clausal) structure. We are now ready to explore the problems of semantic evidence a bit more. If a noun is simply "a person, place, or thing (or idea)," the following definition should be sufficient evidence that *horse* is a noun:

A horse is "a solid-hoofed perissodactyl quadruped (Equus caballus), having a flowing mane and tail, whose voice is a neigh (Horse, n. 1a., OED, 2020).

Well, how about the *horse* in (50)?

(50) That's a nice *horse* barn. (sE)

Does the semantic concept of *horse* still correspond to the OED definition: "a solid-hoofed perissodactyl quadruped (Equus caballus), having a flowing mane and tail, whose voice is a neigh" (Horse, n. 1a., OED, 2020)? After all, the barn is one for these solid-hoofed beings referenced in the definition.

The question for us, however, is the following: Is the word *horse* functioning as a noun when used in the phrase *a nice horse barn*? It describes the next word and tells us about what type of barn we're talking about. So, is it an adjective or a noun? What do you think? Take a moment to jot down your reasoning for or against classifying *horse* as a noun in (50).

Evidence that *horse* in *a nice horse barn* is a **noun**	Evidence that *horse* in *a nice horse barn* is an **adjective**

Chart 5 "Horse"—a noun or adjective?

You will need to stay tuned until Chapter 4 on adjectives, where we will revisit this very question! For now, remember that a dictionary definition is not that reliable in identifying lexical categories.

Let's make this even more fun. How about this sentence:

(51)   The children were *horsing* around when a lamp was broken. (sE)

Now, we have a form of the word *horse* (with the *-ing*), but our word is still semantically referring to our notion of horses—those "solid-hoofed" creatures and especially the actions they do. But this is not clear-cut evidence, really. Good thing you know a variety of tests for nouns! One of our tests from earlier comes in handy: Can you pluralize *horsing* as in *one horsings, two horsings*? We hope you agree that, surely, no, we can't count *horsing*, so there's one piece of evidence against labeling *horsing* as a noun. It also doesn't occur in one of the functional slots like the subject or the DO. Here, this word is not a noun. Rather, it serves as the lexical verb in the verb phrase *were horsing*. Semantic evidence simply is not very reliable in determining the lexical category of a word within a particular sentential context.

We will add one final piece to why semantics is not reliable. After all, the sentiment of "A noun is a person, place, or thing" is so common. But what about words like *idea, love, admiration, confusion, excitement,* and many more. Some of these are ideas, states, concepts, activities, and so on. None of them are places, things, or persons. Given the information presented in this chapter, we can see that using morphology and syntactic information is the reliable way to identify lexical categories. Let's use *idea* as a last illustration. If you relied on semantic meaning only, you likely would be confused since *idea* is not a person, place, or thing. Luckily, we have morphology and syntactic features that can come to our rescue:

- Morphological evidence
  - Can we pluralize *idea*? Yes: *one idea, two ideas*. Check.
- Syntactic environments/syntagmatic evidence
  - Can we place a determiner before *ideas*? Yes: *the idea/an idea*. Check.
  - Can we place a determiner and adjective prior to *ideas*? Yes: *a good idea*. Check.

- Paradigmatic evidence
  - Can we replace *idea* with a word we've already established as being a noun? Yes: *The good idea was mentioned last.* ≤ *The good cat was mentioned last.* Check.
- Evidence from syntactic function
  - Can *idea* function as part of the subject and DO, which are slots nouns can function in? Yes: *The good idea was mentioned last. I mentioned the good idea.* Check.

There you have it. This is why we use morphological and syntactic evidence over semantic evidence to identify lexical categories.

Exercise 2

Provide morphological (form) *and* syntactic (function) evidence for the italicized nouns.

a) My *dog* is sitting by the fire. (sE)

b) We was discussing the *initiative* that Obama curated.[29] (AAE)

c) We Black *folks* be knowin we got some unique *patterns* of language goin on up in here in the U.S. of A.[30] (AAE)

d) *Chickens* are roosting in the barn. (sE)

e) We seek *happiness*. (sE)

f) I heard him a-talkin' about *taxes*.[31] (AE)

g) Farid baked Mary a *cake*. (sE)

h) The little *kid* don't have no *shoes* of his own.[32] (ChE)

Exercise 3

Count nouns versus non-count nouns. Identify all nouns below as count nouns (C) or non-count nouns (NC).

a) My cousin bought apples and milk from the corner store. (sE)

b) I need a little more time to read all the books on grammar I have. (sE)

c) They enjoy eating pizza and pasta with cheese. (sE)

d) The manager purchased furniture, including some chairs, for the new office. (sE)

e) The chef used salt and sugar for their recipe. (sE)

f) We still need water and some plates for the dinner party. (sE)

Exercise 4

Underline as many nouns as you can in the excerpt[33] below. The excerpt is taken from the published convention program for the Conference on College Composition and Communication, and as such represents written AAE.

My dear friends, dear colleagues, dear *CCCC* members, dear honored guests, dear newcomers, dear all: Yay! We is here. We is here! And I for one ain't goin home til we done—til it's ova. Whaboutchu? As I welcome you to Pittsburgh and to 4C19, let me be real wit y'all right from jump. I hope y'all can tell from my call for papers last year, the visuality right here at the conference, from the black feminist program cover, the artist inserts in the program, and much mo'—some of which I highlight below—that dis here C's, dis here conference, is bout honorin, explorin, researchin, and advocatin wit diverse peoples/voices.

Terminology to Know

Term	Working definition	Example/Illustration
Noun		
Syntagmatic evidence		
Paradigmatic evidence		
Derivational suffix		
Inflectional suffix		
Count noun		
Noncount noun		
Subject		
Direct object		
Indirect object		
Subject complement		
Object complement		
Object of the preposition		

Chart 6 Key terminology Chapter 3

Notes

1. W. Beauregard, personal communication, August 29, 2024.
2. Reaser et al., 2017a, p. 37.
3. Ibid., p. 182.
4. Green, 2002, p. 208.
5. Reaser et al., 2017b.
6. Ibid., p. 288.
7. Green, 2002, p. 208/253n2; Bayley, 2012, p. 163.
8. Kendall, Quartey et al., 2018 Transcript ID DCB_se1_ag3_m_03_1.
9. Wood, 2015.
10. University of South Carolina (n.d.).
11. Reaser et al., 2017a, p. 182.
12. Mufwene et al., 1998, p. 74.
13. Green, 2011, p. 196.
14. Kendall, Quartey et al., 2018 Transcript ID DCB_se1_ag2_m_01_1.
15. Ibid., Transcript ID DCB_se1_ag1_m_02_1.
16. Rowe et al., 2018 Transcript ID PRV_se0_ag2_f_02_2.
17. Mufwene et al., 1998, p. 74.
18. Shortened from Reaser et al., 2017b.
19. Green, 2002, p. 77.
20. McMurtry, 2022, p. 42.
21. Baker-Bell, 2020, p. 43.
22. Barrón and San Romón, n.d., pp. 30–1; cited in Bayley, 2012, p. 160.
23. Wood, 2015.
24. Montgomery, 2009; cited in Matyiku, 2011a.
25. Alim, 2004, p. 398, lyric from Busta Rhymes; cited in Zanuttini and Martin, 2017.
26. Kendall, Fasold et al., 2018 Transcript ID DCA_se1_ag1_m_04_1.
27. Farrington et al., 2020 Transcript ID ATL_se0_ag1_f_01_1.
28. Christian et al., 1988; cited in Matyiku, 2011a.
29. Kendall, Quartey et al., 2018 Transcript ID DCB_se1_ag1_m_02_1.
30. Smitherman, 2006, p. 2.
31. Matyiku, 2011a.
32. Bayley, 2012, p. 163.
33. Young, 2019, p. 4.

CHAPTER 4
ENTER MODIFIERS FOR DETAIL: PART 1—ADJECTIVES

Overview

This chapter provides an overview of **morphological and syntactic evidence** for classifying words as **adjectives**. We continue to build on what you already know about morphology. Our objectives are as follows. You'll be able to

- identify words as adjectives based on morphological criteria;
- use syntactic position as well as related syntagmatic and paradigmatic evidence to identify adjectives; and
- build your knowledge about forms and functions of adjectives.

Pre-reading tasks

1. Write down what you know about adjectives. How is your answer different from the one you gave for question 2 from Chapter 2?
2. Combine as many of the following adjectives into one long list following the format of *Adj + Adj + Adj + Adj + Adj + Noun*. How many adjectives did you fit into one list? Can you move the same adjectives around within the list?
   Funny, slow, tiny, round, adorable, lovey-dovey, yellow, square, large, scary, gray, ginormous, orange, talented, fast, impressive, gorgeous, triangular, young, old
3. Compare the following pairs. Which versions do you prefer and why?

   a) calm > calmer vs. calm > more calm

   b) sunny > sunnier vs. sunny > more sunny

   c) fast > faster vs. fast > more fast

   d) clear > clearer vs. clear > more clear

4. Do you think all English speakers choose the same forms in question 3 that you did?

Foundations of Grammar

4.1 Introduction

If you were familiar with the Schoolhouse Rock[1] song about nouns, you may also be familiar with the song about adjectives, in which you may have learned that adjectives describe things. We know from chapter 3 that nouns can be "things," although the category of nouns is not limited to just things. Nevertheless, if we replace *things* with *nouns*, then we have a working hypothesis about what adjectives are:

Adjectives describe nouns.

We can test this hypothesis against a data set. Based on the following data, decide if our hypothesis is accurate.

(1) The *nice* students are on time. (sE)
(2) We *Black* folks be knowin we got some *unique* patterns of language goin on up in here in the U.S. of A.[2] (AAE)
(3) I noticed two *older* girls a-eating something out of a *little* syrup bucket.[3] (AE)
(4) Here's me a *good* pair of jeans.[4] (SAE)
(5) The soul needs fed by *creative, multi-dimensional* teaching.[5] (ME/SAE)
(6) That show was wicked *awesome*.[6] (NEE)

The italicized words, indeed, describe nouns. As a matter of fact, in most cases, the noun comes right after the adjective: *nice* describes *students*, *Black* describes *folks*, *older* describes *girls*, and so on. The adjective *awesome* in (6) does not occur prior to a noun, but it still describes a noun: *show*. Our hypothesis is confirmed, and we can confidently say that one characteristic of adjectives is that they modify nouns. In this chapter, we will systematically review linguistic features that allow us to identify a word as an adjective. We start with morphological features again and then move on to syntactic features.

4.2 Disassembling the Parts: Analysis of Morphological Features

4.2.1 Derivation

Several derivational suffixes are productively used in English to form adjectives. Chart 1 illustrates just a few of these adjective-markers. Add any other derivational suffixes that are adjective markers into the empty rows in Chart 1.

Word (lexical category)	+ derivational suffix	Adjective
child (N)	-ish	*childish*
thought (N)	-ful	*thoughtful*
compare (V)	-able	*comparable*

Word (lexical category)	+ derivational suffix	Adjective
professional (N)	-al	*professional*
eat (V)	-ible	*edible* (note the spelling change)

Chart 1 Some derivational suffixes for adjectives

Suffixes such as the ones in Chart 1 can be used as evidence that a word can be classified as an adjective. Here's how it works for *thoughtful* in (7):

(7) Ali called Riley *thoughtful*. (sE)

We can break *thoughtful* into two parts: *thought* (noun) + *-ful* (derivational suffix, class changing). This is the same process for other words as well: when we add *-ful* to the noun *care*, we end up with the adjective *careful*. This is why productivity is so important: If we can show that the process is productive in English (or whatever language we might be examining), then the evidence is strong.

In English, adjectives sometimes look verb-y. Take a look at this data set:

(8) Our *excited* audience is ready for the show to start. (sE)

(9) I love me some *baked* beans.[7] (AE/SAE)

(10) The grades and the classes was more *interesting*.[8] (AAE)

(11) They'd have a *thrashing* machine to come in and thrash it.[9] (AE)

The italicized adjectives either end in the suffix *-ed* or *-ing*, which are suffixes you were introduced to in Chapter 2 as possible verb suffixes as in *I walk, I had walked, I am walking*. In the examples above, these forms are used as adjectives, however. We know this because each describes a noun:

- *excited* describes *audience*
- *baked* describes *beans*
- *interesting* describes *grades* and *classes*
- *thrashing* describes *machine*

These adjectives are called **participial adjectives**, because the verb forms are participial forms. More on those in Chapter 6. For now, simply remember this term and do a double-take whenever you see an *-ed* or *-ing* word form: it might be a verb, but it might also be an adjective.

We use the same three basic questions as we did in Chapter 3 to help us figure out the composition of adjectives. Chart 2 shows what this looks like for *thoughtful*.

1. How many morphemes?	Two (*thought* + *-ful*)
2. What kind of morphemes?	*thought* (free root) + *-ful* (derivational suffix)
3. What does each morpheme do?	*thought* (N, something in one's mind) + *-ful* (one who is full of thoughts; adjective-marker, class changing)

Chart 2 Breakdown of the word "thoughtful"

Exercise 1

Underline as many adjectives as you can, including participial ones, in the excerpt[10] below. Make a note for all words you're unsure about at this point. Come back to those words after you've worked through the rest of the chapter.

In a quaint little village nestled amidst rolling hills, there lived a colony of feline friends, whose fur ranged from silky black to snowy white, adorned with patterns as intricate as a painter's masterpiece. Their eyes gleamed like polished emeralds, reflecting the moon's silver glow as they prowled through the cobblestoned streets, their nimble paws leaving delicate imprints in the dew-kissed grass. With tails swishing gracefully behind them, they roamed freely, their agile forms darting through alleys lined with colorful blooms. Each cat is distinct; some have playful personalities, some have a mischievous demeanor, while others were regal and dignified, their presence commanding admiration from all who crossed their path.

4.2.2 Inflection: Comparative and Superlative

You will have noticed that not all adjectives contain derivational suffixes. This is why **inflectional morphology** is even more important in identifying adjectives. Remember, certain inflectional processes can occur based on the lexical category a word belongs to: nouns can endure plurality, verbs can endure tense, so what can adjectives endure? The following examples should ring a bell: Remember the **comparative** and **superlative**?

(12)   Bob is a *fast* runner. (sE)
(13)   Sam is a *faster* runner than Bob. (sE)
(14)   Katy is the *fastest* runner of the three. (sE)

Can you identify the inflectional pattern?

- *fast* + *-er* = comparative
- *fast* + *-est* = superlative

The italicized words above are our adjectives, and you can see that the endings *-er* and *-est* can be added to the adjective. The *-er* suffix creates the **comparative form** and conveys that you're comparing something or someone: one person is a *fast runner* and another person is a *faster runner*. The *-est* suffix creates the **superlative form** and conveys that there's a third person who is even faster than the other two! Adjectives that endure comparative and superlative forms are **gradable**.

> **Adjectives**
> - Describe nouns
> - Can form comparatives/superlatives

You're surely familiar with superlatives from your everyday lives because marketers use superlatives constantly in their advertisements. Everyone is trying to sell us the best, the brightest, the most useful, the most impressive, the most life-changing, the boldest product! For instance, a Tropicana® juice ad claimed, "If you want the world's **best** fruit and vegetable juice, look in the cooler." In response, Campbell, which owns V8's V-Fusion® fruit and vegetable juice, took issue with that claim and initiated a complaint with the National Advertising Division (NAD), a self-regulatory program administered by the Better Business Bureau (see NAD Case Report No. 5610, July 3, 2013[11]). While NAD conceded that using the superlative "best" could be actionable, they ruled that Campbell failed to make the case that Tropicana®'s advertisement claimed their juices to be better than all other fruit juices since the advertisement made no objective claims about their juices. So, saying "best" without evidence is just hyperbole.

We'd be remiss to not include the following examples to showcase the variation across American English when it comes to adjectives' comparative and superlative forms. These forms are widespread across many American English dialects and even older forms of English!

(15)   Parents are not less *happier* than non-parents.[12] (sE/non-sE)

(15a) Parents are not least *happiest* than non-parents. (sE/non-sE)

(16)   Does that mean you're two years *taller*? [...] you're *even tallerer*.[13] (sE/non-sE)

(17)   Is that all the *riper* your peaches are?[14] (ME/SAE)

(18)   The Duke of Milan and his *more braver* daughter could controul thee. (Shakespeare, *The Tempest*)[15]

(18a) The Duke of Milan and his *most bravest* daughter could controul thee.

Some dialects allow for the comparative to be formed by adding the suffix *-er* to the adjective **and** either the word *more* or *less*, which means that the comparative is marked twice! This **double comparative** form is found in dialects including AE, AAE,[16] and Newfoundland English.[17] As you can also see, esteemed authors such as Shakespeare have used these double comparatives and double superlatives long before the grammar police got upset about them.

Example (17) is a bit different in that it illustrates a construction known as the *all the + comparative*.[18] Generally, this construction can be rephrased with *as ..... as*: *Is that as ripe as your peaches are?* The *all the + comparative* construction seems to be more common with adverbs, so you'll encounter more of these in Chapter 5!

Foundations of Grammar

Language, essentially, is creative and allows for creative word play. Hence, forms such as *funner* or *tallerer* or *biggerer* can be found online, and we're sure, can be overheard by (or even be used by!) each of us in our everyday lives. And even though the pattern for double comparatives is different from the sE pattern, it is still a systematic pattern!

Here's the morphological analysis for the adjectives *older* and *biggerer*.

1. How many morphemes?	• two (*old* + *-er*) • three (*big* + *-er* + *-er*)
2. What kind of morphemes?	• free root (*old*) + *-er* morpheme • free root (*big*) + *-er* + *-er* morpheme
3. What does each morpheme do?	• *old* (ADJ; beyond middle age) + *-er* (more than old; non-class changing; comparative-marker) • *big* (ADJ; large) + *-er* + *-er* (more than large; non-class changing, double-comparative marker)

Chart 3 Breakdown of the words "older" and "biggerer"

If comparative *-er* and superlative *-est* inflectional suffixes are addable to adjectives, that means we can use these endings to test out whether a word is, or is not, an adjective. Let's try adding the *-er* and *-est* suffix to the next two words:

(19)   because > *becauser/*becausest

(20)   runner > *runnerer/*runnerest

Clearly, performing the comparative/superlative morphological operation on these words results in ungrammatical—really, nonsense—words. You should be able to provide evidence for the fact that *runner* in (20) is a noun (pluralization, for instance) and you may say, wait, *runner* ends in *-er*; doesn't that mean that *run* is an adjective because an *-er* is clearly addable? We hope that you realize by now that this *-er* is the noun-marker suffix; a different kind of *-er*, one that is a noun-marker, not a comparative-marker.

You may not really be tempted to classify *because* and *runner* as adjectives because, after all, they don't describe nouns or come right before nouns. What about the next two sentences?

(21)   I own *more* books. (sE)

(22)   Layla owns *witty* books. (sE)

In both sentences, the italicized words come before the noun and tell you more about that noun, which might make you think that they are both adjectives. Let's try to add *-er* for the comparative form that we know adjectives can endure:

(21a)   *I own *morer* books. (sE)

(22a)   Layla owns *wittier* books. (sE)

As you can see, we can't add -er to *more* since **morer* is not an actual thing; it's ungrammatical! But it works beautifully with *witty* since *wittier* is grammatical (which means that *witty* is an adjective)! Whenever there's a word before a noun and you're not sure if it's an adjective, try the comparative test. Remember the "horse barn"-example from Chapter 3? We're ready to solve the puzzle!

(23) That's a nice *horse* barn. (sE)

We had asked you to jot down your reasoning for classifying *horse* as a noun or an adjective. Well, *horse* really is not an adjective! After all, you can't form structures such as the following:

(23a) That's a nice **horser* barn. (sE)

(23b) That's the nice **horsest* barn. (sE)

Since comparative/superlative forms are not possible, *horse* is not an adjective; it is a noun. We get back to {NPs} that consist of two nouns in Chapter 10.

You may wonder though about words such as *important* in phrases such as *the important meeting*, which modifies a noun, and yet won't let you add -er (**importanter*). This is where our pattern for adjectives gets a bit, but just a tiny bit, more complicated. Let's examine yet another set of data for more details! Look at the italicized words, try to describe a pattern you see, and formulate a hypothesis for the pattern. Underneath each full example sentence, we have invented portions just involving the adjective we're focusing on.

(24) The *funny* teacher is in the classroom. (sE)

(24a) The *funnier* teacher

(24b) The *funniest* teacher

(25) We got some *unique* patterns of language goin on.[19] (AAE)

(25a) some *more unique* patterns

(25b) some *most unique* patterns

(26) I noticed two *older* girls a-eating something ....[20] (AE)

(26a) the two *oldest* girls

(27) It was a *dreadful* sight, fire was a-flamin' everything.[21] (AE)

(27a) a *more dreadful* sight

(27b) a *most dreadful* sight

(28) The *new* set still needs washed to kill germs.[22] (ME/SAE)

(28a) The *newer* set

(28b) The *newest* set

Foundations of Grammar

(29)   Twitter can be a *professional* job anymore.[23] (ME)
(29a)   a *more professional* job
(29b)   a *most professional* job

If you've noticed that some adjectives take the *-er/-est* suffix and some use the words *more/ most*, you're correct. Why not **professionaler* and **professionalest* and why (typically) not **more old* and **most old*? What is the rule here?

Now, do you have a hypothesis that accounts for which pattern is used? If not, develop one before reading further. It boils down to something relatively simple, actually. In most cases, multisyllabic words require the *more/most* (also called **analytic** or **periphrastic** constructions). Short words, monosyllabic ones, usually use the inflectional suffixes *-er/-est* (also called **synthetic** constructions), such as in (30) below:

(30)   Your pie is *sweeter* than mine. (sE).

There are, however, exceptions:

(31)   Today was *fun*. (sE)
(31a) Today was *funner/more fun* than yesterday. (sE)
(31b) Today was *funnest/most fun* of all the days of this week. (sE)

What sounds right to you? Your answer may be different from a classmate's answer! In fact, all dialects of English allow *more/most* forms for many, even short, words depending on the context. This means you'll routinely encounter examples such as *more bad, more calm, more old,* and so on. You may even encounter a double comparative as in *funnerer*!

Two caveats are in order:

- The pattern about *-er/-est* and *more/most* is very robust for all English dialects, but that doesn't mean there aren't exceptions. *good* in (4) is an example of such an exception: *a good pair of jeans* turns into *a better pair* and ultimately into *a best pair of jeans*. No *-er/-est* and no *more/most* in sight. There are several exceptions that exist in all dialects, including sE ones.
- Some adjectives are not gradable, that is, comparatives and superlatives don't apply to them. A person, for instance, can't really be *more/most alive* or *deader/ deadest*. You generally are either alive or dead, not more or less alive or dead. Zombies are another matter entirely of course; a dead person is actually *deader* than a zombie until you drive a spike through the zombie's brain, at which point, we guess, they are *deadest*?

4.2.3 Putting Inflection and Derivation to Work

Both derivational and inflectional morphemes can help us identify a word as an adjective. It works just like the morphological analysis you've done for nouns in Chapter 3. We'll walk you through a few examples before you get to practice yourselves.

(32)   Some folk don't believe fat meat is *greasy*.[24] (AAE)

a. Lexical category: adjective
b. Morphological evidence
   i. derivational evidence

grease	+	-y	=	greasy
Noun: animal fat		derivational **suffix** -y; adjective-marker; class-changing		**Adjective:** full of grease

   ii. inflectional evidence: can endure comparative/superlative forms

greasy	+	-er	=	greasier
		inflectional **suffix** -er; comparative-marker, non-class changing		comparative: more than greasy

greasy	+	-est	=	greasiest
		inflectional **suffix** -est; inflectional suffix; superlative-marker, non-class changing		superlative: highest degree of greasy

c. Additional evidence: this process works for words such as *funny* as well:

   i. derivational evidence

fun	+	-y	=	funny
Noun: a good time		derivational **suffix** -y; adjective-marker; class-changing		**Adjective:** full of fun

   ii. inflectional evidence

funny	+	-er	=	funnier
		inflectional **suffix** -er; comparative-marker, non-class changing		comparative: more than *funny*

funny	+	-est	=	funniest
		inflectional **suffix** -est; inflectional suffix; superlative-marker, non-class changing		superlative: highest degree of *funny*

Let's do another one.

(33) The purple trucks are *cute*. (sE)

a. Lexical category: adjective
b. Morphological evidence:
   i. derivational evidence: Because *cute* isn't a word that was created via derivation, this isn't applicable.
   ii. inflectional evidence: can endure comparative/superlative forms

Foundations of Grammar

cute	+	-er	=	cuter
free root		inflectional **suffix** -er; comparative-marker, non-class changing		comparative: more than *cute*

cute	+	-est	=	cutest
free root		inflectional **suffix** -est; inflectional suffix; superlative-marker, non-class changing		superlative: highest degree of *cute*

    c. Additional evidence: this process works for words such as *new* as well:

new	+	-er	=	newer
free root		inflectional **suffix** -er; comparative-marker, non-class changing		comparative: more than *new*

new	+	-est	=	newest
free root		inflectional **suffix** -est; inflectional suffix; superlative-marker, non-class changing		superlative: highest degree of *new*

How about adjectives that use *more/most* rather than inflectional suffixes for comparative and superlative? Here we go:

    (34)   It was a *dreadful* sight, fire was a-flamin' everything.[25] (AE)

        a. Lexical category: adjective

        b. Morphological evidence

            i. derivational evidence

dread	+	-ful	=	dreadful
Noun: tremendous fear		derivational **suffix** -ful; adjective-marker; class-changing		**Adjective:** full of *dread*

            ii. inflectional evidence: not applicable because there's no *-er/-est*

        c. additional evidence

            i. can endure comparative/superlative periphrastic constructions

dreadful	+	more	=	more dreadful
		comparative-marker		comparative: more than *dreadful*

dreadful	+	most	=	most dreadful
		superlative-marker		superlative: highest degree of *dreadful*

ii. this process works for words such as *professional* as well:

- derivational evidence:

profession +	-al	=	*professional*
Noun: an occupation	derivational **suffix** -*al*; adjective-marker; class-changing		**Adjective:** behaving in such a manner

- can endure comparative/superlative periphrastic constructions

professional +	more	=	*more professional*
	comparative-marker		comparative: more than *professional*
professional +	most	=	*most professional*
	superlative-marker		superlative: highest degree of *professional*

And how about an adjective that uses a double comparative? Here we go:

(35) If anything had to be *biggerer,* betterer, and more badasser?[26] (sE/non-sE)

a. Lexical category: adjective
b. Morphological evidence:
   i. derivational evidence: N/A
   ii. inflectional evidence: can endure comparative/superlative forms

bigger +	+er	=	*biggerer*
	inflectional **suffix** -*er*; comparative-marker, non-class changing		comparative: more than *big*
bigger +	+est	=	*biggerest*
	inflectional **suffix** -*est*; inflectional suffix; superlative-marker, non-class changing		superlative: highest degree of *big*

Exercise 2

Use derivational evidence (if applicable), inflectional evidence, and additional evidence for why the italicized words are classified as adjectives.

a) Latoya is *faster* than the other runners. (sE)
b) I Ø been doing dancing for a *long* time, for eight years already.[27] (ChE)
c) The picnic was *enjoyable*. (sE)
d) Here's me a *good* pair of jeans.[28] (SAE)

Foundations of Grammar

> e) Now that interest rates are wicked *low*.[29] (NEE)
> f) Some folk don't believe *fat* meat is greasy.[30] (AAE)
> g) I noticed two older girls a-eating something out of a *little* syrup bucket.[31] (AE)
> h) I was *afraid* you might couldn't find it?[32] (SAE)

4.3 Just Playing the Role: Analysis of Syntactic Features

4.3.1 Syntactic Environment of Adjectives

It's time to look at **syntactic position**, just like we did for nouns. Adjectives differ from nouns as to where within an English syntactic construction they can occur, and adjectives can thus take on different roles in a sentence or phrase. Where do adjectives occur based on this data set? As a hint, we've bolded some of the verbs in each sentence.

(36) The *important* course. (sE)

(36a) The course **is** *important*.

(37) The *new* set still needs washed …. [33] (ME/SAE)

(37a) The set **is** still *new*.

(38) The *greasy* meat **is** fat.

(38a) Some folk don't believe fat meat **is** *greasy*.[34] (AAE)

In (36), (37), and (38), the adjectives (*important, new, greasy*) come before a noun. Adjectives that come before a noun are called **attributive**, that is, in **attributive** position, because the adjective tells us about an attribute of the noun it precedes. This is one possible **syntactic position** for adjectives, i.e., part of the syntagmatic evidence observed in the order of the words. Seeing this pattern should remind you of the basic {NP} structure from earlier in this text: NP = {(DET), (ADJ+), N} as in this sentence:

(39) The cat jumped over *the lazy dog*. (sE)

In addition to attributive position, adjectives can occur within the predicate as **predicative** adjectives: in (36a), (37a), and (38a), the adjectives come after the verb *is*, i.e., are part of the predicate. This is a second possible **syntactic position** for adjectives, i.e., part of the syntagmatic evidence. You'll be able to rephrase most attributive adjectives as predicative ones by using a verb such as *is* and moving the adjective to after that verb. Here are a few more examples:

(40) The picnic was *enjoyable*. (sE)

(40a) The *enjoyable* picnic.

(41) Here's me a *good* pair of jeans[35] (SAE)

(41a) A pair of jeans is *good*.

(42) We got some *unique* patterns of language.[36] (AAE)

(42a) Some patterns of language are *unique*.

(43) He felt *antsy* because he didn't exercise anymore.[37] (ME)

(43a) The *antsy* person didn't exercise anymore.

Note that the last example uses a linking verb other than a form of *be*; specifically, we have the linking verb *feel*; you may be tempted to think that *antsy* is an adverb telling you more about the verb *feel*. However, it is *he* who is *antsy* rather than the verb *feel* being done in an antsy manner. More on adverbs in the next chapter!

This doesn't mean that all adjectives that occur within predicates are automatically predicative adjectives. Compare *little* and *sturdy*:

(44) The *little* kid don't have no *sturdy* shoes of his own.[38] (ChE)

The adjective *little* is an attributive adjective that tells us more about *kid*. The adjective *sturdy* is also in attributive position to the noun *shoes*, even though the entire constituent *no sturdy shoes of his own* is part of the predicate (the entire predicate is *don't have no sturdy shoes of his own*). This means that attributive adjectives can be embedded within predicates.

We can rephrase the two attributive adjectives in (44) as predicative ones:

(44a) The kid is *little*.

(44b) The shoes are *sturdy*.

The key difference between attributive and predicative adjectives is that the former precedes the noun it describes, and the latter follows a verb **and** the noun it describes.

A final piece of syntagmatic evidence for adjectives is that they can follow words such as *very* or *extremely*. Adjectives can be intensified with these two words (and other similar words, including *wicked* in NEE).

(45) Sam is **very** *funny*. (sE)

(46) Carla is **extremely** *hungry*. (sE)

From this example, can you deduce what the phrase structure rule for an {AdjP} might be?

AdjP = {(Degree ADV) + ADJ}. Chart 4 sums it up. Don't worry too much about this rule; we will get to it in more detail in Chapter 10, including components that can follow the adjective itself!

Syntactic environments	Examples	Notations
in predicative position, alone	Cats are *cute*. Dogs are *adorable*.	Adj
in predicative position, after an adverb	Cats are extraordinarily *cute*. Dogs are very *adorable*.	Adv + Adj

Foundations of Grammar

Syntactic environments	Examples	Notations
in attributive position, alone	*Cuddly* cats are cute. *Fluffy* dogs are adorable.	Adj
in attributive position, after an adverb	The extremely *fluffy* cat is asleep. A very *old* dog was adopted.	Adv + Adj

Chart 4 Syntactic environments for adjectives

> **Exercise 3**
>
> Turn the following predicative adjectives into attributive ones and vice versa.
>
> a) The *loyal* dog wagged its *fluffy* tail when her owner came home. (sE)
> b) After a long day of play, the dogs seemed *tired*, sprawled out on the grass. (sE)
> c) The rescue dog appeared *timid* at first. (sE)
> d) The *tired* dog snoozed on his *favorite* blanket. (sE)
> e) The dogs are *gentle*, despite their size. (sE)
> f) A *playful* puppy chased after a ball in the *sunny* park. (sE)
> g) A *curious* canine sniffed the air, detecting the scent of treats nearby. (sE)
> h) The puppy was *energetic*, bounding across the fields with joy. (sE)

4.3.2 Allowable Number of Adjectives

So far, we have focused on one adjective per example. It is perfectly permissible to add multiple adjectives in a row. In fact, in our pre-reading activity, we asked you to do just that! Here's an example you've already encountered:

(47) The cat jumped over the *little, lazy, gray, old* dog. (sE)

Indeed, there is no grammatical limit on how many attributive adjectives may be placed in front of the noun, or how many predicative adjectives you can combine. In fact, the limiting factor is how many adjectives a listener or reader can put up with. This is part of the *syntagmatic* evidence: where and in what context other syntactic elements occur.

4.3.3 Order of Adjectives

We generally expect a certain order for attribute adjectives. How does (48) sound to you?

(48) The seven, *useful, large, antique, round, green,* city lights are in the garage. (sE)

This should sound like a pretty common English sentence. Now, try to move the adjectives around. Some movement may be acceptable, but certain movements will not be acceptable or, at a minimum, may sound odd:

(48a) The seven *round, green, antique, useful, large* city lights are in the garage. (sE)

Compare these two pairs:

(49) Just eat them *big black* cherries.[39] (AAE)

(49a) Just eat them *black big* cherries.

(50) You could get those *big fat juicy fresh* donuts.[40] (AAE)

(50a) You could get those *fat big fresh juicy* donuts.

You likely will feel that one of the two versions for each sentence just sounds better than the other. These observations lead us to this general order for attributive adjectives:

- Quality or opinion
- Size
- Age
- Shape
- Color
- Proper adjective (often nationality, other place of origin, or material)
- Purpose or qualifier

Next, let's see which kinds of functions adjectives can take on in a sentence or phrase.

4.3.4 Functions of Adjectives

The examples so far in this chapter already demonstrated the functions adjectives can play. Adjectives can function as premodifiers within {NPs} at the phrase level, and they can function as SCs and OCs at the sentence level.

Adjectives in Premodifier Slots in {NPs}

Adjectives can be modifiers of nouns when they are in attributive position prior to a noun. In Chapter 10, you'll learn more about these **premodifiers**. We reproduce just the portion that includes the adjective from some of the previous sentences to illustrate this function.

(51) *funny* teacher

(52) *important* course

(53) *Black* folks

(54) *unique* patterns

(55) *fat* meat

When adjectives are in the premodifying slot within {NPs}, they add additional information and can be dropped without making the {NP} or sentence they are in ungrammatical.

Adjectives in SC Slots

When an adjective is a predicative one, it functions as the SC at the sentence level. The copula, or linking, verb—as you know from Chapter 3—can take an {NP} to serve as an SC (e.g., *Sara is a doctor*). The copula can also select an adjective as its SC to complete the sentence.

(56) Kareem was *afraid*. (sE)

(57) The picnic is *enjoyable*. (sE)

(58) Some iMacs *tangerine*.[41] (AAE)

(59) Your phone bill be *high*.[42] (AAE)

(60) Amos feels *ill*. (sE)

(61) She look *pretty*.[43] (ChE)

The verb *be* is by far the most common linking verb, but there are a few others, including *feel* and *look* ((60) and (61)). Additionally, for AAE, the linking verb *be* is not required, as (58) shows; stay tuned for Chapter 12 for what the *be* in (59) conveys! Since the adjectives here serve as SCs, they are not merely optional but required.

Adjectives in OC Slots

We saw in Chapter 3 that nouns can occur in the OC slot (*We considered Luciana the best doctor*); surprise! Adjectives can do that, too.

(62) Tyrell considers Sam *silly*. (sE)

(63) The child colored the house *purple*. (sE)

(64) It made him *dizzy*.[44] (AAE)

Here, the adjectives *silly*, *purple*, and *dizzy* complete the direct object *Sam*, *the house*, and *him*, respectively. Since the adjectives here serve as OCs, they are not merely optional but required.

Finally, we can use **paradigmatic evidence** for adjectives, just like we did for nouns. When it comes down to it, what this means is that if you can replace a word in question with a word you know is an adjective, then the word in question itself is also an adjective. This is because you can only replace words of the same lexical category in the same syntactic slot without making a sentence ungrammatical. You can try this out yourself with any of the sentences above. Here are just two quick examples:

(65) Mary considers Carlos <u>funny.</u> (sE)

(65a) Mary considers Carlos <u>successful/intelligent/smart.</u>

(66) It made him <u>dizzy.</u>[45] (AAE)

(66a) It made him <u>happy/sad/elated/mad.</u>

Again, the argument would go as follows: Since I know that *successful* and *sad* are adjectives, but I don't know if *funny* and *dizzy* are adjectives, I can try replacing them with the words that I know are adjectives. Since (65a) and (66a) show that I can, indeed,

Enter Modifiers for Detail: Part 1—Adjectives

replace *funny* and *dizzy* with the adjectives I know to be adjectives, that means that *dizzy* and *funny* are adjectives, too.

The main features of adjectives can be summarized as follows:

- belong to an open-class lexical category;
- are able to form comparative and superlative forms via inflectional suffixes *-er/-est* (and, depending on the dialect, also *-erer*) or periphrastic *more/most;*
- can occur in attributive or predicative position in a sentence;
- can follow intensifying adverbs such as *very;*
- can function as premodifiers to a noun;
- can function in the SC and OC slots.

Exercise 4

Identify all the adjectives in the following sentences (there's always just one per sentence). Then label the function for each adjective (attributive, SC, OC).

a) That was the stormiest night was ever in this parish.[46] (AE)

b) My friends made my parents so angry. (sE)

c) Pantyhose are so expensive anymore.[47] (ME)

d) We painted the chairs pink. (sE)

e) He has plenty of free time, so he exercises a lot anymore.[48] (ME)

f) You was pretty weak by the tenth day.[49] (AE)

g) That was the brightest light that ever I seen.[50] (AE)

Exercise 5

Underline as many adjectives as you can in the excerpt[51] below. Label them attributive (A) or predicative (P). The excerpt is taken from the published convention program for the Conference on College Composition and Communication.

My dear friends, dear colleagues, dear *CCCC* members, dear honored guests, dear newcomers, dear all: Yay! We is here. We is here! And I for one ain't goin home til we done—til it's ova. Whaboutchu? As I welcome you to Pittsburgh and to 4C19, let me be real wit y'all right from jump. I hope y'all can tell from my call for papers last year, the visuality right here at the conference, from the black feminist program cover, the artist inserts in the program, and much mo'—some of which I highlight below—that dis here C's, dis here conference, is bout honorin, explorin, researchin, and advocatin wit diverse peoples/voices.

83

Terminology to Know

Term	Working definition	Example/Illustration
Adjective		
Comparative		
Superlative		
Predicative adjective		
Attributive adjective		
Subject complement		
Object complement		
Premodifier		

Chart 5 Key terminology Chapter 4

Notes

1. Warburton and Dorough, 1973.
2. Smitherman, 2006, p. 2.
3. Montgomery, 2009; cited in Matyiku, 2011a.
4. Wood, 2015.
5. Maher and Wood, 2011.
6. Ravindranath, 2011; cited in Wood, 2024.
7. Webelhuth and Dannenberg, 2006; cited in Huang and McCoy, 2015.
8. Quartey et al., 2020 Transcript ID VLD_se0_ag4_m_02_1.
9. Wolfram and Christian, 1976, p. 98.
10. Based on an excerpt produced by OpenAI, 2024.
11. Practical Law Commercial, 2013.
12. Wood, 2012.
13. Ibid.
14. Ashcom, 1953; cited in McCoy, 2016a.
15. Wood, 2012.
16. Wlodarczyk, 2007 and Montgomery, 2008; cited in Wood, 2012.
17. Clarke, 2004; cited in Wood, 2012.
18. McCoy, 2016a.
19. Smitherman, 2006, p. 2.
20. Montgomery, 2009; cited in Matyiku, 2011a.
21. Wolfram and Christian, 1976, p. 69.
22. Maher and Wood, 2011.
23. Maher and McCoy, 2011.
24. Smitherman, 2006, p. 2.
25. Wolfram and Christian, 1976, p. 69.

26. Wood, 2012.
27. Barrón and San Romón, n.d., pp. 30–1; cited in Bayley, 2012, p. 160.
28. Wood, 2015.
29. Wood, 2024.
30. Smitherman, 2006, p. 2.
31. Montgomery, 2009; cited in Matyiku, 2011a.
32. Huang, 2011.
33. Maher and Wood, 2011.
34. Smitherman, 2006, p. 2.
35. Wood, 2015.
36. Smitherman, 2006, p. 2.
37. Murray, 1993; cited in Maher and McCoy, 2011.
38. Bayley, 2012, p. 163.
39. Rowe et al., 2018 Transcript ID PRV_se0_ag3_m_01_1.
40. Kendall, Quartey et al., 2018 Transcript ID DCB_se2_ag4_f_03_2.
41. Green, 2002, p. 52.
42. Ibid, p. 48.
43. Bayley and Santa Ana, 2004, p. 376.
44. Kendall, Fasold et al., 2018 Transcript ID DCA_se1_ag1_m_03_1.
45. Ibid.
46. Doherty, 1993, p. 158; cited in McCoy, 2016b.
47. Murray, 1993; cited in Maher and McCoy, 2011.
48. Ibid.
49. Wolfram and Christian, 1976, p. 71.
50. Ibid., p. 99.
51. Young, 2019, p. 4.

CHAPTER 5
ENTER MODIFIERS FOR DETAIL: PART 2—ADVERBS

Overview

This chapter provides an overview of **morphological** and **syntactic evidence** for classifying words as **adverbs**. Our objectives are as follows. You'll be able to

- identify words as adverbs based on morphological criteria;
- use syntactic position as well as related syntagmatic and paradigmatic evidence to identify adverbs; and
- build your knowledge about form and function of adverbs.

Pre-reading tasks

1. Write down what you know about adverbs. How is your answer different from the one you gave for question 2 from Chapter 2?
2. Compare the following pairs. Which versions do you prefer and why?

    a) drive *safe* vs. drive *safely*

    b) take it *easy* vs. take it *easily*

    c) drive *slow* vs. drive *slowly*

    d) burning *bright* vs. burning *brightly*

    e) sleep *tight* vs. sleep *tightly*

    f) time goes *fast* vs. time goes *fastly*

    g) they'll arrive *soon* vs. they'll arrive *soonly*

3. Do you think all English speakers choose the same forms in question 2 that you did?

5.1 Introduction

The Schoolhouse Rock[1] song about adverbs may once again provide us with an initial idea about what adverbs are. From Lolly's shop, we were introduced to words like *absolutely*, *positively*, and, of course, *very, very, very*, which all add information about words such as adjectives, adverbs, and verbs. An initial working hypothesis about adverbs thus is as follows:

Adverbs can modify verbs, adjectives, or other adverbs.

Go ahead and test this hypothesis against this data set:

(1) Athletes run *fast*. (sE)
(2) Elite athletes run *faster*. (sE)
(3) Olympic sprinters run the *fastest*. (sE)
(4) She was just standin' *quietly* a-hollerin'.[2] (AE)
(5) The neighborhood just look *totally* different.[3] (AAE)
(6) This will be *particularly* important once you're done the tattoo and need to leave the shop.[4] (ECE)
(7) We haven't hung out in a *wicked* long time.[5] (NEE)

In (1)–(4), the adverbs *fast, faster, fastest,* and *quietly* all tell us about the manner in which something was being done, and as such, they are most closely related to the verbs in those sentences. In (5)–(7), the adverbs *totally, particularly,* and—yes—*wicked*, tell us about the adjective, which is placed immediately after the adverb. This means that we have some evidence that adverbs can modify adjectives. Here are three more, with two words each italicized:

(8) John was a-talkin' *so loud* my eardrums hurt.[6] (AE)
(9) Athletes run *extremely fast*. (sE)
(10) Every time you ask me not to hum, I'll hum *more louder*.[7] (AE/AAE)

In (8), *loud* tells us about the verb *a-talkin'*. In (9), *fast* tells us about the verb *run*. In (10), *louder* tells us about how the humming was done. Once again, we have evidence that adverbs can convey more details about verbs. What about *so, extremely,* and *more*? Well, they each intensify the adverb they precede: *so* intensifies *loud*, *extremely* intensifies *fast*, and *more* intensifies *louder* (this is an example of the double comparative, which is something both adjectives and adverbs can do!). This means that adverbs can modify other adverbs. We have evidence for our working hypothesis from above:

Adverbs can, indeed, modify verbs, adjectives, and other adverbs.

A caveat is in order here. For adverbs that intensify other adverbs or modify adjectives, those adverbs belong to one constituent together with the word they modify/intensify. Our question test and movement test come in handy:

(9a) Athletes run *extremely fast.* (sE)

- Q: How do athletes run? A: *extremely fast* [not: Q: *How do athletes run extremely? A: fast]
- It is *extremely fast* that athletes run. [not: *It is *fast* that athletes run extremely.]

So, the adverb *extremely* belongs to the larger {AdvP} *extremely fast*, as evidenced via our two tests. What about the adverb *fast* in (1a), where it tells us more about the manner in which the verb *run* was being done:

(1a) Athletes run *fast.* (sE)

- Q: How do athletes run? A: *fast* [not Q: *How do athletes? A: *run fast.*]
- It is *fast* that athletes run. [not: *It is *run fast* that athletes.]

The adverb *fast* here does not form a constituent together with the verb *run*; rather, it is its own constituent, as evidenced via the two tests we just performed. So, when we say that an adverb modifies verbs, adjectives, and adverbs, really what we mean is that the adverb can modify adjectives and adverbs (i.e., the adverb can form constituents with adjectives and adverbs), and that adverbs can tell us more about verbs (i.e., the adverb does **not** form a constituent with the verb). This distinction between "tells us about" and "modifies" may seem trivial, but the precise relationship and function of adverbs is a bit more nuanced. More on that when we get to functions in a bit.

That's not all there is, though. Take a look at these examples:

(11) *Unfortunately*, Rose can't go home. (sE)

(11a) Rose can't go home, *unfortunately*. (sE)

(11b) Rose, *unfortunately*, can't go home. (sE)

(12) They didn't swear at all, but they, *certainly*, was more careful.[8] (AAE)

(12a) They didn't swear at all, but they was more careful, *certainly*. (AAE)

(12b) They didn't swear at all, but *certainly*, they was more careful. (AAE)

Unfortunately and *certainly* don't modify just one word. There's no adjective or adverb close by that each of them might be modifying, and neither is telling us more about the respective verbs: The verb *go* in (11) is not being done in an "unfortunate manner," and the verb *was* in (12) isn't being done in a "certain manner." These adverbs, then, provide what is called a **stance** about the entire sentence. The speaker or writer of (11) and (12) is telling us about how they felt about what is conveyed in the sentence itself. It looks like our Schoolhouse-Rock-derived hypothesis wasn't complete yet.

Be aware: Adverbs are not as clear-cut as nouns and adjectives! In fact, they've been referred to as the "trash can"[9] category by linguists. Now, this doesn't mean they're less than or not as good as other words; it just means that adverbs are sometimes thought of as a "catch-all"[10] for words that modify all kinds of other words. Because adverbs are more amorphous than the other lexical categories so far, we start with the criterion of **semantics** to get an initial handle on this category. After that, we'll systematically review morphological and syntactic features that allow us to confidently identify a word as an adverb.

5.2 Adverbs—Semantics

Typically, adverbs are grouped into a few major **semantic** categories, according to what they conventionally mean.

Adverbs of Manner

(13) She was just standin' *quietly* a-hollerin'.[11] (AE)
(14) The patients recovered *quickly*. (sE)
(15) That's all the *higher* he can jump.[12] (ME/SAE)

The adverbs *quietly*, *quickly*, and *higher* tell us about how, in which **manner**, something was being done.

Adverbs of Time

(16) The professor teaches *regularly*. (sE)
(17) I just *barely* checked in.[13] (ChE)

The adverbs *regularly* and *barely* tell us about when something happened, and as such have to do with **time**. Note that in ChE, *barely* is used to mean *just recently*.[14] Other examples of time adverbs include *now, later, today, tomorrow, soon, occasionally, frequently*, and so on.

Adverbs of Place

(18) The truck didn't drive *away*. (sE)
(19) I know this lady that she used to live *here*.[15] (ChE)

The adverbs *away* and *here* tell us about location and direction. Anything that has to do with **place** would fall into this category. Other examples are *back, forward, sideways, elsewhere, nearby*, and so on.

Adverbs of Stance

(20) *Fortunately*, the patients recovered quickly. (sE)
(21) They didn't swear at all, but they, *certainly*, was more careful.[16] (AAE)

Stance adverbs are very common. *Fortunately* and *certainly* tell us about how the s or writer felt about what is conveyed in the sentence itself. Other examples in *probably, predictably, undoubtedly, clearly, annoyingly, obviously, ironically,* and so o

Degree Adverbs

(22) The patients recovered *very* quickly. (sE)

(23) The neighborhood just look *totally* different.[17] (AAE)

(24) The idea was so odd that it was *almost* inconceivable. (sE)

(25) The change in temperature was *hardly* noticeable for Serena. (sE)

(26) I was *wicked* stuffed, but it was well worth it.[18] (NEE)

Degree adverbs indicate a certain degree of another word and are sometimes called **intensifiers**. Yet, both upgrades (as in (22) and (23)) and downgrades (as in (24) and (25)) are possible. (26) illustrates the intensifier *wicked*, which is a salient feature of NEE, most common in Massachusetts. It generally expresses the same meaning as *very*; that is, it does not mean "evil." Note that *wicked* indicates even more intensity than *very* does. If someone told you it was *wicked hot*, it would be *hotter* than just *very hot*.[19] Additionally, *wicked* can be used to modify verbs—at least some verbs—just like other adverbs:

(27) I *wicked* want to go to that concert.[20] (NEE)

Wicked can be used as a modifier for some nouns as well, but, chiefly, it's used as an intensifier similar to *very*. As a salient dialect marker for NEE, *wicked* has also been exploited in various marketing campaigns—to the chagrin of many folks who call New England home.

Flat adverbs[21] are a special but widespread form, as our label "sE/non-sE" for these examples illustrates. They are found across many American English dialects. Flat adverbs are those adverbs where the adjective form and adverb form are identical:

(28) Nadia can do this real *quick*. (sE/non-sE)

(29) Kareem finished the reading *fast*. (sE/non-sE)

(30) Pat drove *slow* through the neighborhood. (sE/non-sE)

Now, for *quick* and *slow* (and for *real*, for that matter!), we could change the adverb form by adding an *-ly*, but we couldn't add an *-ly* to *fast*:

(28a) Nadia can do this real *quickly*. (sE/non-sE)

(29a) *Kareem finished the reading *fastly*. (sE/non-sE)

(30a) Pat drove *slowly* through the neighborhood. (sE/non-sE)

Another example that prohibits an *-ly* ending is *soon*. After all, we eat *soon*, not *soonly*. Flat adverbs, then, are adverbs that look like adjectives. They often feel like a new thing in English, and many people will complain about phrases such as *drive slow*, insisting that it should be *drive slowly*. Yet, flat adverbs have been around for a long time. You can

g task 2 and see which adverbs you prefer as flat adverbs and
with an -*ly*.
two examples in detail:

t test was *real* hard. (sE/non-sE)

hat food is *crazy* good. (sE/non-sE)

modifies the adjective *hard*. *Hard* is an adjective, since it describes the noun ould be used in a similar way, as in *The test was real* opposed to some imaginary really, *real* intensifies how hard the test was. So, we have a convergence of the ive and adverb form *real*. Because *real* here is being used before an adjective to dulate the severity of that adjective (*hard*), it is an adverb. While *real* in this usage sn't exactly sE, at least not formal sE, this usage is widespread in essentially all varieties of American English, and it is characteristic of other language change processes. It could be that in a few decades, using the form *real* instead of *really* as the degree adverb may become perfectly acceptable even in formal writing. Those of us who already use *real* in this way are simply ahead of the game!

In (32), the adjective *good* is preceded by *crazy*, which is typically identified as an adjective, but which is used as a degree adverb meaning that the food was *very good*. Together, *crazy good* describes the noun *food* and functions as part of the subject complement in the sentence. Currently, *crazy* as a degree adverb occurs mostly in conversations and in advertising, but this use will likely increase. An increase in its usage as a degree adverb will also contribute to the change in meaning of the word *crazy* as to where it will predominantly be used to indicate *great* or *intense*, which will—in turn— also have the advantage of diminishing its semantic (often pejorative) connection to mental health. This process is similar to the word *cool*, which is now generally used as a marker of positive attribution and has lost its connection to temperature in such contexts completely. This illustrates one way that languages change, and they all change over time.

A final development related to degree adverbs isn't just fascinating, it even comes with a fun name: **Drama SO**. This is another example of how language is inherently creative, as this particular use of *so* is generally thought to have emerged in the 1980s and now is widespread across the United States and even the UK.

(33) People are *so* wearing flip-flops this season.[22] (sE/non-sE)

(34) Jamie has *so* dated that type of guy before.[23] (sE/non-sE)

(35) I am *so* not going to study tonight.[24] (sE/non-sE)

What makes this use of *so* so fascinating is that it is a degree adverb, but unlike other degree adverbs, it now can be used to intensify a verb (*so wearing*) rather than adjectives or adverbs as you saw in the examples earlier in this chapter (or right in this sentence: *so fascinating*, where *fascinating* is an adjective). You'll find many examples by googling it, and we're again sure that you're all using this one yourselves or that you'll have at least heard it in your everyday lives. While this form tends to not be acceptable in academic language, it is used in all American English dialects!

Exercise 1

Label the italicized adverbs below as time adverbs (T), place adverbs (P), manner adverbs (M), or degree adverbs (D).

a) It was so many *darn* good proposals.[25] (AAE)
b) The "spotlight sessions" (…) are ones I *really* want to bring to yo attention.[26] (AAE)
c) Check out too the memoriam (…) to the late and *woefully* underrecognized scholar—Dr. Felipe de Ortego y Gasca.[27] (AAE)
d) We met up with the vet *outside*. (sE)
e) Please go *easy* on the students *tomorrow*. (sE)
f) Some students studied *abroad forever*. (sE)
g) The professors were *so* tired after their *remarkably* long day. (sE)
h) I'll go *upstairs soon*. (sE)

5.3 Disassembling the Parts: Analysis of Morphological Features

5.3.1 Derivation

Several derivational suffixes are productively used in English to form adverbs. Chart 1 illustrates the most common ones.

Word (lexical category)	+ derivational suffix	Adverb
childish (ADJ), *quiet* (ADJ)	-ly	childishly, quietly
length (N)	-wise	lengthwise
noise (N)	-ily	noisily
west (N)	-ward	westward

Chart 1 Some derivational suffixes for adverbs

Only some derivational suffixes can be used as solid evidence for classifying a word as an adverb. *-ily* is one of the suffixes that does indicate you're looking at an adverb. Here is how it works for *heartily*:

(36)   Ainsley laughed *heartily* at the lame joke. (sE)

We could use the derivational suffix *-ily*, which was added to the noun *heart* to form the adverb *heartily* in the same way that the noun *noise* + *-ily* becomes the adverb *noisily*. We use the same three basic questions about morphology to help us figure out the composition of (some) adverbs. Chart 2 shows what it looks like for *noisily*.

1. How many morphemes?	Two (*noise* + *-ily*)
2. What kind of morphemes?	*noise* (free root) + *-ily* (derivational suffix)
3. What does each morpheme do?	*noise* (n., something loud) + *-ily* (in a manner full of *noise*; adverb-marker, class changing)

Chart 2 Breakdown of the word "noisily"

You may have picked up on some of the hedges we've used already: "(some) adverbs" and "only some derivational suffixes" above. The reason for this is that adverbs, as a lexical category, are pretty varied. Many adverbs don't end in one of the suffixes above (as the list of adverbs in Chart 3 shows), and not all *-ly* words are, indeed, adverbs.

deeply	long	accordingly
now	always	mostly
already	occasionally	normally
almost	late	often
eventually	less	soon
hard	near	seldom
never	back	also
more	easily	immediately

Chart 3 A selection of random adverbs

5.3.2 Inflection: Comparative and Superlative

Adverbs

- describe verbs, adjectives, and other adverbs
- express a stance about an entire sentence
- some can form comparatives/ superlatives

To make things even more fun (or *funner*), the inflectional endings that can be added to (some) adverbs are the same as those addable to adjectives: *-er* and *-est*. That also means that some adverbs will use the periphrastic *more/most* rather than inflectional endings to do so. Consider the following examples. Comparative and superlative forms are provided underneath each example.

(37) Athletes run *fast*. (sE)
faster
fastest

(38) She was just standin' *quietly* a-hollerin'.[28] (AE)
more quietly
most quietly

Note that in some dialects, the superlative can be formed slightly differently:

(39) I tried *all the harder* I could.[29] (ME/SAE)

(40) This is *all the tighter* I can tie it.[30] (ME/SAE)

(39) can be rephrased as *I tried as hard as I could* or *I tried the hardest* and (40) can be rephrased as *This is the tightest I can tie it* or *This is as tight as I can tie it*. We provide the morphological analysis for *faster* and *fastest* in Chart 4, but we're pretty confident that you could do this one on your own already!

1. How many morphemes?	• two (*fast* + *-er*) • two (*fast* + *-est*)
2. What kind of morphemes?	• free root (*fast*) + *-er* morpheme • free root (*fast*) + *-est* morpheme
3. What does each morpheme do?	• *fast* (ADV; quick, rapid manner) + *-er* (more than quick/rapid; non-class changing; comparative-marker) • *fast* (ADV; quick, rapid manner) + *-est* (highest level of quick/rapid manner; non-class changing, superlative-marker)

Chart 4 Breakdown of the words "faster" and "fastest"

The limitation of inflectional evidence (i.e., comparative/superlative forms) as a criterion for adverbs becomes apparent when we look at the following examples:

(41) The neighborhood just look *totally* different.[31] (AAE)
*more totally
*most totally

(42) This will be *particularly* important once you're done the tattoo…[32] (ECE)
*more particularly
*most particularly

(43) John was a-talkin' *so loud* my eardrums hurt.[33] (AE)
*more so
*most so

(44) Athletes run *extremely fast*. (sE)
*more extremely
*most extremely

Some adverbs simply aren't gradable, and so the comparative/superlative forms only work for those adverbs that are gradable, like *fast*.

Exercise 2

Underline as many adverbs as you can in the excerpt[34] below. Make a note for all words you're unsure about at this point. Come back to those words after you've worked through the rest of the chapter.

In an incredibly quaint village, many cats lived harmoniously. Their whiskers twitched gently as they lounged sideways in the sun. Occasionally, they would chase rowdily after butterflies. Afterwards, they would nap in the shade of ancient oak trees, snoring very intensely. The remarkably agile cats sometimes fell asleep too soon, not realizing that they missed out on some of the more impressive sunsets.

5.3.3 Putting Inflection and Derivation to Work

Even with the limitations outlined above, both derivational and inflectional morphemes can sometimes help us identify a word as an adverb. It works just like the morphological analysis you've done for nouns in Chapter 3 and adjectives in Chapter 4, and so we'll only show you one example here before you get to practice. Note that the final *-y* in *shabby* changes to an *-i* in *shabbily* because of the addition of the class-changing suffix *-ly*.

(45) My friend was dressed *shabbily* the other day. (sE)

    a. Lexical category: adverb

    b. Morphological evidence

        i. derivational evidence

shabby +	-ly	= shabbily
ADJ: worn, faded	derivational **suffix** *-ly*; adverb-marker; class-changing	**ADV:** in a *shabby* manner

        ii. inflectional evidence: N/A

    c. Additional evidence:

        i. can endure comparative/superlative periphrastic constructions *more/most*

Enter Modifiers for Detail: Part 2—Adverbs

shabbily +	more	=	more shabbily
	comparative-marker		comparative: more than *shabbily*

shabbily +	most	=	most shabbily
	superlative-marker		superlative: highest degree of *shabbily*

    ii. this works for other adverbs such as *speedily*

- derivational evidence

speedy +		-ly	=	speedily
ADJ: quick	derivational **suffix** -*ly*; adverb-marker; class-changing			**ADV**: in a *speedy* manner

- can endure comparative/superlative periphrastic constructions *more/most*

speedily +	more	=	more speedily
	comparative-marker		comparative: more than *speedily*

speedily +	most	=	most speedily
	superlative-marker		superlative: highest degree of *speedily*

Exercise 3

Use—where applicable—derivational evidence, inflectional evidence, and additional evidence for why the italicized words are classified as adverbs.

    a) My momma be running *late* in the morning.[35] (AAE)

    b) She was like a *real* thin lady.[36] (ChE)

    c) She was just standin' *quietly* a-hollerin'.[37] (AE)

    d) The neighborhood just look *totally* different.[38] (AAE)

    e) This will be *particularly* important once you're done the tattoo and need to leave the shop.[39] (ECE)

    f) John was a-talkin' *so loud* my eardrums hurt.[40] (AE)

    g) The movie director is *awfully* polite. (sE)

    h) [H]e's *wicked* selfish.[41] (NEE)

5.4 Just Playing the Role: Analysis of Syntactic Features

5.4.1 Syntactic Environment of Adverbs

It's time to look at **syntactic position**, just like we did for nouns and adjectives. We start with a small data set; what are some observations you can make about adverbs based on this set?

(46) The set *still* needs washed to kill germs.[42] (ME)

(46a) *Still*, the set needs washed to kill germs.

(46b) The set needs washed to kill germs *still*.

(47) He was *really* a-starin' at the picture.[43] (AE)

(47a) He *really* was a-starin' at the picture.

(47b) *Really*, he was a-starin' at the picture.

(48) I had been fixin' to get a new bike for years and *finally* did.[44] (SAE)

(48a) I had been fixin' to get a new bike for years and did *finally*.

(49) The dog *ferociously* barked. (sE)

(49a) The dog barked *ferociously*.

(49b) *Ferociously*, the dog barked.

These examples demonstrate that syntactic position for adverbs is not as limited as it was for adjectives and nouns. In fact, a defining feature for most adverbs is their **flexibility and movability** within a sentence. *Still* in (46) comes before the verb, in (46a) at the beginning of the sentence, and in (46b) at the end of the sentence. (47)–(49) and their additional versions show that various placements are possible for adverbs. This means that most adverbs are syntactically flexible: they can be moved around within the sentence. We can also easily remove most adverbs because they are unnecessary to the grammaticality of the sentence. Syntactic flexibility also supports the view that adverbs or {AdvPs} form their own constituents!

> **Exercise 4**
>
> Add the word *only* to the following sentence in as many spots as possible. How many different positions can you come up with?
>
> The colleagues told her that they appreciate her. (sE)

What do the following data tell you about the movability of adverbs?

(50) Our professor reads *extremely* fast. (sE)

(50a) *Our professor reads fast *extremely*.

(50b) **Extremely, our professor reads fast.

(50c) *Our professor *extremely* reads fast.

(50d) Our professor reads fast.

(51)   A *surprisingly* short introduction to adverbs was part of Chapter 2. (sE)

(51a) *A short *surprisingly* introduction to adverbs was part of Chapter 2.

(51b) *A short introduction *surprisingly* to adverbs was part of Chapter 2.

(51c) A short introduction to adverbs was part of Chapter 2.

It looks like there really is only one possible slot in the sentence where our adverbs fit. In (50), the adverb *extremely* modifies another adverb *fast*, and in (51), the adverb *surprisingly* modifies the adjective *short*. When adverbs occur prior to adjectives or adverbs as modifiers, then we cannot move them around like we did before, because that would result in ungrammatical constructions. Because the adverb together with the adjective or adverb that it modifies forms one constituent (see constituent tests earlier in this chapter!), we can't move them out of that constituent.

While they are fixed to a pre-position to adverbs and adjectives they modify, these adverbs are omittable, which is demonstrated by (50d) and (51c). Chart 5 summarizes some of the main environments for adverbs, but keep in mind that this is not an exhaustive list.

Syntactic environments	Examples	Notations
before an adjective	*extraordinarily* cute	ADV + ADJ
before an adverb	*very* noisily	ADV + ADV
before and after a verb	*ferociously* barked	ADV
	barked *ferociously*	ADV
alone, in various syntactic positions	I *still* need to do this.	ADV
	I need to *still* do this.	
	Still, I need to do this.	
	I need to do this *still*.	

Chart 5 Syntactic environments for adverbs

5.4.2 Functions of Adverbs

The syntactic environment of adverbs is closely related to how adverbs can function. This section reinforces various ideas that have already come up so far. We start with phrase-level functions and end with a sentence-level function.

Premodifier to Adverbs and Adjectives

When adverbs come prior to an adjective or another adverb, they function as a **premodifier** to those adjectives or adverbs at the phrase level:

(52)   My mom drives *extremely* fast. (sE)

(53)   She was like a *real* thin lady.⁴⁵ (ChE)

(54)   John was a-talkin' *so* loud my eardrums hurt.⁴⁶ (AE)

In (52), the adverb *extremely* modifies the adverb *fast*. Mom doesn't just drive fast; no, she drives *extremely fast*. In (53), the adverb *real* modifies an adjective. The lady is not just *thin*, she's *real thin*. Note that the lady isn't *real*; rather, the lady is *thin*, and then *real* intensifies that adjective. And in (54), *so* modifies the adverb *loud*. Fun fact: together, the combination of *so* + *loud* tells us about the verb *a-talkin'*!

Premodifier to Prepositions

To be comprehensive, we'll add one more—fun—function of adverbs (and we'll come back to this in Chapter 10). Sometimes, adverbs can modify a preposition:

(55)   The CEO woke up *just* before dawn. (sE)

(56)   She finished the race *right* behind her best friend. (sE)

(57)   *Right* after school, I go straight to cheerleading practice.⁴⁷ (AAE)

In each example, the adverb modifies the precise meaning of the preposition: Not just *before*, *right*, and *after*, but *just before*, *right behind*, and *right after*.

Adverbial

When adverbs occur on their own as {AdvPs}, they function as an **adverbial** at the sentence level. Usually, they are movable when they function as adverbials. {AdvPs} that function as adverbials can express a stance about the entire sentence, or they can tell us more about a verb. We start with the former:

(58)   *Occasionally*, the teacher left constructive comments for students. (sE)

(59)   It's too late. He done *already* paid for the trip.⁴⁸ (AAE)

(60)   Me and my sister gets in a fight *sometimes*.⁴⁹ (AE)

Once again, these {AdvPs} don't tell us more about any of the verbs: the leaving of comments in (58) wasn't done in an *occasionally* manner; rather, the adverb tells us how often comments were left. In (59), the paying for the trip wasn't done in an *already* manner; rather, the adverb tells us when the paying happened, and so on.

The next three examples include adverbs that tell us more about a verb rather than expressing a stance about the entire sentence:

(61)   Our students studied *diligently* for the exam. (sE)

(62)   She was just standin' *quietly* a-hollerin'.⁵⁰ (AE)

(63)   My grandparents were snoring *contentedly* on the couch. (sE)

In (61), the adverb *diligently* tells you more about the verb *studied*. In (62), the adverb *quietly* tells you more about either the verb *standin'* or the verb *a-hollerin'*—both interpretations would work (how was she standing? Quietly; How was she a-hollerin'? Quietly). And in (63), it's not my grandparents who are *contentedly*; rather, they are *snoring contentedly*. In each example, the adverb describes the manner in which the action of the verb was done, but remember, the adverb doesn't form a constituent together with the verb, which is why they're not modifiers but adverbials!

Finally, we can use **paradigmatic evidence** for adverbs, just like we did for nouns and adjectives. Remember that if you can replace a word in question with a word you know is an adverb, then the word in question itself is also an adverb within that sentence. This is because you can only replace words of the same lexical category in the same syntactic slot within a sentence without making a sentence ungrammatical. You can try this out yourself with any of the adverbs so far. Say you want to test whether *accordingly* in (64) and *real* in (65) are, indeed, adverbs.

(64) Most students revised their essays *accordingly*. (sE)

(65) She was like a *real* thin lady.[51] (ChE)

And let's say that you've already used our evidence in this chapter to confirm that, for example, *quickly* and *awfully* are, indeed, adverbs, then you can use those adverbs and see if they work as replacements for the words in question. Replacing *accordingly* with *quickly* works just fine, as does replacing *real* with *awfully*:

(64a) Most students revised their essays *quickly*.

(65a) She was like an *awfully* thin lady.

Note that semantic restrictions limit this to an extent: *quickly* doesn't work for a replacement for *real* in (65) because the meanings of those words are just too different.

Exercise 5

Identify the functions for the italicized adverbs in the following sentences. Modifier of Adv, modifier of Adj, modifier of preposition, Adverbial.

a) Pantyhose are *so* expensive anymore.[52] (ME)

b) That was the brightest light that *ever* I seen.[53] (AE)

c) You was *pretty* weak by the tenth day.[54] (AE)

d) *Finally* the state come by and pushed it all out.[55] (AE)

e) The cats were *so gloriously* cute. (sE)

f) Our dogs hid *right* behind the corner. (sE)

g) And the water was *real* deep and we swim for about two or three hours.[56] (AE)

5.4.3 -ly Words: A Friend-ly Warning

Let's return to the oft-repeated claim that an adverb is a word that ends in *-ly*. You've seen that many adverbs actually don't end in *-ly*, but what about those words that do end in *-ly*? Are they all adverbs? Drawing from what you've learned about adverbs and adjectives so far, identify the lexical category of the following two *-ly* words.

(66) We *quickly* drove the *costly* car home. (sE)

Foundations of Grammar

How do you know for sure that *quickly* is an adverb and *costly* is an adjective? Both can form comparatives and superlatives:

(67)   We drove *more quickly/most quickly* .... (sE)

(68)   We drove the *more costly/most costly* car home. (sE)

Testing for comparative/superlative forms is important to rule out nouns and verbs. A noun or verb can't form a comparative, so we couldn't use the noun *cat* and say **the cat-er thing* and **the cat-est something* like we can for adjectives as in *the cut-er thing* and *the cut-est something*. This is when you need to figure out what other word in the sentence the word in question tells you more about:

- In (67), *quickly* tells you about how the verb *driving* was done: it is an adverb.
- In (68), *costly* modifies the noun *car*: it is an adjective.

Exercise 6

Decide if the italicized words are adjectives or adverbs. Make sure to provide evidence for your claim.

a) [They] have to start supporting theirselves at an *early* age.[57] (ChE)

b) The new student is *friendly*. (sE)

c) The dogs barked *loudly*. (sE)

d) Couldn't be no *wobbly* switch.[58] (AAE)

e) I ain't *hardly* look at that.[59] (AAE)

f) We finished the task *effortlessly*. (sE)

Exercise 7

Add one or more adverbs to the following sentences.

a) The team scored in the last minute of the game. (sE)

b) The students were finishing the exam in record time during the exam period. (sE)

c) I didn't have no self-confidence.[60] (ChE)

d) I Ø been doing dancing for a long time, for eight years already.[61] (ChE)

e) The racehorse bounds the corner of the track to take lead. (sE)

f) Their car careened into our lane without notice. (sE)

g) My parents be correcting, too.[62] (AAE)

h) Here's me a good pair of jeans.[63] (SAE)

Terminology to Know

Term	Working definition	Example/Illustration
Adverb		
Comparative		
Superlative		
Degree adverb		
Flat adverb		
Premodifier		
Adverbial		
Stance adverb		

Chart 6 Key terminology Chapter 5

Notes

1. Warburton and Dorough, 1973.
2. Wolfram, 1976; cited in Matyiku, 2011a.
3. Kendall, Quartey et al., 2018 Transcript ID DCB_se2_ag2_m_01_1.
4. Wood, 2014.
5. Wood, 2024.
6. Wolfram, 1976; cited in Matyiku, 2011a.
7. Corver, 2005; cited in Wood, 2012.
8. Roger et al., 2023 Transcript ID DTA_se1_ag4_f_03_1.
9. Curzan and Adams, 2012, p. 144.
10. Ibid.
11. Wolfram, 1976; cited in Matyiku, 2011a.
12. Cassidy, 1985; cited in McCoy, 2016a.
13. Fought, 2003, p. 104.
14. Ibid.
15. Bayley, 2012, p. 161.
16. Roger et al., 2023 Transcript ID DTA_se1_ag4_f_03_1.
17. Kendall, Quartey et al., 2018 Transcript ID DCB_se2_ag2_m_01_1.
18. W. Beauregard, personal communication, August 29, 2024.
19. Wood, 2024.
20. Wood et al., 2020; cited in Wood, 2024.
21. Mills, 2022.
22. Gaston, 2011.
23. Ibid.
24. Ibid.

Foundations of Grammar

25. Young, 2019, p. 4.
26. Ibid.
27. Ibid.
28. Wolfram, 1976; cited in Matyiku, 2011a.
29. Thomas, 1993, cited in McCoy, 2016a.
30. Ashcom, 1953, cited in McCoy, 2016a.
31. Kendall, Quartey et al., 2018 Transcript ID DCB_se2_ag2_m_01_1.
32. Wood, 2014.
33. Wolfram, 1976; cited in Matyiku, 2011a.
34. Based on an excerpt produced by OpenAI, 2024.
35. Baker-Bell, 2020, p. 56.
36. Bayley, 2012, p. 164.
37. Wolfram, 1976; cited in Matyiku, 2011a.
38. Kendall, Quartey et al., 2018 Transcript ID DCB_se2_ag2_m_01_1.
39. Wood, 2014.
40. Wolfram, 1976; cited in Matyiku, 2011a.
41. Brown, 2014; cited in Wood, 2024.
42. Edelstein, 2014; cited in Maher and Wood, 2011.
43. Matyiku, 2011a.
44. Staub and Zentz, 2017.
45. Bayley, 2012, p. 164.
46. Wolfram, 1976; cited in Matyiku, 2011a.
47. Kendall, Quartey et al., 2018 Transcript ID DCB_se1_ag1_f_03_1.
48. Baker-Bell, 2020, p. 74.
49. Wolfram and Christian, 1976, p. 78.
50. Wolfram, 1976; cited in Matyiku, 2011a.
51. Bayley, 2012, p. 164.
52. Murray, 1993; cited in Maher and McCoy, 2011.
53. Wolfram and Christian, 1976, p. 99.
54. Ibid., p. 71.
55. Ibid., p. 81.
56. Ibid., p. 82.
57. Bayley, 2012, p. 158.
58. Kendall, Quartey et al., 2018 Transcript ID DCB_se1_ag4_f_01_2.
59. Kendall, Fasold et al. 2018, Transcript ID DCA_se1_ag1_f_02_1.
60. Fought, 2003, p. 97.
61. Barrón and San Romón, n.d., pp. 30–1; cited in Bayley, 2012, p. 160.
62. McMurtry, 2022, p. 42.
63. Wood, 2015.

CHAPTER 6
(EM)POWERING THE CLAUSE: THE VERB

Overview

Verbs are a powerhouse category. Just as we have done for nouns, adjectives, and adverbs, we outline foundational information about **verbs** as a lexical category, including an overview of **morphological and syntactic** features of verbs. Our objectives are as follows. You'll be able to

- identify words as verbs based on morphological criteria;
- use syntactic position as well as related syntagmatic and paradigmatic evidence to identify verbs;
- develop your knowledge about form and function of verbs;
- build an understanding of person, number, tense, and aspect; and
- build an initial understanding of transitivity and verb types.

Pre-reading tasks

1. Write down what you know about verbs. How is your answer different from the one you gave for question 2 from Chapter 2?
2. Compare the following pairs of sentences. Which versions do you prefer and why?

    a) *I seen it.* vs. *I saw it.*

    b) *I had went out.* vs. *I had gone out.*

    c) *I should have wrote the email sooner.* vs. *I should have written the email sooner.*

    d) *I done it.* vs. *I did it.*

3. Do you think all English speakers choose the same forms in question 2 that you did?
4. Write down three of your favorite nouns. Now, try verbing those nouns, i.e., use those nouns as verbs in a sentence! Did it work for all of your nouns?

Foundations of Grammar

6.1 Introduction

The verb, more specifically the {VP}, is the powerhouse of the clause. Similar to other lexical categories, verbs are often presented simplistically, leading to a very narrow understanding. Many of us were taught through our elementary grammar lessons that words which show action are verbs. And, if you watched Schoolhouse Rock's[1] cartoon Grammar Rock, like we did, the verb is brought to life, personified, as a superhero whose power is to grant characters (or subjects) the ability to perform actions: to run, to sing, to dream. We expand the superpowers of the verb here and in later chapters, but, first, let's start by applying and testing this semantic power of the verb *run*. In the process, we will also see what other powers such words have.

(1)   I *run* every day. (sE)

(2)   Antonia *ran* yesterday. (sE)

(3)   We are *running* the race tomorrow. (sE)

(4)   Johnny *run* down the hill a-aiming to go to his uncle's.[2] (SAE)

To run is an action. But what about *running* in the following sentence?

(5)   *Running* is my favorite exercise. (sE)

On the one hand, semantically, we are still talking about the action of running, but, on the other hand, *running* doesn't behave like other verbs in this sentence. For one, we can replace it with a pronoun:

(5a)   *It* is my favorite exercise. (sE)

The tag-question test demonstrates that *running* is the subject (because *it* in the tag refers back to *running*):

(5b)   *Running* is my favorite exercise, isn't *it*? (sE)

So not only does *running* endure one of our noun-tests (replaceable with a pronoun), it also serves as the subject of the sentence, and we know that {NPs} can function as subjects, not {VPs}. These types of *-ing*-words are called **gerunds**—verbs that serve as nouns in a slot for nouns, such as the subject. You'll see later that gerunds exhibit features tied to nouns and tied to verbs. The debate about gerunds as nouns or verbs is certainly not a settled one!

What about *running* in (6)?

(6)   I like the movie *The Running Man*. (sE)

Running is still an action semantically, but the word *running* in this sentence gives us a detail about the noun *man*: it's an attributive adjective, and more specifically, it is one of those participial adjectives. It's not just any man—it's a running man.

So, classifying a word as a verb simply based on its meaning is shaky at best. We must use syntactic and morphological evidence to be certain, which is what we turn to next.

6.2 Disassembling the Parts: Analysis of Morphological Features

6.2.1 Derivation

Several derivational suffixes are used productively in English to form verbs. Chart 1 illustrates some of them, but it is by no means a complete list. Can you add some yourself?

Word (lexical category)	+ derivational suffix	Verb
threat (N); *bright* (ADJ)	*-en*	*threaten, brighten*
ample (ADJ)	*-ify*	*amplify*
custom (N), *standard* (N)	*-ize*	*customize, standardize*

Chart 1 Some derivational suffixes for verbs

We can use derivational suffixes as a first indication for a word's lexical category. For the word *amplify* in (7), the suffix *-ify* is a first clue that it is a verb because it turned the adjective *ample* into the verb *amplify*:

(7) Ainsley and Taylor *amplify* each other's voices. (sE)

We again use the same three basic questions as we did in previous chapters to help us figure out the composition of verbs. Chart 2 shows the verb *standardized* as an example. If you want to know more about the oft-contested verb *to conversate*, check out the companion website!

1. How many morphemes?	Two (*standard* + *-ize*)
2. What kind of morphemes?	*standard* (free root) + *-ize* (derivational suffix)
3. What does each morpheme do?	*standard* (N, some criterion) + *-ize* (to make something fit that *standard*; verb-marker, class-changing)

Chart 2 Breakdown of the word "standardize"

6.2.2 Inflection

It is not very efficient to memorize all possible derivational verb suffixes to be able to identify words as verbs. This is why inflectional morphology is much more important as evidence. Which verb forms can you identify in the following data set?

(8) Malika and Nadia want *to cuddle* with my cats all day. (sE)

(9) Do you want *to come* with?[3] (ME)

(10)   Martin is done his bass tracks and we are ready *to start* vocals.[4] (ECE)

(11)   Alls I *want* to do is have fun.[5] (ME)

(12)   The chef *cooks* her showstopper on Tuesdays. (sE)

(13)   My dad *use* both [Black Language and White Mainstream English].[6] (AAE)

(14)   I *picked* her because she nice and calm.[7] (AAE)

(15)   Then after that I *talk* English.[8] (ChE)

(16)   We *danced* all night long at the party. (sE)

(17)   He's *smiling* to the cat.[9] (ChE)

(18)   Fire was *a-flamin'* everything.[10] (AE)

(19)   We were *dancing* last night. (sE)

(20)   We have *eaten* already. (sE)

(21)   Cameron and Samir have *worked* together for years. (sE)

(22)   We been *done* with our project.[11] (AAE)

While this collection of verb forms does not represent complete paradigms, we're confident that you can identify what the base form of verbs is and the specific inflectional suffixes that can be added to verbs. The base form, also called **infinitive**, is represented in examples (8)–(10). When the infinitive is preceded by the infinitive marker *to*, it is called **full infinitive**. The verbs in (11) and (13) are present-tense forms without suffixes, and (12) is a present-tense form with an *-s*-suffix.

Our data set above shows the inflectional suffixes that can be added to a verb: *-s*, *-ing*, *-ed*, and *-en*. Recall that the *-s* is required in sE dialects and other American English dialects as a way to mark that the verb corresponds to subjects that are *she/he/it*—also known as **third person singular -s**. In some dialects, this particular *-s* is optional (see *use* in (13)), which means that it can be used but is not required. Researchers have found that this third-person *-s* suffix is a morphological feature that children acquire well before they are four years old when the dialect they are exposed to has this feature.[12] Gender-neutral third person singular pronouns such as *ze* would also take the third person singular agreement marker *-s* as in *Ze cooks*; however, singular *they* presently does not take the *-s* suffix (as in *I met Taylor. They cook a lot.*).

In sE dialects, **simple past tense** is indicated most often via an *-ed* suffix, which turns the verb into the **past tense form** (see (14) and (16)). This knowledge is acquired even before the present-tense agreement *-s* marker—likely before age two. In some non-sE dialects, the *-ed*-suffix, similar to the *-s* verb suffix, is optional and not required (see (15) above). For those of you who speak AAE or ChE, this is likely not a surprise. For those of you who speak an sE dialect, this might seem surprising at first. We hope that you're starting to see already that no matter which dialects, these forms are all part of a grammatical system.

The *-ing* suffix is a possibility for verbs across the represented dialects ((17)–(19)). This suffix indicates that something is happening right now or is/was ongoing for a while (this is called **progressive aspect**, something we will add more nuance to in Chapter 12!). This -*ing* form is called **present participle**.

Finally, a verb can form the **past participle** ((20)–(22)). The -*ed*-suffix is used to form past participles for regular verbs such as *work* in (21) (past tense form is *worked* and past participle is *worked*). For irregular verbs, a few different patterns exist, including the -*en*-suffix in *eaten* in (20). The past tense form is *ate* (not the regular **eated*), and the past participle is *eaten*. For *do*, the past tense form is *did* and the past participle form is *done* (as in (22)). The past participle is used to form **present perfect** and **past perfect** as well as a variety of other aspects. For the various irregular verbs in English, different options for the past participle exist. More on the **aspectual system** for verbs in Chapter 12!

> **Verb forms**
> - infinitive
> - third person -*s* form
> - present participle
> - past tense form
> - past participle

A total of four possible inflectional suffixes for verbs exist in English. What this means is that these suffixes can be used as tests to identify words as verbs. We'll use the -*ing*-suffix as an example. Compare (23) and (24) to (23a) and (24a).

(23)　He's *smiling*.

(23a)　**He-ing* is smiling.

(24)　We were *dancing*.

(24a)　We were dancing last **night-ing*.

Adding -*ing* to *he* and *night* results in the nonsense, ungrammatical words **he-ing* in (23a) and **night-ing* in (24a), but it works for *smile* and *dance* in (23) and (24), so we can be sure that *smile* and *dance* are verbs in those sentences.

Most verbs are **regular verbs** in that they each will be able to endure these suffixes (not all at once, of course). **Irregular verbs** also have these forms, but they might look different, such as *to drive* (infinitive), *drives* (third person singular form), *driving* (present participle), *drove* (past tense form), and *driven* (past participle). Past tense forms and past participles can be confusing because for regular verbs, the two forms look identical (*hiked/hiked*). Yet, they are distinct forms that do distinct grammatical work. The pairs below feature irregular verbs to better illustrate these two forms:

(25)　We *learned/learnt* new things last night. (sE)

(25a)　We *had learned/learnt* new things before we applied them. (sE)

(26)　They *taught* me, so at every game, I be winning.[13] (AAE)

(26a)　They *have taught* economics ever since they started out. (sE)

(27)　A friend was with, and she *drove* me home.[14] (ME)

(27a)　A friend had been with, and she *had driven* me home.[15] (ME)

(28)　We *went* into Cartier where she spent a wicked amount of money.[16] (NEE)

(28a) We *had gone* into Cartier where she spent a wicked amount of money.[17] (NEE)

(29) I *put* the cup on the shelf last night. (sE)

(29a) I *have put* the cup on the shelf just now. (sE)

Some irregular verbs feature a vowel change (*sing/sung*), some feature entirely new forms (*went/gone*), and some feature a zero-morpheme suffix (*put/put*). Because irregular verbs endure such radical changes in form, they are called **strong verbs**: they are strong enough to go through a change. Contrastingly, verbs that cannot endure such a change, i.e., regular ones, are called **weak verbs**. While we do not attempt to give an exhaustive overview of irregular verbs in English here, Chart 3 illustrates the main processes/patterns for how irregular verbs are formed (based on Quirk et al.[18]).

	Infinitive	Past tense	Past participle
past tense form and past participle variation possible	*burn*	*burned/burnt*	*burned/burnt*
	learn	*learned/learnt*	*learned/learnt*
	spill	*spilled/spilt*	*spilled/spilt*
past participle variation possible	*saw*	*sawed*	*sawed/sawn*
	strew	*strewed*	*strewed/strewn*
	mow	*mowed*	*mowed/mown*
vowel change; past tense and past participle variation possible	*buy*	*bought*	*bought*
	creep	*crept*	*crept*
	dream	*dreamt/dreamed*	*dreamt/dreamed*
vowel change; past tense form and past participle form differ	*break*	*broke*	*broken*
	bite	*bit*	*bitten*
	know	*knew*	*known*
all forms are the same	*put*	*put*	*put*
	cost	*cost*	*cost*
	shut	*shut*	*shut*
vowel change; past tense and past participle are the same; no suffix	*bleed*	*bled*	*bled*
	cling	*clung*	*clung*
	win	*won*	*won*
same as above, but past tense and past participle are different	*begin*	*began*	*begun*
	drink	*drank*	*drunk*
	run	*ran*	*run*

Chart 3 Major patterns for irregular verbs in English

(Em)Powering the Clause: The Verb

Exercise 1

Identify verb forms. Label the italicized verb forms in the excerpt[19] below as infinitive (I), 3rd person singular (3rd ps sg), past tense (PT), present participle (pres. part.), or past participle (past part.).

In a quaint little village *nestled* amidst rolling hills, there *lived* a colony of feline friends, whose fur *ranged* from silky black to snowy white. After they had *prowled* through the cobblestoned streets, they *came* to lie down in the dew-kissed grass. As their tails were *swishing* gracefully behind them, they were *roaming* freely through the colorful blooms. Each cat *is* distinct, and each cat *moves* in a distinct manner. They *have* playful personalities and some of them *display* mischievous demeanors. Their presence *commanded* admiration from all who had *gotten to know* them.

6.2.2.1 Person and Number

Person and **number** are grammatical categories relevant to verbs. "Person" simply refers to *first, second, third* and "number" refers to *singular* and *plural*. The grammatical category of singular and plural for verbs simply distinguishes whether we are talking about a single person or multiple people. The pronouns *I, you, she/he/it*, and gender-neutral *they* all refer to one person, whereas *we, you,* and *they* refer to more than one person; hence, they are plural. Chart 4 illustrates present tense paradigms for sE and non-sE dialect verbs.

	Person	sE dialects	Non-sE dialects
singular	1st person	**I** play	**I** play
	2nd person	**You** play	**You** play
	3rd person	**She/he/it** plays	**She/he/it** play(s)
	3rd person, gender neutral	**They** play	**They** play
plural	1st person	**We** play	**We** play
	2nd person	**You** play	**You** play
	3rd person	**They** play	**They** play

Chart 4 Person and number—sE and non-sE dialects

As Chart 4 shows, 2nd person singular refers to *you* and the 2nd person singular verb form is *play*. 1st person singular refers to *I* and the 1st person singular verb form is *play*. 1st person plural is *we* and the 1st person plural verb form is *play*. The pronoun *you* can refer to either one person or multiple people depending on whether it is used as the 2nd person singular or 2nd person plural form. Because this can create some ambiguity, many American English dialects have created separate 2nd person plural forms such as *y'all*, which removes such ambiguity, meaning that *you* is the 2nd person singular form and *y'all* is the 2nd person plural form. More on this and other variations with pronouns in Chapter 8!

Foundations of Grammar

You may notice that the 3rd person singular -s in sE dialects really is an outlier. sE uses the base form for all present tense forms except for the 3rd person singular form; non-sE uses the base form for all forms and makes the -s for the 3rd person form optional. If you know an additional language other than English, chances are (depending on the actual language, of course) that you are familiar with conjugation patterns that require different suffixes depending on person/number for that language.

Exercise 2

Identify person (1st, 2nd, 3rd) and number (singular, plural) for the italicized verbs in the sentences below.

a) My friends *sing* joyfully in the choir. (sE)
b) The new set still *needs* washed to kill germs.[20] (ME/SAE)
c) You all *play* the guitar beautifully. (sE)
d) [W]e *went* to the Capital Burger restaurant and had a wicked delicious burger.[21] (NEE)
e) I *read* a fascinating book last night. (sE)
f) Y'all *come* back.[22] (AE/SAE)
g) My best friend Rhys *bakes* delicious cookies for me. (sE)
h) Maybe it is what he *like* or even all he *know*.[23] (AAE)

6.2.2.2 Tense

Tense is another relevant grammatical category for verbs. For regular verbs, the past tense suffix -ed in most dialects distinguishes present tense from past tense, but remember that irregular verbs follow different patterns (see Chart 3 from earlier).

(30) Then after that I *talk* English.[24] (ChE)
(31) We *danced* all night long at the party. (sE)
(32) Yesterday, we *play* another team for the championship.[25] (AAE)
(33) I *picked* her because she nice and calm.[26] (AAE)

Chart 5 shows the paradigms for present and past tense for sE and some non-sE dialects for regular verbs.

	Present tense		**Past tense**	
	sE dialects	some non-sE dialects	sE dialects	some non-sE dialects
1st ps sg	I play	I play	I played	I play(ed)
2nd ps sg	You play	You play	You played	You play(ed)
3rd ps sg	She/he/it plays	She/he/it play(s)	She/he/it played	She/he/it/play(ed)
	They play	They play	They played	They play(ed)
1st ps pl	We play	We play	We played	We play(ed)
2nd ps pl	You play	You play	You played	You play(ed)
3rd ps pl	They play	They play	They played	They play(ed)

Chart 5 Present and past tense paradigms—sE and some non-sE regular verbs

Now, it's important to point to a possible reason for this: Phonology, one's language sound system that guides the pronunciation of words, influences morphology here. In most dialects, including sE, consonant clusters (when there are more than two consonants in a row) are reduced in spoken language. For example, in *I tasked her with writing the report*, the combination of "tasked" and "her" results in four (!) consonants in a row: "tasked" ends in three consonants (represented by "s," "k," and "ed;" the "ed" is pronounced as just one sound: "t"). This final "t" sound is followed by the initial "h" consonant in "her." Because there are four consonants in a row, most speakers (regardless of dialect) will skip at least one of those four sounds when they say the word, resulting in something like "tassed her" or "tasked 'er" or "task her" or "task 'er" or "tas' 'er". You get the idea. Some speakers may skip the "h," some the "k," and some the "t." This means that the consonant that represents the past tense *-ed* ending may be what gets skipped in oral language production, resulting in "task her." Not pronouncing the past tense *-ed* ending doesn't mean a speaker doesn't have an understanding that the verb is past tense. For more on the interplay of pronunciation and orthography, check out Lisa Green's explanation[27] in her introduction to AAE or Reaser et al.'s[28] discussion of the same.

6.2.3 Putting Inflection and Derivation to Work

Evidence from inflectional morphology is more important to classify a word as a verb, simply because many verbs aren't derived by derivational processes. Here is how our analysis works for verbs:

(34) We *hospitalized* the patient in time. (sE)

    a. Lexical category: verb

    b. Morphological evidence

        i. derivational evidence

hospital	+	-ize	=	hospitalize
Noun: a place where people get medical treatment		derivational suffix; verb-marker; class-changing		**Verb**: to be admitted as a patient in a hospital

ii. inflectional evidence: can endure past tense form

hospitalize +	-ed	=	hospitalized
Infinitive	inflectional suffix; past-tense marker; non-class changing		past tense: to be admitted as a patient in a hospital, but in the past

c. Additional evidence: this process works for verbs such as *customize* as well
   i. derivational evidence

custom	+	-ize	=	customize
Noun: a widely accepted behavior		derivational suffix; verb-marker; class-changing		**Verb**: to modify something

ii. inflectional evidence

customize +	-ed	=	customized
infinitive	inflectional suffix; past-tense marker; non-class changing		past tense: to modify something, but in the past

In what follows, we focus on **inflectional** morphology of verbs. We believe you're ready for an abbreviated morphological analysis! The point of our morphological analysis is to be able to provide evidence that the italicized words are, in fact, verbs. We know that verbs can endure various inflectional suffixes, and so that's our most important evidence. So, let's start.

(35) She *plays* soccer. (sE)

play	+	-s	=	she plays
Infinitive		inflectional suffix; 3rd person singular marker		3rd person singular form

(36) We *play* soccer. (sE)

play	+	-Ø	=	play
Infinitive		inflectional suffix: Ø-morpheme		1st person plural form

(37) Then she *get* some soap.[29] (AAE)

get	+	-Ø	=	get
Infinitive		inflectional suffix: -Ø-morpheme		3rd person singular form

(38) He's *smiling* to the cat.[30] (ChE)

smile	+	-ing	=	smiling
Infinitive		inflectional suffix: present participle marker		present participle form

(39) Fire was *a-flamin'* everything.[31] (AE)

a-flame +	*-in'*	=	*a-flamin'*
Infinitive	inflectional suffix: present participle marker		present participle form

(40) He *start* playing the piano [last year].[32] (AAE)

start +	-Ø	=	start
Infinitive	inflectional suffix: -Ø-morpheme		past tense form

(41) Cameron and Samir have *worked* together for years. (sE)

work +	-ed	=	worked
Infinitive	inflectional suffix: past participle marker		past participle form

(42) We have *eaten* already. (sE)

eat +	-en	=	eaten
Infinitive	inflectional suffix: past participle marker		past participle form

Knowing what you know about verbs by now should make it easier to figure out if something is a verb or not. To test if a given word is a verb, see if it can form 3rd person singular verb forms, past tense forms, present participle forms, and past participle forms. We'll use *eaten* from (42) as an example:

- 3rd person singular form: *she/he/it eat(s)*—check!
- Past tense form: I *ate*—check!
- Present participle form: I am *eating*—check!
- Past participle form: I have *eaten*—check!

Eaten is definitely a verb! The same isn't possible for, say, the word *horse*: *She/he/it horse(s)*; *I horsed*; *I am horsing*; *I have horsed*.

Exercise 3

Use inflectional morphology (and derivational, where applicable) to provide evidence that the italicized words are all verbs.

a) We *provided* access to treatments. (sE)
b) And he *get* what you mean.[33] (AAE)
c) She *retire* last year.[34] (AAE)

d) Our friends have *ridden* the bus to the fair. (sE)

e) I saw some girl, she *look* pretty.[35] (ChE)

f) Then after that I *talk* English.[36] (ChE)

g) We were *dancing* last night. (sE)

h) Yesterday, we was *conversating* with Mr. B. about the war.[37] (AAE)

6.2.4 Past-tense Variation

You already saw many examples of Ø-morpheme past tense forms across some dialects of American English. Here are a few more.

(43) I just *learn* to shut my mouth.[38] (AAE)

(44) After I *graduate* from there, ….[39] (AAE)

(45) I just *start* yesterday.[40] (AAE)

(46) We *dance* in Mayfair.[41] (AAE)

While the -ed suffix is not required in AAE and ChE, for instance, it is certainly possible in these dialects:[42]

(47) Where else have you *lived*?[43] (AAE)

(48) I *talked* to my mom about my career.[44] (AAE)

(49) Certain people *cooked* certain foods.[45] (AAE)

Irregular verb forms such as *give/gave, leave/left,* and *go/went* are generally used in the same way across dialects:

(50) He *gave* me a hand.[46] (AAE)

(51) I *left* Hyattsville.[47] (AAE)

We spent a bit of time on past-tense -ed because when AAE or ChE speakers do use Ø-morpheme past tense forms on regular verbs in English, it stands out to those who do not speak AAE or ChE. In other words, this is a salient feature, and many people assume it is incorrect or ungrammatical, when in reality, it is perfectly grammatical (it is a systematic feature of these dialects). Even in sE, some verbs use Ø-morpheme past tense forms:

(52) They *beat* us in the game yesterday. (sE)

(53) I *put* the cat in the carrier five minutes ago. (sE)

The verb *beat* features no past tense -ed suffix and neither does *put*, and yet both still denote past tense in such sentences. Conveniently, bare past-tense forms such as *beat* and *put* are generally seen as "exceptions" in sE dialects, and yet, bare past-tense forms such as *graduate* in non-sE dialects such as (44) above are seen as "mistakes." Again, our hope is that you're starting to see that these forms are all parts of patterns, each of which is part of a dialect's grammatical system, and as such, are grammatically correct.

An additional variation is the use of the past form as the past participle:[48]

(54)   I had *ate* a snack by the time they delivered pizza.[49] (AAE)

(55)   I haven't *wrote* in a long time.[50] (ChE)

(56)   I know of all the things that could have *went* wrong.[51] (sE)

(57)   None of these folks have *drove* a truck in their lives.[52] (sE)

The simple past form can be used in places where, traditionally, the past participle is expected. This pattern is *not* a feature relegated to non-sE dialects; especially in informal sE dialects, this feature pops up as well. In fact, this is an area where language change is happening all around us! In a few generations, we might all be using past tense forms in all instances, i.e., we might be phasing out the past participle forms altogether. For regular verbs such as *walk*, the past tense form and past participle form already look the same:

(58)   I *walked* yesterday. (simple past form)

(59)   I had *walked* for five miles before I found my friend. (past participle form)

This also helps explain why the use of the past-tense form of irregular verbs is increasing in places where the past participle form might be expected: The two forms look the same in the vast majority of all verbs!

Another feature related to past-tense forms where there is variation, and where that variation can be explained, in part, via ongoing, current language change is the use of regularized past-tense forms.

(60)   It *spinned*.[53] (ChE)

(61)   It *spinned* perfectly.[54] (sE)

(62)   Those were the most people that I *hanged* around with.[55] (ChE)

(63)   Melbourne always *striked* me as weird.[56] (sE)

It's important to remind you that the dialect variation forms we present to you are not relegated to just spoken conversations. You might hear them more frequently in spoken conversations and you might not see them as often in written texts, but that doesn't mean they are less grammatical or not grammatical at all. We simply live in a world where written texts are, by and large, still, expected to be produced in what is considered to be sE. Maybe those conventions and expectations will change if more people understand that all dialects are equally grammatical and valid!

6.3 Just Playing the Role: Analysis of Syntactic Features

6.3.1 Syntactic Environment of Verbs

It's time to look at **syntactic position**, just like we did for the other lexical categories so far. Verbs are a bit more complicated all around than the other classes, and we'll build up all the necessary knowledge step by step. A relatively simple way to describe the syntactic environment of where verbs can occur is summarized in Chart 6:

Foundations of Grammar

Syntactic environment	Example
alone in imperative constructions	*Bake!*
alone after a subject	We *bake*.
after auxiliary verb(s)	We have *baked*. We must *bake*. We *should be baking* etc.
after a subject and before other syntactic constituents (see subsequent sections in this chapter!)	We *bake* daily. We *may bake* cakes etc.

Chart 6 Syntactic environments of verbs

While this may look simple at first, the complexity comes into play, especially with the last row in Chart 6. As we will discover next, it is the lexical verb that selects what is or isn't included in the predicate. The subject has little—grammatical—power at the sentential level.

6.3.2 Verb Choice and Choices of the Verb: Verbs and What Follows Them

Remember from Chapter 2 that the English sentence consists of minimally a subject (S) and a verb, or, put differently, a sentence can be broken into the following parts:

- sentence = subject + predicate

This means that the subject will always be a noun-y thing, that is, an {NP}, and that the predicate is everything else to the right of the subject, including the {VP}. There are really two uses of the notation {VP}: it can be used narrowly to refer to just the verbal elements in sentences. In this way, we could refer to *must bake* in *We must bake cakes* as the {VP}. What can go into the narrow {VP} is limited to auxiliary verbs and lexical verbs only (more on this in Chapter 10). The same notation, {VP}, can also be used more broadly, in the sense of "predicate," and in that sense, it refers to *must bake cakes* in *We must bake cakes*. To keep things consistent, we use "predicate" for the broad sense and {VP} for the narrow sense.

A verb selects certain constituents required for the predicate in order for a sentence to be grammatically complete. Consider the first data set below. We've italicized the verbs and underlined the predicate.

(64) My very talented sister *had been honored*. (sE)
(65) I *had ate* a snack.[57] (AAE)
(66) He *gave* me a hand.[58] (AAE)
(67) I *bought* my horse a new bridle. (sE)
(68) She *look* pretty.[59] (ChE)
(69) The students *found* the quiz difficult. (sE)

Notice that some predicates consist of just the {VP} and others include {VP} and other constituents. Sometimes, the predicate includes more than one additional constituent. Chart 7 summarizes verb types based on how many constituents are required as part of the predicate; we go over each type in turn next.

Verb type	Number of required constituents in predicate
Intransitive verb	0
Monotransitive verb	1
Ditransitive verb	2
Copula verb	1
Complex transitive verb	2

Chart 7 Overview of verb types

6.3.2.1 Intransitive Verbs

Intransitive verbs don't require a constituent of any kind in the predicate for sentence completion:

(70)   I _run_. (sE)

(71)   My very talented sister _had been honored_. (sE)

Both sentences consist of only a {VP} after the subject:

(70a)   I   +   run. (sE)

        {NP}   +   {VP}

        S   +   predicate

(71a)   My very talented sister   +   had been honored. (sE)

        {NP}   +   {VP}

        S   +   predicate

Position, or syntagmatic clues, helps us identify the main lexical verb. Since all English sentences require a subject and knowing that the subject is nearly always in first position, the verb exists in second place/position after its subject. In (70a), the pronoun _I_ is the subject, and in (71a), the {NP} _My very talented sister_ is the subject. In both examples, the predicate consists of just the {VP}.

An **intransitive verb** is a verb that doesn't require an object to be grammatically complete. Sentences with intransitive verbs can include components to the right of the verb, but those components are always optional, not required, for the sentence to be grammatical:

(72)   Alejandra   +   runs   daily. (sE)

       {NP}   +   {VP}   {AdvP}

       S   +   predicate

(73)	We	+	dance in Mayfair.[60] (AAE)
	{NP}	+	{VP} {PP}
	S	+	predicate

Each of the sentences above can end after the main verb, i.e., we can delete *daily* and *in Mayfair*, and each sentence would still be grammatical. This means that the verb doesn't require an object or another constituent to be complete, and that means, in turn, that each verb above is an intransitive one.

6.3.2.2 Monotransitive Verbs

When the verb requires just one object for grammatical completion, it will be a **direct object**. This type of verb is called **monotransitive**:

(74) I *bought* a horse. (sE)

(75) I *had ate* a snack.[61] (AAE)

(76) Certain people *cooked* certain foods.[62] (AAE)

Each predicate here consists of the {VP} and an {NP}; those {NPs} all function as DOs. How do we know they function as DOs? The question test:

(74a) I bought *a horse*. (sE)

   Q: Whom/what did I buy? A: *A horse.*

(75a) I had ate *a snack*.[63] (AAE)

   Q: I had ate what? A: *A snack.*

(76a) Certain people cooked *certain foods*.[64] (AAE)

   Q: What did certain people cook? A: *Certain foods.*

It is the verb that expresses the action that selects what is necessary in the predicate, and these verbs here each select a DO as necessary for grammatical completion for that verb in that specific sentence. Keep in mind that, really, what needs the object is the verb itself. The subject could, literally, care less about whether there is an object or not.

6.3.2.3 Ditransitive Verbs

A verb can also select both DO and **indirect object (IO)**, in the predicate. How do we know there is an IO and a DO? Constituent tests such the question test and one-word replacement test allow us to determine how many constituents there are in the predicate.

(77) He gave [*me*   ] [a hand].[65] (AAE)

(77a) He gave [her   ] [it   ].

(78) I bought [*my horse*] [a new bridle]. (sE)

(78a) I bought [it   ] [something].

The IO is what conveys the beneficiary or receiver (*my horse, me*) of the direct object (*a new bridle, a hand*). Here, the verb has selected both a DO (the item being bought or given; here *a new bridle* and *a hand*) and an IO (the thing benefiting from or receiving the DO; here *my horse* and *me*). In these cases, because the verb selects two objects (both IO and DO), we call the verb **ditransitive**.

A note about the term *transitivity*. *Transitivity* means "transfer to or selection of." Knowing what you know about morphological analyses of words, the internal composition of our transitivity labels helps explain their meaning, too:

- Transitive: movement or transfer of action;
- Intransitive: prefix *in* means *no*, so: no movement/action onto anything, no objects;
- Monotransitive: prefix *mono* means *one*, so: movement or action of the verb affecting one object;
- Ditransitive: prefix *di* means *two*, so: movement or action of the verb affecting two objects

6.3.2.4 Copula Verbs (aka: Linking Verbs)

Monotransitive verbs require one constituent as part of the predicate. There's yet another type of verb that requires one constituent as part of the predicate: **copula verbs** (aka **linking verbs**). Can you describe in your own words how the next examples are different from monotransitive verbs? How does the constituent in the predicate differ from a DO?

(79) They *are* professors. (sE)

(80) Most movies *have been* very engaging. (sE)

(81) She *look* pretty.[66] (ChE)

We can reproduce these sentences as follows:

(79a) They = professors. (sE)

(80a) Most movies = very engaging. (sE)

(81a) She = pretty. (ChE)

In each case, we can replace the verb with an equal sign because the constituent that follows the verb completes our understanding of the subject. In (79a), the word *professors* tells us what *they* are, in (80a) *very engaging* tells us what *Most movies* have been, and in (81a), *pretty* tells us what *she* is. In other words, the verb closely links or couples the subject to its complement. For this reason, this verb type is called **copula** or **linking verb**. The constituent a copula verb requires is called **subject complement (SC)**. A DO does not complete the subject; rather, the DO expresses whom/what is affected by the action, and so this is why we differentiate monotransitive verbs from copula verbs.

The *be* verb is the most frequent copula verb, and it has many forms because it is the most irregular verb in English: *am, is, are, was, were, been, being*. When a *be* verb is used as the main verb, then this is the copula verb. *Be* can be used as a helping verb as in *We were running when the rain hit* where the main verb is *running* and *were* is the helping, the auxiliary, verb, which means as an auxiliary verb, the *be* verb is not a copula verb. There are some other linking verbs, including *look* in (81) above. *Feel, become, seem*, and *appear* are just a few other ones. We come back to them in Chapter 11!

6.3.2.5 Complex Transitive Verbs

Complex transitivity exists when the verb requires a DO followed by another required constituent:

(82) Sam called [Dakota] [their friend]. (sE)

(83) They called [us] [Hotlanta].[67] (AAE)

(84) The students found [the quiz] [difficult]. (sE)

We can rephrase the constituents on the right side of the verb as follows:

(82a) Dakota = their friend

(83a) us = Hotlanta

(84a) the quiz = difficult

It's almost as if there's a copula-verb-type construction on the right side of verb, just without an actual copula verb! The two constituents required by complex transitive verbs complete each other, or more precisely, the second completes the first one. The first one is the DO, and so the constituent that completes the DO is called **object complement (OC)**. In the same way, the SC completes our understanding of the subject, the OC completes our understanding of the DO. When you encounter sentences with two required constituents as part of the predicate, you must determine if those two constituents are IO + DO, or if they are DO + OC. We get into that in Chapter 11.

These five verb types—intransitive, monotransitive, ditransitive, copula, complex transitive—correspond to sentence patterns. We will build on this knowledge in Chapter 11. For now, what's important is that verbs are a lexical category that can select additional constituents in a sentence. Being able to identify these constituents helps us to identify the verb type in a sentence, and that, in turn, can be evidence that a particular word is a verb.

Exercise 4

Verb types. Identify the verb type for the italicized verbs in each of the sentences (the first has been done as an example) and label all required constituents correctly.

a) The students *took* the exam. (sE) monotransitive (*the exam* = DO)

b) The students *had studied*. (sE)

c) This will be particularly important once you're *done* the gorgeous tattoo.[68] (ECE)

d) The professor *gave* the students the exam. (sE)

e) The park *has* two basketball hoop.[69] (AAE)

> f) The students *called* the professor a genius. (sE)
>
> g) Your phone bill be *high*.[70] (AAE)
>
> h) My neighbor *painted* my cat statue green. (sE)
>
> i) That *don't give* her no money.[71] (AAE)

6.3.3 Paradigmatic Evidence

We provided Chart 4 about person and number earlier not just to illustrate the patterns for different dialects, but also because it can provide **paradigmatic evidence** to classify a word as a verb. Words that are verbs can be conjugated. Let's illustrate this with just one example:

(85) I compete with my horse. (sE)

The word *compete* is a verb because you can conjugate it:

- I compete
- You compete
- She/he/it competes
- They compete
- We compete
- You compete
- They compete

Let's say you're not sure if *horse* is a verb, and so you try conjugating that word, but the verbal paradigm *I horse/you horse/she horses/we horse* and so on is not possible! This demonstrates that *horse* is not a verb in (85).

In addition to the conjugation paradigm, you can also simply try to replace a word in question with a word you know for sure is a verb as evidence. If we can replace the word in question with a known verb in the same syntactic environment, we have "circumstantial" evidence. If we know that *to train* is a verb, we can slot it in for *bought* in (86), and if we know that *to prepare* is a verb, we can slot that in for *cooked* in (87), giving us (86a) and (87a):

(86) I *bought* a horse. (sE)

(87) Certain people *cooked* certain foods.[72] (AAE)

(86a) I *trained* a horse. (sE)

(87a) Certain people *prepared* certain foods. (AAE)

Of course, semantics will make us reach our limits fast. We couldn't replace *cooked* with *trained*: *Certain people trained certain foods* is simply nonsensical. We could, if we wanted to, simply switch out the two verbs in the original sentences:

(86b)   I *cooked* a horse

(87b)   Certain people *bought* certain foods.

Then again, we are not proponents of cooking horses, so other verbs would be more appropriate! We can use the substitution of a known verb as a first step in confirming the word in question as a verb. However, how do you know the known verb is, indeed, a verb? You must establish that your test-word is a verb, and so you won't be able to get around using morphological analysis, syntactic function, and position as evidence!

6.3.4 Rocking Out Together: Nouns, Adjectives, Adverbs, and Verbs

We have covered a lot of ground about identifying lexical categories from a linguistic perspective. We have taken apart, quite literally, all open-class words: Nouns, adjectives, adverbs, and verbs. To recap, both morphology (about form) and syntactic information (about position and function) can help us confidently identify a given word as a noun, adjective, adverb, or verb.

For each lexical category so far, we introduced you to some derivational suffixes such as *-ment*, *-ful*, *-ly*, and *-ify* that can be useful to classify words. Because derivational suffixes don't have a solid, 1:1 correspondence to lexical categories, inflectional morphology is better suited to distinguish word classes from one another. Chart 8 summarizes the possible inflectional suffixes for the four lexical categories covered so far.

Inflectional suffix	Grammatical information	Examples
Noun		
-s	Plural	One cat—two *cats*
's	Possessive	The *cat's* fur is soft.
Adjective		
-er	Comparative	The *cuter* cat
-est	Superlative	The *cutest* cat
Adverb		
-er	Comparative	We drove *faster*.
-est	Superlative	They drove *fastest*.
Verb		
-s	Third person singular	She/he/it *purrs/eats*.
-ed	Past tense form	They *purred/ate*.
-ing	Present participle	We are *purring/eating*.
-ed/-en	Past participle	We have *purred/eaten*.

Chart 8 Inflectional morphemes

Exercise 5

Identify the lexical category of the italicized word(s) in each sentence below and support your claim with morphological evidence and syntactic evidence by filling in the chart. For sentence a), we have provided answers. Complete the rest!

a) The dog *chased* the cat under the *table*. (sE)
b) He *bring* the *food* yesterday.[73] (AAE)
c) He got *sick* a-workin' *so hard*.[74] (AE)
d) The *new student* is *bilingual*. (sE)
e) We are *running* around the lake. (sE)
f) For she won't *feel guilty*.[75] (ChE)
g) They drove too *slow*. (sE)
h) Emilia *swims* every day. (sE)
i) Here's me a *good* pair of *jeans*.[76] (SAE)

Word	Morphological evidence	Syntactic evidence
a) chased = V	past-tense inflectional suffix -ed; could also add -ing: *The dog is chasing.*	monotransitive verb (takes DO); occurs after subject and before DO
a) table = N	inflectional plural -s suffix possible: *one table—two tables.*	occurs after determiner *the*; functions as part of object of prep
b) bring		
b) food		
c) sick		
c) so		
c) hard		
d) new		
d) student		
d) bilingual		
e) running		
f) feel		
f) guilty		
g) slow		
h) swims		
i) good		
i) jeans		

Terminology to Know

Term	Working definition	Example/Illustration
Verb		
Person		
Number		
Tense		
Infinitive (full)		
Aspect		
Progressive aspect		
Present participle		
Past participle		
Transitivity		
Intransitive		
Monotransitive		
Ditransitive		
Copula verb/linking verb		
Complex transitive		

Chart 9 Key terminology Chapter 6

Notes

1. Warburton and Dorough, 1973.
2. Montgomery, 2009; cited in Matyiku, 2011a.
3. Spartz, 2008, cited in Kaplan, 2015.
4. Wood, 2014.
5. Putnam and van Koppen, 2011; cited in Wood, 2013.
6. Baker-Bell, 2020, p. 57.
7. Ibid., p. 76.
8. Barrón and San Romón, n.d., pp. 30–1; cited in Bayley, 2012, p. 158.
9. Ibid., p. 162.
10. Wolfram and Christian, 1976, p. 69.
11. Baker-Bell, 2020, p. 43.
12. Brown, 1973; but see Green (2011) on language acquisition of AAE.
13. T. McMurtry, personal communication, March 30, 2025.
14. Kaplan, 2015.
15. Adapted from Ibid.
16. W. Beauregard, personal communication, August 29, 2024.

17. Adapted from Ibid.
18. Quirk et al., 1985.
19. Based on an excerpt produced by OpenAI, 2024.
20. Edelstein, 2014; cited in Maher and Wood, 2011.
21. W. Beauregard, personal communication, August 29, 2024.
22. University of South Carolina (n.d.).
23. Baker-Bell, 2020, p. 45.
24. Barrón and San Romón, n.d., pp. 30–1; cited in Bayley, 2012, p. 158.
25. Kendall, Fasold et al., 2018 Transcript ID DCA_se1_ag1_m_05_1.
26. Baker-Bell, 2020, p. 76.
27. Green, 2002.
28. Reaser et al., 2017a.
29. Green, 2011, p. 208.
30. Barrón and San Romón, n.d., pp. 30–1; cited in Bayley, 2012, p. 162.
31. Wolfram and Christian, 1976, p. 69.
32. Kendall, Fasold et al., 2018 Transcript ID DCA_se1_ag1_m_05_1.
33. Ibid., Transcript ID DCA_se2_ag2_m_02.
34. Rowe et al., 2018 Transcript ID PRV_se0_ag1_f_02_1.
35. Bayley and Santa Ana, 2004, p. 376.
36. Barrón and San Romón, n.d., pp. 30–1; cited in Bayley, 2012, p. 158.
37. Baker-Bell, 2020, p. 43.
38. Kendall, Quartey et al., 2018 Transcript ID DCB_se2_ag4_m_01_1.
39. Ibid.
40. Ibid., Transcript ID DCB_se1_ag1_f_03_1.
41. Ibid.
42. For more info on variation of *-ed* markers, see Green, 2002; Kohn et al., 2020.
43. Kendall, Quartey et al., 2018 Transcript ID DCB_se2_ag4_m_01_1.
44. Ibid., Transcript ID DCB_se1_ag1_f_03_1.
45. Ibid.
46. Ibid., Transcript ID DCB_se2_ag4_m_01_1.
47. Ibid.
48. Green, 2002.
49. Ibid., p. 95.
50. Fought, 2003, p. 94.
51. Davies, 2018.
52. Ibid.
53. Fought, 2003, p. 94.
54. Davies, 2018.
55. Fought, 2003, p. 94.

56. Davies, 2018.
57. Green, 2002, p. 95.
58. Kendall, Quartey et al., 2018, Transcript ID DCB_se2_ag4_m_01_1.
59. Bayley and Santa Ana, 2004, p. 376.
60. Kendall, Quartey et al., 2018 Transcript ID DCB_se1_ag1_f_03_1.
61. Green, 2002, p. 95.
62. Kendall, Quartey et al., 2018 Transcript ID DCB_se1_ag1_f_03_1.
63. Green, 2002, p. 95.
64. Kendall, Quartey et al., 2018 Transcript ID DCB_se1_ag1_f_03_1.
65. Ibid., Transcript ID DCB_se2_ag4_m_01_1.
66. Bayley and Santa Ana, 2004, p. 376.
67. Farrington et al., 2020 Transcript ID ATL_se0_ag1_m_01_1.
68. Adapted from Wood, 2014.
69. Reaser et al., 2017a, p. 182.
70. Green, 2002, p. 48.
71. Kendall, Fasold et al., 2018 Transcript ID DCA_se2_ag1_f_03_1.
72. Kendall, Quartey et al., 2018 Transcript ID DCB_se1_ag1_f_03_1.
73. Reaser et al., 2017a, p. 284.
74. Wolfram, 1976; cited in Matyiku, 2011a.
75. Barrón and San Romón, n.d., pp. 30–1; cited in Bayley, 2012, p. 160.
76. Wood, 2015.

CHAPTER 7
LENDING A HELPING HAND: THE AUXILIARY VERB

Overview

You already know a lot about the lexical category of verbs, which belong to open-class words. This chapter is about **auxiliary verbs**, which are a word type that rarely adds new words and belongs to the closed-class words. You'll learn about the forms of primary and modal auxiliary verbs and the work they help accomplish (i.e., their functions), including marking tense, emphasis, and negation, as well as forming questions. Our objectives are as follows. You'll be able to

- better understand characteristics of primary and modal auxiliaries;
- build your knowledge of forms and functions of auxiliary verbs.

Pre-reading task

1. For those who are native speakers of any variety of English, the selection and use of auxiliary verbs is automatic. For the most part, we never think about which to use. Take, for example, the sentences below. Which auxiliaries would you use in the blanks?

    a) My spouse and I _____ dropping off the prescription when our friend called. (sE)

    b) I know he _____ a-tellin' the truth, but I _____ a-comin' home.[1] (AE)

    c) The group of friends _____ _____ meeting regularly at the park on Sundays. (sE)

    d) They _____ giving him the recognition.[2] (AAE)

    Once you select the auxiliary, try to express what the auxiliary adds to the sentence. In other words, what does the auxiliary tell you that other parts of the sentence don't? Be sure to come back to your answers after you've worked through this chapter!

7.1 Introduction

Auxiliary verbs are sometimes called **helping verbs**, which is an intuitive term, since auxiliary verbs do just that: they help the main verb, or lexical verb, in various ways. How do you know if a verb is an auxiliary verb or a main verb? Take a look at these two examples:

(1) Yesterday, Carlos and Diego *had been cuddling* with my cats all day. (sE)

(2) Yesterday, we *was conversating* with Mr. B. about the war.[3] (AAE)

Is the {VP} in (1) about "having," "being," or "cuddling"? In other words, are you *having with your cats all day* or *are you being with your cats all day*? Surely, you'll agree that the sentence is about *cuddling with the cats all day*. So, our main verb is *cuddling*. In (2), is the sentence about "was-ing" or "conversating"? Again, surely, you agree that it is the latter, and thus, the main verb in (2) is *conversating*. This means that whenever we have a {VP} with more than one verb, the last verb is the main verb. All other verbs in that same {VP} are auxiliary verbs. Your evidence to identify main verbs and auxiliary verbs, thus, is pretty simple:

- If the {VP} consists of just one verb, that verb is the main verb.
- If the {VP} consists of more than one verb, the last verb in the {VP} is the main verb.

Two types of auxiliary verbs exist: **modal** auxiliaries and **primary** auxiliaries. We'll start with primary auxiliaries. Get ready: This chapter is chock-full with information about variation when it comes to auxiliaries!

7.2 Primary Auxiliary Verbs

The three primary auxiliary verbs in English are *be*, *have*, and *do*. These auxiliaries are called primary auxiliaries because they help {VPs} do some very important work.

7.2.1 The Primary Auxiliary Be

We need the *be* auxiliary, chiefly, for two purposes: to form the progressive aspect and to form passive voice. You already know a little bit about the **progressive aspect** from the chapter on verbs. It requires a form of *be* and the present participle of the main verb (the -*ing* form). Here are a few examples:

(3) I *am preparing* for my exams. (sE)

(4) He *is smiling* to the cat.[4] (ChE)

(5) Fatima and Amir *are dancing* today. (sE)

(6) Fire *was a-flamin'* everything.[5] (AE)

(7) Yesterday, we *was conversating* with Mr. B. about the war.[6] (AAE)

(8) You *writing* all this.[7] (AAE)

In (3)–(7), the present participle in each {VP} is preceded by a form of *be*: *am*, *is*, *are*, *was*, and *was*. The auxiliary here, then, is helping to index progressive aspect in our {VP}. In (8), there is no form of *be* prior to the main verb *writing*. This is a grammatical feature called **zero copula** or **null copula**. It is common in AAE and other dialects, and in fact, many languages other than English have this feature in their standardized version of their languages. Stay tuned for more information about progressive aspect, its nuances, and its dialect variations!

Be is also required for **passive voice**:

(9)   Many books *are read* by Hunter. (sE)

(10) A book *is read* to Isabel's child every night. (sE)

(11) The reports *were written* by the project manager. (sE)

(12) We *was taught* that there is no such thing.[8] (AAE)

Here, the form of *be* precedes the past participle of the main verb: *read*, *written*, and *taught*. Combining a form of *be* with the past participle is how passive voice in English dialects is formed. For now, just keep in mind that the passive voice is a way to move the object of the sentence to the subject position and omit or de-emphasize the agent or doer of the action. So, in (9), the phrase *many books* occupies the subject slot, whereas *Hunter*, the reader of those books, has been relegated to the optional {PP}. In active voice, the doer of the action, *Hunter*, occupies the subject slot and *many books* the object slot: *Hunter read many books*. We cover passive voice in more detail in Chapter 13.

When a form of *be* is used as an auxiliary, it causes the next verb form to either be the past participle (usually an *-ed/-en* form but other forms exist) or present participle (the *-ing* form). The *be* auxiliary is our helper to indicate either progressive aspect or passive voice—without them, you wouldn't be able to talk about things that *are happening* right now or things that *were done* by you or to you, for example.

7.2.2 The Primary Auxiliary Have

The auxiliary *have* is needed to form **perfective aspect**, which requires a form of *have* and the past participle. The auxiliary *have* comes in just three forms: *have* and *has* for present tense and *had* for past tense.

(13) Blake *has eaten* their ice cream already. (sE)

(14) Amos and Kori *have driven* the cats to the vet already. (sE)

(15) We *have seen* many beautiful flowers this summer. (sE)

(16) I *had ate* a snack by the time they delivered pizza.[9] (AAE)

(17) Samir *had walked* the dog before dinner. (sE)

The auxiliary *have* precedes the main verb. When a form of *have* is used as an auxiliary, it causes the next verb form to be the past participle (or the past form, depending on the dialect). This means that *have* is the auxiliary, our helper, to indicate perfective aspect. Without it, you wouldn't be able to indicate that something *has happened* in the past and still has relevance for right now!

The tricky thing about *be* and *have* is that when these verbs are the only verb in the {VP}, then they are the **main verb**:

(18)   I *am* happy.

(19)   The teachers at South High *is* cool.[10] (AAE)

(20)   Since my grandmother *is* the only one Ø has a Nintendo.[11] (ChE)

(21)   Sarah and Blake *were* tired. (sE)

(22)   I *have* many clients. (sE)

(23)   You *had* a great time. (sE)

In each example, the form of *be* or of *have* is the only verb in the {VP}. As such, the sentences now really are about "am-ing," "is-ing," "have-ing" in that *I have many clients* is about, well, having many clients. *I am happy* is about, well, being happy. So, it is only when the form of *be* or *have* is followed by another verb in the {VP} that it functions as an auxiliary verb.

7.2.3 The Primary Auxiliary Do

The *do* auxiliary isn't quite as irregular as the *be* verb, but it still has a few forms: *do, does, doing, did, done*. The next data set illustrates the use of *do* as an auxiliary:

(24)   But Ms. Nicks *do be trippin'* sometimes.[12] (AAE)

(25)   The candidate *did win* after all. (sE)

(26)   When I *don't have* hockey and I'm done my homework, I go there ....[13] (ECE)

(27)   They *didn't know* nothing about me.[14] (AAE)

(28)   *Does* she *know* that she works too hard? (sE)

(29)   *Did* the candidate *win*? (sE)

These sentences are not about "doing." Instead, they are about *tripping, winning, having, knowing,* and *winning*. Another obvious clue is that each of the {VPs} consists of two or more verbs:

(24a)   do + be + tripping

(25a)   did + win

(26a)   do + n't + have

(27a)   did + n't + know

(28a)   does + know

(29a)   did + win

The forms of *do,* above, all function as auxiliary verbs. You'll likely have noticed that the *do* verb has different kinds of jobs, or functions. In (24) and (25), *do* emphasizes something, in (26) and (27), *do* helps negate something, and in (28) and (29), it helps formulate questions. Now, *be* and *have* also have a couple of these superpowers.

Like the *be* and *have* auxiliary, *do* can also occur as the main verb of the sentence. (30)–(33) are truly about "doing." Plus, the form of *do* is the only verb in the {VP} in each, making it the main verb:

(30)   The candidate *did* it! (sE)

(31)   Ali and Moesha always *do* a good job. (sE)

(32)   She *do* well.[15] (AAE)

(33)   She *does* it all. (sE)

As auxiliaries, *be*, *have*, and *do* accomplish work like indicating aspect, voice, emphasizing something, negating something, and turning a statement into a question, which are all important **functions** within a language. Hence, the label **primary auxiliary** is well-deserved. In addition to these primary auxiliaries, we have a plethora of modal auxiliaries, which can do a whole of things, too! We turn to them next.

Exercise 1

Identify the auxiliary verb(s) and main verb in each verb phrase below.

a) Yesterday, I *had been cuddling* with my cats all day. (sE)

b) Yesterday, we *was conversating* with Mr. B. about the war.[16] (AAE)

c) I *had wrote* a letter to the editor. (sE)

d) The cops *had went* to my house.[17] (ChE)

e) Martin *is done* his bass tracks and we are ready to start vocals.[18] (ECE)

f) Javier *has walked* six miles every Saturday for many years. (sE)

g) He *has been walking* for a long time. (sE)

h) He *don't be barking* at nobody.[19] (AAE)

7.3 Modal Auxiliary Verbs

Modal auxiliary verbs include both nine **central** modal verbs as well as a few other **marginal** modal verbs (see Chart 1 for an overview).

Central modal verbs	Marginal modal verbs
can	dare
could	need
may	ought
might	used
must	liketa
shall[20]/should	
will	
would	

Chart 1 Central and marginal modal verbs

These two types of modal auxiliaries behave somewhat differently. Let's dig into some data to get a handle on them:

(34)   Karigan *will deliver* the pens. (sE)

(35)   Casey *must be* on time. (sE)

(36)   Avery *may be* at home. (sE)

(37)   Hunter *might arrive* on time. (sE)

(38)   Pat *can go* to the movies. (sE)

(39)   Taylor *can explain* things straightforwardly. (sE)

(40)   He *could talk* smart ... He's like a straight-A student.[21] (ChE)

(41)   Katy *should go* home tonight. (sE)

The fact that the modal verb comes prior to the main verb shouldn't be a surprise given that we saw this same pattern with primary auxiliaries. After all, we don't come across sentences where the auxiliary comes after the main verb such as **Karigan deliver will the pens*. However, look again at the main verb's form: It's different from what we saw with primary auxiliaries. Rather than a present participle or past participle, for central modal auxiliaries, what follows next is the **bare infinitive** form of the main verb, such as *deliver, be, arrive, go, talk*.

Let's see if this is the same for marginal modal verbs:

(42)   She *needs to go* home. (sE)

(43)   She *need to stay* in the boat.[22] (AAE)

(44)   They *dared to overstay* their welcome. (sE)

(45)   We *used to go* dancing every weekend. (sE)

(46)   You *ought to read* some good fiction every now and then. (sE)

(47)   The soul *needs fed* by creative, multi-dimensional teaching.[23] (ME)

(48)   And it *liketa scared* him to death![24] (AE/AAE/WSE)

This data set shows two patterns: Examples (42)–(46) show that marginal modal verbs are followed by the full infinitive of the main verb: *to go, to stay, to overstay,* and *to read*. Examples (47)–(48) show the constructions *needs fed* and the marginal modal *liketa*—two dialect variations. Both require the simple past form of the main verb. The form *needs fed* is a feature of non-sE dialects found in the Midwest, and chiefly, it is almost exclusively found in White Midwestern English and virtually absent in AAE dialects.[25] *Liketa* is also a fascinating (and systematic!) regional and social dialect variant. *Liketa* may also be spelled as *like to* or *liked to*. People use this construction to indicate that "an event that was likely to happen but did not actually happen."[26] This form is used mostly in AE, White Southern English (WSE), and AAE, but also occurs in some varieties of British English.[27]

Another difference compared to *be, have,* and *do* is that central modal verbs (and the marginal modal *ought*) are limited when it comes to the forms they can take. Specifically, central modals

- cannot occur as full infinitives (**to must/to might/to may/etc.*),
- cannot occur as present participles (**is musting/is mighting/is maying/etc.*),
- cannot occur as past participles (**has musted/has mighted/has mayed/etc.*),
- cannot occur as 3rd person singular forms (**she wills/musts/mights/mays/etc.*).

Compare that to the primary modals, which can occur as infinitives (*to be/to have/to do*), as present and past participles (*being/been; having/had; doing/done*), and have a 3rd person singular form in sE (*is/has/does*).

Central modal auxiliaries are, still, helping verbs, of course. Just like primary auxiliaries. That means they help us do something; they have a function: They tweak the meaning of a verb in various ways, some of which are as follows:

- *Liketa*: In *It liketa scared him to death* (48), *liketa* conveys that someone was almost scared to death, not actually scared to death.
- *May/might*: In *Avery may be at home* in (36), *may* expresses that there's a possibility that Avery is not actually at home. Hence, *may* helps the writer express a personal assessment of the likelihood of Avery's presence at home. In *Hunter might arrive on time* in (37), *might* expresses that *Hunter* won't necessarily arrive on time. *Might*, thus, expresses a possibility rather than a fact. *May* can also be used to ask for permission as in *May I have a second portion of ice cream cake?*
- *Can/could*: In *Taylor can explain things straightforwardly* in (39), *can* conveys Taylor's ability to explain things. This is different from *Pat can go to the movies* in (38), where *can* expresses that permission has been granted for Pat to go to the movies rather than expressing Pat's ability to physically do so. Note that quite a while ago, *can* was overwhelmingly used to express that someone had the capability to do something. Over time, the usage has shifted to where we now use it very regularly in permission-seeking contexts.[28] The older usage, dare we say more outdated usage, rears its head in the oft-repeated back-and-forth in

classrooms that goes something like this: Student: "Can I go to the bathroom?"—Teacher: "I don't know. Can you?" This means that both *can* and *may* are quite common in contemporary usage to seek permission. However, a ChE dialect variation uses *could* to convey capabilities, abilities, and accomplishments. Example (40) demonstrated this: *He could talk smart* ....[29] In sE, we might use *can* as in *He can talk smart*, pointing to the person's abilities. This use of *could* is unique to ChE.[30] Here are two more examples of this usage:

(49)   I learned that people that are left-handed *could draw* better than ....[31] (ChE)

(50)   Nobody believes that you *could fix* anything.[32] (ChE)

- *Must/shall/should/ought*: These modals generally have to do with obligation or duty. In (35), *Casey must be on time*, the modal *must* conveys that Casey has an obligation to be on time. At the same time, in a sentence such as *Casey isn't here yet. They must be working late today*, there's not an obligation that they're working late. Rather, *must* expresses the speaker's relative certainty about Casey working late. This relative certainty is sometimes referred to as **epistemic** meaning. When a modal verb is used to convey certain cultural norms, moral imperatives, or speaker expectations—as in (46) *You ought to read some good fiction every now and then*—this is referred to as **deontic** meaning.

As you can see, while there are broad categories of how a modal can tweak the semantic meaning of sentence, depending on context, a modal auxiliary can sometimes be used to express different aspects of these broad categories of meaning. *Can/could* and *may/might* as well as *must* are just a couple of examples for that variability in semantic meaning and use. We will see soon that modal auxiliaries can sometimes also do some of the fundamental tasks like negation or question formation. Stay tuned!

Exercise 2

Create one sentence using each of following modals: *can, could, may, might, ought, shall, should, will, would, need, liketa*. That means you'll be writing eleven sentences. For each sentence, describe what kind of meaning the modal ads (obligation, permission, epistemics, something else).

Another feature of central modal auxiliaries is that they can **co-occur** with primary auxiliaries:

(51)   I *might be studying* for my exams. (sE)

(52)   He *could be smiling* to the cat.[33] (ChE)

(53)   We *must be dancing* today. (sE)

(54) We *should have been dancing* last night. (sE)

(55) A book *would be read* to Sandy's child every night. (sE)

(56) Blake *shall have eaten* their ice cream already. (sE)

(57) I *liketa got run* over by 'em![34] (AE/AAE/WSE)

(58) I know of all the things that *could have went* wrong.[35] (sE)

(59) Samir *must have walked* the dog before dinner. (sE)

When both central and modal auxiliaries co-occur in a {VP}, the modal auxiliary comes first, followed by the primary auxiliary, followed by the main verb:

(51a) I *might be studying* for my exams. (sE)
modal + primary + main verb

(52a) He *could be smiling* to the cat.[36] (ChE)
modal + primary + main verb

(54a) We *should have been dancing* last night. (sE)
modal + primary + primary + main verb

Liketa is a little different from other modal auxiliary verbs because the only primary auxiliary verb that can co-occur with it is *have*, though *got* can co-occur with it as well.

You saw earlier that the main verb following a modal auxiliary will be in its infinitive form (in most dialects). So, when we add a modal auxiliary to a {VP} that includes a primary auxiliary and a main verb, there's a change in verb form. You may have caught on to this already! If not, here is a direct pair:

(60) We *are relaxing* on the couch. (sE)

(60a) We *might be relaxing* on the couch. (sE)

Adding the word *might* requires us to change *are* to *be*, again, because (in most dialects, including sE) the verb that follows a modal must be in its infinitive form.

In many dialects of English, predominantly in SAE, speakers can also double up on modals. That is, they can place two modal auxiliaries right next to one another prior to the main verb. While it is most common in SAE, speakers ranging from areas from Florida to West Texas and further north up into Pennsylvania and New Jersey have been found to use this feature; some AAE speakers may use it, too.[37] Here are some examples:

(61) I don't think I have any grants you *might could apply* for.[38] (SAE)

(62) We *might can go* up there next Saturday.[39] (SAE)

(63) This thing here I *might should turn over* to Ann.[40] (SAE)

The data above demonstrates that using more than one modal is a common occurrence. In each example, *might* is followed by yet another modal (*could, can, should,* and *would*). The examples are not an exhaustive list of possible combinations. In fact, sometimes, even three modals can co-occur (Huang, 2011):

(64) Sorry, we don't carry them anymore, but you know, you *may might can get* one right over there at Wicks.[41] (SAE)

Double/multiple modals are fascinating! They are an excellent example of how dialect variations simply reveal different underlying structures, which in turn are responsible for the difference in how modals can be used. We'll unpack this in Chapter 10 in more detail when we look at phrases and phrase-internal structure.

> **Exercise 3**
>
> For each sentence identify each component of the {VP} as a central modal auxiliary, a marginal modal auxiliary, a primary auxiliary, and a main verb. Provide evidence for your claims.
>
> Example: *We <u>should have called</u> the veterinarian.* (sE)
>
> - *should*: central modal; first slot in VP; next verb is in bare form;
> - *have*: primary auxiliary; next verb is the past participle form
> - *called*: main verb; last verb in VP; this is what the sentence is about (it is about "calling," not "having" or "should-ing")
>
> a) My spouse and I were dropping off the prescription when our friend called. (sE)
>
> b) We might have been dancing until the sun came up. (sE)
>
> c) I know he was a-tellin' the truth, but I was a-comin' home.[42] (AE)
>
> d) They was giving him the recognition.[43] (AAE)
>
> e) Once we get under way, it shouldn't ought to take us very long.[44] (SAE)
>
> f) We Black folks be knowin we got some unique patterns of language goin on up in here in the U.S. of A.[45] (AAE)
>
> g) You be doing a classwork in class, and she used to tell me: "Do this."[46] (ChE)
>
> h) We might could do that.[47] (ChE)
>
> i) None of these folks would have drove a truck in their lives.[48] (sE)

7.4 Auxiliary Verbs and Their Superpowers

Now that you know that the main verb always comes last in a {VP} and that there can be multiple auxiliaries, including modal ones, in a single {VP}, it's time to look a bit more at the first auxiliary in a {VP}. You'll see that this first auxiliary comes equipped with a bunch of superpowers.

7.4.1 The Auxiliary Verb's First Superpower: Tense

You already know from previous chapters that main verbs can express present and past tense:

(65) Cats *clean* themselves. (sE)

(65a) Cats *cleaned* themselves. (sE)

But what if there is an auxiliary prior to the main verb? In those instances, it is the first auxiliary in the {VP} that carries tense-marking, which means that the main verb actually doesn't tell you whether the verb's action was done in the past or present:

(66) Denzel and Booker *are walking*. (sE)

(66a) Denzel and Booker *were walking*. (sE)

(67) They *is making* stuff up.[49] (AAE)

(67a) They *was making* stuff up.[50] (AAE)

(68) The doctor *has been working*. (sE)

(68a) The doctor *had been working*. (sE)

(69) The new set still *needs washed* to kill germs.[51] (ME)

(69a) The new set still *needed washed* to kill germs.[52] (ME)

This ability to turn a {VP} from past to present or vice versa is the first superpower of auxiliaries. All primary auxiliaries can do this; some of the modals can as well. Let's move on to superpower number 2.

7.4.2 The Auxiliary Verb's Second Superpower: Questioning

Enabling us to talk about things in the past by enduring past tense marking is an important job auxiliaries perform. Of course, we don't just go through life talking about things that happen in the present or past. Sometimes, we also like to question things, like *Are auxiliaries really this important?* Queue the auxiliary once again! The next data set shows how a statement (declarative) can be turned into a question (or interrogative):

(70) I <u>*was*</u> wicked *stuffed*.[53] (NEE)

(70a) *Was* I wicked *stuffed*?

(71) Twitter <u>*can*</u> be a professional job anymore.[54] (ME)

(71a) *Can* Twitter *be* a professional job anymore?

(72) [T]he witch <u>*had*</u> *gave* Snow White [an apple].[55] (ChE)

(72a) *Had* the witch *gave* Snow White an apple?

Surprise: The first auxiliary (we told y'all that it's got powers!) does the heavy lifting: It moves all the way to the front of the sentence to form a question. It switches places with the subject.

Foundations of Grammar

When you have a declarative that doesn't include an auxiliary, the syntactic operation is a different one:

(73) Cats *clean* themselves. (sE)

(73a) **Clean* cats themselves?*

(73b) *Do* cats *clean* themselves?

(74) My spouse *works* very hard. (sE)

(74a) **Works* my spouse very hard?*

(74b) *Does* my spouse *work* very hard?

Initially, it might seem like we're in a conundrum: There's no auxiliary we can move to the beginning of the sentence. Plus, we can't just move the main verb to the front because that results in an ungrammatical structure (see (73a) and (74a)). Because we don't have the superpower-filled first auxiliary, what we need is a stand-in. A Robin to Batman. Or a Lois to Superman. You get the idea. This "stand in" is a form of the primary auxiliary verb *do* (*do, does, did*). It simply does the work an auxiliary would do if there were one: It moves to the front of the sentence, with the main verb remaining in its original slot after the subject. Because grammarians apparently aren't very creative, we don't have a cool name for this most awesome *do*! Instead, we call this *do* a **dummy do**, **dummy operator**, or **do-support**.

In our examples so far, we included mostly sE examples and some non-sE dialect variations. This is because question formation can differ from sE patterns. For AAE, question formation looks both a bit different and a bit similar to sE. We provide a few examples here, but this is by no means an exhaustive treatment of how questions are formed in AAE (or in sE for that matter).

(75) Bob *gon' leave*.[56] (AAE)

(75a) *Is* Bob *gon' leave*?[57] (AAE)

(76) They *BIN running*.[58] (AAE)

(76a) *Have* they *BIN running*?[59] (AAE)

(77) They *be running*.[60] (AAE)

(77a) *Do* they *be running*?[61] (AAE)

You can see that inversion—moving the first auxiliary to the front is possible. Remember the feature called **zero copula** from earlier? (75) is another example. While *is* (the form of *be*) is not required in the declarative, it re-emerges in initial position of the interrogative. In (76a), the auxiliary *have* is added so that inversion can happen. Additionally, using the dummy *do* for question-formation is also possible in AAE as in (77a).

7.4.3 The Auxiliary Verb's Third Superpower: Emphasis

Imagine that you run into someone who's reading this book as well. They say *This book is getting interesting. Don't you think?* and you want to agree, but you *really* want to emphasize that this book *really* is getting interesting. You might say *It IS getting interesting*. You wouldn't even have to add any additional words: all you must do is stress/emphasize *is* and you'd be getting your point across. Guess what! It is again the first auxiliary that we can emphasize in this way to convey this. To our knowledge, this holds across all American English dialects. This means that the first auxiliary is once again the one that does the heavy lifting; we've capitalized each to represent the added stress/emphasis:

(78) I *WAS* wicked *stuffed*.[62] (NEE)

(79) [T]he witch *HAD gave* Snow White [an apple].[63] (ChE)

(80) She *IS a-goin'* to the show.[64] (AE)

(81) You still *CAN play* many game.[65] (SAE/ChE/AAE/others)

What if we don't have an auxiliary? You guessed it: *dummy do*:

(82) Cats *DO clean* themselves. (sE)

(83) My spouse *DOES work* very hard. (sE)

One more superpower to go. Maybe the most important one, especially for naysayers among us!

7.4.4 The Auxiliary Verb's Fourth Superpower: Negation

When we negate something, we have to add a negative element like *not* to our sentence. If you guessed that the negation gets added to the auxiliary, you'd be right:

(78a) I *was* wicked *stuffed*.[66] (NEE)

(78b) I *wasn't* wicked stuffed.[67] (NEE)

(84) The stove *is being cleaned*. (sE)

(84a) The stove *isn't* being cleaned. (sE)

(85) Twitter *can be* a professional job anymore.[68] (ME)

(85a) Twitter *can't* be a professional job anymore.[69] (ME)

Like with the other superpowers, it's the first auxiliary that is crucial: *not* latches on to that first auxiliary, not the main verb or one of the other auxiliaries. After all, we don't say any of the following:

(84b) *The stove is *beingn't* cleaned.

(84c) *The stove is being *cleanedn't*.

When there isn't an auxiliary, *dummy do* comes to our rescue because we can't form {VPs} such as *cleannot* or *jumpsn't*:

(82a) Cats *clean* themselves. (sE)

(82b) *Cats *cleannot* themselves. (sE)

(82c) Cats *don't* clean themselves. (sE)

(83a) My spouse *works* very hard. (sE)

(83b) *My spouse *worksn't* very hard. (sE)

(83c) My spouse *doesn't* work very hard. (sE)

7.4.4.1 Negation in Non-sE Dialects

This is not the end of the story quite yet when it comes to negation. For sE dialects and many other non-sE dialects, one negative element such as *not* is all that is required to negate something. Look at the sentences below and see if you can find a pattern for how negation is done in other dialects. This particular feature spans across all American English dialects—you may be using it yourself (do you think you're making a mistake when you do? Rest assured, you're not!). We label the examples below based on which dialects the feature has been attested to in published work. Consider these questions as you examine the next data set. Can the negative element be added to an auxiliary? We've italicized relevant portions. Can it be added to *dummy do*? What else do you notice?

(86) Bruce *don't want no* teacher telling him *nothing* about *no* books.[70] (AAE)

(87) I *ain't never lost* a fight.[71] (AAE)

(88) I *don't eat no* biscuit.[72] (AAE)

(89) We *ain't never* really had *no* tornadoes in this area here that I *don't* remember.[73] (White Alabama English)

(90) *Nobody couldn't handle* him.[74] (AE)

(91) Things *ain't gonna never change* in L.A. *no* more.[75] (ChE)

(92) *None* of the girls *don't like* her.[76] (ChE)

(93) I *don't* feel like *nobody* pets me.[77] (WSE)

Some of your observations might be similar to these:

- A negative element can be added to *do*, *can*, and *could*.
- *Do* can be used when there is no other auxiliary.
- A negative element is not added to main verbs (so we do not have something like *lostn't* or *handlen't*).
- The word *ain't* often occurs as a negative element in negations.
- In addition to *not* (and its contracted version *n't*), other negative elements can be added: *nothing, no, none, nobody*.

Overall, you should notice that it is perfectly fine to have more than one negative element in the same sentence; the reason we gave this many examples is to underscore how prevalent this feature is. We could have filled up this entire book with examples of just this one feature! This construction is known as **multiple negation**, **double negation**, or **negative concord**. It is often associated with AAE, ChE, and SAE. However, it is a common feature of other dialects as well, including WSE, AE, and West Texas English.[78] When features such as the double negative are shared among so many varieties of English, will it lose the stigma associated with it and be accepted as standard?

Contrary to popular belief, in languages, a negative and another negative do not equal a positive. Some people take issue with multiple negation claiming precisely that. They claim that two negatives make a positive (applying some logic from math to language). This would mean that for those people, this is how the following sentence would be interpreted:

(88a)   I don't eat no biscuits.[79] (AAE) = I eat biscuits.

Clearly, that is not the meaning of *I don't eat no biscuits*. You would likely never assume (unless you were trying to be difficult) that the person who says *I don't eat no biscuits* is telling you that they actually do eat biscuits! Imagine you're having someone over and offer the person some biscuits. The person says *I don't eat no biscuits*. It would be wild if you then proceeded to hand them biscuits, saying "Great. Here you go! Enjoy the biscuits!" It's preposterous, really.

While applying the rules of math to language should be a non-starter, we can humor this line of thinking to further illustrate its shortcomings. Let's multiply sets of two and sets of three numbers:

- $(-2) * (-2) = 4$ a positive number.
- $(-2) * (-2) * (-2) = -8$ a negative number.

So, for all those folks out there who claim that multiple negation doesn't make sense because two negatives make a positive, well, they would have to be okay with sentences that contain **three** negatives, since—according to their own (misguided) logic—three negatives make a negative! Then, sentences such as (91) above should be acceptable to those folks. Surprise—they ain't! Even triple negatives are not acceptable to people who take issue with multiple negation. At this point in the book, you should know that language has its own structures, its own underlying rules. It does not work like math. And different dialects of a language have their own underlying rules. This is why multiple negation is perfectly grammatical in many English dialects. It just happens to be the case that multiple negation, which is also used by folks who consider themselves users of sE, is seen as somehow bad, as unacceptable.

We would be remiss to not point out that many languages around the world form the standardized version of negation via multiple negation, French being just one example. In fact, in conversational French, people often drop one of the negative elements and use—hold the mustard—just simple negation. Prescriptivists in France will comment on how **single negation** is "broken French," whereas prescriptivists here in the United States will comment on how **multiple negation** is "broken English." Funny how that goes. Each type of negation is just fine, and grammatical, in its respective language and dialect! If a feature like multiple negation is this frequent and common in a language, what is the more likely explanation?

- Everyone who uses multiple negation is making mistakes left and right; they clearly don't know anything about English grammar; or

- It's unlikely that millions of people are making mistakes. Multiple negation must be a permissible structure based on grammatical structures of English.

Again, when you think about it, is it more likely to think that millions of people are making errors all the time in a language they acquired as children? By the way, this is not an opinion-based question either; we asked you to think about these two possible perspectives to reveal how preposterous the claim is that argues that people are making grammar mistakes when they use multiple negation; but rest assured, research shows that this feature is perfectly grammatical! It simply is a feature that by and large is currently not accepted *socially* in various contexts, but *grammatically*, it is perfectly fine.

Another grammatical feature related to negation is called **positive anymore**; it is chiefly associated with ME dialects. You've encountered many of those examples already. Compare (94) to (95) below:

(94) Gas is pretty expensive *anymore*.[80] (ME)

(95) Gas isn't expensive *anymore*. (sE)

Pronouns such as *anyone, anything*, and *anymore* typically occur in clauses that have negation elements as in (95). In (94), however, the word *anymore* occurs in a positive statement—hence its name! Generally, this construction means that gas is pretty expensive *nowadays*.

7.4.4.2 The Case of *Ain't*

Last but not least, we turn to the infamous word *ain't*. You've already seen it in some example sentences above; and we snuck one in ourselves a little while ago—go figure! That should tell you already that it's a common feature of many English dialects. Again, it simply is a **socially derided** form, not a **grammatically incorrect** one. You yourself probably have used it in your life before now. Yet, the famous saying *Ain't ain't a word and I ain't gonna use it* is a reminder that for many people, it is an unacceptable word. Nevertheless, it is a well-established and grammatical feature in many English dialects, where *ain't* can be used for all subject pronouns, not just for *I*:

- I *ain't* reading.
- You *ain't* reading.
- He/she/it *ain't* reading.
- They *ain't* reading.
- We *ain't* reading.
- You *ain't* reading.
- They *ain't* reading.

It isn't unusual to have the same form for an auxiliary across a paradigm:

- I *won't* read.
- You *won't* read.

- She/he/it *won't* read.
- They *won't* read.
- We *won't* read.
- You *won't* read.
- They *won't* read.

Nobody takes issue, as far as we're aware, with the form *won't* being used for all subject pronouns, yet *ain't* is criticized for being used across the paradigm and for not having one designated subject pronoun. This criticism of *ain't* falls short, since this exact criticism isn't leveled against *won't*!

So, *ain't* is a perfectly systematic form, one that has existed for a long time, one that used to be considered "standard" in previous points in time, and one that is currently being used across the board in many, if not all, American English dialects. If you want to learn more about *ain't* including where it came from, check out the companion website!

Terminology to Know

Term	Working definition	Example/Illustration
Auxiliary verb		
Modal auxiliary		
Primary auxiliary		
Main verb		
Zero or null copula		
Bare infinitive		
Question formation		
Negation (including multiple negation)		
Dummy *do*		

Chart 2 Key terminology Chapter 7

Notes

1. Wolfram and Christian, 1976, p. 70.
2. Kendall, Quartey et al., 2018 Transcript ID DCB_se1_ag2_m_01_1.
3. Baker-Bell, 2020, p. 43.
4. Slightly adapted from Barrón and San Romón, n.d., p. 30–1; cited in Bayley, 2012, p. 162.
5. Wolfram and Christian, 1976, p. 69.
6. Baker-Bell, 2020, p. 43.
7. Farrington et al., 2020 Transcript ID ATL_se0_ag1_f_03_1.

8. Kendall, Quartey et al., 2018 Transcript ID DCB_se1_ag3_m_02_1.
9. Green, 2002, p. 95.
10. Baker-Bell, 2020, p. 43.
11. Bayley, 2012, p. 164.
12. Green, 2002, p. 95.
13. Wood, 2014.
14. Baker-Bell, 2020, p. 52
15. Kendall, Quartey et al., 2018 Transcript ID DCB_se2_ag2_f_01_1.
16. Baker-Bell, 2020, p. 43.
17. Fought, 2003, p. 96.
18. Yerastov, 2010; cited in Wood, 2014.
19. T. McMurtry, personal communication, March 30, 2025.
20. *Shall* is a becoming rare in both discourse and written language. It does, however, remain part of legal language. See Garner (1995) for more information on *shall* in legal contexts.
21. Fought, 2003, p. 100.
22. Kendall, Quartey et al., 2018 Transcript ID DCB_se1_ag2_f_02_1.
23. Maher and Wood, 2011.
24. Ruffing, 2012.
25. Maher and Wood, 2011.
26. Ruffing, 2012.
27. Johnson, 2013; cited in Ruffing, 2012.
28. Merriam-Webster (n.d.).
29. Fought, 2003, p. 100.
30. Ibid.
31. Ibid.
32. Ibid.
33. Slightly adapted from Barrón and San Romón, n.d., pp. 30–1; cited in Bayley, 2012, p. 162.
34. Feagin, 1979; cited in Ruffing, 2012.
35. Davies, 2018.
36. Slightly adapted from Barrón and San Romón, n.d., pp. 30–1; cited in Bayley, 2012, p. 162.
37. Huang, 2011.
38. Ibid.
39. Ibid.
40. Ibid.
41. Ibid.
42. Wolfram and Christian, 1976, p. 70.
43. Kendall, Quartey et al., 2018 Transcript ID DCB_se1_ag2_m_01_1.
44. Slightly adapted from Huang, 2011.
45. Smitherman, 2006, p. 2.
46. Bayley, 2012, p. 158.

47. Ibid., p. 163.
48. Davies, 2018.
49. Kendall, Fasold et al., 2018 Transcript ID DCA_se1_ag4_m_02_1.
50. Slightly adapted from Kendall, Fasold et al., 2018 Transcript ID DCA_se1_ag4_m_02_1.
51. Maher and Wood, 2011.
52. Slightly adapted from Maher and Wood, 2011.
53. W. Beauregard, personal communication, August 29, 2024.
54. Maher and McCoy, 2011.
55. Bayley and Santa Ana, 2004, p. 378.
56. Based on Green, 2002, p. 36ff.
57. Green, 2002, p. 42.
58. Analogous to *Bruce BIN running* from Green, 2002, p. 69.
59. Green, 2002, p. 68.
60. Analogous to *Bruce be running* from Green, 2002, p. 69.
61. Green, 2002, p. 68.
62. W. Beauregard, personal communication, August 29, 2024.
63. Bayley and Santa Ana, 2004, p. 378.
64. Slightly adapted from Christian et al., 1988; cited in Matyiku, 2011a.
65. Reaser et al., 2017b.
66. W. Beauregard, personal communication, August 29, 2024.
67. Slightly adapted from W. Beauregard, personal communication, August 29, 2024.
68. Maher and McCoy, 2011.
69. Slightly adapted from Maher and McCoy, 2011.
70. Green, 2002, p. 77.
71. Labov, 1972; cited in Matyiku, 2011b.
72. Ibid.
73. Feagin, 1979; cited in Matyiku, 2011b.
74. Wolfram and Christian, 1976; cited in Matyiku, 2011b.
75. Fought, 2003, p. 97.
76. Ibid.
77. Feagin, 1979; cited in Matyiku, 2011b.
78. Matyiku, 2011b.
79. Labov, 1972b; cited in Matyiku, 2011b.
80. Maher and McCoy, 2011.

CHAPTER 8
RESPECTFULLY REPLACING NOUNS: THE PRONOUN

Overview

The lexical category of **pronouns** has a special relationship with nouns, and more specifically, the noun phrase {NP}. We build on what you know about {NPs} as well as the analytical skills you have gained for identifying lexical categories through morphological and syntactic evidence and their corresponding tests. How many pronouns did we use in the second sentence of this paragraph? Four (*we, what, you, you*). If we didn't have pronouns, our second sentence would be *Dr. Stickle and Dr. Drake build on concepts the readers know about {NPs} as well as the analytical skills the readers have gained …* Quite cumbersome, we believe! This chapter explores ways to identify different types of pronouns. Our objectives are as follows. You'll be able to

- recognize different types of pronouns;
- acquire the skills to test for pronouns; and
- build your knowledge of forms and functions of pronouns.

Pre-reading tasks

1. Make a list of any- and everything you know about pronouns and determiners.
2. Identify all pronouns in the following sentences:
    a) Anyone can do that.
    b) Those over there are for you'uns.
    c) He gave y'all a hat.
    d) Isabella talked to herself.
    e) That book is theirs.
    f) No, that's ourn, not hern!
    g) What are youse talking about?
    h) I want these flavors and one of those.
    i) You guys are out of line.
    j) Yinz are making the best ice cream ever.
3. What kind of information is contained within each pronoun in question 2?
4. If you know something about any other languages, are there differences in how pronouns work in those languages compared to English?

8.1 Introduction

Pronouns belong to the **closed class** of words, which means that it is generally very difficult to add new words to this particular category. This also means that in English, we have had a largely stable set of pronouns. The term pronoun intrinsically shows its relationship to nouns. The prefix *pro* comes from Latin and means "for the sake of" or put differently, "instead of." We believe that even if we were aliens coming to earth, we'd be able to see from the data set below that pronouns can replace nouns:

(1) [Mary] went to the store. (sE)
(1a) [She] went to the store.
(2) [My brother] slept on the chair. (sE)
(2a) [He] slept on the chair.
(3) She spent [a wicked amount of money] for this ....[1] (NEE)
(3a) She spent [it] for this....

And, yes, this is the pronoun-replacement test (aka one-word replacement test) that you should be plenty familiar with by now! Since replacing nouns with pronouns serves as evidence for nouns, the reverse test serves as evidence for pronouns. If you're not sure that you're looking at a pronoun, try replacing it with an {NP}:

(4) [It] was a dreadful sight, fire was a-flamin' everything.[2] (AE)
(4a) [The blaze] was a dreadful sight, fire was a-flamin' everything.
(5) I bought [him/zim] a new shirt. (sE)
(5a) I bought [Pat] a new shirt.
(6) Nadia and Rhonda baked [them] a cake for [their] birthday. (sE)
(6a) Nadia and Rhonda baked [Mati] a cake for [their] birthday.
(6b) Nadia and Rhonda baked them a cake for * [Mati] birthday.
(7) Watch out when [yinz] go outside ...[3] (Pittsburghese)
(7a) Watch out when [your brother and Taylor] go outside ...

Our reverse-engineered test for pronouns works beautifully, except for (6b): replacing *their* with an {NP} (here, *Mati*) results in an ungrammatical structure. This means that *their* in (6) is actually not a pronoun (it's a determiner, more on that later). Notice that we could not use the pronoun to fill in simply for the noun when the noun is part of a more complex {NP}. In other words, when the noun is accompanied by other elements (e.g., determiner, adjectives) in the {NP}, replacing just the noun with a pronoun results in the following ungrammatical sentences:

(2b) *My brother* slept on the chair. (sE)
(2c) *My <u>he</u> slept on the chair.

(3b) She spent *a wicked amount of money* for this....[4] (NEE)

(3c) *She spent a *wicked it of money* for this... (NEE)

So, what these data show is that pronouns don't simply replace nouns, but, rather, pronouns replace the entire {NP}: the noun and everything that goes with the noun as one constituent. Because pronouns replace entire {NPs}, they can't be preceded by

- a determiner (*My/The/That *he* slept on the chair in (2c)), and
- an adjective (*wicked *it* in (3c))—unless you are a language-rules-bending poet such as e.e. cummings.

That said, pronouns can function in the same roles as nouns, including but not limited to subject (8a) and direct objects (9a):

(8) *Bob* went to the store. (sE)

(8a) *He* went to the store.

(9) She spent *a wicked amount of money* ....[5] (NEE)

(9a) She spent *it* ....[6] (NEE)

Pronouns are ubiquitous! But don't worry—we'll describe the different types of pronouns one by one next.

Exercise 1

Substitute the italicized {NPs} in the chart below with an appropriate pronoun.

Function	Sentence with NP	Pronoun Substitution
Subject	a) *The little kid* don't have no sturdy shoes of his own.[7] (ChE)	
Direct object	b) Mary baked *cookies*. (sE)	
	c) You could get *those big fat juicy fresh donuts*.[8] (AAE)	
Indirect object	d) Here's *Sam* a good pair of jeans.[9] (SAE)	
	e) Mary baked *Cheryl* cookies. (sE)	
Subject complement	f) Ted is *a chef* by training. (sE)	
Object complement	g) We called Betty *a genius*. (sE)	
Object of the preposition	h) These gravels are hard on *your feet*.[10] (AE)	

8.2 Types of Pronouns

8.2.1 Personal Pronouns

Personal pronouns convey information about people, or persons, hence the name: **Personal pronoun.** The form of the personal pronoun depends on the function it performs in the sentence (for some personal pronouns, that is!). The following sentence pairs illustrate this:

(10) *I* was just telling people last night, they was talking about how ....[11] (AAE)

(11) We sitting there talking, and he come hitting on *me* for some money.[12] (AAE)

(12) *You* are a talented singer. (sE)

(13) Here's *you* a piece of pizza.[13] (SAE)

(14) *She* was a-goin' to the show.[14] (AE/OE)

(15) That don't give *her* no money.[15] (AAE)

(16) *He* could talk smart.[16] (ChE)

(17) I told *him* you done changed.[17] (AAE)

(18) *It* is nice and warm today. (sE)

(19) He's a-gonna try *it*.[18] (AE/OE)

(20) *We* adopted two new cats. (sE)

(21) We'd be mad if they left *us*.[19] (AAE)

(22) *You* offered Samir and Hassam a fair deal. (sE)

(23) LeBron and Denzel gave *you* their favorite book to read. (sE)

(24) *They* are proud of their accomplishments. (sE)

(25) I met *them* four mile down the road.[20] (AAE)

Despite the variety of dialects and feature represented in the lists above, you'll probably have noticed that the patterns for pronouns are consistent across all examples: With the exception of *you* and *it*, the forms for personal pronouns differ depending on whether the pronoun occurs in the **subject slot** (*I, she, he, we, they*) or in the **object slot**, including object of the preposition (*me, her, him, us, them*). The fact that there are different forms for subject/object slots is solid **morphological evidence** for claiming that a given personal pronoun is, indeed, a pronoun. Such a change in form based on syntactic function does not happen to other noun-y things. In English, then, personal pronouns (and the relative pronoun *whom*) are really the last noun-y things that have different subject and object forms. Chart 1 summarizes these pronoun paradigms for sE.

Respectfully Replacing Nouns: The Pronoun

Person	Number	Subject form	Object form
First	singular	I	Me
Second		You	You
Third		She/he/it/they	Her/him/it/them
First	plural	We	Us
Second		You	You
Third		They	Them

Chart 1 Personal pronouns sE

Notice, too, that the pronoun *you* in sentences (12), (13), (22), and (23) is the same for singular and plural. Based on just the pronoun itself, you wouldn't have a clue if *you* refers to one person or multiple people. Multiple non-sE American dialects have reduced this ambiguity by creating separate forms for second person plural personal pronouns, which we think is awesome! Chart 2 presents that variety.[21] Which ones do you use?

Dialect	Standard English	Southern	Appalachian	Pittsburgh and Western Pennsylvania	Philadelphia, New York, and parts of New Orleans	Midwest
2nd person plural pronoun	You	Y'all	You'uns	Yinz	Youse	You guys

Chart 2 Dialect variation of second person plural pronoun *You*

When we said that pronouns are the last noun-y things in the English language that have actual different forms for object/subject slots, we meant it. Compare the two sets of sentences below.

(26)   *We* bought cookies. (sE)

(26a) *The family* bought cookies. (sE)

(27)   Morgan bought *us* cookies. (sE)

(27a) Morgan bought *the family* cookies. (sE)

While the pronoun changes its form based on the slot it is in (again, *we* for subject, *us* for indirect object), the form of the noun *family* stays the same! No separate form for whether the noun occurs in subject or object slots. If you're familiar with languages other than English, you might be familiar with what are called **case-endings** that are added to nouns to indicate which role in a sentence the noun plays. Luckily, or unfortunately (depending on your perspective), English has lost all those case-endings over time for nouns. We want to point out one more wrinkle related to this. Technically, when a pronoun occurs in subject complement (SC) slots, the subject form is required:

(28)   This is *she*. (sE)

(29)   That is *they* on the cover of the book. (sE)

However, these subject forms (*she* in (28) and *they* in (29)) come across as somewhat stilted. In fact, we usually encounter object forms *her* and *them* in this position, especially in conversations:

(28a) This is *her*. (sE)

(29a) That is *them* on the cover of the book. (sE)

Frankly, the title of the popular TV show *This is us* should, technically, be *This is we*. If you're like us, *This is we* just doesn't sound all that great; likely something the creators and marketers of that show also realized, going with the much more natural sounding *This is us* as the title.

Exercise 2

Identify all personal pronouns in this excerpt and label each by person (first, second, third) and number (singular, plural). Indicate if the pronoun is in subject form or object form.

a) As I welcome you to Pittsburgh (…), let me be real wit y'all right from jump.[22] (AAE)

b) Now that y'all right here, what all you gon do?[23] (AAE)

c) It was so many darn good proposals.[24] (AAE)

d) Among the spotlights, we got some real special ones.[25] (AAE)

e) We met up with the vet outside. (sE)

f) He often stops by the bakery on our way home. (sE)

g) They made us dinner. (sE)

h) She asked her an excellent question. (sE)

8.2.2 Reflexive Pronouns

Reflexive pronouns come in different forms that correspond to person and number once again. What do you notice about these reflexive pronouns in the next data set?

(30) I took care of *myself*. (sE)

(31) You can make pancakes *yourself*. (sE)

(32) She call *herself* a queen.[26] (AAE)

(33) We supported *ourselves* from an early age. (sE)

(34) They have to start supporting *theirselves* at early ages.[27] (ChE)

Once again, morphology provides evidence for what kind of word we're looking at. If a pronoun has a *-self/-selves* suffix, it's a **reflexive pronoun**. A second characteristic of reflexive pronouns is illustrated in the examples below:

(31a)   You can make pancakes *yourself*. (sE)

(31b)   Carlos can make pancakes **yourself*.

(35)   They make their juice *theirself*.[28] (AAE)

(35a)   We make their juice **theirself*.

In (31a), *yourself* refers back to *you*. Switching out *you* with another word as we did in (31b) with *Carlos*, the sentence becomes ungrammatical because *yourself* now has no other noun or pronoun it can refer to anymore. In (35), *theirself* refers to *they*. Replacing *they* with *we* leaves the reflexive pronoun without a possible referent (35a). *We* and *theirself* simply can't refer to the same people. This means that a core feature of reflexive pronouns is that they must have a pronoun or noun in the same sentence that they can refer to. No matter what your own English variety is, the reflexive pronouns are always co-referenced with another pronoun or noun.

Based on the sentences above, we can see that there's a difference in some pronoun **forms** depending on the dialect someone speaks. We provide full paradigms in Chart 3.

	Reflexive pronouns—sE dialects	**Reflexive pronouns—various non-sE dialects**
singular	myself yourself herself/himself/itself/themself	myself yourself herself/hisself/itself/theirself
plural	ourselves yourselves themselves	ourselves yourselves theirselves/theyselves

Chart 3 Reflexive pronouns in sE and various non-sE dialects

If you're an sE dialect speaker, the forms *hisself* and *theirself* might seem unusual. If you're an AAE or ChE speaker, they will sound perfectly normal, since those (and other) dialects use these forms. Remember also that speakers who use sE may use non-sE forms and that non-sE speakers may use sE forms! This serves as our regular reminder that the forms we introduce you to are not unique to just one dialect and that no dialect is monolithic; there are many nuances and variations in real life. We'd be remiss if we did not point out, again, that both patterns are perfectly grammatical!

Another variation involving reflexive pronouns is called **personal dative**, a feature that occurs primarily in ChE and SAE, including AE:

(36)   I got *me* some candy.[29] (SAE)

(37)   You got *you* some candy.[30] (SAE)

(38)   He got *him* some candy.[31] (SAE)

(39) She got *her* some candy.³² (SAE)

(40) We got *us* some candy.³³ (SAE)

(41) They got *them* some candy.³⁴ (SAE)

In (36), the candy was for the speaker of that sentence, not for some other person. In this construction, the personal pronoun forms do the work of a reflexive pronoun. In (36) and also (40), this meaning is easily understood even by those who didn't acquire this feature as part of their grammar system as children. Other examples, such as (41) could cause some confusion as to whether *they* bought some other people (*them*) some candy, or if *they* got *themselves* some candy. For this dialect feature, for personal datives, the meaning is the latter. Who does the pronoun *him* refer to in (42)?

(42) *He* was looking to buy *him* a house for his family.³⁵ (SAE)

Him refers to *he*, i.e., the sentence means that *he* was looking to buy himself a house, not some other person (e.g., maybe his brother). The italicized pronouns above then are **co-referenced** with the subject pronoun in each sentence—they share the same referent, which is a hallmark feature of reflexive pronouns as such. These personal dative pronouns, then, can also do this reflexive work in the dialects they are a part of!

Exercise 3

Identify all reflexive pronouns; include person and number information! Be on the lookout for some personal datives from AE and ChE dialects as well!

a) Now, while you at the convention center itself, check out at least one of dem dere sessions I spotlighted.³⁶ (AAE)

b) Have yo'self a grand great time!³⁷ (AAE)

c) Sometimes individuals come there with issues at home theirselves.³⁸ (AAE)

d) I had me a pair of crutches.³⁹ (AE)

e) They found them an apartment.⁴⁰ (ChE)

f) She taught herself to play the piano. (sE)

g) They built the house themselves. (sE)

h) I prepared the meal by myself. (sE)

8.2.3 Possessive Pronouns

Possessive pronouns are pronouns that indicate some kind of possession. We start with so-called **freestanding possessives**, since they share the hallmark feature of pronouns:

they replace {NPs}. Consider the sentences below, all as responses to the question *Whose computer is where?*

(43) *Mine* is right here. (sE)

(43a) *My computer* is right here. (sE)

(44) *Yours* is over there. (sE)

(44a) *Adley's computer* is over there. (sE)

(45) *His/hers/theirs* is on the couch. (sE)

(45a) *Sam's computer* is on the couch. (sE)

(46) *Ours* is under the table. (sE)

(46a) *Dan's and my computer* is under the table. (sE)

(47) *Yours* is behind the shelf. (sE)

(47a) *Anna and Rose's computer* is behind the shelf. (sE)

(48) *Theirs* is on the desk. (sE)

(48a) *Sue and Sherry's computer* is on the desk. (sE)

Each pronoun above can be replaced with an {NP}, which is again evidence for clarifying them as pronouns. Except for first person singular (*mine*), all **freestanding possessive pronouns** feature a final *-s* in sE dialects. In some dialects, a final *-s* or a final *-n* can be added to freestanding possessives:

(49) She had her birth night de day befo' *mines*.[41] (AAE)

(50) *Her'n* on December 31, and *mine's* January 1.[42] (AAE)

(51) I don't know just how he made *hisn*.[43] (AE)

(52) [We] generally sold *ourn* to a man on Coopers Creek.[44] (AE)

The second type of possessive pronoun is also called **dependent possessive**. Based on the following data set, make some observations about where these dependent possessives occur and what forms they take.

(53) I've call her *my* sister.[45] (AAE)

(54) You stay in *your* office too late anymore.[46] (ME)

(55) Martin is done *his* bass tracks and we are ready to start vocals.[47] (ECE)

(56) The baby wants cuddled by *her* mother.[48] (ME)

(57) *Our* event was a huge success. (sE)

(58) Derek and Tammy enjoyed *your* performance a lot. (sE)

(59) They make *their* juice theirself.[49] (AAE)

(60) If they wanna go out and do something else with it, that's *they* business.[50] (AAE)

Foundations of Grammar

The data show that dependent possessives occur **prior** to a noun, such as *my sister, your performance, their juice, they business*, which means they are part of the {NP}. Chart 4 exemplifies the paradigms, highlighting that this type of pronoun is pretty uniform across dialects across the United States, with an exception in dialects such as AAE where both *their* and *they* can be used.

	Dependent possessive—sE dialects	**Dependent possessives—various non-sE dialects**
singular	my your her/his/its/their	my your her/his/its/their
plural	our your their	our your their/they

Chart 4 Dependent possessives

Now, you may be thinking "Wait. I thought pronouns *replace* nouns/{NPs}, but here, the pronouns *aren't* replacing any nouns!" And you are correct! For **dependent possessives**, the term *possessive pronoun* is a misnomer. Rather than doing the work of a pronoun—that is, replacing an {NP}—they do the work of pointing to or specifying a noun, which is something determiners do. This is an incredibly important distinction. For this reason, it is better to label these as **possessive determiners**, but there are still many sources that rely on the misleading label "possessive pronoun." For an argument that the non-sE reflexive pronoun patterns are more systematic than sE reflexive pronouns patterns, check out the website!

While pronouns are an example of a closed-class type of word, pronouns have allowed new members into the pronoun club on a limited basis. Adding gender-neutral pronouns to our language is a social attempt to make our communication more inclusive to persons who use pronouns that do not split on the male-female dichotomy. *They* and *them* are by far the most commonly used, currently, which is why we included them as the default gender-neutral pronouns in our charts. Chart 5 provides a sampling of other inclusive pronouns that have been suggested (but you likely will be able to find an even greater variety, including *e/ey, per, ve,* and *xe*, by conducting an internet search).[51]

Number	**Subject form**	**Object form**	**Possessive forms**	**Reflexive form**
singular	(f)ae	(f)aer	(f)aer/(f)aers	(f)aerself
	e/ey	em	eir/eirs	eirself
	he	him	his	himself
	per	per	pers	perself
	she	her	her/hers	herself
	they	them	their/theirs	themself

Number	Subject form	Object form	Possessive forms	Reflexive form
plural	ve	ver	vis	verself
	xe	xem	xyr/xyrs	xemself
	ze/zie	hir	hir/hirs	hirself

Chart 5 Gender-neutral pronoun options—a selection

It is worth noting that the most used inclusive pronoun, *they/them*, is one that has been part of the English language for centuries, so we're familiar with it. It is easier to incorporate a familiar pronoun to be used in new contexts than to incorporate a new pronoun altogether. Here are some examples of singular *they*:

(61) Javier has *a student* this quarter who keeps forgetting *their* backpack …[52] (sE)

(62) *Someone* suggested their doctor to me. (sE)

(63) *Rhys* suggested *their* doctor to me. (sE)

In (61), *their* refers to *a student*; in (62), *their* refers to *someone*. The gender of *someone* and *student* is either not relevant or we don't know. Using *their* in such instances is not only very common, but well-established for English.[53] It is only a relatively new usage when we use *they/them* in contexts where the pronoun refers to someone who is trans or non-binary, as in (63). While it is relatively new, this second, inclusive, usage, is very much on the rise.

Exercise 4

Identify all possessive pronouns (independent possessives) and possessive determiners (dependent possessives). Include information about person and number for each.

a) That cat over there on the couch is mine. (sE)

b) You can pet yours any time you want to. (sE)

c) John was a-talkin' so loud my eardrums hurt.[54] (AE)

d) They want to do they own thing, and you steady talking to them.[55] (AAE)

e) Her biggest fan saved enough money to go to her concert. (sE)

f) The white mare is hern.[56] (AE)

g) Your brain needs fed to work out.[57] (ME)

h) Did that person forget their coat?[58] (sE)

8.2.4 Demonstrative Pronouns

Next are the **demonstrative pronouns** *this/that* and *these/those*:

(64)   *This* is my sweater. (sE)
(65)   *That* is Santiago's sweater. (sE)
(66)   *These* are my sweaters. (sE)
(67)   *Those* are your sweaters. (sE)

We can observe a difference in number: (64) and (65) refer to singular referents, (66) and (67) refer to plural referents. Each time, *this, that* and *these, those* occur alone in a syntactic slot. We could replace each of them with an {NP}:

(64a)   [*This*   ] is my sweater. (sE)
(64b)   [*The little grey sweater*] is my sweater. (sE)

(66a)   [*These*   ] are my sweaters. (sE)
(66b)   [*The little grey sweaters*] are my sweaters. (sE)

This constitutes definite proof that **demonstrative pronouns** are, in fact, pronouns because they can stand in for {NPs}. *This/that* and *these/those* also convey information about what is closer/further away from the speaker:

(68)   *This* is my truck <u>right here</u>. (sE)
(69)   *That* is your truck <u>over there</u>. (sE)
(70)   *These* are my reports <u>right here</u>. (sE)
(71)   *Those* are your reports <u>over there</u>. (sE)

In (68) and (70), *right here* is closer to the speaker than *over there* in (69) and (71). Chart 6 shows that from the speaker's perspective, then, *this/these* refers to something that is closer while *that/those* refers to something that is farther away.

	Closer relative to speaker	Farther away relative to speaker
Singular	*this*	*that*
Plural	*these*	*those*

Chart 6 Demonstrative pronouns

Now, let's look at another data set:

(72)   *This* thing here I might should turn over to Ann.[59] (SAE)
(73)   I'm fixin' to finish *that* budget proposal today.[60] (SAE)
(74)   *These* gravels are hard on your feet.[61] (AE)
(75)   They building *these* condos.[62] (AAE)
(76)   We saw *those* movies a long time ago. (sE)
(77)   She ate *them* tomatoes.[63] (sE/non-sE dialects)

The demonstratives here all occur as *part of* an {NP}, rather than *replacing* an {NP}. As such, they are **dependent demonstratives** and function as determiners! We again have singular and plural forms depending on the noun that follows: singular *this/that* for singular nouns as in *This thing* (72) or *that budget proposal* (73) and plural *these/those/them* for plural nouns as in *these condos* (75), *those movies* (76), and *them tomatoes* in (77). Note that in various dialects across the United States, *them* can be used in place of the demonstrative determiners *these* and *those*.[64] *Them tomatoes*, then, corresponds to *those/these tomatoes*, not to *the tomatoes*.

Exercise 5

Identify all demonstrative pronouns and demonstrative determiners. Determine if the demonstratives are singular or plural.

a) Y'all may be [needing] it one of these days.[65] (AE)
b) Not to mention those who be sayin ain no such thang as Black Language.[66] (AAE)
c) Those adorable cats over there are very energetic. (sE)
d) I love this cat so much. (sE)
e) I done already finished that.[67] (AAE)
f) We had several rock on that trail.[68] (AE)
g) Rowan prefers these over there. (sE)
h) Them cars are fancy.[69] (sE/non-sE)

8.2.5 Quantifying Pronouns

Broadly speaking, **quantifying pronouns** (aka **indefinite pronouns**) are words that have to do with the number or amount of something. There are quite a few of them, and what we present is not an exhaustive list. Similar to demonstratives and possessives, they can be dependent and independent: Independent quantifying pronouns replace an {NP}, dependent quantifying pronouns precede a noun inside an {NP}, where they function as a determiner. The following data set illustrates a variety of **independent quantifying pronouns**:

(78) *Everybody* got in the middle of the street.[70] (ChE)
(79) I forgot *everything*. (sE)
(80) I noticed two older girls a-eating *something* out of a little syrup bucket.[71] (AE)
(81) *Someone/Somebody* was at the door just now. (sE)

(82) *Anyone/Anybody* can do *anything* they set their mind to. (sE)

(83) I can't say *nothing/anything*.[72] (ChE)

(84) *Nobody* ain't doin' nothing' wrong.[73] (West Texas English; SAE)

(85) I like all cats, but I prefer the fluffy *one/ones*. (sE)

(86) *All* I want is ice cream for dinner. (sE)

(87) *Alls* Greg and Marsha want to do is kiss each other ....[74] (ME)

Many quantifying pronouns are compounds derived from *every, some, any,* and *no*. (85) shows that *one* can be a singular pronoun (*one*) or a plural pronoun (*ones*). This is different from the numeral *one* as in *one cat, two cats*. (87) shows the dialect variation *alls*. This *alls* pronoun has some unique features. For instance, it is restricted to environments where it could be replaced with *what*:

(88) What Amy got from Grace was a box of chocolates. (sE)

(88a) *Alls* Amy got from Grace was a box of chocolates.[75] (SAE)

The next data set illustrates **dependent quantifiers**, each of which is followed immediately by the noun they quantify:

(89) A *few* days ago, I went to *several* stores. (sE)

(90) We sitting there talking, and he come hitting on me for *some* money.[76] (AAE)

(91) I don't think I have *any* grants you might could apply for.[77] (SAE)

(92) *Many* athletes stretch their muscles after *every* workout. (sE)

(93) That don't give her *no* money.[78] (AAE)

(94) It was nice meeting you the *other* day. (sE)

(95) Those were the *most* people that I hanged around with.[79] (ChE)

You may be wondering about how *few* (89) and *most* (95) function as determiners, when there are other determiners—*a* and *the*—prior to them. We come back to this in the next chapter, so stay tuned!

Exercise 6

Identify all quantifying pronouns and quantifying determiners in the sentences below.

a) Someone needs to get a move on. (sE)

b) Nobody believes that you could fix anything.[80] (sE)

c) Everybody took care of their own self.[81] (AE)

d) Some guys I find that I can't trust them.[82] (ChE)

e) I was getting closer and more closer with every step I took.[83] (AE)

f) They enjoy everything they do. (sE)

g) We Black folks be knowin we got some unique patterns of language.[84] (AAE)

h) My dad use both [Black Language and White Mainstream English].[85] (AAE)

8.2.6 Relative Pronouns

Relative pronouns introduce relative clauses. For now, we just expect you to be able to identify and name these pronouns; we'll explain relative clauses in much more detail in Chapter 14. In the next data set, pay attention to the italicized relative clauses and the underlined relative pronouns. Which {NPs} do the pronouns refer to?

(96) Athletes <u>who</u> *train consistently* win the most prizes. (sE)

(97) The athletes <u>whom</u> *we met last week* won the prizes. (sE)

(98) I learned that people <u>that</u> *are left-handed* could draw better than people <u>who</u> *are right-handed*.[86] (ChE)

(99) It was in the apple <u>that</u> *the witch had gave Snow White* …[87] (ChE)

(100) We ain't never really had no tornadoes (…) <u>that</u> *I don't remember*.[88] (SAE)

(101) Our neighbors' tree, <u>which</u> *was struck by lightning during the storm*, crashed onto the road. (sE)

(102) Our friends, <u>whose</u> *cats are still very young*, adopted a dog recently. (sE)

The **forms** of relative pronouns are *who, whom, that, which,* and *whose*; their **function** is to introduce a relative clause that refers back to another {NP} in the sentence. In (96), *who* refers to *athletes*; in (97), *whom* refers to *the athletes*; in (98), *that* refers to *people* and *who* to *people,* and so on. The {NP} that the relative pronoun refers to is called **antecedent**. Rather than repeating that antecedent in the relative clause, a relative pronoun replaces the antecedent. Otherwise, our sentences would read something like this: **Athletes athletes train consistently win the most prizes*, which is ungrammatical! *Whose* in (102) is a bit different, since *whose* occupies the determiner slot prior to the noun and as such doesn't replace *our friends*. *Whose*, nevertheless, introduces the relative clause *whose cats are still very young,* and for this reason, is a relative pronoun.

Exercise 7

Identify all relative pronouns in the sentences[89] below. Name the antecedent for each relative pronoun as well.

a) Dogs, which are often considered our best friends, exhibit remarkable loyalty. (sE)

b) The breed of dog that is known for its intelligence is the Border Collie. (sE)

Foundations of Grammar

> c) The family fed the stray puppy that they found wandering in the park. (sE)
>
> d) People who have allergies may opt for hypoallergenic dog breeds. (sE)
>
> e) The German Shepherd, whose origins trace back to Germany, is renowned for its versatility. (sE)
>
> f) Dogs that receive proper training tend to be well-behaved in various situations. (sE)
>
> g) Owners who understand their dog's needs can foster a strong bond with their pet. (sE)
>
> h) She treated the injured dog that the animal control officer had brought in earlier. (sE)

8.2.7 Interrogative Pronouns

The last type of pronouns in this chapter are the **interrogative pronouns** *what, who, whom, which,* and *whose*. The name already reveals what these pronouns do: They help us form interrogatives, i.e., questions:

(103) *What* did you do today? (sE)

(104) *Who* you be talking to like that?[90] (AAE)

(105) *Whom* did you give it to? (sE)

(106) *Which* is nicer? (sE)

(107) *Whose* is that car over there? (sE)

(108) *What all* did you get for Christmas?[91] (SAE)

Note that you already encountered the words *which, who, whom,* and *whose* as relative pronouns. Comparing the examples in that section on relative pronouns to the examples here illustrates the difference between them. While the form for *who* as a relative pronoun and the form for *who* as an interrogative pronoun is the same (it's the same word after all), you can see that the word *who* can function differently depending on how it is used (one introduces a relative clause and the other starts a question). (108) shows a dialect variation where *what* can co-occur with *all*.

When you come across a *who, whom, which,* or *whose,* you can't assume it's one or the other; you have to look at the sentential context in which it occurs: Does it introduce a relative clause (where it has an antecedent it refers back to), or does it simply introduce a question?

What, which, and *whose* can also function as, surprise, determiners, where they precede a noun in an {NP} (note that (112) and (113) demonstrate that the combination of *what + all* can function as a determiner as well):

(109) <u>*What*</u> artist do you like best? (sE)

(110) <u>*Which*</u> movies are currently popular? (sE)

(111) <u>Whose</u> *precious cat* is this? (sE)
(112) <u>What all</u> *ice cream flavors* do you like?[92] (ME)
(113) I don't know <u>what all</u> *jobs* she's had in the last year.[93] (ME)

For more information about the value of pronouns and some tidbits about pronouns in other languages, check out the companion website.

Exercise 8

Identify all interrogative pronouns and interrogative determiners in the sentences[94] below.

a) Who is responsible for feeding the dogs while we're away? (sE)
b) Whose idea was it to adopt a rescue dog from the shelter? (sE)
c) What kind of treats does your dog enjoy the most? (sE)
d) Which dog breed is known for its gentle nature and patience with children? (sE)
e) Whom did you consult when deciding on the best training methods for your puppy? (sE)
f) Whose leash is this tangled mess in the hallway? (sE)
g) Which veterinarian did you take your dog to for its annual check-up? (sE)
h) What time does the dog obedience class start at the community center? (sE)

Exercise 9

Pronounpalooza. Identify all pronouns in the sentences[95] below. Label them as personal, possessive, indefinite, reflexive, demonstrative, relative, interrogative. Whenever one of them functions as a determiner, label it as such.

a) *They* took *his* energetic Labrador for a walk, during *which they* encountered a stray dog *that* immediately caught *her* attention. (sE)
b) The dog, *which* scratched *itself* constantly, seemed lost, so *they* decided to take *it* to the nearest animal shelter. (sE)
c) At the shelter, *they* asked the vet if *anyone* had reported a missing dog; *her* answer was no. (sE)
d) *No one* had come forward, so *they* adopted the stray as *their* own, naming *him* Max. (sE)
e) Max quickly became accustomed to *his* new home, exploring *every* corner and making *himself* comfortable on *his* new bed. (sE)

> f) *We* often wondered *what* Max's life was like before he was found by *us*. (sE)
> g) Max seemed to have quickly forgotten *those* days. (sE)
> h) As the vet reflected on *their* decision to adopt Max, *she herself* knew *it* was the right choice; *her* clients vowed to give him *all* the love and care *he* deserved. (sE)

Terminology to Know

Term	Working definition	Example/Illustration
Personal pronoun		
Possessive pronoun		
Interrogative pronoun		
Reflexive pronoun		
Dependent possessives		
Object form of pronouns		
Subject form of pronouns		
Quantifying pronouns		
Relative pronouns		
Antecedent		
Demonstrative Pronouns		

Chart 7 Key terminology Chapter 8

Notes

1. W. Beauregard, personal communication, August 29, 2024.
2. Wolfram and Christian, 1976, p. 69.
3. Johnstone, 2013, p. 189.
4. W. Beauregard, personal communication, August 29, 2024.
5. Ibid.
6. Ibid.
7. Bayley, 2012, p. 163.
8. Kendall, Quartey et al., 2018 Transcript ID DCB_se2_ag4_f_03_2.
9. Slightly adapted from Wood, 2015.
10. University of South Carolina (n.d.).
11. Kendall, Quartey et al., 2018 Transcript ID DCB_se1_ag2_m_01_1.
12. Spears, 1982, p. 852; cited in Green, 2002, p. 22.
13. Wood, 2015.
14. Christian et al., 1988; cited in Matyiku, 2011a.
15. Kendall, Fasold et al., 2018 Transcript ID DCA_se2_ag1_f_03_1.

16. Adapted from Fought, 2003, p. 100.
17. Green, 2002, p. 60.
18. Christian et al., 1988; cited in Matyiku, 2011a.
19. Green, 2002, p. 40.
20. Reaser et al., 2017a, p. 37.
21. Wolfram and Schilling-Estes, 2000.
22. Young, 2019, p. 4.
23. Ibid.
24. Ibid.
25. Ibid.
26. Green, 2002, p. 21.
27. Fought, 2006, p. 85.
28. Kendall, Quartey et al., 2018 Transcript ID DCB_se2_ag2_f_01_1.
29. Christian, 1991, and Webelhuth and Dannenberg, 2006; cited in Huang and McCoy, 2015.
30. Ibid.
31. Ibid.
32. Ibid.
33. Ibid.
34. Ibid.
35. Huang and McCoy, 2015.
36. Young, 2019, p. 4.
37. Ibid.
38. Kendall, Quartey et al., 2018 Transcript ID DCB_se3_ag3_m_02_1.
39. University of South Carolina (n.d.).
40. Bayley, 2012, p. 163
41. Green, 2002, p. 183.
42. Ibid.
43. University of South Carolina (n.d.).
44. Ibid.
45. Farrington et al., 2020 Transcript ID ATL_se0_ag1_f_01_1.
46. Maher and McCoy, 2011.
47. Wood, 2014.
48. Ibid.
49. Kendall, Quartey et al., 2018 Transcript ID DCB_se2_ag2_f_01_1.
50. Green, 2002, p. 103.
51. LGBTQ+ Resource Center, 2021.
52. Conrod, 2022, p. 151.
53. Conrod, 2022; Curzan, 2003.
54. Christian et al., 1988; cited in Matyiku, 2011a.
55. Green, 2002, p. 103.
56. University of South Carolina (n.d.).

57. Wood, 2014.
58. Conrod, 2022, p. 143.
59. Huang, 2011.
60. Staub and Zentz, 2017.
61. University of South Carolina (n.d.).
62. Kendall, Quartey et al., 2018 Transcript ID DCB_se3_ag3_m_02_1.
63. Reaser et al., 2017a, p. 70.
64. Ibid.
65. University of South Carolina (n.d.).
66. Smitherman, 2006, p. 3.
67. Green, 2002, p. 60.
68. University of South Carolina (n.d.).
69. Reaser et al., 2017a, p. 70.
70. Callahan, 2017.
71. Montgomery, 2009; cited in Matyiku, 2011a.
72. Fought, 2003, p. 147; cited in Bayley and Santa Ana, 2004, p. 385.
73. Foreman, 1999; cited in Matyiku, 2011b.
74. Putnam and van Koppen, 2011; cited in Wood, 2013.
75. Wood, 2013.
76. Spears, 1982, p. 852; cited in Green, 2002, p. 22.
77. Huang, 2011.
78. Kendall, Fasold et al., 2018 Transcript ID DCA_se2_ag1_f_03_1.
79. Fought, 2003, p. 94.
80. Ibid, p. 100.
81. University of South Carolina (n.d.).
82. Bayley, 2012, p. 160.
83. University of South Carolina (n.d.).
84. Smitherman, 2006, p. 2.
85. Baker-Bell, 2020, p. 43.
86. Fought, 2003, p. 100.
87. Bayley and Santa Ana, 2004, p. 378.
88. Feagin, 1979; cited in Matyiku, 2011b.
89. Sentences produced with the help of OpenAI, 2024.
90. Green, 2002, p. 86.
91. McCloskey, 2000, p. 58; cited in Lindemann, 2018.
92. Putnam and van Koppen, 2011; cited in Wood, 2013.
93. Ibid.
94. Sentences produced with the help of OpenAI, 2024.
95. Ibid.

CHAPTER 9
CONNECTING EVERYTHING: FUNCTIONAL WORD CATEGORIES

Overview

Function words are closed-class words. When compared to open-class words such as nouns and adjectives, function words convey less semantic meaning but more grammatical information. **Function words** are a category that includes pronouns, auxiliary verbs, determiners, prepositions, conjunctions (both coordinators and subordinators), numerals, and interjections. This is the last chapter on word classes as such, and so we close this chapter with a summary of all word classes! Our objectives are as follows. You'll be able to

- identify words as determiners, prepositions, conjunctions, and numerals; and
- build your knowledge of forms and functions of function words.

Pre-reading task

1. Take a look at the following two groups of words.
    - Group 1: In, a, amidst, there, a, of, whose, from, to, with, as, as, a
    - Group 2: quaint, little, village, nestled, rolling, hills, lived, colony, feline, friends, fur, ranged, silky, black, snowy, white, masterpiece

   What kinds of information do these words convey? Jot down a few observations:

    - Observations about group 1:
    - Observations about group 2:

   Next, can you combine *all* the words from both groups into one big sentence? Write it down and, if possible, compare it with a classmate's.
   Sentence: _____
   _____
   _____
   _____

9.1 Introduction

When was the last time you heard a new preposition added to English? In fact, little has changed with prepositions after the year 1500, and prior to that, English saw the pruning away of many Old English prepositions.[1] It does, however, happen that functional classes add new words or borrow forms from other languages, but not frequently. For example, in Middle English, the preposition "during" entered English via a calque from Old French.[2] This chapter focuses on just those kinds of stable, grammatical words: the **function words**. We essentially have built up your understanding of determiners stealthily, under the radar so to speak, in the chapter on pronouns, and so we start with determiners.

9.2 Determiners

The most common **determiners** are the **definite article** *the* and the **indefinite articles** *a* and *an*. Compare the two sentences below.

(1)   Riley met *a* client the other day. (sE)

(2)   *The* client that Riley met is desperate. (sE)

The indefinite article *a* in (1) doesn't clearly identify a specific client; it simply introduces *a client* as a general topic. If a noun begins with a vowel, *an* is typically used over *a* as in *an apple*. Compare the indefinite article *a* in (1) to the definite article in (2): *the* now clearly identifies *the client* as the one Riley met the other day. Once something has been introduced, definite articles are used to refer back to those things.

We use the term "determiner" as a broad function label to refer to any word that can occur in the determiner slot of an {NP}. We include definite and indefinite articles, demonstrative determiners, possessive determiners, and so on as determiners—something you should be remembering from Chapter 8 on pronouns! Below are the first few examples of words that can function as determiners:

(3)   *Your* essay is better than *those* essays. (sE)

(4)   Here's you *some* money.[3] (SAE)

(5)   I noticed *two* older girls a-eating something out of *a* little syrup bucket.[4] (AE)

(6)   *Any* man can't fight for *his* friends had better be dead.[5] (AE/AAE)

(7)   *The* little kid don't have *no* sturdy shoes of *his* own.[6] (ChE)

(8)   *Chiara's* essay is extremely good. (sE)

(9)   Just eat *them* big black cherries.[7] (AAE)

(10)   Miles read *all the* books that were assigned by *several* professors. (sE)

Your in (3) as well as *his* in (6) are examples of possessive determiners. *Those* in (3) is a demonstrative determiner, and (9) shows that *them* is a variant for *these* in AAE.

Quantifying words (*some* (4), *any* (6), *no* (7), and *all* in (10)), numerals (*two* (5)), and possessive nouns (*Chiara's* (8)) are more examples of words that can function as determiners. Essentially, **determiners** specify the scope of reference for a particular noun: not just any essay, but *your* essay, for instance; not the older girls, but *two* older girls, and so on.

9.2.1 Four Crucial Features

Because determiners are so closely connected to nouns, some features of determiners have already been discussed in the context of nouns. We reiterate the four central features for determiners all in one spot here, one by one. The data set below illustrates the first important feature:

(11) *The cat* jumped over *the lazy dog*. (sE)

(11a) **Cat the* jumped over *lazy dog the*. (sE)

As (11) and (11a) demonstrate, when there is a determiner, it must come prior to the noun, not after it.

On to the second feature:

(11b) **Cat* jumped over *lazy dog*. (sE)

(12) *Cats* are notorious for killing *mice*. (sE)

(12a) ~*The cats* are notorious for killing *the mice*. (sE)

> Remember these **symbols**:
> * = something is ungrammatical.
> ~ = something may or may not be acceptable.

Nouns that are singular (as in 11b) require a determiner, while those that are plural as in (12) do not require a determiner for the structure to be grammatical. What if, however, we have a plural noun that we want to specify with a determiner?

(13) Jayden took *those cats* to three veterinarians. (sE)

(13a) Jayden took *the cats* to the veterinarian. (sE)

(13b) I took *the cats* from the shelter—not my own cats—to the veterinarian. (sE)

(14) *Cats* are Layla's favorite pets. (sE)

(15) Quinn appreciate *veterinarians* so much. (sE)

You can see that when you want to specify a plural noun, you can do so (as in (13)–(13b)), but when you talk about cats as such (as in (14)) or veterinarians as such (as in (15)), no determiner is required.

What about abstract nouns?

(16) *Honesty* is the best policy. (sE)

(16a) **An honesty* is the best policy. (sE)

(16b) **The honesty* is the best policy. (sE)

(17) *Beauty* is in the eye of the beholder. (sE)

(17a) *A beauty* is in the eye of the beholder. (sE)

(17b) *The beauty* is in the eye of the beholder. (sE)

As you can see, abstract nouns do not need determiners. Adding *the* or *a* results in the ungrammatical {NPs} in (16a/16b) and (17a/17b), at least for the examples so far. But not so fast, as some abstract nouns *can* take determiners. And, some nouns can be, depending on context, abstract as in (18) and (19), or concrete as in (19a):

(18) *Truth* is expected. (sE)

(19) *The truth* will set you free. (sE)

(19a) *The truths* of the case will set the defendant free. (sE)

The third feature of determiners has to do with number agreement. This really only applies to demonstrative determiners, where there's a choice between singular and plural determiners: *this/that* for singular nouns and *these/those* for plural nouns:

(20) *This* thing here I might should turn over to Ann.[8] (SAE)

(21) *These* gravels are hard on your feet.[9] (AE)

Thing in (20) is singular, so we have the singular form for the determiner (i.e., *this*), and *gravels* in (21) is plural, which means we have the plural form for the determiner (i.e., *these*).

The last feature for determiners is related to how many determiners a noun can take:

(22) *The* dog slept in *its* doghouse. (sE)

(22a) **The my* dog slept in its doghouse. (sE)

(22b) **The a* dog slept in its doghouse. (sE)

(22c) *My dog slept in *its that* doghouse. (sE)

Based on these examples, only one determiner can precede a noun. Now, technically speaking, determiners can actually be broken down into pre-, post-, and central determiners, which can occur together, but there can't ever be more than **one** central determiner, so our fourth feature is a bit of a simplification. Anyway, take a look at the following {NPs} where two determiners co-occur:

(23) *a few* days ago (sE)

(24) *the most* people (sE)

(25) *all my* cats (sE)

(26) *both my* cats (sE)

You can see that quantifying determiners can co-occur with articles as in (23) and (24) or with possessive determiners as in (25) and (26). Other combinations are possible, but what is *never* possible is to double up by combining an article with a possessive or an article with a demonstrative or an article with another article (see (22a-c). This is because articles are central determiners, and you can't have more than one of those in an {NP}.

Our four features can be summarized as follows:

1. In an {NP}, a determiner (if present) comes first.
2. Single count nouns require a determiner, but plural nouns do not require determiners.
3. Some determiners show number agreement with the noun they specify.
4. Only one per given noun within an {NP} (but with exceptions, because it wouldn't be fun otherwise; remember the pre-, central, and post-determiners from above!).

We can always use **paradigmatic evidence** as well by replacing the word in question with another determiner to see if the sentence remains grammatical:

(27) *My* bird is sick. (sE)

(27a) *The* bird is sick. (sE)

(28) Here's you *some* money.[10] (SAE)

(28a) Here's you *the* money.[11] (SAE)

We can replace *my* with *the* in (27), which means that *my* is a determiner. Likewise, *some* can be replaced with *the*, which means *some* is a determiner in (28). The only morphological, or morphosyntactic, evidence is our rule that for sE, some determiners must agree in number—singular or plural—with their noun.

Exercise 1

Identify all determiners in the sentences below. Bonus points for finding the one example with a pre-determiner followed by a central determiner!

a) My parents be correcting, too.[12] (AAE)
b) These shoes are better than the ones advertised by several companies. (sE)
c) All the construction of our house is finished. (sE)
d) The cats are more funnier than the dogs. (various sE and non-sE dialects)
e) Twitter can be a professional job anymore.[13] (ME)
f) Many geese are flying home. (sE)
g) We went to the Capital Burger restaurant and had a wicked delicious burger.[14] (NEE)
h) Here's me a good pair of jeans.[15] (SAE)

9.2.2 Adjectives vs. Determiners (one more time)

Since we can have both determiners and adjectives prior to a noun in an {NP}, let's take another look at how we can figure out if a word is functioning as a determiner or an adjective. Compare the next two examples. Can you identify the determiner(s)? What evidence can you use?

(29)   The big, red balloon popped. (sE)

(29a)   *The that big, red balloon popped. (sE)

What makes (29a) ungrammatical? While we can stack attributive adjectives in front of a noun ad infinitum or ad nauseum (your choice), as in *The lovely, big, old, round, red, plastic balloon*, only one determiner is allowed per noun. In the following sentence, identify the determiner (remember, only one allowed) and adjectives (more than one allowed):

(29b)   The one, big, red balloon popped. (sE)

We can see that the noun *balloon* is a single count noun, so it must have a determiner. What happens to the word *One* when *The* is deleted?

(29c)   One big, red balloon popped. (sE)

Here, *one* has been promoted to the determiner slot since the single, count noun must have a determiner for the sentence to be grammatical. If you are unsure, delete the word *one* and see whether the sentence is grammatical:

(29d)   *Big, red balloon popped. (sE)

Without *one* or *the* or another word functioning as a determiner, the sentence is ungrammatical, so you can be confident that *one* functions as the determiner in *One big, red balloon*. Here are the essential differences between determiners and adjectives:

- The determiner will be the first in the sequence: NP = {DET, ADJ + N}.
- There can only be one determiner (but again, pre-, central, and post-determiners are possible), but many adjectives are allowed.
- Replacing the word in question with a known determiner (definite and indefinite articles are a safe bet) can be helpful to identify determiners from adjectives. (This is paradigmatic evidence.)
- Finally, determiners cannot form comparatives (*The oner/onest red balloon*), but adjectives can.

Exercise 2

Underline as many determiners as you can in the excerpt[16] below.

In a quaint little village nestled amidst our rolling hills, there lived a colony of feline friends, whose fur ranged from silky black to snowy white, adorned with many patterns as intricate as a painter's masterpiece. Their eyes gleamed like polished emeralds, reflecting the moon's silver glow as they prowled through the cobblestoned streets, their nimble paws leaving delicate imprints in the dew-kissed grass. With tails swishing gracefully behind them, they roamed freely, their agile forms darting through alleys lined with colorful blooms.

9.3 Relationship Builders: Prepositions

If you learned about prepositions in your K-12 education, you probably learned something like this: a preposition is anywhere a mouse/a bunny/an ant can go:

(30) *in* a house > The mouse is in a house.
(31) *under* the stairs > The mouse is under the stairs.
(32) *on* a chair > The mouse is on a chair.
(33) *behind* a door > The mouse is behind a door.
(34) *between* the curtains etc.
(35) *below* the stoop
(36) *above* the clock
(37) *at* the kitchen sink

These are called **locative prepositions**. They are a subset of prepositions that help convey information related to locations.

Now, prepositions don't all have to do with location. Take a look at the next few examples.

(38) The dog needs scratched *for* an hour.[17] (ME)
(39) Latoya and James are happy *for* her. (sE)
(40) We're really supposed to get out of here *on* June.[18] (ChE)
(41) We witnessed much anxiety *over* the final exam. (sE)
(42) Here's you a piece *of* pizza.[19] (SAE)
(43) Sandy and Pat are angry *about* the last-minute assignment. (sE)

None of these examples have to do with location. For instance, in both (38) and (40), the prepositions *for* and *on* are tied to time in some way (duration, a date). Even the preposition *in* could be used in a similar way as in *in a minute* (rather than be tied to location!). Now, what's crucial is that this information, or this meaning related to time or location, is expressed not by the preposition itself, but rather by the connection the preposition creates between the words prior to the preposition and the nouns that follow it.

Let's break that down a bit more. In (38) and (39), the same preposition (*for*) is used in very different ways, and so the preposition *for* on its own does not mean "duration." The semantic meaning of duration in (38) is created via the connection that *for* establishes between the verb *needs scratched* and the {NP} *an hour*. In (39), the same preposition creates a different modifying connection, this time between the adjective *happy* and the pronoun *her*. The phrase *for her* gives us more details about *happy*. In (41), the connection that the preposition *over* creates is between the noun *anxiety* and the {NP} *the final exam*. In our initial examples about location, this applies, too: In *The mouse is in the house*, the preposition *in* creates a connection between the nouns *mouse* and *house*.

So, rather than trying to locate semantic meaning in prepositions themselves, it's more productive to think of prepositions as function words that create connections between the noun that follows it to other elements in a clause or sentence. Chiefly, prepositions make connections between

- a verb and an {NP}:

    (44)   He's *smiling   to   the cat*.[20] ChE)
                verb   prep   {NP}

    (45)   A person *ran   by   us*. (sE)
                    verb prep {NP}

- an adjective and an {NP}:

    (39a) Latoya and James are *happy   for   her*. (sE)
                               adjective prep {NP}

    (43a) Sandy and Pat are *angry   about   the last-minute assignment*. (sE)
                             adjective prep   {NP}

- a noun and an {NP}:

    (41a) We witnessed much *anxiety   over   the final exam*. (sE)
                             noun   prep   {NP}

    (46)   That's the *street   behind   my mom and dad house*.[21] (AAE)
                      noun   prep   {NP}

In contrast to other function words which don't form their own phrases, prepositions do head their own phrases, specifically, the prepositional phrase {PP}. For now, simply remember that a preposition is always followed by an {NP}, and that the preposition owns that {NP}. In other words, the basic structure for {PPs} is this: P + {NP}. We provide a full picture of {PPs}, including their functions, in Chapter 10.

Exercise 3

Underline all prepositions in the sentences below.

a) My sister studies engineering in college. (sE)

b) This thing here I might should turn over to Ann.[22] (SAE)

c) I was able to find the information about determiners in this chapter. (sE)

d) I'm gonna write me a letter to my cousin.[23] (AE)

e) We sitting there talking, and he come hitting on me for some money.[24] (AAE)

f) Ann and Maria bought new furniture at the warehouse during the sale. (sE)

g) They are leaving on a great adventure; you should go with.[25] (ME)

h) I had been fixin' to get a new bike for years and finally did.[26] (SAE)

Exercise 4

Label the underlined words as either a determiner (DET) or a preposition (PREP) in the excerpt[27] below. The excerpt is taken from the published convention program for the Conference on College Composition and Communication, and as such represents written AAE.

<u>My</u> dear friends, dear colleagues, dear *CCCC* members, dear honored guests, dear newcomers, dear all: Yay! We is here. We is here! And I <u>for</u> one ain't goin home til we done—til it's ova. Whaboutchu? As I welcome you <u>to</u> Pittsburgh and to 4C19, let me be real <u>wit</u> y'all right <u>from</u> jump. I hope y'all can tell <u>from</u> <u>my</u> call <u>for</u> papers last year, the visuality right here <u>at</u> the conference, <u>from</u> <u>the</u> black feminist program cover, <u>the</u> artist inserts <u>in</u> the program, and much mo'—some <u>of</u> which I highlight below—that dis here C's, <u>dis</u> here conference, is <u>bout</u> honorin, explorin, researchin, and advocatin <u>wit</u> diverse peoples/voices.

9.4 Conjunctions and Coordinators: Equality and Inequality in Connection

The next section helps us move from the simple sentences we have mostly been using to more complex structures. In particular, we are moving from sentences with just one {VP} to sentences with more than one {VP}. Put differently, we are moving on to multi-clausal sentences. Compare the **simple sentences** in (47) and (48) with the **compound sentences** in (49) and (50).

(47) The students *met* for the exam. (sE)
         {VP}

(48) They *done tore* it down.[28] (AAE)
         {VP}

(49) The students *met* for the exam, but they *had arrived* much too early. (sE)
         {VP$_1$}   {VP$_2$}

(50) They *done tore* it down, but the building *is* still there.[29] (AAE)
         {VP$_1$}   {VP$_2$}

Simple sentences have only one {VP}. Simple sentences consist of a subject and a predicate. (Remember from Chapter 2 that everything to the right of the subject in a clause is considered the predicate.) **Compound sentences** consist of two clauses and as such have two {VPs}. In other words, there are two subjects and two predicates:

(49a) [The students]   [met for the exam],
           subject 1 +   predicate 1
                  clause 1

        but [they]   [had arrived much too early]. (sE)
              subject 2 +   predicate 2
                       clause 2

(50a) [They] [done tore it down], but [the building] [is still there].[30] (AAE)
         subject 1 +   predicate 1   subject 2   +   predicate 2
                    clause 1   clause 2

Clause 2 in both (49a) and (50a) is introduced with *but* and can stand on its own. They are independent. (Remember independent and dependent clauses from Chapter 2?) Because each clause can stand on its own and because neither is dependent on the other, these kinds of sentences are called **compound sentences**.

9.4.1 Coordinators

Coordinators allow us to join constructions of **like status**. One type of coordinator is the **coordinating conjunction (CC)**, which must join the same types of constructions. This restriction is very important. You can join the same grammatical classes (e.g., nouns, adjectives, verbs), the same type of phrases (e.g., {PPs}, {NPs}), or the same types of clauses. Since conjunctions are a closed class, we do not add more of them. In fact, the list forms an easy acronym, a mnemonic device, for remembering all of them:

- For
- And
- Nor
- But
- Or
- Yet
- So

FANBOYS conjunctions can be used to link like grammatical classes. We have underlined the respective coordinating conjunction and italicized the constituents each CC links in the examples below. For independent clauses, we simply italicized the conjunction. You'll see that commas can be replaced by *and* as in (52), where *Kim, Alex, and Sandy* can be rephrased as *Kim and Alex and Sandy*. Likewise, a comma alone (without a conjunction such as *and*) can connect words, as is shown in (57).

Connecting Nouns and {NPs}

(51) *Chiara and Matteo* are both sleeping. (sE)

(52) It needs checked by *Kim, Alex, and Sandy*.[31] (ME)

(53) Darius and Hassan bought *honey-baked ham and delicious rolls* at the store. (sE)

(54) I ain't really thinking about getting with *Jay or any other guy*.[32] (ChE)

Connecting Adjectives and {AdjPs}

(55) The cake was *sweet but yummy*. (sE)

(56) I picked her because she *nice and calm*.[33] (AAE)

(57) The soul needs fed by *creative, multi-dimensional* teaching.[34] (ME)

Connecting Adverbs and {AdvPs}

(58) The neighborhood just look *big and empty*.[35] (AAE)

(59) Yegor reviewed the examples *quickly and thoroughly*. (sE)

(60) My dog runs *extremely fast, yet very bizarrely*. (sE)

Connecting Verbs and {VPs}

(61) They *flipping and flopping*.[36] (AAE)

(62) Our guests *drink and eat* a lot. (sE)

Connecting Prepositions and {PPs}

(63) The students went *above and beyond* my expectations. (sE)

(64) I wanted to buy ice cream which was *in the store yet above my reach*. (sE)

(65) The car needs washed, not necessarily *by you, but by someone*.[37] (ME)

Connecting Independent Clauses

(66) Blake walked to the store, *so* they could get Ainsley treats. (sE)

(67) I know he was a-tellin' the truth, *but* I was a-comin' home.[38] (AE)

(68) He has plenty of free time, *so* he exercises a lot anymore.[39] (ME)

9.4.2 Creating Dependencies: Subordinators

Subordinators, also called **subordinating conjunctions**, allow us to join clauses as well. Joining two clauses with a subordinating conjunction results in a **complex sentence**. In contrast to the compound sentences in Section 9.4.1, these conjunctions link a dependent clause with an independent clause. The next data set shows some of the many words that can function as subordinators (see italicized words):

(69) *Before* it goes out, it needs checked by Kim, Alex, and Sandy.[40] (ME)

(70) Samir watched all of the Women's March Madness games, *even though* he had so much work to do. (sE)

(71) *If* he'd be here right now, he'd make me laugh.[41] (ChE)

(72) I ain't saying *that* these linguists have not discussed these frameworks.[42] (AAE)

(73) This will be particularly important *once* you're done the tattoo and need to leave the shop.[43] (ECE)

(74) *Since* my cats are the cutest in the world, I talk about them all the time. (sE)

Many subordinators exist. Chart 1 provides you with quite a few of them, but it is not an exhaustive list! Are there any in this list that you rarely use, but you could add to your own writing tool repertoire?

after	if	provided	whenever
although	if only	provided that	where
as	if then	rather that	whereas
as if	if when	since	where if
as long as	inasmuch	so that	wherever
as much as	in order that	supposing	whether
as soon as	just as	than	which
as though	lest	that	while
because	now	though	who
before	now since	till	whoever
even	now that	unless	why
even if	now when	until	
even though	once	when	etc.

Chart 1 Subordinators—a selection

Subordinators combine two previously independent clauses into one complex clause:

(75) Sarah likes pistachios. (sE)   *Independent clause 1*

(76) She will eat peanuts. (sE)   *Independent clause 2*

(77) [*Although*] [Sarah likes pistachios], [she will eat peanuts]. (sE)

   SUB   +   Independent clause 1   +   Independent clause 2

While *Sarah likes pistachios* can stand alone, *Although Sarah likes pistachios* **cannot** stand alone as its own sentence, not with the *although* included.

Types of sentences	
Simple sentence	one independent clause
Compound sentence	two independent clauses linked
Complex sentence	contains a dependent clause

Let's look at one more example.

(78) Vanilla ice cream will be fine for my party. (sE)   *Independent clause 1*

(79) I like all ice cream. (sE)   *Independent clause 2*

(80) Vanilla ice cream will be fine for my party *because* I like all ice cream.

   Independent clause 1   +   SUB   +   *Independent clause 2*

Again, just like above, we have two independent clauses, one of which is turned into a dependent clause once we add the subordinator *because*. *Because*, then, makes the second clause a dependent one. This is the function of subordinators. Can *Because I like all ice cream* stand on its own as a sentence? No. Not with the *because* included in the clause.

Notice that only (77) includes a comma; (80) has no punctuation mark other than a final period. The pattern is that when subordination comes before the main clause, a comma is always needed to set the dependent clause off as introductory. When subordination comes after the main clause, it's different. While some subordinate clauses that follow the main clause could require a comma (i.e., the subordinate clause is deemed to be extra material and not essential), the lack of comma is more common.

> **Exercise 5**
>
> Identify the italicized conjunctions as either coordinating (co) or subordinating (sub) conjunctions in the sentences below.
>
> a) *As* I welcome you to Pittsburgh *and* to 4C19, let me be real wit y'all right from jump.[44] (AAE)
>
> b) And *when* and *if* you find some, make sure to tell me about it.[45] (AAE)
>
> c) And when *and* if you find some, make sure to tell me about it.[46] (AAE)
>
> d) I was president of the council four years *and* that liketa worked the pants off of me![47] (SAE)
>
> e) He asked me *where* did I live.[48] (ChE)
>
> f) Our car broke down, *and* Croton was the farthest we got.[49] (ME)
>
> g) We used to have four cats *but* now we have just two. (sE)
>
> h) *After* we adopted two cats, we took in two more cats from the neighbor. (sE)

9.5 Numerals and Interjections

We include numerals and interjections together in a sort of **peripheral class** of words, following Quirk et al.[50] **Numerals** are, in a way, open classes of words because we can continue counting infinitely, meaning that if we add +1 to any existing number, we'll always get yet another number. Yet, we hope you agree that these new numbers are not new in the same way as new nouns or new verbs are new. **Interjections**, too, are sort of in between open and closed classes. We can interject with new expressions and words (an argument for considering them as open-class words), but generally, interjections that have been established or agreed upon are a relatively fixed group of words. Either way, both numerals and interjections are words that we use, and as such, are part of language and grammar. Hence, we must account for them.

9.5.1 Numerals

Two types of numerals exist:

- **Cardinal numerals**: one, two, three, four, five, ...
- **Ordinal numerals**: first, second, third, fourth, fifth, ...

Here are a few examples of where and how they crop up in sentences:

(81) I met them *four* mile down the road.[51] (SAE/ChE/AAE/others)

(82) We used to have *three* tablets. (sE)

(83) The park has *two* basketball hoop.[52] (SAE/ChE/AAE/others)

(84) The *second* cat we adopted took a while to warm up to us. (sE)

(85) After we saw Star Wars for the *37th* time, I have had enough. (sE)

(86) Cindy, this *one* just woke up and probably wants fed.[53] (ME)

(87) If you are the age of *60* or *80*, you still can play many game.[54] (SAE/ChE/AAE/etc.)

(88) *Thousands* are signing up for the grammar course. (sE)

In (81)–(85), the numerals (both cardinal and ordinal) occur as determiners prior to a noun. In (86)–(88), the numerals function as the head word in an {NP}. In fact, in (86), the numeral *one* gets its own determiner *this*. Both ordinals and cardinals can function as heads in {NPs}. That's it for the concept of numerals—at least for our purposes! If you were to consult a comprehensive grammar such as Quirk et al.'s work, you would be able to read about a whole lot more nuances and details.

9.5.2 Interjections—Extra Expressions

Interjections are words that express emotions. These words occur outside the grammatical clause, serving as an addition to it; hence, they are not required by the syntax of the sentence. Any word, really, could be turned into an interjection with the right placement and intonation (for spoken sentences). In written sentences, the exclamation point (!) often follows them as a visual cue to their emotive content. Here's a (non-exhaustive) list!

- **Ahem**—A clearing of the throat in an attempt to get attention
- **Aah**—A call for help or when someone is scared or in trouble
- **Boo**—Used to scare someone or to voice disapproval
- **Eh**—Used when one didn't hear or understand what someone said or, more recently, indicates one is not impressed
- **Eww**—Conveys dislike or disgust
- **Hmm**—Indicates one is thinking or hesitating
- **Jeez**—Indicates disbelief or exasperation
- **Oh**—Expresses surprise, hesitation, or contemplation
- **Oops**—Indicates an accidental or misfortunate event
- **Phew**—Expresses relief or gladness something is over
- **Whoa**—Shows surprise or amazement
- **Wow**—Expresses amazement

- **Yay**—Expresses joy or happiness
- **Yeah**—Demonstrates a very strong affirmation or approval
- **Yoo-hoo**—Seeks someone's attention
- **Zing**—Usually used comically to emphasize a clever statement or comeback

Of course, we're pretty confident that you could add to this list of interjections a plethora of taboo words that are regularly used as interjections. As an alternative to taboo interjections, try to create new interjections, like this:

(89)   *Pumpkins*! I forgot to do my homework. (sE)

Exercise 6

Create three example sentences each for coordination and subordination (so six sentences total). Once you've created your sentences, identify functional categories such as coordinators, subordinators, determiners, and prepositions. Did you have any interjections? If not, can you add one or two?

9.6 Word Classes—Taking Stock

These last few chapters covered a wealth of information about English word classes (Chart 2 summarizes the open-class and closed-class words) as well as many variations within the use of those word classes. We provide a quick summary of the word classes together with a couple of quick tests (but remember *all* the tests you learned in each chapter; you'll have to supply them for exercise 7).

Open-class words	Closed-class words
Nouns	Auxiliary verbs
Adjectives	Pronouns (mostly)
Adverbs	Determiners
Verbs	Prepositions
	Conjunctions
	Numerals (peripherally)
	Interjections (peripherally)

Chart 2 Open and closed word classes

Below are some of the main features and tests for the lexical categories in the open class and the functional categories in the closed class.

- Nouns can be preceded by a determiner; you can count them (i.e., pluralize them).
- Adjectives can form comparatives/superlatives; they modify nouns.

Foundations of Grammar

- Adverbs can form comparatives/superlatives; they modify adjectives and adverbs, and they can tell you about verbs.
- Verbs can occur in past and present tense.
- Pronouns can replace nouns and noun phrases; many of them can also function as determiners. There are many of them!
- Determiners specify the reference of a noun; they precede nouns.
- Prepositions own a noun phrase; they create connections between nouns and nouns, verbs and nouns, and adjectives and nouns.
- Conjunctions create connections between larger units such as clauses (but coordinators can also connect just two nouns or verbs and so on).

Once you have completed exercise 7 below, sit back and contemplate how much you have learned already, or have been reacquainted with in this short time. You should treat yourself!

Exercise 7

Provide the missing information in the chart below. Make sure to go beyond what is listed above and make sure to provide an example. Where possible, include examples from non-sE and sE dialects.

Word category	Definition	Sentence	Test
Noun			
Adjective			
Adverb			
Verb			
Auxiliary			
Modal			
Pronoun			
Determiner			
Preposition			
Coordinator			
Subordinator			

Terminology to Know

Term	Working definition	Example/Illustration
Determiner		
Preposition		
Coordinator		
Subordinator		
Numeral		
Interjection		
Open-class word		
Closed-class word		

Chart 3 Key terminology Chapter 9

Notes

1. Weber, 2012.
2. Mustanoja, 1960, p. 376.
3. Wood, 2015.
4. Montgomery, 2009; cited in Matyiku, 2011a.
5. Doherty, 1993, p. 158; cited in McCoy, 2016b.
6. Bayley, 2012, p. 163.
7. Rowe et al., 2018 Transcript ID PRV_se0_ag3_m_01_1.
8. Huang, 2011.
9. University of South Carolina (n.d.).
10. Wood, 2015.
11. Slightly adapted from Wood, 2015.
12. McMurtry, 2022, p. 42.
13. Maher and McCoy, 2011.
14. W. Beauregard, personal communication, August 29, 2024.
15. Wood, 2015.
16. Based on an excerpt produced by OpenAI, 2024.
17. Tenny, 1998, p. 592.
18. Fought, 2003, pp. 100–1.
19. Wood, 2015.
20. Barrón and San Romón, n.d., p. 30–1; cited in Bayley, 2012, p. 162.
21. Rowe et al., 2018 Transcript ID PRV_se0_ag2_f_02_2.
22. Di Paolo, 1989; cited in Huang, 2011.
23. Christian, 1991; cited in Huang and McCoy, 2015.
24. Spears, 1982, p. 852; cited in Green, 2002, p. 22.

25. Spartz, 2008; cited in Kaplan, 2015.
26. Staub and Zentz, 2017.
27. Young, 2019, p. 4.
28. Kendall, Quartey et al., 2018 Transcript ID DCB_se1_ag4_f_01_1.
29. Ibid.
30. Ibid.
31. Whitman, 2010; cited in Maher and Wood, 2011.
32. Bayley, 2012, p. 163.
33. Baker-Bell, 2020, p. 76.
34. Maher and Wood, 2011.
35. T. McMurtry, personal communication, November 27, 2024.
36. Kendall, Quartey et al., 2018 Transcript ID DCB_se2_ag4_f_04_1.
37. Shortened from Whitman, 2010; cited in Maher and Wood, 2011.
38. Wolfram and Christian, 1971, p. 77; cited in Matyiku, 2011a.
39. Maher and McCoy, 2011.
40. Whitman, 2010; cited in Maher and Wood, 2011.
41. Bayley, 2012, p. 158.
42. Baker-Bell, 2020, p. 15.
43. Wood, 2014.
44. Young, 2019, p. 4.
45. Ibid.
46. Ibid.
47. Ruffing, 2012.
48. Bayley, 2012, p. 164.
49. McCoy, 2016a.
50. Quirk et al., 1985.
51. Reaser et al., 2017a, p. 37.
52. Ibid., p. 182.
53. Maher and Wood, 2011.
54. Reaser et al., 2017b.

CHAPTER 10
HOW WORDS STICK TOGETHER: THE CASE FOR PHRASES

Overview

By now, you have a good grasp on how words are formed, and you know some things about identifying words as belonging to a particular word class. In this chapter, we expand on what you know about phrases—the larger chunks of language. We cover, in detail, both form and function of the five phrase types: Noun Phrases {NP}, Adjective Phrases {AdjP}, Adverb Phrases {AdvP}, Prepositional Phrases {PP}, and Verb Phrases {VP}. Our objectives are as follows. You'll be able to

- identify phrase types;
- analyze the internal structure of phrases; and
- build your knowledge of the forms and functions of phrases.

> **Pre-reading tasks**
>
> 1. Take a moment and recall all the information about nouns, adjectives, adverbs, prepositions, and verbs. Then, write down your initial ideas about what the difference between these word classes and the corresponding phrase types ({NP}, {AdjP}, {AdvP}, {PP}, and {VP}) might be. Think of both form and function!
> 2. Take a look at the sentences below. Each can be interpreted in at least two different ways. The ambiguity comes down to how you group the words. Can you group the words into different phrases for each sentence so that you can illustrate the different meanings?
>   a. We bought her books.
>   b. I cuddled with the cats in pajamas.
> 3. Identify as many phrases as you can in the following excerpt, which is the opening paragraph of the tale "The Garden of Paradise" by Hans Christian Anderson.[1] After you work through the chapter, revisit the phrases you identified. Are modifications necessary? Did you miss some phrases the first time around?
>   There was once a king's son; nobody had so many or such beautiful books as he had. He could read about everything which had ever happened in this world and

> see it all represented in the most beautiful pictures. He could get information about every nation and every country; but as to where the Garden of Paradise was to be found, not a word could he discover, and this was the very thing he thought most about. His grandmother had told him, when he was quite a little fellow and was about to begin his school life, that every flower in the Garden of Paradise was a delicious cake, and that the pistils were full of wine. In one flower, history was written, in another, geography or tables; you had only to eat the cake, and you knew the lesson. The more you ate, the more history, geography, and tables you knew. All this he believed then; but as he grew older and wiser and learnt more, he easily perceived that the delights of the Garden of Paradise must be far beyond all this.

10.1 Introduction

Recall that phrases are groups of words that together form a chunk, i.e., groups of words that are more closely connected to one another than to the other remaining words in a sentence. Together, these chunks (i.e., phrases) take on a function in a clause/sentence or within another, larger phrase. Consider these short example sentences and pay extra attention to the bracketed words:

(1) [Kanesha] likes [grammar]. (sE)
(2) [He] was a-huntin'.[2] (AE)
(3) [We] invited [Taylor]. (sE)
(4) [I] got [me] [some candy].[3] (SAE/AE)
(5) [Hassan and Santiago] are [incredibly nice]. (sE)
(6) [The teachers at South High] is [cool].[4] (AAE)
(7) [In the morning], [Carlos] needs [hot coffee]. (sE)
(8) [They] celebrated [after class]. (sE)

Many of the bracketed phrases above consist of just one word, such as *Kanesha* and *grammar* in (1), *We* and *Taylor* in (3), *I* and *me* in (4), *cool* in (6), and so on. Some consist of two words: *incredibly nice* in (5), *some candy* in (4), and *hot coffee* in (7). Another one consists of three words: *in the morning* in (7). Finally, *the teachers at South High* in (6) consists of five words! You will see even longer phrases in this chapter! Most of the phrases above are {NPs}, one is an {AdjP} (*cool* in (6)), one is an {AdvP} (*incredibly* in (5)), and two are {PPs} (*In the morning* in (7) and *after class* in (8)). If you're somewhat unsure about any of this so far (which we hope you're not!), then you'll want to review the previous chapters before you move on.

Reserving the label **phrase** exclusively for word groups that are two words or longer would mean that a one-word phrase would not be considered a phrase. This would result in cumbersome formulations such as "Nouns and noun phrases can function as subjects" or "Adjectives and Adjective Phrases can function as premodifiers" when talking about both one-word and multi-word phrases. Additionally, the main difference between word classes such as nouns, adverbs, and adjectives and phrases such as {NPs}, {AdvPs}, and {AdjPs} is that phrases—not words—are

> **Phrases**
> - May consist of just one word, or multiple words
> - A grouping of words that is closely related

what take on functions in a larger phrase, clause, or sentence; thus, the word class of the most important word in the phrase determines the phrase type.

10.2 Noun Phrase {NP}

10.2.1 Noun Phrase {NP}—Form

Earlier in this book, you learned that {NPs} can be made up of {DET} + {ADJ+} + N. We briefly review some basic information about {NPs} before we expand this initial structure so that we can account for words that belong to the {NP} but come *after* the noun. This internal phrase structure for {NPs} holds for all dialects of English. Remember the one basic and easy test to figure out which words form a constituent is the one-word replacement test: Because it is so important to figure out which words all belong to an {NP}, especially when you are looking at even longer {NPs}, here are two examples:

(9)   *The cute cats*   chase   *the tiny mouse.* (sE)

(9a)   *They*   chase   *it.* (sE)

(10)   I had like, three weeks that I had came out of *the hospital.*[5] (ChE)

(10a)   *it*

> **Exercise 1**
>
> Rewrite the sentences by replacing as many words as you can with pronouns such as *I, you, he/she/it, we, you, they* or *something* or *someone* (the first sentence has been done as an example). This also works with one-word time and place references such as *there* and *then*.
>
> a) Many athletes stretch their muscles after every workout. (sE)
>   *They stretch them then.* Many athletes = They; their muscles = them; every workout = it; after every workout = then;
> b) The basketball players won the very important game. (sE)
> c) Gas is pretty expensive anymore.[6] (ME)

d) The most talented player was named the tournament's MVP. (sE)

e) The clever students were planning their linguistic projects carefully. (sE)

f) The cats are more funnier than the dogs. (AE & other dialects)

g) We was at Lisa's house last night.[7] (AAE)

h) I don't think I have any grants you might could apply for.[8] (SAE)

Now that you've refreshed your knowledge of how to test for which words belong to a given phrase, it's time to look inside the phrase. The **deletion test** identifies which word is the most important one in a phrase: the word that cannot be deleted without making the phrase/sentence ungrammatical is the **head** word. We can test this ourselves:

(9b) *The cute cats* chase the tiny mouse. (sE)

(9c) *(The) cats* chase the tiny mouse. (sE)

(9d) **The cute* chase the tiny mouse. (sE)

(9e) **The* chase the tiny mouse. (sE)

(9f) **Cute* chase the tiny mouse. (sE)

> **Head of a phrase**
>
> - The most important word of a phrase
> - The one you cannot delete and still have a grammatical structure

Clearly, we can cut either *the* or *cute* or both *the* and *cute* (as in (9c)), but when we cut *cats*, ungrammatical sentences are the result (see (9d)–(9f)). This means that *cats* is the most important word in the phrase *the cute cats*. The phrase is about the *cats*, after all, not about the adjective *cute* or the determiner *the*. *Cats* is the head word, and because the word *cats* is a noun, the entire phrase is an {NP}. Now, we've been using the one-word replacement test to figure out which words belong together to form an {NP}. You might be wondering what kind of phrases pronouns such as *they* or *I* form in the following examples:

(9g) *They* chase the tiny mouse. (sE)

(11) *I* had came out of *it*.[9] (ChE)

(12) *We* was at Lisa's house last night.[10] (AAE)

Each of the italicized pronouns is the head of its own {NP}. In addition to nouns, pronouns can also function as heads in an {NP}. Remember that pronouns are noun-y, since the main work they do is replace nouns (but remember those dependent pronouns that function as determiners from Chapter 9!).

10.2.1.1 Premodifiers

Let's go back to the following sentence one more time. In addition to *The cute cats*, the clause has another {NP} within it:

(9h)   The cute cats chase the tiny mouse. (sE)

The {NP} *the tiny mouse* follows the identical structure:

       the + tiny + mouse
       DET   ADJ   N

Mouse is, like *cats* in the other {NP}, the head because it cannot be deleted without making the {NP} ungrammatical: *the tiny is incomplete.

So far, we have encountered {NPs} that have the headword and another word before it: *cute* and *tiny*. These two adjectives **modify** the headword, that is, they describe the headword. And they both occur **prior** to the head, not after it. If we move these kinds of modifiers after the headword as in (9j), the structure becomes ungrammatical:

(9i)   The cute cat

(9j)   *The cat cute

Because these adjectives occur prior to the headword, that is, they are in **pre** position, they are called *premodifiers* (**PREs**). You know from Chapter 4 that adjectives often function in these slots as premodifiers. Here are a few more examples (this structure applies to all dialects!):

> **Premodifiers (PREs)**
>
> - Placed prior to the head within a phrase
> - {NPs} can have multiple PREs

(13)   extremely *hungry* dogs

(14)   many *angry* customers

(15)   the *helpful* teachers

(16)   an incredibly *outspoken* candidate

(17)   our *affordable* insurance

Chart 1 represents the (so-far) three-part structure of {NPs}:

DET	Premodifier	HEAD
	extremely hungry	dogs
many	angry	customers
the	helpful	teachers
an	incredibly outspoken	candidate
our	affordable	insurance

Chart 1 {NP}-structure based on Det + Premodifier + Head

What about expanded phrases such as the ones below?

(13a)   *extremely hungry, impatient* dogs

(14a) many *angry, annoyed* customers

(15a) the *helpful, experienced, empathetic, talented* teachers

It is possible to have more than one PRE in {NPs}. Chart 2 represents this structure. Each of the words prior to the head (and after the determiner) adds more information about the head, so each of them is a PRE.

DET	PRE 1	PRE 2	PRE 3	PRE 4	HEAD
	extremely hungry	impatient			dogs
many	angry	annoyed			customers
the	helpful	experienced	empathetic	talented	teachers

Chart 2 {NP}-structure with multiple PREs

The PRE 1 *extremely hungry* consists of two words and you may be wondering why *extremely* isn't its own PRE. Well, it's not that the head *dog* is *extremely*; it's that the dog is *extremely hungry*, so *extremely* actually premodifies the adjective *hungry* (how hungry?—extremely!). We'll get to the internal structure of {AdjPs} soon!

Of course, the number of PREs in {NPs} is not limited to just four; you can theoretically have an infinite number of PREs. Can you come up with an {NP} that contains more than four PREs?

10.2.1.2 Postmodifiers

What about words that occur **after** the head and still belong to that same {NP}? Using the one-word replacement test, we can determine again precisely which words belong to the phrase and which ones don't:

(18) *The cuddly cats that sleep a lot* are very cute. (sE)

(18a) *They* are very cute.

If we only replace a portion of this long {NP} with the pronoun *they*, we end up with ungrammatical sentences such as this one:

(18b) The ~~cuddly~~ cats that sleep a lot are very cute. (sE)

(18c) *The **they** cats that sleep a lot are very cute.

Again, only when we replace the entire {NP} with the pronoun *they* do we get a grammatically correct sentence:

(18d) ~~The cuddly cats that sleep a lot~~ are very cute. (sE)

(18e) *They* are very cute.

This shows that additional words after the head in an {NP} can belong to that {NP}. When words that follow the head further describe (i.e., modify) that head, they are called, surprise, **postmodifiers** (or **POST**, for short). So, words that modify prior to the head = premodifier, words that modify after the head = postmodifier; pretty intuitive, right?

Find all pre- and postmodifiers in the following, longer {NPs}! Your first step should be identifying the head in your quest for modifiers!

(19) *Some books about grammar* include *information on dialects.* (sE)

(20) Alls Amy got from Grace was *a box of chocolates.*[11] (ME)

(21) I don't think I have *any grants you might could apply for.*[12] (SAE)

(22) *A tree to decorate* is *my favorite part of the holidays.* (sE)

(23) *The vet examining my cat* is new. (sE)

(24) We Black folks be knowin we got *some unique patterns of language.*[13] (AAE)

Each {NP} above includes modifiers. This is how the {NP} in (24) breaks down:

- *patterns* = head
- *unique* = modifier before the head (i.e., a PRE)
- *of language* = modifier after the head (i.e., a POST)

Here, *of language* specifies which patterns we're talking about: those *of language*. The POST specifies precisely what kind of patterns are being referenced. Same with the POST *about grammar* in (19): it is not just any books, but, rather, it is those books *about grammar* that include information on dialects.

Postmodifier (POSTs)

- Placed after the head within a phrase
- {NPs} can have multiple POSTs

In phrases such as *A tree to decorate* in (22), we also have something that specifies in more detail what kind of tree: one *to decorate*, not just any tree. Same for *the vet examining my cat* in (23): *examining my cat* specifies again which vet is new: the one examining my cat (as opposed to maybe the one who is examining my neighbor's dogs). If you're wondering about these two particular structures—*to decorate* and *examining my cat*—don't worry, we will explain them in more detail in Chapter 14. For now, simply focus on the fact that they modify the {NP}-head.

The one-word replacement test once again confirms that the entire phrase *a box of chocolates* below must be replaced with *it* instead of just one portion of it:

(20a) Alls Amy got from Grace was *a box of chocolates.*[14] (ME)

(20b) Alls Amy got from Grace was   *it.*   (ME)

(20c) *Alls Amy got from Grace was   *it*   *of chocolates.*[15] (ME)

You can see that the pronoun replaces *a box* AND *of chocolates* together; if it replaces just a portion such as only *a box* as we did in (20c), the result is ungrammatical. Based on the examples above, we can establish the basic structure for {NPs}:

NP = DET + PREmodifier + HEAD + POSTmodifier

Many different types of structures can occupy the postmodifier slot. Note, too, that not all the slots in an {NP} must be filled. Only the head must be filled at all times. Break

Foundations of Grammar

down the longer {NPs} in (25) and (26) and the {NP} examples in (27)–(30) into the basic structure. Then, check Chart 3 for the answer.

(25) *The cuddly cats that sleep a lot* are very cute. (sE)
(26) I don't think I have *any grants you might could apply for*.[16] (SAE)
(27) the horse which wins many prizes
(28) the complex structures of noun phrases
(29) the vet to go to
(30) the gregarious person introducing your friend

Chart 3 represents the internal structure of the {NPs} from above:

DET	Premodifier	HEAD	Postmodifier
the	cuddly	cats	that sleep a lot
any		grants	you might could apply for
the		horse	which wins many prizes
the	complex	structures	of noun phrases
the		vet	to go to
the	gregarious	person	introducing your friend

Chart 3 Full {NP}-structure

Exercise 2

Break down each of the italicized {NPs} below by determining which words are in which {NP} slot and fill in the chart accordingly.

a) *Taylor* worked hard to get *the big promotion at work*. (sE)
b) This beat be *the beat for the street*.[17] (AAE)
c) We noticed *the new car that was parked in the driveway* right away. (sE)
d) *Cats* jumped over *lazy dogs lying on the floor*. (sE)
e) Alls I want is *some new shoes*.[18] (ME)
f) *The horses in the barn* whinnied loudly. (sE)
g) I had been fixin' to get *a new bike* for *years* and finally did.[19] (SAE)
h) *The first scientist to discover a cure* will win *a prestigious award*. (sE)

	DET	PRE	HEAD	POST
a)				
a)				
b)				

194

c)	
d)	
d)	
e)	
f)	
g)	
g)	
h)	
h)	

10.2.1.3 When a Noun Modifies Another Noun

So far, all our PREs were adjectives, such as *cute* and *tiny* in *the cute cats* and *the tiny mouse*. What about examples like these:

(31) The park has two *basketball hoop*.[20] (AAE)

(32) I'm fixin' to finish that *budget proposal* today.[21] (SAE)

(33) They took part of the *mummification process*.[22] (ChE)

(34) People live in densely populated *human communities* around the world. (sE)

(35) Ahmed and Hassan have a beloved *house cat*. (sE)

In each example, there are two nouns: *basketball* and *hoop* in (31), *budget* and *proposal* in (32), and so on. Apparently, there are {NPs} where a noun can function as a PRE itself within a larger {NP}. This kind of thing is actually very common in all American English dialects. How do we know which word is the head word? After all, there are two nouns right next to one another. Well, let's see what happens when we delete one of those two nouns (i.e., the deletion test):

(31a) two *basketball* ~~hoop~~ (AAE)

(31b) two ~~basketball~~ *hoop* (AAE)

(32a) that *budget* ~~proposal~~ today (SAE)

(32b) that ~~budget~~ *proposal* today (SAE)

(33a) the *mummification* ~~process~~ (ChE)

(33b) the ~~mummification~~ *process* (ChE)

(34a) densely populated *human* ~~communities~~ around the world. (sE)

(34b) densely populated ~~human~~ *communities* around the world. (sE)

(35a) a beloved *house* ~~cat~~. (sE)

(35b) a beloved ~~house~~ *cat*. (sE)

The noun that modifies the head word can be deleted easily, as this gives us (31b)–(35b), which are all perfectly grammatical and don't change the meaning of the original phrase drastically (we lose some meaning, since the modifiers are gone, but the essential meaning is preserved). This is not the case when we delete the head noun, as that gives us (31a)–(35a). Note that *a beloved house* (35a) is a grammatical structure, but the deletion of *cat* changes the meaning of our original phrase drastically! The same goes for (32a) and (33a)—you could imagine a situation where *I'm fixin' to finish that budget today* and *They took part of the mummification* can work; it's just that the original sentences were about a *proposal* and a *process*, respectively.

Because sometimes, as in *house cat*, *budget proposal*, and *mummification process*, deleting the head word does give us, technically, a grammatically correct sentence, we need another, second, test as a back-up: **the plural test**. It's pretty straightforward and requires you to pluralize the {NP} in question. Here's how it works:

(32c) finish that *budget **proposal*** today (SAE)

(32d) finish *two budget **proposals*** today (SAE)

(32e) *finish *two **budgets** proposal* today (SAE)

The head word, not the modifying noun, is the one that gets the plural -*s* in dialects that have overt pluralizations. If the modifying noun gets the -*s* as in (32e), the structure is ungrammatical. This is how we know that *proposals* is the head in the above example. Let's apply the plural test to the remaining sentences (if the {NP} is already a plural one, you go from plural to singular):

(31c) *two* basketball ***hoop(s)*** (AAE)

(31d) *one* basketball ***hoop***

(31e) **two **basketball(s)** hoop*

(33c) *one* mummification ***process*** (ChE)

(33d) *two* mummification ***processes***

(33e) **two **mummifications** process*

(34c) *many* densely populated human ***communities*** around the world (sE)

(34d) *one* densely populated human ***community***

(34e) **many* densely populated ***humans*** community*

(35c) *a* beloved house ***cat*** (sE)

(35d) *two* beloved house ***cats***

(35e) **two* beloved ***houses*** cat*

Clearly, it is the head word, not the modifier, that is pluralized with a plural -*s* in sE and an optional plural -*s* in dialects such as AAE.

Why not treat the PRE *human* and the PRE *house* and the PRE *basketball* as adjectives, like the other PREs we've already seen, you might ask? *house* and *human* do—after all—describe the head word, just like an adjective, right? Well, not so fast! Yes, it is true that these PREs describe the head word, but other than that, they do not behave at all like adjectives. Remember again our lovely horse-barn sentence from Chapters 3 and 4 *That's a nice horse barn*?

We established in Chapter 4 that *horse* is not an adjective, even though it describes another noun (*barn*). Let's apply evidence for determining a word's class, specifically, evidence for adjectives and nouns. Compare the {NP} in (36) with the one in (37):

(36)   the cute cat

(37)   a horse barn

In (36), *cute* is a PRE and it describes the head *cat*. We can add the premodifier *very* or *extremely* to *cute*, showing us that *cute* is an adjective (remember, adding *very* is something we can add before adjectives!):

(36a)   The *very cute* cat

(36b)   The *extremely cute* cat

Remember that *very* and *extremely* are adverbs, and that adverbs can modify other adverbs, verbs, and adjectives, but not nouns. In the {NP} *a horse barn*, *horse* is a PRE and it describes the head *barn*. However, we cannot add *very* or *extremely* as a premodifier to *horse*:

(37a)   *the *extremely horse* barn

(37b)   *the *very horse* barn

Adding *very* here only works if *very* were to mean "this particular, this specific horse" as in *This very horse that I just saw is gorgeous*. But if *very* is an intensifier as it was in *the very cute cat*, it cannot be used in sentence (37b) above.

And there's more! Remember from Chapter 4 that we can't form the comparative/superlative either as in *the horser barn* or *the horsest barn* like we can with actual adjectives (*cute; cuter; cutest*). This shows us that *horse* is, in fact, not an adjective. Nouns as PREs simply do not behave like adjectives, and so they are not adjectives. This means that we have incontrovertible evidence that you can have a noun functioning as a PRE inside an {NP}.

To recap, the {NP} in English consists of four slots (DET + PRE + HEAD + POST), and other than the head, not all slots must be filled. The label PRE is more general than *ADJ* and allows us to account for the fact that in addition to adjectives, nouns can also occupy this PRE slot. The label POST is similar in that it labels the function within the {NP}, not the specific *form* that can occupy it. You've already seen a variety of *forms* occupy the POST slot, including but not limited to {PPs}.

Exercise 3

Identify all {NPs} in the sentences below. Then, label all DETs, PREs, HEADs, POSTs in each (as applicable).

a) Although he has an extra thumb, Mr. Kitty can't hold a spoon. (sE)

b) Because Fluffy has a mean streak, he chases Norma Jean a lot around the house. (sE)

c) I have a cat whose paws are extremely big. (sE)

d) The newest show on Netflix is very popular. (sE)

e) After the show, viewers frequently continue to watch entertaining movies on TV. (sE)

f) Everybody got in the middle of the street.[23] (ChE)

g) I met them four mile down the road.[24] (AAE)

h) [H]e ain't ask you no questions.[25] (AAE)

10.2.2 Noun Phrase {NP}—Functions

10.2.2.1 Functions of {NPs} at the Phrase Level
  A. {NP} as PRE in {NP}

As you saw above, a noun can occur in the PRE-slot within an {NP}. Those nouns are themselves {NPs}:

(38)   The park has *two **basketball** hoop*.[26] (AAE)

This means that the noun *basketball* **first** functions as the head in its own {NP} *basketball*. This {NP} then functions as the PRE in the larger {NP} *two basketball hoops*. This is sometimes confusing. If the {NP} were *two new hoop*, then the adjective *new* would be its own {AdjP}, consisting just of the head *new*, and then this {AdjP} would function as the PRE in the {NP} *two new hoop*. That's exactly how it works when you have an {NP} in the PRE slot of another {NP}!

So, how many {NPs} are in (38)? The answer is three, not two: the {NP} *the park* that functions as the subject, the {NP} *basketball* that functions as the PRE in the larger {NP} *two basketball hoop*, which in turn functions as the direct object.

  B. {NP} as Object of the Preposition in {PP}

Prepositions lead {PPs}, and they own the {NP} that follows inside that {PP}. Put differently, an {NP} can function as the **object of the preposition** within a {PP}. Here are some examples. The bold portions are the {NPs}, the italicized portions the entire {PPs}:

(39)   Here's you a piece *of **pizza***.[27] (SAE)

(40)   The dog needs scratched *for **an hour***.[28] (ME)

(41)   He's smiling *to **the cat***.[29] (ChE)

10.2.2.2 Functions of {NPs} at the Sentence Level
Nouns can be a part of the following syntactic slots: Subject, Subject Complement, Direct Object, Indirect Object, and Object Complement. We'll review this information and add

two more functions for {NPs}: That of Adverbial and Adverbial Complement. Consult Chapter 3 for a basic refresher on some of these functions but also stay tuned for Chapter 11, where we do a deep dive into sentence-level functions and sentence patterns as such. Here is a quick overview for each function (the italicized portion in each example is the {NP}):

A. {NP} as Subject
    (42)   *Scary movies on the internet* are easy to find. (sE)

    (43)   *Your phone bill* be high.[30] (AAE)

B. {NP} as Direct Object
    (44)   He's a-gonna try *it*.[31] (AE/OE)

    (45)   Some books about grammar include *information on dialects*. (sE)

C. {NP} as Indirect Object
    (46)   That don't give *her* no money.[32] (AAE)

    (47)   The presidential candidate gave *the press* several riveting interviews. (sE)

D. {NP} as Subject Complement
    (48)   She *a chairwoman*.[33] (AAE)

    (49)   My sister is *an engineer*. (sE)

E. {NP} as Object Complement
    (50)   We considered Sarah *a genius*. (sE)

    (51)   I've call her *my sister*.[34] (AAE)

F. {NP} as Adverbial
    (52)   I was just telling people *last night*, they was talking about how ....[35] (AAE)

    (53)   *Last year*, we adopted two new cats. (sE)

G. {NP} as Adverbial Complement
    (54)   The period to get the cats used to each other lasted *three hours*. (sE)

    (55)   The flowerbed goes *all the way around the porch*. (sE)

Adverbials (As) and Adverbial Complements (ACs) can seem tricky at first glance. The difference between an A ((52) and (53)) and an AC ((54) and (55)) is that an A is *not* necessary to complete the sentence while an AC is. This means that when we delete *last year* in (53), a grammatically correct sentence remains (see (53a)), but if we delete *three hours* in (54), the result is an ungrammatical sentence:

    (53a)   We adopted two new cats. (sE)

    (54a)   *The period to get the cats used to each other lasted. (sE)

Here are two more examples:

(56) Don't he live *next door*?³⁶ (AAE)

(57) We found the cats *next door*. (sE)

In (56), if we delete *next door*, the meaning is drastically changed from *where* the person lives to the person simply *living*, as in *existing/being alive*. Because of this, *next door* in (56) is an AC. In (57), in contrast, we can delete *next door*, and because it's optional, it's an A.

10.3 Adjective Phrase {AdjP}

10.3.1 Adjective Phrase {AdjP}—Form

As always, let's start with some data! Pay attention to the italicized portions. Which words are the heads of the phrases and what's the lexical category of each?

(58) He could talk *smart*.³⁷ (ChE)

(59) The cats find their owners *lovable*. (sE)

(60) She *smart*.³⁸ (AAE)

(61) I had been fixin' to get a *new* bike for years and finally did.³⁹ (SAE)

(62) The drop-off in performance was *quite precipitous*. (sE)

(63) The students are *extremely nice*. (sE)

(64) The carryout food made me *unbelievably sick*. (sE)

In (58)–(61), the italicized portion consists just one word, an adjective. In (62)–(64), it's two words: an adjective and another word prior to it. When there is more than one word, we can use the **deletion test** to determine which of the two words is more important:

(62a) The drop-off in performance was ~~quite~~ *precipitous*. (sE)

(62b) *The drop-off in performance was *quite* ~~precipitous~~. (sE)

Here, *precipitous* is clearly the more important of the two italicized words. After all, it's not that the **drop-off was quite*; no, *the drop-off was precipitous*. Because deleting *precipitous* results in an ungrammatical structure, we know that it is required, and since only head words are—minimally—required in a phrase, it must be our head word. Since *precipitous* modifies the noun *drop-off*, it is an adjective, which means the entire phrase is an {AdjP}. When you only have one word in the {AdjP}, that word functions as the head. Our examples include several intensifying adverbs in the PRE slot in {AdjPs}, including *quite*, *extremely*, and *unbelievably*. In fact, you could add *very* to each of the {AdjPs} that don't have a PRE already! *very* and *extremely* are particularly common PREs in {AdjPs}!

{AdjPs}, like {NPs}, can be expanded with a postmodifier (the head is bolded below). Note that *happy for to go* in (67) is a dialect construction mostly used in southern regions, including the Ozarks and Smoky Mountains. This structure would work differently in sE (in sE, you'd need to add something like a pronoun, as in *Fifi was happy for you to go*).⁴⁰

(65) The journalists were *extremely **tired** of the candidates*. (sE)

(66) The friends are **excited** to go dancing. (sE)

(67) Fifi was **happy** for to go.[41] (SAE)

Rather than the one-word replacement test we used to identify what belongs to the {NP}, we use the question test to identify where an {AdjP} starts and ends. Compare the two question-answer pairs below (the second one will be an ungrammatical question):

(65a) Q: The journalists are what?—A: *extremely tired of the candidates.*

(65b) Q: *The journalists are what *of the candidates*?—A: *extremely tired.*

(66a) Q: The friends are what?—A: *excited to go dancing.*

(66b) Q: *The friends are what *to go dancing*?—A: *very excited.*

(67a) Q: Fifi was what?—A: *happy for to go.*

(67b) Q: *Fifi was what *for to go*?—A: *happy.*

In (65b), (66b), and (67b), the portion that together forms an {AdjP} is divided with one portion being included in the question and the rest of the portion being included in the answer. Both portions need to be part of the answer for the test to work, as is shown in (65a), (66a), and (67a). This illustrates that *of the candidates*, *to go dancing*, and *for to go* are closely connected to the head, and as such belong in the respective {AdjP} rather than functioning as their own constituents outside of the {AdjPs}. Chart 4 illustrates the structure of the {AdjPs} in the last three examples as well as some of the {AdjPs} from earlier.

Premodifier	HEAD	Postmodifier
extremely	tired	of the candidates
	excited	to go dancing
	happy	for to go
quite	precipitous	
extremely	nice	
	smart	
unbelievably	sick	
	new	

Chart 4 {AdjP} structure

Exercise 4

Find all {AdjPs} in the sentences below. Then, identify all PREs, HEADs, POSTs (as applicable). There might be more than one {AdjP} in a sentence.

a) Although he has an extra thumb, Mr. Kitty can't hold even the tiniest spoon. (sE)

b) Because our ridiculously adorable cat Fluffy has an unbelievably tremendously mean streak, he chases Norma Jean a lot around the house. (sE)

c) The cops had went to my super comfortable house.⁴² (ChE)
d) Alejandra has a cat whose paws are extremely big. (sE)
e) The newest show on Netflix is very popular. (sE)
f) This will be particularly important once you're done the gorgeous tattoo and need to leave the shop.⁴³ (ECE)
g) The audience was exceedingly eager to watch the show. (sE)
h) I'm ready for to fade.⁴⁴ (SAE)

10.3.2 Adjective Phrase {AdjP}—Functions

10.3.2.1 Function of {AdjPs} at the Phrase Level: PRE in {NP}

You can probably guess by now that the function of an {AdjP} as a PRE within an {NP} is probably the most common function of an {AdjP} at the phrase level.

(68) *extremely hungry* dogs

(69) many *angry* customers

(70) the *incredibly helpful* teachers

(71) the *cuddly* cats

(72) the *talented* horses

(73) the *complex* structures

(74) a *very delightful* evening

Once again, you can see that {AdjPs} often consist of just the head, or of a PRE + head. You can also see that phrases are embedded within other phrases: The {AdjP} *cuddly* is embedded in the {NP} *the cuddly cats*. The {AdjP} *extremely hungry* is embedded in the {NP} *extremely hungry dogs*. We can represent this embedded structure via brackets with superscript phrase labels:

(68a) [[extremely hungry]_AdjP dogs]_NP

(71a) [the [cuddly]_AdjP cats]_NP

The embedded {AdjP} *extremely hungry* functions as the PRE in the {NP} *extremely hungry dogs*, and the embedded {AdjP} *cuddly* functions as the PRE in the {NP} *the cuddly cats*. Additionally, the noun (*dogs, cats*) functions as the head in each {NP}. For another way to visually represent both form and function for phrases, check out the companion website.

10.3.2.2 Functions of {AdjPs} at the Sentence Level: Subject Complement and Object Complement

When the {AdjP} comes after a linking verb (which are most commonly a form of *be* as well as verbs such as *seem, become,* and *appear*) in sE and other dialects, and when the

{AdjP} comes right after the subject of a sentence in AAE/ChE, the {AdjP} functions as a **Subject Complement** (SC).

(75) She *smart*.[45] (AAE)

(76) The students are *extremely nice*. (sE)

(77) The teacher is *funny*. (sE)

(78) Fifi was *happy for to go*.[46] (SAE)

An {AdjP} can also function as an **Object Complement** (OC). For this function, {AdjPs} come after a direct object and are necessary to make the sentence complete:

(79) The carryout food made Hassan *unbelievably sick*. (sE)

(80) The cats find their owners *lovable*. (sE)

Remember that we'll focus on sentence patterns in more detail in the next chapter. For now, simply take note of these two sentence-level functions of {AdjPs}.

> **Functions of {AdjP}**
> - PRE in {NP} (phrase-level)
> - Subject Complement (sentence-level)
> - Object Complement (sentence-level)

10.4 Adverb Phrase {AdvP}

10.4.1 Adverb Phrase {AdvP}—Form

We have some good news: The structure of {AdvPs} is the same as that of {AdjPs} and {NPs}: PRE, head, and POST. You've already encountered several {AdvPs} embedded in {AdjPs} throughout this chapter, such as *extremely* in *extremely hungry*, where *extremely* is the PRE in the larger {AdjP}. The form of this PRE is itself an {AdvP}. As an {AdvP}, *extremely* consists of just the head.

Let's look at a few more {AdvPs} that include PREs and/or POSTs. The head is bolded in each:

(81) The furry kitten purrs *very **loudly** indeed*. (sE)

(82) I'll hum *more **louder***.[47] (AE/AAE)

(83) He runs *so **funnily***. (sE)

(84) She runs ***quickly** enough*. (sE)

Let's establish again that all the bolded portions are one phrase. You guessed it! Question test!

(81a) Q: The furry kitten purrs how?—A: *very loudly indeed*

(82a) Q: I'll hum how?—A: *more louder*

(83a) Q: He runs how?—A: *so funnily*

(84a) Q: She runs how?—A: *quickly enough*

Once again, you won't be able to delete the head (bolded above) because doing so would result in the following ungrammatical structures:

(81b)   *The furry kitten purrs *very* ~~loudly~~ *indeed*.

(82b)   *I'll hum *more* ~~louder~~.

(83b)   *He runs *so* ~~funnily~~.

(84b)   *She runs ~~quickly~~ *enough*.

Note that *I'll hum more* (82b) is a grammatical sentence, but only if we let the meaning change drastically compared to the original sentence *I'll hum more louder*. *I'll hum more* is no longer about loudness, but about how much the person hums. In the same vein, *She runs enough* (84b) is a grammatical sentence but—again—its meaning is drastically different from the original sentence *She runs quickly enough*. *She runs enough* is no longer about her speed but about the amount she's running.

How do we know the heads of these phrases are adverbs to begin with? Easy: they all describe how the action expressed via the verb is being done, which is illustrated in the questions (81a)–(84a). Keep in mind that adverbs can also modify adjectives and other adverbs. We'll get to that in the section on functions. Chart 5 visualizes the internal structure of the {AdvPs} from above.

PRE	HEAD	POST
very	loudly	indeed
so	funnily	
more	louder	
	quickly	enough

Chart 5 {AdvP}—full structure

Exercise 5

Find all complete {AdvPs} in the sentences below. Then, label all PREs, HEADs, and POSTs. There might be more than one {AdvP} in a sentence.

a) These were expensive when they barely came out.[48] (ChE)

b) Rhys rarely spoke about their family. (sE)

c) The movie corresponded loosely to the novel it was based on. (sE)

d) John wasn't a-talkin' loud enough to hear.[49] (AE)

e) She was just standin' quietly a-hollerin'.[50] (AE)

f) She practiced her skills daily. (sE)

g) This will be particularly important once you're done the tattoo and need to leave the shop.[51] (ECE)

h) You stay in your office too late anymore.[52] (ME)

10.4.2 Adverb Phrase {AdvP}—Functions

10.4.2.1 Functions of {AdvPs} at the Phrase Level

The {AdvP} can function as a PRE inside another phrase, either inside a larger {AdvP} or inside an {AdjP}. You've seen many, many examples of these two {AdvP}-functions, so we limit ourselves to a handful of examples here.

    A. {AdvP} as PRE inside an {AdvP}

We've bolded the {AdvP} in each sentence that functions as the PRE below:

(85)   She snores **extremely** *quietly*. (sE)

(86)   They run **so** *funnily*. (sE)

The {AdvP} *extremely* functions as the PRE in the bigger {AdvP} *extremely quietly* in (85). The same applies to (86): the {AdvP} *so* functions as the PRE in the bigger {AdvP} *so funnily*. We can, again, represent this via brackets:

(85a)   She snores [[extremely]$_{AdvP}$ quietly]$_{AdvP'}$ (sE)

(86a)   They run [[so]$_{AdvP}$ funnily]$_{AdvP'}$ (sE)

    B. {AdvP} as PRE inside an {AdjP}

When an {AdvP} is embedded in an {AdjP}, it functions as the PRE:

(87)   The course is *super important*. (sE)

(88)   *extremely hungry* dogs

(89)   They *very friendly*.[53] (AAE)

In (87), *important* is the head of the {AdjP}, and the {AdvP} *super* functions as the PRE within that {AdjP}. In (88), the {AdvP} *extremely* functions as a PRE within the {AdjP} *extremely hungry*, and in (89), the {AdvP} *very* in *very friendly* functions as the PRE within that bigger {AdjP}. We can again represent this visually as follows:

(87a)   The course is [[super]$_{AdvP}$ important]$_{AdjP'}$ (sE)

(88a)   [[extremely]$_{AdvP}$ hungry]$_{AdjP}$ dogs

(89a)   They [[very]$_{AdvP}$ friendly]$_{AdjP'}$[54] (AAE)

Before we move on, let's visualize how this embedding works in a bit more detail by breaking down this larger {NP} that you've already seen earlier (Figure 10.1):

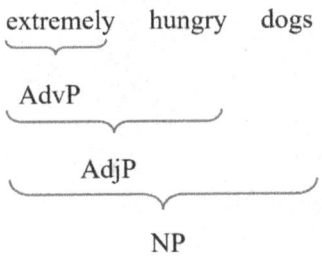

Figure 10.1 {NP} Dogs.

Foundations of Grammar

What this illustrates is the following:

- The {AdvP} *extremely* modifies *hungry* and as such functions as a PRE in the {AdjP} *extremely hungry*.
- That entire {AdjP} modifies *dogs* and as such functions as the PRE in the overall {NP} *extremely hungry dogs*.

This is why it is important to keep function and form strictly separate. You can see now that phrases are hierarchical chunks, with other phrases embedded inside. Words make up phrases and those phrases can function as PREs or POSTs in other phrases, and so on. Remember the **grammatical hierarchy** from Chapter 2? No? Here it is again (Figure 10.2):

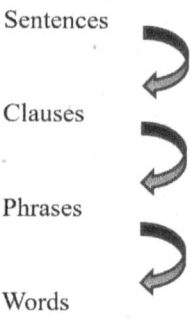

Figure 10.2 Grammatical Hierarchy.

Words make up phrases, phrases make up clauses, and clauses make up sentences. We have climbed up to the second wrung—phrases—just now!

10.4.2.2 Function of {AdvPs} at the Sentence Level
In the examples provided in Section 10.4.1, each {AdvP} takes on the function of **adverbial** in the sentence. We reproduce some of them here, with {AdvPs} italicized, and add two more:

(81c) The furry kitten purrs *very loudly indeed*. (sE)
(82c) I'll hum *more louder*.[55] (AE/AAE)
(83c) They run *so funnily*. (sE)
(84c) She runs *quickly enough*. (sE)
(90) We finna leave out of here *early*.[56] (SAE/AAE)
(91) I had been fixin' to get a new bike for years and *finally* did.[57] (SAE)

When an {AdvP} functions as an adverbial, this means that the {AdvP} can be left out of the sentence without resulting in an ungrammatical sentence; it is optional in its entirety:

> **Functions of {AdvP}**
> - Adverbials (sentence-level)
> - PRE in {AdjP} (phrase-level)
> - PRE in {AdvP} (phrase-level)

(81d) The furry kitten purrs ~~very loudly indeed~~. (sE)

(82d) I'll hum ~~more louder~~.[58] (AE/AAE)

(83d) They run ~~so funnily~~. (sE)

(84d) She runs ~~quickly enough~~. (sE)

(90a) We finna leave out of here ~~early~~.[59] (SAE/AAE)

(91a) I had been fixin' to get a new bike for years and ~~finally~~ did.[60] (SAE)

10.5 Prepositional Phrase {PP}

10.5.1 Prepositional Phrase {PP}—Form

Prepositional phrases are similar and a bit different from the phrases you've encountered so far. Like the other phrases, they include a head (the preposition), but in contrast to the other phrases, what comes after the head is not called a postmodifier, but the **Object of the Preposition (OP)**. Another term commonly used for the OP is **prepositional complement (PC)**. Remember how a subject complement completes the subject? Well, a PC completes the {PP} rather than modifying it like postmodifiers do. Both terms—OP and PC—convey the close relationship between the head (the preposition) and the rest of the {PP}.

Let's look at a few {PPs}. The phrase is italicized, and the head is bolded.

(92) LeBron finished the homework ***after*** *class.* (sE)

(93) She was a-goin' ***to*** *the show.*[61] (AE)

(94) Yegor scored ***in*** *time.* (sE)

(95) This machine is ***for*** *to drill with.*[62] (SAE)

(96) Yesterday we play another team ***for*** *the championship.*[63] (AAE)

(97) The cookie ***on*** *the table* is mine! (sE)

(98) He's smiling ***to*** *the cat.*[64] (ChE)

(99) He's pointing ***from*** *the cat.*[65] (ChE)

In each example, the head (the preposition) is followed by the PC. The PC almost always is an {NP}, which means that when you have a {PP}, you'll always have another phrase embedded in it:

(96a) Yesterday we play another team [***for*** [*the championship*]$_{NP}$]$_{PP}$.[66] (AAE)

(97a) The cookie [***on*** [*the table*]$_{NP}$]$_{PP}$ is mine! (sE)

Like other phrases, {PPs} can include a premodifier. Below, we've added a PRE (*right* in both (92a) and (93a), *just* in (94a)) right before the head to three of the examples from above (did you notice we just used a PRE before a preposition right here in this very sentence: *right before the head?*):

(92a)   LeBron finished the homework **right** *after class.* (sE)

(93a)   She was a-goin' **right** *to the show.*[67] (AE)

(94a)   Yegor scored **just** *in time.* (sE)

Just like the PRE *extremely* modifies the headword *hungry* in the {AdjP} *extremely hungry*, so do the PREs *right* and *just* modify the heads of their {PPs}: not *after class*, but *RIGHT after class*; not *in time*, but *JUST in time*. The PRE gives a tiny bit more info about that headword, just like *extremely* gives more information about the headword *hungry* in *extremely hungry*. If you're not sure if the PRE really does belong to the {PP}, you can use the question test to isolate this constituent. Compare the sentence pairs below (the second one is always an ungrammatical question):

(92b)   Q: When did LeBron finish the homework?—A: *right after class.*

(92c)   Q: *When did LeBron finish the homework *right*?—A: *after class.*

(93b)   Q: Where was she a-goin'?—A: *right to the show.*

(93c)   Q: *Where was she a-goin' *right*?—A: *to the show.*

(94b)   Q: When did Yegor score?—*just in time.*

(94c)   Q: *When did Yegor score *just*?—*in time.*

This shows you that the *right* belongs to the {PP} for both (92a) and (93a) and not to some other constituent of the sentence, and that *just* belongs to the {PP} in (94a). Chart 6 illustrates the structure for {PPs}.

PRE	HEAD	PC
right	after	class
	on	the bed
just	in	time
	of	this music
	on	the table

Chart 6 {PP}—full structure

We have used the question-test quite a bit in this chapter to figure out which words constitute constituents, but remember, there are more tests! Remember the movement test? When we can move a group of words together as one chunk to elsewhere in the sentence, then we know that those words function together, that they are a constituent. Let's try this with some of the {PPs}.

(100) We're really supposed to get out of here *on June*.⁶⁸ (ChE)

(100a) *On June*, we're really supposed to get out of here.

(101) The kitten sleeps *on the bed*. (sE)

(101a) *On the bed*, the kitten sleeps.

(102) Yesterday we play another team *for the championship*.⁶⁹ (AAE)

(102a) Yesterday, *for the championship*, we play another team.

You can move the entire {PP} to a different location in the sentence, which is evidence that the words in the {PP} all belong together. This test doesn't work for all {PPs}; it depends on the function it plays in the sentence (more on that right after the next exercise).

Exercise 6

Identify the {PPs} by performing the movement test. Identify the head, PC, and any PREs (if included).

a) Right after the game, we went out to celebrate. (sE)

b) He's pointing from the cat.⁷⁰ (ChE)

c) We planned to meet right by the library. (sE)

d) I said I would call by noon. (sE)

e) I ain't got no friends at this school.⁷¹ (AAE)

f) The house was built by my grandfather. (sE)

g) What all did you get for Christmas?⁷² (ME)

h) We are moving toward the semester's end. (sE)

10.5.2 Prepositional Phrase {PP}—Functions

10.5.2.1 Functions of {PPs} at the Phrase Level

The {PP} can function as a POST inside another phrase—either inside an {NP} or inside an {AdjP}. When it functions as a POST within another phrase, it's **not** freely movable to another location in the sentence, in contrast to the examples you saw in the previous section.

A. {PP} as POST inside an {NP}

You've encountered many {PPs} as POSTs within {NPs} in the section on {NPs} earlier in this chapter. Here are just three examples:

(103) The cookie *on the table* is mine! (sE)

(104) We found a cat *behind the couch*. (sE)

(105) They bought gifts *for the neighbors*. (sE)

Bracketing can be a great visual aid to represent the embeddedness of phrases:

(103a) [The cookie [*on the table*]$_{PP}$]$_{NP}$ is mine! (sE)

(104a) We found [a cat [*behind the couch*] $_{PP}$]$_{NP}$. (sE)

(105a) They bought [gifts [*for the neighbors*] $_{PP}$]$_{NP}$. (sE)

In each example, the {PP}, as a POST within an {NP}, specifies exactly which cookie is, which cat is, or which gift is being referenced. And of course, in each {PP}, we have another embedded {NP} (which we didn't bracket for now)! Try using the question test on your own to isolate the entire {NPs}!

B. {PP} as POST inside an {AdjP}

You've also encountered many {PPs} as POSTs within {AdjPs} in the section on {AdjPs} earlier in this chapter. Here are some more examples:

(106) I am tired *of this music*. (sE)

(107) They are excited *about the candidates*. (sE)

(108) Latoya is suspicious *of the calm weather*. (sE)

(109) You are happy *for her*. (sE)

In each example, the {PP}, as a POST within an {AdjP}, specifies exactly what someone is tired of, excited about, suspicious of, and happy for. In each {PP}, we of course have an additional embedded {NP}, and in *of the calm weather*, that embedded {NP} even has its own embedded {AdjP}. Can you identify which word that embedded {AdjP} is?

Let's bracket the {AdjPs} and embedded {PPs}:

(106a) I am [tired [*of this music*]$_{PP}$]$_{AdjP}$ (sE)

(107a) They are [excited [*about the candidates*]$_{PP}$]$_{AdjP}$ (sE)

(108a) Latoya is [suspicious [*of the calm weather*]$_{PP}$]$_{AdjP}$ (sE)

(109a) You are [happy [*for her*]$_{PP}$]$_{AdjP}$ (sE)

10.5.2.2 Functions of {PPs} at the Sentence Level

{PPs} can also take on sentence-level functions: Adverbial, SC, and OC. The **adverbial** function is likely the most common one, and we limit our discussion to adverbials here. The {PP} can take on this function across all English dialects. Here are some examples. The {PPs} functioning as adverbials are italicized.

(110) LeBron finished the homework *right after class*. (sE)

(111) We're really supposed to get out of here *on June*.[73] (ChE)

(112) The kitten sleeps *on the bed*. (sE)

(113) Yegor scored *just in time*. (sE)

These italicized {PPs} are the ones that we can move around (Section 10.5.1). We could also leave them off entirely and still have grammatically correct sentences.

Just like with the adverbials that are in the form of {AdvPs} in Section 10.4.1, we can target the constituent that functions as the adverbial with a *wh*-question, such as *When did LeBron finish the homework?* for (110) and *Where did the kitten sleep?* for (112) and so on.

Functions of {PP}

- POST in {NP} (phrase-level)
- POST in {AdjP} (phase-level)
- Adverbials (sentence-level)
- SC (sentence-level)
- OC (sentence-level)

10.6 An Intermezzo: A Very Long {NP}

Now that we have covered the main phrase types with the exception of {VPs}, let's have some fun with this and break down one very, very long {NP} that has embedded in it {AdvPs}, {AdjPs}, and {PPs}:

(114) An unbelievably adorable kitten on the pillow behind the couch

Can you draw a picture of what you're envisioning? Where is the pillow, where is the kitten, and where is the couch? Now, the picture you likely have drawn includes a couch. Behind the couch is a pillow and on top of that pillow is the cat.

Here's a visual of the embedding that is going on in the phrase (HEAD is bolded) (Figure 10.3):

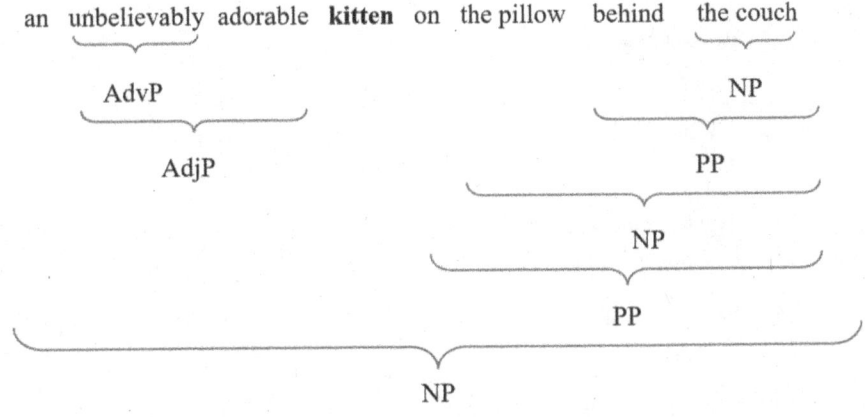

Figure 10.3 Embedded Phrases.

Foundations of Grammar

10.7 Verb Phrase {VP}

The {VP} is a little different from the other phrases. No more PRE, HEAD, or POST! What is allowed in the {VP} are main verbs, regular auxiliaries, and modal auxiliaries; sometimes, all three occur simultaneously. The sentences below demonstrate some of the variety of verbs and verb combinations possible in {VPs}. Focus on the italicized {VPs}, with main verbs bolded; additionally, we use the label *mv* for "main verb," "aux" for "auxiliary verb," and "mod" for "modal auxiliary."

(115) I **saw** some girl, she **look** pretty.[74] (ChE)
       mv   *mv*

(116) The fish *is* happy. (sE)
             mv

(117) Our neighbors **called** our house a zoo. (sE)
                   mv

(118) The dog *is **barking**. (sE)
              aux + mv

(119) Yesterday, we *was **conversating** with Mr. B. about the war.[75] (AAE)
                   aux + mv

(120) They *should be **sleeping** in their beds. (sE)
           mod + aux + mv

(121) The apple that the witch *had **gave** Snow White.[76] (ChE)
                              aux + mv

(122) We *had **fed** them already. (sE)
         aux + mv

(123) Blake *might **do** that themselves. (sE)
            mod + mv

(124) I don't think I have any grants you *might could **apply** for.[77] (SAE)
                                         mod 1 + mod 2 + mv

(125) The cats *had been **chased** by the dogs. (sE)
              aux 1 + aux 2 + mv

(126) We *was **taught** that there is no such thing.[78] (AAE)
         aux + mv

(127) My cat *may have been being **examined** while I was on the phone. (sE)
             mod + aux 1 + aux 2 + aux 3 + mv

A {VP} must—minimally—contain a main verb for the phrase to be a {VP} (see (115)–(117)). If a {VP} has more than one verb in it, the main verb is always the last one (see (118)–(127)). If a modal auxiliary and other auxiliaries co-occur, the modal auxiliary comes first (e.g., (124) and (127)). For sE dialects (and most non-sE dialects as well), the underlying rule for the internal structure of {VPs} is as follows:

VP → (modal) + (aux 1) + (aux 2) + (aux 3) + main verb
perfective + progressive + passive + main verb

What this notation means is that a {VP} consists of (the arrow means "consists of")—minimally—the main verb. The other elements are optional, which is indicated by the parentheses. Depending on what exactly we want to communicate (perfective and passive, just passive, progressive, etc.), we choose the respective modal and auxiliary verbs, which is why we have various possible combinations at our disposal. When multiple auxiliaries co-occur, the order is as shown above, with perfective aspect coming first. There can be up to three auxiliaries after the modal; (127) was one such example:

(127a) My cat *may have been being examined* by the vet while I was … (sE)

VP → modal + aux 1 + aux 2 + aux 3 + main verb
may   have   been   being   examined

Alright, so, for sE, the underlying rule for {VPs} is that only one modal can precede the other auxiliaries and the main verb. Now, for SAE and other non-sE dialects, where double modals are possible, the underlying structure, roughly, looks like this:

VP → (modal 1) + (modal 2) + (modal 3) + (aux 1) + (aux 2) + (aux 3) + main verb

Again, the parentheses simply mean that the respective elements are not required for a {VP} to be grammatical, but each could be included in a grammatically correct {VP}. A closer look at one of the examples above, from SAE, shows that they correspond to this underlying rule, making them perfectly grammatical:

(124a) I don't think I have any grants you *might could apply* for.[79] (SAE)

VP → modal 1 + modal 2 + main verb
might   could   apply

And here are two more examples with double modals:

(128) You *may might can get* one right over there at Wicks.[80] (SAE)

VP → modal 1 + modal 2 + modal 3 + main verb
may   might   can   get

(129) We *might can go* up there next Saturday.[81] (SAE)

VP → modal 1 + modal 2 + main verb
might   can   go

Put differently, the reason we can observe double modal constructions at all isn't because someone is making a mistake; rather, someone is producing a linguistic structure based on the underlying grammatical rule for {VPs} for their specific dialect of English!

Exercise 7

Identify the {VPs}. Label the main verb and all auxiliary verbs, including modal auxiliary verbs.

> Example ({VPs} bolded, main verbs underlined):
> We **had been <u>walking</u>** for a while before we saw a car on the road.

a) We start on July.[82] (ChE)
b) She was a-goin' to the show.[83] (AE)
c) Alls Alice brought to the party was bread.[84] (ME)
d) Yesterday we play another team for the championship.[85] (AAE)
e) Many talented soccer players have received competitive offers from multiple teams. (sE)
f) They are leaving on a great adventure; you should go with.[86] (ME)
g) He yelled at John for fixin' to change the plan.[87] (SAE/AAE)
h) We might can go up there next Saturday.[88] (SAE)

Exercise 8

You've already seen these sentences earlier and you were asked to find all {NPs}. This time, find any and all phrases and label them {AdjP}, {AdvP}, {NP}, {PP}, {VP}. If there is a phrase embedded within another phrase, explain the function of the embedded phrase (see example below).

a) Although he has an extra thumb, Mr. Kitty can't hold a spoon. (sE)
   NPs: he, an extra thumb, Mr. Kitty, a spoon
   AdjP: extra (functions as a PRE in the NP)
   VPs: has, can't hold
b) Because Fluffy has a mean streak, he chases Norma Jean a lot around the house. (sE)
c) I have a cat whose paws are extremely big. (sE)
d) The newest show on Netflix is very popular. (sE)
e) After the show, viewers frequently continue to watch entertaining movies on TV. (sE)
f) Everybody got in the middle of the street.[89] (ChE)
g) I met them four mile down the road.[90] (AAE)
h) [H]e ain't ask you no questions.[91] (AAE)

Terminology to Know

Term	Working definition	Example/Illustration
Phrase		
PRE		
HEAD		
POST		
DET		
Prepositional complement		
Embedded phrase		
Function		
Form		
{NP}		
{AdjP}		
{AdvP}		
{PP}		
{VP}		

Chart 7 Key terminology Chapter 10

Notes

1. Anderson, 1839.
2. Christian et al., 1988; cited in Matyiku, 2011a.
3. Huang and McCoy, 2015.
4. Baker-Bell, 2020, p. 43.
5. Fought, 2003, p. 94.
6. Maher and McCoy, 2011.
7. Baker-Bell, 2020, p. 74.
8. Huang, 2011.
9. Based on Fought, 2003, p. 94.
10. Baker-Bell, 2020, p. 74.
11. Wood, 2013.
12. Huang, 2011.
13. Smitherman, 2006, p. 2.
14. Wood, 2013.
15. Based on Wood, 2013.
16. Huang, 2011.
17. Alim, 2004, p. 398, lyric from Busta Rhymes; cited in Zanuttini and Martin, 2017.

18. Wood, 2013.
19. Staub and Zentz, 2017.
20. Reaser et al., 2017a, p. 182.
21. Staub and Zentz, 2017.
22. Bayley, 2012, p. 162.
23. Callahan, 2017.
24. Reaser et al., 2017a, p. 37.
25. McMurtry, 2023, p. 7.
26. Reaser et al., 2017a, p. 182.
27. Wood, 2015.
28. Tenny, 1998, p. 592.
29. Barrón and San Romón, n.d., pp. 30–1; cited in Bayley, 2012, p. 162.
30. Green, 2002, p. 48.
31. Christian et al., 1988; cited in Matyiku, 2011a.
32. Kendall, Fasold et al., 2018 Transcript ID DCA_se2_ag1_f_03_1.
33. Ibid., Transcript ID DCA_se1_ag1_m_04_1.
34. Farrington et al., 2020 Transcript ID ATL_se0_ag1_f_01_1.
35. Kendall, Quartey et al., 2018 Transcript ID DCB_se1_ag2_m_01_1.
36. Ibid., Transcript ID DCA_se2_ag3_m_02_1.
37. Adapted from Fought, 2003, p. 100.
38. Kendall, Quartey et al., 2018 Transcript ID DCB_se2_ag4_f_01_1.
39. Staub and Zentz, 2017.
40. Bayley and Santa Ana, 2004, p. 376.
41. Carroll, 1983; cited in Kaplan, Scruton, and Wood, 2017.
42. Slightly adapted from Fought, 2003, p. 96.
43. Adapted from Wood, 2014.
44. "Mr. Tambourine Man;" cited in Kaplan, Scruton, and Wood, 2017.
45. Kendall, Quartey et al., 2018 Transcript ID DCB_se2_ag4_f_01_1.
46. Carroll, 1983; cited in Kaplan, Scruton, and Wood, 2017.
47. Wood, 2012.
48. Fought, 2003, p. 106.
49. Matyiku, 2011a.
50. Ibid.
51. Adapted from Wood, 2014.
52. Maher and McCoy, 2011.
53. Kendall, Fasold et al., 2018 Transcript ID DCA_se1_ag1_f_03_1.
54. Ibid.
55. Wood, 2012.
56. Staub and Zentz, 2017.
57. Ibid.

58. Wood, 2012.
59. Staub and Zentz, 2017.
60. Ibid.
61. Christian et al., 1988; cited in Matyiku, 2011a.
62. Carroll, 1983; cited in Kaplan, Scruton, and Wood, 2017.
63. Kendall, Fasold et al., 2018 Transcript ID DCA_se1_ag1_m_05_1.
64. Bayley, 2012, p. 162.
65. Ibid.
66. Kendall, Fasold et al., 2018 Transcript ID DCA_se1_ag1_m_05_1.
67. Slightly adapted from Christian et al., 1988; cited in Matyiku, 2011a.
68. Fought, 2003, p. 101.
69. Kendall, Fasold et al., 2018 Transcript ID DCA_se1_ag1_m_05_1.
70. Bayley, 2012, p. 162.
71. Baker-Bell, 2020, p. 74.
72. McCloskey, 2000, p. 58; cited in Lindemann, 2018.
73. Fought, 2003, p. 100.
74. Bayley and Santa Ana, 2004, p. 376.
75. Baker-Bell, 2020, p. 43.
76. Bayley, 2012, p. 163.
77. Huang, 2011.
78. Kendall, Quartey et al., 2018 Transcript ID DCB_se1_ag3_m_02_1.
79. Huang, 2011.
80. Ibid.
81. Ibid.
82. Bayley and Santa Ana, 2004, p. 382.
83. Christian et al., 1988; cited in Matyiku, 2011a.
84. Wood, 2013.
85. Kendall, Fasold et al., 2018 Transcript ID DCA_se1_ag1_m_05_1.
86. Kaplan, 2015.
87. Staub and Zentz, 2017.
88. Huang, 2011.
89. Callahan, 2017.
90. Reaser et al., 2017a, p. 37.
91. McMurtry, 2023, p. 7.

CHAPTER 11
HOW PHRASES STICK TOGETHER: SENTENCE PATTERNS

Overview

Phrases are used to build larger units: clauses and sentences. Some of this will be familiar because you've already learned some things about a verb and its transitivity! After we review how phrases differ from clauses, we move on to identifying sentence patterns based on sentence constituents such as subject, direct object, indirect object, subject complements, and so on. If you need a refresher, go back to Chapter 2 for some fundamentals! Our objectives for this chapter are as follows. You'll be able to

- deepen your understanding of form and function;
- develop your knowledge about syntactic roles of constituents;
- break down sentences into their syntactic sentence patterns; and
- apply tests to confidently identify syntactic functions of constituents.

Pre-reading tasks

1. Write down what you know about constituents and constituent tests by now.
2. Take a look at the sentence below (we asked ChatGPT to create a sentence Gen Z would find funny). Can you identify phrases and the roles they play in the sentence? If you're not sure, try to make several observations!

   After realizing their avocado toast photoshoot didn't go viral, they consoled themselves with a marathon of TikTok dances and ironic memes, questioning their existence while sipping oat milk lattes.[1]

3. Break down the following sentences into their constituents. Can you identify all constituents and label their syntactic function (i.e., the role they play in the sentence)? Don't worry if you're not sure—we'll do a deep dive in this chapter and will come back to these examples throughout the chapter.

   a) The talented athlete won. (sE)

   b) Gas is pretty expensive anymore.[2] (ME)

   c) We was at Lisa's house last night.[3] (AAE)

> d) My dad baked banana bread. (sE)
>
> e) My dad baked his neighbors banana bread. (sE)
>
> f) She look pretty.[4] (ChE)
>
> g) They called us Hotlanta.[5] (AAE)

11.1 Introduction: Revisiting Some of the Basics

11.1.1 Clauses and Phrases

While phrases can consist of just one word (the head of the phrase), phrases often consist of multiple words. Clauses, too, consist of multiple words. What differentiates these two types of multi-word constructions is the presence or absence of a verb: A clause is a group of words that contains a {VP}. A phrase is a structure that does not contain a verb (unless of course we're looking at a {VP}). Chart 1 provides some initial examples of phrases and clauses.

Phrases		Clauses	
(1)	the talented athlete	(5)	The talented athlete *won*. (sE)
(2)	pretty expensive	(6)	Gas *is* pretty expensive anymore.[6] (ME)
(3)	very fast	(7)	The athlete *runs* very fast. (sE)
(4)	at Lisa's house last night	(8)	We *was* at Lisa's house last night.[7] (AAE)

Chart 1 Phrases vs. clauses—initial examples

> **Phrase vs Clause**
>
> - Clause: contains a {VP}
> - Phrase: no {VP} (except when the phrase itself is a {VP})

None of the four phrases in Chart 1 includes a {VP} anywhere. We can use these phrases to construct a clause by adding, minimally, a verb as you can see in example (5). Adding the {VP} *won* to the {NP} *the talented athlete* results in a clause that can stand alone as a complete sentence. Of course, when creating clauses, more than just a {VP} can be added; (6)–(8) illustrate this.

A clause needs a {VP}. Yet, having a {VP} does not guarantee that the group of words can stand on their own as a sentence. As you know, a **dependent clause** cannot stand on its own as a sentence, while an **independent clause** can. All examples in Chart 1 are examples of independent clauses. In this chapter, we focus on sentence patterns for independent clauses; later, we will see that these patterns are also found in dependent clauses.

How Phrases Stick Together: Sentence Patterns

Exercise 1

Phrase or Clause? Label the italicized portions in the examples below as either a phrase or a clause.

a) *The car* raced *down the street*. (sE)

b) *You be doing a class work in class*.[8] (ChE)

c) *Although we business professional*, our goal is to work with underprivileged youth.[9] (AAE)

d) *A few years ago*, I didn't have no confidence.[10] (ChE)

e) Alls Greg and Marsha want to do is kiss each other *when no one else is around*.[11] (ME)

f) The playlist was curated *by a pop music fan*. (sE)

g) Over by the couch we found *two cat toys*. (sE)

h) *When I don't have hockey and I'm done my homework*, I go there and skate.[12] (ECE)

11.1.2 Locating the Subject: Another Test

We know from Chapter 2 that an English sentence requires a subject and a verb, and that in English, subjects come before verbs because English has a relatively fixed word order. In Chapter 2, we introduced you to a variety of tests that help us identify constituents as such (question-test, movement test, and one-word replacement test), and a test that helps you identify subjects (tag-question test), and we've been using them repeatedly throughout the last several chapters! As sentences become more complex, locating the subject can become a little tricky. This is why we start with a brief review of the question test and tag-question test before we show you one more way of identifying subjects—the inversion test.

The **question test** is a test that allows you to identify constituents in general, not just subjects:

(9) A few years ago, I didn't have no confidence.[13] (ChE)

    Q & A: Who didn't have no confidence a few years ago?—I

(10) The car raced down the street. (sE)

    Q & A: What raced down the street?—The car

Now, remember that this test can also isolate non-subject sentence constituents, but since you know that subjects come before verbs, you'll be able to identify *I* and *the car* as the subjects and rule out *no confidence* as the subject (it comes after the verb after all!).

If you're still not sure, then you can rely on the **tag-question test**, which will always identify the subject:

(9a)   A few years ago, I didn't have no confidence.[14] (ChE)

(9b)   A few years ago *I* didn't have no confidence, did *I*?

(11)   Gas is pretty expensive anymore.[15] (ME)

(11a) *Gas* is pretty expensive anymore, isn't *it*?

(12)   Down the road, the traffic light that lost power has flickered back. (sE)

(12a) Down the road, *the traffic light that lost power* has flickered back, hasn't *it*?

> **Tag:** little phrases such as:
> *isn't it?*   *aren't you?*
> *are you?*   *is he?*
> *didn't they?* *did we?*

The pronoun in the added little tag will always refer to the subject. Sometimes, if the subject is a pronoun itself, such as *I*, the pronoun in the tag simply repeats that pronoun. So, if you have a sentence where you find that you can form *who/what*-questions for more than one constituent, then you can add on the tag-test and that will disambiguate which of those two is the subject. Then again, the subject will be the constituent prior to the verb!

The **inversion test** is yet another test that can help identify the subjects of sentences. All you must do is turn a statement into a question, but without adding any additional words to the sentence, such as question words or *dummy do*; instead, you'll be switching the subject and the verb of a sentence:

(13)   **The editor** *is* detail-oriented. (sE)

(13a) *Is* **the editor** detail-oriented? (sE)

(11b) **Gas** *is* pretty expensive anymore.[16] (ME)

(11c) *Is* **gas** pretty expensive anymore? (ME)

Because we flipped the position of the subjects with their verbs to form questions, we know that *the editor* is the subject in (13) and *gas* is the subject in (11b). This is one of the underlying principles of English: One way to form questions is by **inverting** the subject with the verb or auxiliary verb (hence: inversion test). What if the sentence is less straightforward? It still works!

(14)   **It** *was* the detail-oriented editor who worked all day. (sE)

Which is the subject: *it* or *the detail-oriented editor*? Let's do the test!

(14a) *Was* **it** the detail-oriented editor who worked all day? (sE)

Since *it* changed place with *was*, we know that *it* is the subject of our overall sentence, not *the detail-oriented editor*. Let's look at one more example with a longer subject:

(12b) Down the road, **the traffic light that lost power** *has* flickered back. (sE)

(12c) *Has* **the traffic light that lost power** flickered back down the road? (sE)

Once again, the words in bold switched places with the auxiliary verb *has* (remember the auxiliary's superpowers?), and so that's how we know that the bold portion is the subject. An important caveat is in order though: if the {VP} consists of just the main verb and that main verb is something other than a form of *be* (and some limited examples of *have*), this test doesn't work. After all, we can't say *Worked the editor all day?* In those cases, the *dummy do* swoops in so that we can form the question as *Did the editor work all day?* When a form of *have* is the main verb, this test works only sometimes (for some differences between British and American English when it comes to *have*, see the companion website). Despite these limitations, this test works well for sentences that have an auxiliary verb or use a form of *be* as the main verb.

> **Exercise 2**
>
> Find the subject in each sentence. Apply the inversion test to at least four of the examples and pick your test of choice for the remaining ones.
>
> a) The dog was envious of the cat's food. (sE)
> b) The dog and the parrot complained about the cat. (sE)
> c) Today, the dog was sleeping in the cat's basket. (sE)
> d) The dog and cat fought over the basket. (sE)
> e) It was in the apple that the witch had gave Snow White that wasn't poisonous.[17] (ChE)
> f) He was really a-starin' at the picture.[18] (AE)
> g) Yesterday we play another team for the championship.[19] (AAE)
> h) They are leaving on a great adventure; you should go with.[20] (ME)

11.2 Sentence Patterns

We have some good news: While the number of specific sentences we can form is infinite, the number of possible **sentence patterns** in English is quite limited. It is out of this limited number of sentence patterns that we form the infinite number of actual sentences, which is amazing in our view! So, let's get at it.

11.2.1 Subject–Verb (S-V)

The type of verb in **S-V** patterns is called **intransitive** verb, which means that the verb does not select any object. Here are some initial examples (we have italicized the subject):

(15) *Derek* cooked. (sE)
(16) *We* studying.[21] (AAE)
(17) *I* read. (sE)
(18) *He* been chilling.[22] (AAE)

(19) *My dad* baked. (sE)

(20) *The car* needs repaired.²³ (ME)

The verb can be just the main verb, or it can include one or more auxiliary verbs such as *been* in (18) and *needs* in (20). **S-V** type sentences can of course be longer. Identify the complete subject in the somewhat longer sentences below before reading further. We're confident you can do this quite easily now.

(21) My dear friend Frankie had been studying. (sE)

(22) A colleague who had just come back from their break left. (sE)

(23) Mistakes had been made. (sE)

Did you come up with the following?

(21a) [My dear friend Frankie] [had been studying]. (sE)
                     S   V

(22a) [A colleague who had just come back from their break] [left]. (sE)
                             S   V

(23a) [Mistakes] [had been made]. (sE)
                S   V

Note that the subject in (22a) consists of a long {NP}: it has a long POST (*who had just come back from their break*) after its head *colleague*. Even though the sentences are longer, they break down into a pattern that consists of just two constituents: S-V.

One type of variation when it comes to subjects is the **zero subject pronoun**:

(24) I tried that door. (…) I moved the lock. Ø locks from the inside.²⁴ (ChE)

(25) Ø is washing the hair.²⁵ (ChE)

This structure occurs in many American English dialects, especially in conversations. The zero subject pronoun is, however, chiefly associated with ChE. Spanish syntax helps explain where subject pronouns are optional. This means that this particular structure in ChE could be the influence of Spanish. Essentially, as you can see in (24) and (25), the pronoun in subject position is not necessary; instead, it is optional, indicated by the Ø-symbol. This means that there is a tiny exception to the mantra "Minimally, an English sentence must consist of a subject and a verb." An exception doesn't mean that a structure isn't rule-governed though. The subject slot can only be unoccupied, even in ChE, when it is a pronoun that would fill it (not any {NP}). Plus, even in sE, there's an exception to needing the subject slot filled: imperatives (i.e., commands) such as *Run!* or *Go now!* consist of just the verb because in the imperative, the implied subject is always the pronoun *you* as in *You run!* and *You go!*

11.2.2 Subject–Verb–Direct Object (S-V-DO)

When a sentence contains a **monotransitive verb**, it will consist of a subject, verb, and **direct object (DO)**. S-V-DO patterns are illustrated below; DOs are italicized.

(26) Harper cooked *dinner*. (sE)

(27) He's a-gonna try *it*.[26] (AE)

(28) They building *these condos*.[27] (AAE)

(29) Salim read *the book*. (sE)

(30) My dad baked *banana bread*. (sE)

Here, the additional phrases that follow the subject and verb function as DOs. Notice that these additional constituents are affected by the action of the verb and are necessary to complete the precise meaning of each verb; in other words, the verb **selects** the DO, and as such, the DO is grammatically necessary.

Just like with the S-V pattern, the **S-V-DO** pattern can also give us longer sentences. Before reading further, identify the subject and DO in each:

(31) The attentive students asked many complicated questions. (sE)

(32) The helpful neighbor shoveled the heavy snow in our driveway. (sE)

(33) We was discussing the initiative that Obama curated.[28] (AAE)

(34) Fatima has been eating the most delicious cookies. (sE)

(35) Nobody believes that you could fix anything.[29] (ChE)

Did you come up with the following?

(31a) [The attentive students] [asked] [many complicated questions]. (sE)
                     S   V   DO

(32a) [The helpful neighbor] [shoveled] [the heavy snow in our driveway]. (sE)
             S   V   DO

(33a) [We] [was discussing] [the initiative that Obama curated]. (AAE)
        S   V   DO

(34a) [Fatima] [has been eating] [the most delicious cookies]. (sE)
        S   V   DO

(35a) [Nobody] [believes] [that you could fix anything]. (ChE)
        S   V   DO

All DOs and Ss here are {NPs}. You should be able to break down each {NP} into their component parts (DET, PRE, HEAD, POST) by now, and so you'll see that we have several embedded phrases in our larger {NPs}. For example, there is a {PP} that functions as a POST in the {NP} *the heavy snow in our driveway*; the entire {NP} is what functions as a DO. The {PP} *in our driveway* specifies which snow the neighbor shoveled (the snow in our driveway, not hers) rather than the location of where the neighbor did the shoveling.

11.2.3 Subject–Verb–Indirect Object–Direct Object (S-V-IO-DO)

A **ditransitive verb** requires two constituents following the verb: an **indirect object (IO)** followed by the DO. IOs are italicized in the sentences below.

(36) Harper cooked *their friend* dinner. (sE)
(37) Santiago read *the children* the book. (sE)
(38) My dad baked *his neighbors* banana bread. (sE)
(39) He give *me* five dollar.[30] (AAE)
(40) I'ma tell *you* this.[31] (AAE)
(41) They found *them* an apartment.[32] (ChE)
(42) They found *themselves* an apartment. (sE)
(43) I'm gonna write *me* a letter to my cousin.[33] (AE)

How do we know that the words on the right side of the verb aren't just one constituent? We can do the pronoun replacement test (we told you: it's your best friend!). For instance, *the children* in (37) and *five dollar* in (39) can be replaced by *them*, and so on. Because English has fixed word order, if there are two objects, then the IO will always come before the DO: **S-V-IO-DO**. Just like with the other patterns so far, the S-V-IO-DO pattern can give us longer sentences as well. Again, before you continue reading further along, identify the sentence constituents. Which words function as the S, the IO, the DO? What phrases are they?

(44) Our new colleague bought their boss, whom they admired very much, a perfect gift. (sE)
(45) We asked the students at the top of the class the hardest questions. (sE)
(46) The newly licensed realtor showed the interested and motivated buyers the houses that were on the market. (sE)

Did you come up with the following?

(44a) [Our new colleague] [bought] [their boss, whom they admired very much,]
   S   V   IO
[a perfect gift]. (sE)
   DO

(45a) [We] [asked] [the students at the top of the class]
   S   V   IO
[the hardest questions]. (sE)
   DO

(46a) [The newly-licensed realtor] [showed] [the interested and motivated buyers]
   S   V   IO
[the houses that were on the market]. (sE)
   DO

How Phrases Stick Together: Sentence Patterns

Each sentence can be reduced to merely the head words of the phrases (sometimes with a determiner). This should help in illustrating again that all constituents that function as S, IO, and DO in the above examples are {NPs}:

(44b) [Our colleague] [bought] [their boss] [a gift]. (sE)

(45b) [We] [asked] [the] [students] [questions]. (sE)

(46b) [The realtors] [showed] [the buyers] [the houses]. (sE)

Keep in mind that a verb can be used intransitively, monotransitively, and ditransitively. In (47), the verb doesn't select any objects, in (48), the verb selects one object, and in (49), the verb selects two objects:

(47) Harper cooked. (sE)
      S   V

(48) Harper cooked dinner. (sE)
      S   V   DO

(49) Harper cooked their friend dinner. (sE)
      S   V   IO   DO

Testing for IO and DO

If you're not sure which constituent functions as the DO and which functions as the IO, one straightforward type of evidence is simply **word order**. Because word order is fixed, we know IOs come before DOs. So, if you know that you have a sentence that includes two objects, the first one is always going to be the IO.

Because not all sentences that contain two constituents after the verb are S-V-IO-DO patterns, it's useful to know another test to identify the IO and DO: **the *for/to*-rephrasing test**. Because semantically, the IO expresses who/what benefits from the action expressed by the verb, we can rephrase the IO as a *for/to*-phrase:

(49a) Harper cooked *their friend* dinner. (sE)

(49b) Harper cooked dinner *for their friend*.

(50) Constanza read *the children* the book. (sE)

(50a) Constanza read the book *to the children*.

(51) He give *me* five dollar.[34] (AAE)

(51a) He give five dollar *to me*.

Let's try using this *to/for*-rephrasing test for our DOs in the same sentences:

(49c) Harper cooked their friend *dinner*. (sE)

(49d) ~Harper cooked their friend *for dinner*.

(50b) Constanza read the children *the book*. (sE)

(50c) *Constanza read the children *to the book*.

(51b) He give me *five dollar*.[35] (AAE)

(51c) *He give me *to five dollar*.

We can't simply plop the DO into the *to/for*-phrase in the same way as we were able to do for the IO. The DO is not the beneficiary. The only reason we didn't place an * in front of (49d) is that we can imagine a cannibal-inspired horror story where someone may, in fact, cook their friend for dinner, but this sentence clearly is a huge departure from our original sentence, which is about cooking dinner for a friend (not the other way around!).

An important note is in order: Once you rephrase an IO as a *to/for*-phrase, that *to/for*-phrase no longer functions, syntactically, as an IO. The **form** of this constituent now is a {PP}, and the **function** is adverbial–it is optional and movable:

(49e) Harper cooked *their friend* dinner. (sE)

(49f) Harper cooked dinner ~~for their friend~~. (sE)

(49g) *For their friend*, Harper cooked dinner. (sE)

(49h) *Harper cooked dinner *their friend*. (sE)

(50d) Constanza read *the children* the book. (sE)

(50e) Constanza read the book ~~to the children~~. (sE)

(50f) *To the children*, Constanza read the book. (sE)

(50g) *Constanza read the book *the children*. (sE)

(51d) He give *me* five dollar.³⁶ (AAE)

(51e) He give five dollar ~~to me~~. (AAE)

(51f) *To me*, he give five dollar. (AAE)

(51g) *He give five dollar *me*. (AAE)

In each example, the *to/for*-phrase itself can be left out without making the sentence overall ungrammatical, and more importantly, we can move the {PP} to the beginning of the sentence. In other words, these {PPs} do not need to come before the DO. However, the IO as an {NP} must come after the verb and before the DO because English word order makes it so: S-V-IO-DO. This means that the {PPs} here do not behave how IOs behave, syntactically speaking. Therefore, we treat these {PPs} as adverbials, not IOs (we'll get back to adverbials in a little bit). You should know that some grammar books treat these kinds of *to/for*-phrases as IOs still (based on semantic meaning, not systematic criteria). It's an example of how not everything about grammar and syntax is settled; researchers debate this quite lively sometimes at conferences!

Our examples so far have been taken from a few American English dialects already. We want to highlight a few additional dialect structures. The first one is common especially in conversations across many sE and non-sE dialects. It involves {PPs} that could be interpreted as IOs (italicized below):

(52) Ahmed cooked *for his friend* a huge, expensive dinner.

(53) Carlos read *to the children* the most incredibly funny book.

(54) My dad baked *for his neighbors* an elaborate, three-layer, chocolate cake.

You can see that the {PPs} occur where {NP}-IOs occur in a sentence (after the verb and before the DO). We could simply delete the prepositions and be left with the {NP} in the IO slot. Since there *is* a preposition though, and the phrase in this slot is therefore in the form of a {PP}, these {PPs} function as adverbials as they can easily be moved to other positions in the sentence, including sentence-final position as in *Ahmed cooked a huge, expensive dinner for his friend*. Researchers have found that—instead of using an {NP}-IO—placing a *to/for*-phrase prior to a heavy, or multi-word, DO is the most common pattern.[37]

There is another variation that has to do with objects, and specifically with DOs, that we have not included in the examples so far. This feature is attested in ChE, and it is sometimes called "**direct object absence**."[38]

(55) He took a bath. I gave him Ø to eat.[39] (ChE)

(56) Close that back window. If you ever open Ø again, I'm gonna kill you![40] (ChE)

The Ø-symbol, as a quick reminder, indicates an absence of some kind (an absence when compared to sE, that is!). In this instance, it marks the slot in the sentence where, in sE, one would expect a DO. This DO in ChE, however, is not necessary. In (55), you have an IO (*him*) followed by Ø. In sE, you might say something closer to these versions of the same sentences:

(55a) I gave him *something* to eat. (sE)

(56a) If you ever open *it* again … (sE)

For a syntactic breakdown of personal datives, common in ChE and SAE and covered in Chapter 8 alongside reflexive pronouns, check out the companion website. Another variation, common in SAE, specifically in Kentucky English,[41] involves pronouns in the IO slot, which are followed by a DO:

(57) Here's *you* a piece of pizza.[42] (SAE)

(58) Here's *me* a good pair of jeans.[43] (SAE)

(59) Here's *him* a nice cup of coffee.[44] (SAE)

(60) Here's *us* a gas station—pull over![45] (SAE)

Because this construction involves getting someone's attention about something that is being presented to them (i.e., *a piece of pizza* or *a gas station*), it is called **dative presentative**. In sE, these sentences would likely be rephrased with a *to/for*-phrase as in *Here's a piece of pizza for you* and so on.

Keep in mind that while some American English dialects may show variation when it comes to some of the sentence patterns, all sentence patterns exist in all dialects! So far, you've seen three sentence patterns in English dialects: S-V, S-V-DO, S-V-IO-DO. Good news: These patterns don't have additional names, so you don't have to memorize another technical term!

Foundations of Grammar

> **Exercise 3**
>
> How many and which objects do the following sentences contain? Provide a test of how you know which constituent is which object, as well as any additional evidence you can think of.
>
> a) The parrot made the dog a mimosa. (sE)
> b) I didn't see nothing.[46] (AAE)
> c) The cats caught the owner two mice. (sE)
> d) The cats caught the owner's mice. (sE)
> e) He was a-tellin' the truth.[47] (AE)
> f) We bought Gregory two cats. (sE)
> g) A few years ago, I didn't have no confidence.[48] (ChE)
> h) Here's John a glass of iced-tea.[49] (SAE)

11.2.4 Subject–Verb–Subject Complement (S-V-SC)

In S-V-SC sentences, **linking verbs** (or **copula verbs**) select an SC. These copula verbs are not all that numerous, but we use the limited number of linking verbs quite a lot, and so you'll encounter S-V-SC sentences (or S-SC sentences in various dialects) quite frequently. The verb *be* is by far the most common one. Other examples of copula verbs include *look, become, seems*, and *appear* (not a complete list!).

(61) Fatima is *nice*. (sE)
(62) My spouse seemed *frightened*. (sE)
(63) Moesha became *a professor*. (sE)
(64) He *a expert*.[50] (AAE)
(65) He *nice*.[51] (AAE)
(66) Some iMacs *tangerine*.[52] (AAE)
(67) She look *pretty*.[53] (ChE)
(68) She is *funny*.[54] (New Orleans YAT)
(69) You *right*.[55] (New Orleans YAT)

The first three examples show the structure for sE, where you have three components: subjects, verbs, and **subject complements** (SCs). The other examples show dialect variation where the verb is not necessary, which is called **zero/null copula** or **copula absence**. What this means is that in these dialects, a verb *can* occur between the subject and SC, but it is optional and can be left out. For instance, in the New Orleans dialect called YAT, structures such as *You right* are used frequently, but speakers only use an S-SC structure rather than an S-V-SC structure when the subject is *you*. This means that speakers include the verb in sentences such as *She is funny*.[56]

How Phrases Stick Together: Sentence Patterns

The SC describes or completes the subject; it *matches* the subject (*Moesha* and *professor* are a match for the same referent, as is *Fatima* and *nice*). This is why it is called a **subject complement**. In a way, the AAE and ChE examples demonstrate this very close relationship between the S and SC even more, since the S and the SC are placed directly next to one another, without a verb intervening.

Each of the sentences above would be incomplete without the SC:

(61a) *Fatima is.
(62a) *My spouse seemed.
(63a) *Moesha became.
(64a) *He.
(65a) *He.
(66a) *Some iMacs.
(67a) *She look.
(68a) *She is.
(69a) *You.

> **Complement:** not to be confused with *compliment*
> **Complement** = matching something

In other words, the SC is needed to complete the sentence. Note that *She look* would be grammatical in ChE and AAE, but in a drastically different sense, where *look* becomes the action of looking (maybe in a direction or at something) rather than a way of describing a person's looks.

Because an S-V-SC sentence consists of a verb and two constituents, you may be tempted to think it is an S-V-DO pattern rather than a pattern with an SC. Luckily, there's a quick and easy test that can help clear things up: Replace the verb with an equal sign:

(61b) Fatima = *nice*. (sE)
(62b) My spouse = *frightened*. (sE)
(63b) Moesha = *a professor*. (sE)
(64b) He = *a expert*. (AAE)
(65b) He = *nice*. (AAE)
(66b) Some iMacs = *tangerine*. (AAE)
(67b) She = *pretty*. (ChE)
(68b) She = *funny*. (New Orleans YAT)
(69b) You = *right*. (New Orleans YAT)

Because the S and SC match, or put differently, the SC complements the S, we can replace the verbs with an equal sign. Let's see if we can do this for sentences with DOs as well:

(70) Amos cooked *dinner*. (sE)
(70a) *Amos = *dinner*. (sE)
(71) They building *these condos*.[57] (AAE)

(71a) *They = these condos. (AAE)

(72) Amina read the book. (sE)

(72a) *Amina = the book. (sE)

Because in (70), *Amos* is—crucially—**not** *dinner*, and *they* in (71) are—crucially—**not** *these condos*, and *Amina* in (72) is definitely **not** *the book*, these three sentences are not S-V-SC sentences. To recap, the test is simple: If you have a sentence with two constituents (and a verb) and you can replace the verb with an equal sign, the two constituents complement each other, and the sentence pattern is S-V-SC. If you cannot replace the verb with an equal sign, the constituents don't complement each other, and the sentences are not S-V-SC.

Let's look at the **form** of the SCs. Identify the SC in each sentence below and then determine the SC's form (i.e., what phrase is it).

(73) The newly adopted cat became more relaxed. (sE)

(74) Your mama a weight-lifter.[58] (AAE)

(75) My siblings seem overwhelmed. (sE)

(76) Many of the new students are commuters. (sE)

(77) You right about that.[59] (AAE)

Compare your answers with the information here:

(73a) [The newly adopted cat] [became] [more relaxed]. (sE)
                S   V   SC = {AdjP}

(74a) [Your mama] [a weight-lifter].[60] (AAE)
         S   SC = {NP}

(75a) [My siblings] [seem] [overwhelmed]. (sE)
         S   V   SC = {AdjP}

(76a) [Many of the new students] [are] [commuters]. (sE)
                S   V   SC = {NP}

(77a) [You] [right about that].[61] (AAE)
         S   SC = {AdjP}

This shows that {NPs} and {AdjPs} can function as SCs.

Exercise 4

Locate the SC, if there is one, in the below sentences.

a) Saige is my neighbor's friend. (sE)
b) Asher composed a stunning piece of music. (sE)
c) Bob and Sam visit me nearly every week. (sE)

d) At the vet, my cat felt very frightened. (sE)
  e) He nice.[62] (AAE)
  f) She was like a real thin lady.[63] (ChE)
  g) Pantyhose are so expensive anymore.[64] (ME)
  h) He felt antsy because he didn't exercise anymore.[65] (ME)

11.2.5 Subject-Verb-Direct Object-Object Complement (S-V-DO-OC)

The next sentence pattern also involves a constituent that matches, or complements, another constituent in the sentence. Take a look at the italicized portion and see if you can tell which constituent it complements:

  (78)   Saarik labeled my friend *a beast*. (sE)
  (79)   I keep the house *clean*. (sE)
  (80)   The jury found the defendant *guilty*. (sE)
  (81)   They make it *crystal clear*.[66] (AAE)
  (82)   Scott making us *better*.[67] (AAE)

In each example, the italicized portion complements the DO that comes directly before it; hence the name **object complement (OC)**. Let's illustrate this in detail with the first sentence:

  (78a)   [Saarik] [labeled] [my friend] [*a beast*.] (sE)
            S   V   DO   OC

Here, *a beast* describes *my friend* (the DO), not *Saarik* (the S). In other words, it is my friend who is a beast, not Saarik! The same applies to the rest of the sentences. Because the OC matches, or complements, the DO, you cannot ever have an OC without a DO. Recall that the verb that requires both a DO and an OC is called **complex transitive**.

> Without a DO, there can be no OC!

Another feature of S-V-DO-OC patterns that will help you **test** for, i.e., identify, the pattern is that we can easily turn the constituents to the right of the verb into their own mini-sentence if we add a copula verb:

  (78b)   My friend is *a beast*. (sE)
  (79a)   The house is *clean*. (sE)
  (80a)   The defendant is *guilty*. (sE)
  (81a)   It (is) *crystal clear*. (AAE)
  (82a)   We (are) *better*. (AAE)

You can see that the underlying structure of (DO-OC) and (S-SC) is extremely similar. This comes in handy for yet another **test**! How do you know that the two constituents after the verb are **not** IO and DO? That they are DO and OC? Consider the next two sentences, which look very similar at first:

(80b) [The jury] [found] [the defendant] [guilty]. (sE)

(83) [The jury] [found] [the defendant] [a chair]. (sE)

Here's how the test works: Isolate the two components after the verb and try turning them into an S-V-SC sentence, like so:

(80c) The defendant is guilty. (sE)

(83a) The defendant is a chair. (sE)

Now, we're pretty sure you can immediately see that this only works for sentences that feature a DO-OC structure, since *the defendant* clearly isn't *a chair*. Just like we were able to distinguish between an S-V-SC and an S-V-DO sentence pattern by testing whether the SC truly is matched to the S, we can do the same test to see if the OC is matched to the DO (in other words, complements the DO).

A final test is using the IO-test, the *to/for*-**rephrasing test** to rule out that the component right after the verb isn't an IO. Remember, if it's an IO, we should be able to rephrase that IO into a *to/for*-phrase! Let's test it, just to make sure:

(80d) *The jury found guilty *for the defendant*. (sE)

(83b) The jury found a chair *for the defendant*. (sE)

The IO test only works for sentences that include, surprise surprise, an IO! It won't work for a DO-OC pattern, as (80d) illustrates. Let's apply these tests one more time:

(84) Derek made the students food. (sE)

(84a) Derek made food *for the students*. (result of IO-test)

(84b) *The students are food. (result DO-OC test)

(85) Derek made the students team leaders. (sE)

(85a) *Derek made team leaders *for the students*. (result of IO-test)

(85b) The students are team leaders. (result DO-OC test)

Because of the two tests we just performed, we can confidently say that (84) is a S-V-IO-DO sentence and that (85) is a S-V-DO-OC sentence. Note that both {NPs} and {AdjPs} can function as OCs. Identify both the DO and OC constituents below and label the phrase for each (i.e., their forms) before reading on:

(86) We painted the wall behind the bed an extremely bright yellow. (sE)

(87) The citizens of the newly formed democracy elected a complete newcomer president. (sE)

(88) Binge-watching movies makes my family super sleepy. (sE)

Did you come up with the following?

(86a) [We] [painted] [the wall behind the bed] [an extremely bright yellow]. (sE)
        S   V   DO = {NP}   OC = {NP}

(87a) [The citizens of the newly formed democracy] [elected]
           S   V
[a complete newcomer] [president]. (sE)
   DO = {NP}   OC= {NP}

(88a) [Binge-watching movies] [makes] [my family] [super sleepy]. (sE)
              S   V   DO = {NP}   OC = {AdjP}

> **Exercise 5**
>
> Locate the OC, if there is one, in the following sentences.
>
> a) I considered the dog my best friend. (sE)
> b) Alls I want is new shoes.[68] (ME)
> c) There's me some fantasy points.[69] (Kentucky English/SAE)
> d) The dog called the cat his mortal enemy. (sE)
> e) The parrot considered us silly. (sE)
> f) He call me son.[70] (AAE)
> g) Together, we sat on the porch nightly. (sE)
> h) She made her intentions clear. (sE)

11.2.6 Subject–Verb–Adverbial Complement (S-V-AC)

A final pattern that involves a complement is exemplified in the data below. As you look at the italicized portions, can you explain why these are **not** S-V-SC sentences? What about the component after the verb is different from/similar to an SC?

(89) This road goes *to Midland*. (sE)
(90) The meeting lasted *four hours*. (sE)
(91) New York lies *north of Washington D.C.* (sE)
(92) It last *a year and a half or so*.[71] (AAE)
(93) She *here*.[72] (AAE)

Here's what's similar to an SC structure: The italicized constituents are needed to complete the sentence because without them, the sentences would be incomplete:

(89a) *This road goes.
(90a) *The meeting lasted.
(91a) *New York lies.
(92a) *It last.
(93a) *She.

This particular component is also very different from an SC. For one, we can't use the SC test (replacing the verb with equal signs):

(89b)   *This road = *to Midland*. (sE)

(90b)   *The meeting = *four hours*. (sE)

(91b)   *New York = *north of Washington D.C.* (sE)

(92b)   *It = *a year and a half or so*. (AAE)

(93b)   *She = *here*. (AAE)

The equal sign means that the subject **is the same as** the SC. However, *This road* isn't the same as *to Midland* (this road simply *leads* to this particular city; it's not the city itself). *The meeting* isn't the same as *four hours* (the meeting simply *lasted* for this long); *New York* isn't the same as *north of Washington D.C.*; *it* isn't the same as *a year and a half or so*; and *she* isn't the same as *here*.

Compare this to just one S-V-SC structure:

(94)   This road is a highway. (sE)

Here, *This road* is, in fact, the same as *a highway*. It is a very different structure from saying that a road *leads* somewhere, which means that *somewhere* and the *road* are not the same thing. Having ruled out SC as the function for our italicized constituent, we should also rule out the possibility of it being a DO. Remember that a DO is a constituent that can be singled out with a *what/who* question, as illustrated below:

(95)   Luca cooked dinner. (sE)
         Q & A: What did Luca cook?—dinner

Let's see if we can apply this to our sentences in questions:

(89c)   This road leads to Midland. (sE)
         Q & A: *What does this road lead?—to Midland

Using the question test leads to nonsensical and/or ungrammatical questions, which tells us that *to Midland* is not a DO. Because we don't have a DO, we also can't have an OC (remember that an OC completes a DO).

So, what is it then? A closer look at these constituents reveals that they tell us information about **location** (*to Midland/here*), **duration/time** (*four hours/a year and a half or so*), and **direction** (*north of DC*). Components that tell us this kind of information are referred to as **adverbials**. Adverbials are usually optional/additional elements that can be added to any of the six sentence patterns (more in the next section). When adverbials are necessary to complete a sentence, to make it grammatical, we call them (you might have guessed already again!) **adverbial complements (AC)**.

The ACs above come in different forms. The one in (89), *to Midland*, is a {PP}, while *four hours* in (90), *north of Washington D.C.* in (91), and *a year and a half or so* in (92) are all {NPs}. *Here* in (93) is an {AdvP}. To figure out ACs, the best way is to rule out SCs and DOs using the tests described above because then all you have left is the AC (remember, without a DO, there is no IO, and without a DO, there's no OC either).

Our six sentence patterns are summed up in Chart 2 below.

---

intransitive verbs: S + V

We		studying.[73] (AAE)
The students	study. (sE)	
S	V	

monotransitive verbs: S + V + DO

My dad	baked	banana bread. (sE)
The CEO	wrote	the report. (sE)
S	V	DO

ditransitive verbs: S + V + IO + DO

My dad	baked	his neighbors	banana bread. (sE)
A couple	fed	the cats	some food. (sE)
S	V	IO	DO

linking/copula verb: S + (V) + SC

The essays	are	excellent. (sE)
You		right.[74] (New Orleans YAT)
She	look	pretty.[75] (ChE)
S	V	SC

complex transitive verbs: S + V + DO + OC

Derek	labeled	my friend	a beast. (sE)
The reports	keep	me	busy. (sE)
S	V	DO	OC

transitive verbs: S + (V) + AC

This road	goes	to Midland. (sE)
She		here.[76] (AAE)
S	V	AC

Chart 2 Summary of sentence patterns

11.2.7 The Optional Adverbial

To any of the patterns we described in this chapter, we can add optional elements. These optional elements are **adverbial (A)**. They are not selected by the verb. Adverbials are not demanded by the verb, and, as such, are not required to make a sentence grammatically complete. These adverbials are ubiquitous, and you could go through all example sentences in this chapter and add one or even more than one adverbial to each of them. We did just that to a few of the sentences you already encountered to give you a taste of where adverbials can be placed and just how ubiquitous they are. As you read through the data set below, make some observations about the italicized adverbials. A complete breakdown of patterns for these sentences and several additional examples are available on the companion website.

(96) The alarm at the detailing place next door had went off *a few minutes ago*.[77] (AAE)

(97) The soul needs fed *by creative, multi-dimensional teaching*.[78] (ME)

(98) *All throughout the night*, the cats chased the mice. (sE)

(99) They *quickly* found them an apartment.[79] (ChE)

(100) *After years in grad school*, my sister finally became a professor. (sE)

(101) For she won't feel guilty *forever*.[80] (ChE)

(102) *The other day*, I've call her my sister.[81] (AAE)

(103) The reports *always* keep me busy *in the mornings*. (sE)

(104) The road goes *directly* to New York. (sE)

As you can see in this data set, semantically, adverbials convey information about when, where, how, for how long, and so on something did happen. Syntactically, adverbials are not confined to a specific position in a sentence. Some adverbials in the sentences above come in initial position, before the S, some come in the middle of the sentence, after the V, some come at the very end of a sentence. This is what sets them apart from all the other constituents we've covered. The position of the other constituents is clearly confined to a specific spot in the sentence: The IO comes before the DO. The DO comes before the OC. The SC comes after the V, the S comes before the V, and so on. If you tried to move the IO, for instance, to the beginning of a sentence, you'd end up with this:

(105) My dad baked *my neighbors* banana bread. (sE)

(105a) *My neighbors my dad baked banana bread. (sE)

The same goes for other constituents, including the DO:

(106) Bruce ain't taking *calculus* this semester.[82] (AAE)

(106a) *Bruce *calculus* ain't taking this semester. (AAE)

To reiterate, with (almost all) adverbials, you have some flexibility as to where in the sentence you want to place them. This is a defining feature and will allow you to identify adverbials. The **test** is simple: try to move it elsewhere in the sentence; if you can, it's almost always an adverbial.

(106b) Bruce ain't taking calculus *this semester*.[83] (AAE)

(106c) *This semester*, Bruce ain't taking calculus. (AAE)

You may have noticed that, semantically, As and ACs convey similar information. To recap, the two crucial syntactic differences between an AC and an adverbial are that adverbials can be left out completely or moved around in a sentence whereas ACs cannot be left out and are (usually) not movable.

Exercise 6

Determine which sentences feature an AC and which ones feature an adverbial. Identify all ACs and all adverbials. Provide evidence for your answers.

a) My friends live in Germany. (sE)
b) My friends travelled to Germany. (sE)
c) They stayed very quiet. (sE)
d) Breakfast be cooked at 8 o'clock.[84] (AAE)
e) Breakfast is at 8am. (sE)
f) Ms. Helen be correcting us all the time.[85] (AAE)
g) They hiked up on the trail. (sE)
h) Middlesboro is on yan side of Cumberland Gap.[86] (AE) [note: *yan* is a demonstrative determiner here; in sE, it would correspond to *that*]

In this chapter, we have identified syntactic functions of constituents in simple sentences to be able to arrive at specific sentence patterns. In Chapter 14, we'll look at complex sentences, i.e., sentences that include dependent and embedded clauses, where you'll learn that clauses themselves can also function as sentence-level constituents, not just phrases. So, stay tuned for that, but also enjoy the extravaganza that Exercise 7 is!

Exercise 7

Identify the sentence patterns of the sentences below, including any optional adverbials. Make sure to indicate where each constituent begins and ends (brackets, slashes, etc.)

a) The project manager wanted a raise. (sE)
b) We immediately bought the cats several treats. (sE)
c) The board named the new hire executive vice president. (sE)
d) He working during the day.[87] (AAE)
e) She bin at work.[88] (AAE)
f) Then after that I talk English.[89] (ChE)
g) I haven't wrote in a long time.[90] (ChE)
h) He give me a holler.[91] (AAE)
i) Bruce BIN putting those glasses on the shelves.[92] (AAE)
j) We like them molasses.[93] (AE)

k) The performance will be next month. (sE)
l) It was a lot of fights and stuff.[94] (ChE)
m) The cute cats eat constantly. (sE)
n) Every week, my spouse baked cookies. (sE)
o) The cats got their fuzzy paws wet this morning. (sE)
p) She was right on time. (sE)
q) We real cool.[95] (AAE)
r) The presidential candidates gave the press several interviews. (sE)
s) We start on July.[96] (ChE)
t) My colleagues are the most talented colleagues in the world. (sE)
u) The little kid don't have no sturdy shoes of his own.[97] (ChE)

Exercise 8

Provide your own example sentences for all six sentence patterns. Make sure you include an optional adverbial in each one! Identify each constituent by drawing vertical lines and labeling the constituents. Hint: Keep it simple and use simple verbs. Feel free to use whichever dialect you're most comfortable with!

Terminology to Know

Term	Working definition	Example/Illustration
Clause vs phrase		
Constituent		
SC		
OC		
IO		
DO		
AC		
Adverbial		
Intransitive verb		
Copula/linking verb		
Ditransitive verb		
Monotransitive verb		
Complex transitive verb		

Chart 3 Key terminology Chapter 11

Notes

1. Produced by OpenAI, 2024.
2. Maher and McCoy, 2011.
3. Baker-Bell, 2020, p. 74.
4. Bayley and Santa Ana, 2004, p. 376.
5. Farrington et al., 2020 Transcript ID ATL_se0_ag1_m_01_1.
6. Maher and McCoy, 2011.
7. Baker-Bell, 2020, p. 74.
8. Bayley, 2012, p. 158.
9. Kendall, Quartey et al., 2018 Transcript ID DCB_se2_ag2_f_01_1.
10. Adapted from Fought, 2003, p. 97.
11. Putnam and van Koppen, 2011; cited in Wood, 2013.
12. Wood, 2014.
13. Adapted from Fought, 2003, p. 97.
14. Ibid.
15. Maher and McCoy, 2011.
16. Ibid.
17. Bayley and Santa Ana, 2004, p. 378.
18. Matyiku, 2011a.
19. Kendall, Fasold et al., 2018 Transcript ID DCA_se1_ag1_m_05_1.
20. Kaplan, 2015.
21. Kendall, Fasold et al., 2018 Transcript ID DCA_se3_ag1_m_05_1.
22. Farrington et al., 2020 Transcript ID ATL_se0_ag1_f_01_1.
23. Maher and Wood, 2011.
24. Bayley, 2012, p. 157.
25. Ibid., p. 163.
26. Christian et al., 1988; cited in Matyiku, 2011a.
27. Kendall, Quartey et al., 2018 Transcript ID DCB_se3_ag3_m_02_1.
28. Ibid., Transcript ID DCB_se1_ag1_m_02_1.
29. Fought, 2003, p. 100.
30. Kendall, Fasold et al., 2018 Transcript ID DCA_se1_ag4_m_02_1.
31. Kendall, Quartey et al., 2018 Transcript ID DCB_se2_ag4_f_05_1.
32. Bayley, 2012, p. 163.
33. Christian, 1991; cited in Huang and McCoy, 2015.
34. Kendall, Fasold et al., 2018 Transcript ID DCA_se1_ag4_m_02_1.
35. Ibid.
36. Ibid.
37. Anttila, Adams, and Speriosu, 2010; Bresnan, Cueni, Nikitina, and Baayen, 2007.
38. Bayley and Santa Ana, 2004, p. 379.

39. Ibid.
40. Ibid.
41. Wood, 2015.
42. Ibid.
43. Ibid.
44. Ibid.
45. Ibid.
46. Green, 2002, p. 76.
47. Wolfram and Christian, 1976, p. 71.
48. Adapted from Fought, 2003, p. 97.
49. Wood, 2015.
50. Bender, 2000, p. 84; cited in Parsard, 2016.
51. Kendall, Fasold et al., 2018 Transcript ID DCA_se1_ag1_m_04.
52. Green, 2002, p. 52.
53. Bayley and Santa Ana, 2004, p. 376.
54. Coles, 2001.
55. Ibid.
56. Ibid.
57. Kendall, Quartey et al., 2018 Transcript ID DCB_se3_ag3_m_02_1.
58. Labov, 1969, p. 720; cited in Parsard, 2016.
59. Baker-Bell, 2020, p. 74.
60. Labov, 1969, p. 720; cited in Parsard, 2016.
61. Baker-Bell, 2020, p. 74.
62. Kendall, Fasold et al., 2018 Transcript ID DCA_se1_ag1_m_04.
63. Bayley, 2012, p. 164.
64. Murray, 1993; cited in Maher and McCoy, 2011.
65. Parker, 1975; cited in Maher and McCoy, 2011.
66. Becker et al., 2021 Transcript ID LES_se0_ag4_f_01_2.
67. Kendall, Quartey et al., 2018 Transcript ID DCB_se1_ag2_m_01_1.
68. Wood, 2013.
69. Wood, 2015.
70. Kendall, Fasold et al., 2018 Transcript ID DCA_se1_ag4_m_02_1.
71. Ibid., Transcript ID DCA_se3_ag3_m_04_1.
72. Green, 2002, p. 3.
73. Kendall, Fasold et al., 2018 Transcript ID DCA_se3_ag1_m_05_1.
74. Coles, 2001.
75. Bayley and Santa Ana, 2004, p. 376.
76. Green, 2002, p. 3.
77. Ibid., p. 91.
78. Maher and Wood, 2011.

79. Adapted from Bayley, 2012, p. 163.
80. Adapted from Barrón and San Romón, n.d., pp. 30–1; cited in Bayley, 2012, p. 162.
81. Slightly adapted from Farrington et al., 2020 Transcript ID ATL_se0_ag1_f_01_1.
82. Green, 2002, p. 41.
83. Ibid.
84. Ibid., p. 98.
85. Baker-Bell, 2020, p. 52.
86. University of South Carolina (n.d.).
87. Kendall, Fasold et al., 2018 Transcript ID DCA_se2_ag1_m_01_1.
88. Harris and Wood, 2013.
89. Barrón and San Romón, n.d., pp. 30–1; cited in Bayley, 2012, p. 158.
90. Fought, 2003, p. 94.
91. Quartey et al., 2020 Transcript ID VLD_se0_ag3_m_01_1.
92. Green, 2002, p. 58.
93. University of South Carolina (n.d.).
94. Bayley, 2012, p. 163.
95. Parsard, 2016.
96. Bayley and Santa Ana, 2004, p. 379.
97. Bayley, 2012, p. 163.

CHAPTER 12
TIME AND TIME AGAIN: TENSE, ASPECT, FINITENESS

Overview

In this chapter, you'll expand your understanding of verbs and verb phrases {VPs} by looking at **tense** and **aspect** across a multitude of American English dialects. As such, this chapter will demonstrate additional powers of the verb phrase! Our objectives are as follows. You'll be able to

- solidify your knowledge about verbs;
- identify tense and aspect of a {VP}; and
- recognize some of the rich variation of the aspectual system in American English dialects.

Pre-reading tasks

1. Write down all characteristics of verbs that you remember from previous chapters. How do you know something is a verb? What inflectional and derivational suffixes can verbs endure? What are the different forms verbs can occur in (provide the label and give an example for each)?
2. What do you know about the aspectual system of verbs so far? In your own words, what are *progressive aspect* and *perfective aspect*?
3. Nouns can be verbed, such as using the noun *heart* as a verb: *I heart ice cream.* Create your own sentences that feature verbed nouns!

12.1 Introduction

Verb forms
Full infinitive	*to walk*
Bare infinitive	*walk*
Present tense	*walk*
3rd person sg present	*walks*
Simple past form	*walked*
Present participle	*walking*
Past participle	*walked*

In this chapter, we focus on **tense** and **aspect**. We'll be referencing the five verb forms a lot. You already know that tense is marked either on the main verb, or—when there is an auxiliary verb in a {VP}—on the auxiliary. In addition to **simple present tense** verb forms (in (1) and (2)) and **simple past tense** verb forms (in (3) and (4)), we distinguish **simple future tense** forms as well (in (5) and (6)):

(1) You *walk* three miles every day. (sE)
(2) Latoya *walks* three miles every day. (sE)
(3) We *danced* all night long at the party. (sE)
(4) She *striked* me with that.[1] (ChE)
(5) They *will walk* with me later today. (sE)
(6) This *will be* particularly important once you're done the tattoo …[2] (ECE)

Note that some grammarians distinguish between just present tense and past tense. Their reasoning (which is sound!) goes something like this: Tense, as a **grammatical category**, is exclusively about what main verbs can endure morphologically. In (2) and (3) above, the main verbs endure the *s*-suffix and *ed*-suffix, for instance. This perspective is very strict in separating **semantic** and **grammatical** components when it comes to tense. There is no inflectional suffix such as *-uth* (we made that one up just now!) that would morphologically mark future tense as in **We walkuth tomorrow*. Because of this, the reasoning goes, there really isn't a **future-tense-ness** in English when compared to past-tense-ness and present-tense-ness, again, because it's not marked via inflection on the main verb. Yet, we can express future-tense-ness just fine in English via auxiliary verbs, and so we include future tense as one of the tenses.

Tense indicates **when** something happens: past time, present time (or non-past), or future time. **Aspect** indicates other information relevant to the verb, including whether an action is ongoing, completed, or habitual. Aspect can reveal if an action took a while or if it was a one-and-done kind of action; aspect can also reveal if an action is still relevant for the present moment. Other than tense, what do the next four {VPs} convey about the action of *walking*?

(7) Blake *walks* three miles every day. (sE)
(8) I *am walking* to the store right now. (sE)
(9) Fatima *walked* three miles with me yesterday. (sE)
(10) Denzel *was walking* to the store last night when you called him. (sE)

Example (7) expresses a general action while (8) shows that the act of *walking* is ongoing currently. (9) is about a general action that happened in the past, while (10) conveys that the act of *walking* was ongoing in the past. This aspect—something is/was ongoing—is called *progressive* aspect.

> **Tense** – *when* something happened: past, present, future
> **Aspect** – *how* a particular event is being viewed with respect to time

The next data set features more complex {VPs} from a variety of American English dialects, most with some form of auxiliary preceding the main verb. This is a preview of the myriad ways in which the grammatical categories of tense and aspect help us convey all kinds of semantic meaning regarding when events occur, how they are related to other events, and how these events are experienced in regard to time.

(11) I *might walk* later today if it doesn't rain. (sE)
(12) The cops *had went* to my house.³ (ChE)
(13) They care about it now that you *done moved* everybody out.⁴ (AAE)
(14) Martin *is done* his bass tracks and we are ready to start vocals.⁵ (ECE)
(15) Sam *has walked* six miles every Saturday for many years. (sE)
(16) We *been married* almost twenty-six years.⁶ (AAE)
(17) Hassan *is walking* now. (sE)
(18) He *don't be barking* at nobody.⁷ (AAE)
(19) Sarah and Alejandra *were walking* earlier today. (sE)

Next, we'll examine exactly how {VPs} convey meaning such as whether an action is in progress, complete, or habitual, or how two or more events are related in time.

12.2 Simple Tenses

12.2.1 Simple Present

You may be tempted to think that **simple present tense** conveys actions that take place in the present. Not so fast! Take a look at the following sentences and decide what **time frame** is being expressed.

(20) I *walk* for my health. (sE)
(21) Juan *jogs* at 6 a.m. Monday through Friday. (sE)
(22) She *teaches* second grade.⁸ (AAE)
(23) My dad *use* both [Black Language and White Mainstream English].⁹ (AAE)

Simple present tense is rarely about something that happens in the present moment. Instead, it expresses a regular, habitual action. One context where a present-tense {VP} actually is about something that happens in the present comes from sports commentators: When they narrate a soccer match, for instance, they'll use present-tense verbs as in *She passes the ball*.

12.2.2 Simple Past

Same question, different tense: What's the **time frame** that is being expressed in these next sentences that feature **simple past tense** {VPs}?

(24) Amos *walked* to the store. (sE)

(25) The bear *weighed* four hundred and seventy-five pound.[10] (AE)

(26) I *picked* her because she nice and calm.[11] (AAE)

(27) Then after that I *talk* English.[12] (ChE)

(28) They *taught* me, so at every game, I be winning.[13] (AAE)

(29) A friend was with, and she *drove* me home.[14] (ME)

(30) We *went* into Cartier where she spent a wicked amount of money.[15] (NEE)

Simple past tense {VPs} denotes one-time events that took place in the past. So, the term "past tense" does match the semantic meaning of "past"! What **simple present** and **simple past** have in common is that the {VPs} consists of just one verb, the main verb, which is the one that has all the semantic meaning; no auxiliary is required to form this tense. This is why these verb forms are called **simple**. Remember that in some dialects, including ChE and AAE, an overt past-tense *-ed* marking is not required, as you can see in (27), where *talk* does not have the past-tense morphological *-ed* suffix.

12.2.3 Simple Future

Now, **simple future** {VPs} consist of two verbs: the **modal *will*** + **the bare infinitive form of the main verb**:

(31) Samir *will walk* tonight. (sE)

(32) Every time you ask me not to hum, I'*ll hum* more louder.[16] (AE and other dialects)

(33) Sarah *will run* in the Boston Marathon. (sE)

(34) Over on (…) the mountains you *will see* a little house on (…) postes.[17] (AE)

Semantically, this two-word construction is how we express that something will take place at some point in the future.

12.3 Progressive (aka Continuous) Aspect

Tenses can be combined with **aspect** in the {VP}. **Progressive aspect** is one such type of aspect, and it allows us to indicate that an action is in progress. Because it can be combined with tense, we have three distinct progressive forms: present progressive, past progressive, and future progressive. Let's get into it.

12.3.1 Present Progressive

Based on the next data set, what is required in the {VP} to form **present progressive**?

(35) I *am walking* to the store. (sE)
(36) He's *smiling* to the cat.[18] (ChE)
(37) He *is walking* now. (sE)
(38) They *building* these condos.[19] (AAE)

In this two-verb construction, the *be* auxiliary verbs (i.e., *am*, *is*) are followed by the main verbs. The auxiliary gives the {VP} its tense. Note that for some dialects, like AAE, the *be* auxiliary is optional (more on this later!). The main verbs end in the inflectional suffix *-ing*. The *-ing* form is called *present participle*. This is simply nomenclature. The fact that the word "present" is part of this term does not mean that the present participle is present tense; in fact, the present participle is not marked for tense at all (tense is marked on the auxiliary). The combination of *be* plus main verb ending in *-ing* is what encodes *progressive* or *continuous* meaning. What does that mean? Compare the following two sentences:

(39) I *drink* coffee. (sE)
(40) I *am drinking* coffee. (sE)

In (39), I'm expressing that, generally, I drink coffee. In (40), however, I'm expressing that the action of drinking is in progress at this very moment. It is this continuous meaning that the present participle encodes.

Present progressive =
present tense *be* + present participle of main verb

- *am* read*ing*
- *are* examin*ing*
- *is* writ*ing*

12.3.2 Past Progressive

Past progressive should be pretty easy now, we hope! We need a *be* **verb in past tense** + *present participle* **of main verb**, which the next data set confirms:

(41) Sarah *was walking* earlier today. (sE)
(42) Fire *was a-flamin'* everything.[20] (AE)
(43) We *were dancing* last night. (sE)
(44) Yesterday, we *was conversating* with Mr. B. about the war.[21] (AAE)

What this means again is that the action of the verb was ongoing at some point in the past. The action of *walking* wasn't an instantaneous one-and-done kind of action; neither was *a-flamin'* or *dancing* or *conversating*. So, it's once again the *-ing*-form of the verb that encodes this **aspect** of the {VP}'s meaning, this ongoing nature of the verb; it's the auxiliary that encodes **tense**. Many times, progressive {VPs} occur in clauses that contrast with a simple {VP} in another clause:

Past Progressive =
past tense *be* + *present participle* of main verb

- *was* read*ing*
- *were* examin*ing*
- *was* writ*ing*

(45) I *was talking* when the teacher entered the room. (sE)
(46) People *were dreaming* of brighter futures before they arrived in their new homeland. (sE)

Foundations of Grammar

In (45), one action was in progress when another, second action took place. The action of *talking* provides a backdrop for the teacher entering the room; both actions were completed in the past. In (46), the action of dreaming was in progress before the people left their homes to go to a new place to live, but the act of dreaming is complete as is the second action, the arrival to a new place of residency. Rather than providing a backdrop, here, *past progressive* shows an ongoing action in the past that took place prior to another action in the past. Notice how these complex {VPs} allow us to express more than one action's timeline in relation to another event's timeline.

12.3.3 Future Progressive

Now this construction is a little more complex because we must use the modal *will*, which will require the next verb to be in bare infinitive form, which doesn't have any inflectional affixes. To make a verb progressive, however, we need the main verb to have an *-ing* suffix. Because we can't add the *-ing* suffix to the bare infinitive *be*, this *-ing* affix hops on to the next verb in the {VP}. The affix hops to the next verb as instructed by the verb in front of it. We'd say this process is its own kind of club dance! It sounds complicated, but this is what it looks like:

(47) LeBron *will be reading* the next chapter soon. (sE)

(48) We *will be dancing* tonight. (sE)

(49) Fatima *will be selecting* her vice president soon. (sE)

Semantically, the **future progressive** conveys that an event will be in progress in the future. And to form future progressive, we need the following: **modal *will* + bare infinitive *be* + present participle of the main verb**. For some American English dialects, the modal *will* is not required.[22]

To recap, we can add the **progressive aspect** to our three tenses to form **present progressive**, **past progressive**, and **future progressive**. That means that we have a grammatical form that allows us to express that the action of the verb is either happening right now (when the *be* auxiliary verb is in present tense), or that the action of the verb happened in the past and was ongoing at some point in the past (when the *be* auxiliary verb is in past tense), or that the action of the verb will be ongoing at some point in the future (when we have the combination of modal *will* + *be* prior to the main verb).

Knowing what you know about progressive aspect, we can go over two more constructions that technically are in present tense and to which we have nevertheless granted semantic meaning of future. The first of those two is often called ***going-to* future**:

(50) Bob *is going to jog* every day this week. (sE)

(51) Sarah *is gonna run* a marathon. (sE)

(52) He's *a-gonna try* it.[23] (AE)

(53) It's a long way and he might will can't come, but I'*m going to ask*.[24] (SAE)

***Going-to* future** {VPs} consist of a form of *be* + *going to* +infinitive. Because the auxiliary *be* is in present tense, the {VP} is in present tense, and because we have the present participle *going*, we have progressive aspect. Notice that *going* is not what the sentences are about; the main verb comes last in the {VP}. A time-referencing adverbial, such as *this week* in (50) that conveys when in the future the action of the verb is going to happen, is often included but isn't required for the sentences to express future-ness. Notice, too, that *going* and *to* can be contracted across dialects to form *gonna*. Even though the auxiliary *be* is in present tense, as a community of speakers, we've given this construction the ability to index future-ness!

And because we, as users of a language, are ultimately in control of how we end up using various grammatical constructions, we have yet another way of indexing future time. This one simply uses **present progressive** verb forms:

(54)   I *am walking* tonight. (sE)

(55)   Bob *is jogging* every day this week. (sE)

(56)   I'*m going* to my father house for the summer.[25] (AAE)

(57)   Tammy and Maria *are going* for a record at the competition. (sE)

Because the form of the auxiliary *be* is in present tense, the {VP} is in present tense, and because we have the present participle of the main verb, we have progressive aspect. While contractions are possible for the *going-to* future {VPs} from earlier, *going* can't be contracted for these examples now. This is because *going* is the main verb now:

(56a)   *I'*m gonna* my father house for the summer. (AAE)

(57a)   *Tammy and Maria *are gonna* for a record at the competition. (sE)

We'd have to build it up into the *going-to* future to be able to use a contraction as in *We're going to go for a record at the competition*, which could then be rendered as *We're gonna go* ... All this is a lot to take in, so let your neurons process that while we move on to the next tense-and-aspect pairings.

Exercise 1

Create your own sentences, Round 1. Provide present, past, and future progressive {VPs} for the following verbs. Then, create an example sentence for each of those {VPs}.

talk, sing, jump, dream, appoint

verb	{VP} present progressive	{VP} past progressive	{VP} future progressive
talk			
sing			
jump			
dream			
appoint			

Example sentences for all progressive {VPs}:

12.4 Perfect (aka Completive) Aspect

We turn now to the **perfect aspect**. Colloquially, the word "perfect" means without flaws; its etymology shows that its Latin roots mean "complete." This non-colloquial meaning of *completion* is what's important for perfect aspect: when a {VP} is grammatically marked for perfect aspect, semantically, what that {VP} conveys is that the {VP}'s action has been completed. Often, perfect aspect sentences include two clauses that involve two actions in which one is complete at the time of another. Like our progressive aspect, perfect aspect can be combined with all three tenses: present, past, and future.

12.4.1 Present Perfect

Now, the way people use this tense and aspect combination is currently undergoing some linguistic change, which has led to some variability for its use, and so we'll focus on the fundamental semantic properties here. What are some observations about the meaning of the {VP}, again as it relates to time and timeframes, that you can make based on the data set below?

(58) Blake *has eaten* oatmeal every morning for five years as of this Saturday. (sE)

(59) I *haven't been* through none of that.[26] (AAE)

(60) I *haven't wrote* in a long time.[27] (ChE)

(61) We *have seen* many beautiful flowers this summer. (sE)

Semantically, the present perfect conveys that the action of the {VP} happened in the past, but that it still is relevant for the present moment. There's an implication of those completed actions in the past for the present time. Blake has eaten oatmeal every morning for five years in (58), so now their heart health is really top notch. Not having written in a long time in (60) has an implication that now, at the time of speaking or writing, no written products can be shared. So, each action has taken place in the past, yet there's an implication for now.

The grammatical components required for **present perfect** are a form of *have* + past participle (at least for most dialects). The auxiliary *have* is marked for tense and will thus be either *have* or *has* for present perfect. Don't let the term **present perfect** get the better of you: even though the word "present" is in this label, present perfect {VPs} convey that an action did take place in the past!

Note that while the *have* auxiliary generally requires the **past participle** in sE dialects, it can be paired with the simple past form in some non-sE dialects. The past participles in the examples above are *eaten*, *been*, and *seen*; example (60) features the simple past tense form *wrote*. What does that mean? Generally, in sE (and especially in academic, formal written language use), the perfect aspect requires the past participle of the verb, but in many non-sE dialects and to some extent in some informal sE dialects, the simple past tense form can also be used.

When people increasingly use forms such as *have drove* and *have went* and *should have spoke,* language change can occur which may result in widespread acceptance. One reason for the increasing use of simple past tense form over the past participle in perfect aspect {VPs} might be that past tense form and past participle forms look identical for regular verbs (and for many irregular verbs such as *met*), and so folks start using the simple past form of irregular verbs for perfect aspect by extension. It is more noticeable for irregular verbs when a past tense form (i.e., *have wrote*) is used over a past participle form (i.e., *have written*). Compare the three verb forms for regular and irregular verbs in Chart 1—using the past tense form *jogged* over the past participle form *jogged* isn't even noticeable, since they're the same form!

> **Present Perfect =**
> Auxiliary *have* in **present** tense + *past participle* of main verb (or *past tense* form in some cases)
>
> - *have/has* + *taught/gone/ watched/sung/cuddled*
> - *have/has sang/drove/ate*

Infinitive form	*Past tense* form	*Past participle* form	
eat	ate	eaten	
write	wrote	written	irregular verbs
meet	met	met	
jog	jogged	jogged	
participate	participated	participated	regular verbs
cuddle	cuddled	cuddled	

Chart 1 Verb forms: regular vs irregular verbs

To recap, we need a **present tense form of the auxiliary** *have* **+ past participle** (or past tense form, depending on dialect) to form present perfect. Remember that the term "past participle," just like with the term "present participle," doesn't mean that the past participle itself is past tense (it's simply nomenclature). The {VPs} in our examples in this section are all in present tense because the auxiliary *have* is in present tense!

12.4.2 Past Perfect

You probably guessed it. To change a present perfect {VP} to a **past perfect** {VP}, all we need to do is change our auxiliary from present-tense *have* or *has* to past-tense *had*:

(62) Blake *had devoured* their dessert before they ate their supper. (sE)

(63) The jury *had deliberated* for five hours before returning a verdict. (sE)

(64) I had like, three weeks that I *had came* out of the hospital.[28] (ChE)

(65) Before we *had fought*, she *had came* up to see me.[29] (ChE)

(66) I was really shocked because you *had wrote* me.[30] (AAE)

(67) I *had ate* a snack by the time they delivered pizza.[31] (AAE)

> Past Perfect = Auxiliary *have* in **past** tense + *past participle* of main verb (or *past tense* form in some cases)
>
> - *Had taught/gone/sung*
> - *Had wrote/ate/drove*

We can see that we need the **past tense of the auxiliary *have* + past participle** (or past tense form, depending on dialect) to form past perfect as in *had fought* and *had ate*. Again, the past participle of the main verb is required in sE dialects while in other dialects, such as AAE and ChE, the past tense form of the main verb can be used. Note that in some informal sE dialects though, the past tense form (*had spoke*) might be used as well. While these are valid and grammatical ways of forming past perfect, we'd be remiss not to point out that, once again, in edited formal written sE, the past participle is required.

Semantically speaking, in (62), *devour* and *eat* both happened in the past, with Blake's act of devouring having been completed prior to Blake's act of eating. Once the jury deliberations had been completed in (63), the jury returned; so, completing deliberations had the implication that a verdict could be rendered. Finally, the act of eating a snack and that of delivering pizza both happened in the past, but the eating of the snack was complete prior to the pizza delivery in (67).

12.4.3 Future Perfect

Just like future progressive was a bit more complex, so is **future perfect**, but at least it's analogous!

(68) People *will have talked* for three days about citizen's rights once the conference ends tomorrow. (sE)

(69) Sarah *will have jogged* every day for five weeks by March. (sE)

(70) We *will have understood* everything about grammar by the end of the semester. (sE)

(71) Our cat *will have eaten* all the treats by the end of the day. (sE)

To form **future perfect**, we need the **modal *will* + base form *have* + past participle of the main verb**. And again, we can see that the theme of some action being complete comes through. This time, the action will have been completed by some time in the future; hence: future perfect. Once the act of talking is complete in (68), the conference ends, so one action starts after another will have ended in the future. Even without a second action, we can still see in our examples how each {VP} conveys that the act of jogging in (69) and the act of understanding in (70) will have been completed at some future point.

Main takeaways so far?

- aspect: is marked on the main verb
- tense: is marked on the auxiliary verb (or, for simple tenses, the main verb itself)
- progressive aspect: form of *be* + present participle (*-ing*)
- perfect aspect: form of *have* + past participle

Exercise 2

Tense and Aspect, Round 1. Label tense (past, present, future) and aspect (simple, progressive, perfect) for each of the italicized {VPs} below.

Example:
It ***was*** in the apple that the witch ***had gave*** Snow White that wasn't poisonous.[32] (ChE)

- *was*: tense—past; aspect: simple
- *had gave*: tense—past; aspect: perfect

a) They *was giving* him the recognition.[33] (AAE)

b) Daisy May *had purred* loudly before she stopped when the vet came in. (sE)

c) Once we *get* under way, it shouldn't ought to take us very long.[34] (SAE)

d) I've *written up* the document, but before it *goes out*, it needs checked by Kim, Alex, and Sandy.[35] (ME)

e) I *will have taken* my medicine once a day for 2 weeks tomorrow. (sE)

f) I *was* afraid you might couldn't find it.[36] (SAE)

g) Many celebrities *will be auditioning* for this role. (sE)

h) Fluffy *has been* such a patient little kitty lately. (sE)

12.5 Complex Tense and Aspect

What if you want to express that something was ongoing in the past **and** completed in the past? We could use *be* and the *-ing* form (and thus progressive aspect) to index the ongoing nature of an action, but then how do we add *have* and the past participle to index that while it was ongoing, it's also complete? Well, we can combine all these components into complex {VPs}. As we work through each of our three tenses that can be combined with both progressive and perfect aspect, remember our affix hop and the potential for a new club dance.

12.5.1 Present Perfect Progressive

Let's look at our first data set. Can you identify progressive and perfect aspect in each?

(72) I *have been watering* the flowers all week. (sE)

(73) Tammy *has been waiting* for months for a response. (sE)

(74) People *have been planning* this for the last fifteen to twenty year.[37] (AAE)

(75) They *have been working* hard to succeed in the course. (sE)

(76) I *Ø been doing* dancing for a long time, for eight years already.[38] (ChE)

Each {VP} includes a form of *have*, a form of *be*, and both present participles and past participles, with one exception (i.e., (76)) where there is no initial auxiliary. Exactly how it all comes together is something our affix hop can help with. Let's take on the first example:

(72a) I *have been watering* the flowers all week. (sE)

Our form of *have* is *have*, so it's in present tense. The auxiliary *have* requires a past participle (remember, *have* + past participle = perfect aspect). Good thing we have a past participle in *been*, which also comes right after the auxiliary *have*. Now, we also have a present participle (*watering*). What causes a main verb to take on the *-ing* suffix? A form of *be*, exactly! And that past participle, *been*, is exactly that—a form of *be*. So, *have* causes the past participle affix to hop to the next verb (here, *been*), and *be* causes the present participle affix to hop to the next verb (here, *watering*). The form of *be* does double duty here: it's the past participle required for perfect aspect, and it's the form of *be* required for progressive aspect! And this is exactly what we can observe in all other examples. So, when you have a {VP} with an *-ing* form, do a double-take to make sure you didn't miss a past participle in that {VP}; if there are both, you're looking at a {VP} that is marked for both progressive and perfect aspect.

12.5.2 Past Perfect Progressive

The only difference between **present perfect progressive** and **past perfect progressive** is the tense of the first auxiliary *have* in the {VP}:

(77) We *had been watering* the flowers all week before we realized they were getting too much water. (sE)

(78) There were files that *had been missing* for five year, ten year, twenty years.³⁹ (AAE)

(79) I *had been a-fighting* a bear.⁴⁰ (AE)

(80) The cats *had been trying* to open the treat bags for hours when I finally started to notice what was going on. (sE)

(81) We *had been paying* attention all semester. (sE)

So, *had* (the past tense form of *have*) is followed by *been* (the past participle), which is followed by the present participle. If this complex {VP} is used in a complex or compound sentence, the relationship between the clause with the past perfect progressive {VP} and the other clause is often one of sequence, where something had been going on for some time before something else took place.

12.5.3 Future Perfect Progressive

One more form! This one lets us move both progressive and perfect aspects into the future realm:

(82) They *will have been singing* for five hours by midnight. (sE)

(83) We *will have been watering* the flowers for 5 hours by the time it gets dark. (sE)

Because the modal auxiliary *will* is what indexes future tense, and because it requires the next verb to be in its bare infinitive form, we have *have* next, rather than *has* or *had*. To check off our perfect aspect, we'll need *have* and a past participle. *Been* checks that box for the past participle. *Been* also checks the box for one of our progressive aspect requirements, since it's a form of *be*. And, of course, our present participles *singing* and *watering* check the box for progressive aspect.

Exercise 3

Tense and Aspect, Round 2. Label tense (past, present, future) and aspect(s) (progressive, perfect, simple) for each of the italicized {VPs} below (all sE; produced with the help of OpenAI⁴¹).

a) She *will be attending* the conference next week.

b) We *have learned* many things about cats since we *adopted* our first one years ago.

c) They *had been living* in that house for ten years before they decided to move.

d) They *were playing* soccer when it started to rain.

e) By the end of the month, she *will have completed* her project.

f) By next year, she *will have been working* at the company for a decade.

g) We *had left* the office already when the meeting started.

h) I *am reading* a book right now.

Foundations of Grammar

> **Exercise 4**
>
> Create your own sentences, Round 2. Provide {VPs} that are present perfect progressive, past perfect progressive, and future perfect progressive for each of the following verbs. Then, create an example sentence for each of those {VPs}.
>
> *talk, sing, jump, dream, appoint*
>
> | verb | {VP} present perfect progressive | {VP} past perfect progressive | {VP} future perfect progressive |
> |---|---|---|---|
> | *talk* | | | |
> | *sing* | | | |
> | *jump* | | | |
> | *dream* | | | |
> | *appoint* | | | |
>
> Example sentences for all fifteen {VPs}:

12.6 Variation in Aspect

With everything you know about tense and aspect by now, you're ready for some of the rich variation in the aspectual system across some American English dialects.

12.6.1 Progressive Aspect

12.6.1.1 AAE Paradigms

Recall that the term "aspect" refers to how a particular event is being viewed in respect to time. Since this entire section is about AAE paradigms, we don't provide dialect labels for each example. Do keep in mind that SAE, ChE, and to an extent AE, allow for similar patterns. For AAE and some SAE dialects, the pattern for **present progressive** can look slightly different from the sE pattern. Can you spot the pattern based on this data set?

(84) They *is making* stuff up.[42]

(85) They say it's a party tonight. *Is* you *going*?[43]

(86) I *am moving*.[44]

(87) You feel like *you getting* something.[45]

(88) She *making* us eat healthy.[46]

(89) He *working* during the day.[47]

(90) Our mind tricks us to think that *we going* to sleep and *we waking* up.[48]

(91) They *building* these condos.[49]

These example sentences indicate that there is some variation in AAE for present progressive verb forms, since a form of *be* is included (either *am* or *is*) only in (84)–(86).

How about the pattern for **past progressive** based on the next data set?

(92) I *was walking* past the bathroom.[50]
(93) I *was aksing* you about the traditions you *was talking* about.[51]
(94) She *was getting* older.[52]
(95) He *was reading* in the library.[53]
(96) We *was discussing* the initiative that Obama curated.[54]
(97) Grandma and grandpa decided y'all *was coming* to DC.[55]
(98) They *was waiting* on the other side.[56]

The *be* auxiliary's form is *was* in all instances. Chart 2 summarizes the paradigms for present and past progressive[57]:

	Person	AAE present progressive	AAE past progressive
singular	1st	I am growing.	I was drinking.
	2nd	You (is) growing.	You was drinking.
	3rd	She/he/it/they (is) growing.	He/she/it/they was drinking.
plural	1st	We (is) growing. / We growing.	We was drinking.
	2nd	You (is) growing. / You growing.	You was drinking.
	3rd	They (is) growing. / They growing.	They was drinking.

Chart 2 Present/past progressive paradigms AAE

Past progressive uses the form *was* as the auxiliary. Present progressive requires *am* for first-person singular (i.e., *I*) while *is* (a form of *be*) is optional (as indicated by the parentheses) for the remainder of the paradigm. Green notes that *is* is usually not omitted in sentences such as *it is growing*.[58] A related feature is shown in the sentences below:

(99) They fools *steady hustlin'* everybody they see.[59]
(100) They want to do they own thing, and you *steady talking* to them.[60]
(101) *He *steady having* money.

According to Green, adding *steady* to the progressive paradigm means that "an action or process (…) is carried out in an intense, consistent and continuous manner."[61] As such, it is incompatible with verbs that do not denote an action such as in (101).

Exercise 5

Tense and Aspect, Round 3. Identify tense and aspect in the AAE examples below.

a) You gotta make sure they *doing* this right.[62]
b) They *was telling* the truth.[63]

Foundations of Grammar

> c) You *was working*.[64]
> d) At the awards ceremony—you *comin* to that ain't you?[65]
> e) Dave Bartholomae (...) *is retirin* and his peeps *honorin* him here.[66]
> f) Rhetoric and writin prof Todd Craig *is dee-jayin* all night too.[67]

12.6.1.2 Appalachian English and a-prefixing

Now, AAE isn't the only dialect that shows some variation when it comes to the *-ing* verb. You've encountered many related examples throughout this book from Appalachian English (AE). It's time to fill you in on the grammatical pattern of **a-prefixing**! As you look at the data set below, pay attention to which ones are grammatical and which ones are ungrammatical (marked with an *). What does each group have in common?

(102) I know he *was a-tellin'* the truth, but I was *a-comin'* home.[68]
(103) Fire was *a-flamin'* everything.[69]
(104) He was *a-huntin'*.[70]
(105) John was *a-talkin'* so loud my eardrums hurt.[71]
(106) **A-dancin'* is a lot of fun.
(107) **The book is a-thrillin'*.
(108) **After a-tellin'* the truth, I forgave him.
(109) **They were a-considerin'* all the facts.

The a-prefixing is possible for verbs only. When an *-ing*-verb functions as a noun as in **A-dancin'* in (106), it becomes ungrammatical. The same goes for adjectives (*thrilling* in (107)). So that's the first part of the grammatical rule for a-prefixing: it only works on verbs. Next, when the *-ing* verb comes after a preposition (*after* in (108)), the a-prefix cannot be added. And finally, the a-prefix is only addable to verbs that have a primary stress on the first syllable. The primary stress is on the second syllable for *considering* (*conSIdering*) in (109), and because of that, the *a*-prefix can't be added.[72] When the *-ing* form does endure the a-prefix, it can be combined with a form of *be* to form present and past progressive; the *be* form is not always necessary, similar to the AAE pattern from earlier.

12.6.1.3 Fixing to do/finna

Finally, you might have heard about this construction, or you might be using this construction yourself:

(110) I'*m fixin'* to finish that budget proposal today.[73] (SAE)
(111) He *was fixing to* go to Korea.[74] (AAE)
(112) Now I'*m finna get* into some more general topics.[75] (AAE)
(113) Daisy's *fixin to* tell the story.[76] (SAE)
(114) I'*m fixin' to* wash the dishes.[77] (SAE)

This form requires progressive aspect (notice the present participle form of the verbs), which means that something like *He fixed to go to Korea* would be ungrammatical. Overall, this particular feature is most used in present tense.[78] Semantically, it indicates that something is about to happen or that someone is planning on doing something; in other words, something is imminent.[79] This grammatical feature is widely used by speakers in the Southern states of the United States.

12.6.2 Perfective Aspect

In addition to the perfect aspect already covered above, many American dialects have specific, additional verb constructions that express a range of semantic meaning.

12.6.2.1 Completive done in AAE

Our next data set illustrates **completive done**, which is common (and grammatical!) in AAE.

(115) I *done killed* five of my years being in Lorton.[80]

(116) You *done did* all the work.[81]

(117) My mama *done tol'* me when I was in pigtails. (Johnny Mercer, "Blues in the Night," as sung by Ella Fitzgerald.)[82]

(118) Y'all *done* already *jumped*.[83]

(119) They *done tore* it down but the building is still there.[84]

This verb construction consists of the auxiliary *done* followed by the past tense form of the verb. The fact that the past tense form of the verb is used becomes especially clear in *done did* and *done tore*: the past participle would result in *done done* and *done torn*. Sometimes, this construction is represented as *dən did*, which highlights the pronunciation of the auxiliary *done* with a reduced vowel (which is similar to the initial vowel in *again*). This construction emphasizes that an action has been **fully** completed. In other words, in comparison to perfect aspect, which would use the auxiliary *have* + past participle (i.e., *have torn*), **completive done** *done tore* adds this semantic nuance to the {VP}. Generally, this form is associated with AAE. However, it is a feature of SAE as well and used by white Southerners.[85]

> **Completive done** =
> *Done/ dən*+ simple past form

12.6.2.2 Another *done*

This next *done* is called **done my homework** and is found in East Coast English dialects (ECE), such as in Philadelphia, southern New Jersey, Delaware, Maryland, and the northern part of New England. It's even more common in Canada.[86] Here are some examples:

(120) When I don't have hockey and *I'm done* my homework, I go there and skate.[87]

(121) Martin *is done* his bass tracks and we are ready to start vocals.[88]

(122) So many bloggers I read are doing this. One *is already done* her 50,000 words![89]

(123) This will be particularly important once you*'re done* the tattoo and need to leave the shop.[90]

This feature requires a form of *be* plus the participle *done* or *finished*. Because this form indicates that an action has been completed, we include it in this section in this chapter, since it fits in with other constructions that indicate that an action has been completed. It's a bit different from the other perfective {VPs} because we need a form of *be*. Compare these two sentences:

(124) I*'m* all *ready* for school.

(124a) I*'m* all *done* my homework.

In (124), we have a form of *be* (in this case *am*) followed by *ready*, which is an adjective that is intensified by *all*. In (124a), we have the same combination, just with the past participle *done* instead of *ready*. This points to the fact that this dialect feature shares similarities with adjectives more so than with verbs. More on this in Chapter 13!

12.6.2.3 *After*-perfect

We turn to another perfective construction which is called ***after*-perfect**—can you guess why?

(125) Charlie said I*'m after learnin'* a French song while I was in there.[91]

(126) If you said to me last year, I'd be after having the year I*'m after having*, I would have laughed at you basically.[92]

(127) I *am after cooking* in the kitchen.[93]

The other {VPs} that indicate that an action is completed so far have looked like this:

- form of *have* + past participle as in *I have planted several flowers.*
- *done* + simple past tense as in *I done told you.*
- Form of *be* + participle *done* as in *I'm done my homework.*

In the ***after*-perfect**, we need a bit more: ***be* + *after* + present participle**. This feature conveys that an action has happened in the recent past, and that it has implications for the present, something this feature has in common with other perfect aspect constructions. For (125), the semantic meaning is similar to *I have (just) learned a French song*, for (126) it would be like *the year I just had*, and for (127) it would be close to *I have cooked dinner*.

While this feature is common in various areas within the United States,[94] it is more common in Canada and even more common in Ireland and some areas of Scotland. Interestingly, in areas in Canada in which this feature occurs, Irish English is widely used. People who use this form and who emigrated to Canada brought this form with them, which is why we can find it in those areas today.

12.6.3 Even More Possibilities: Moving beyond Perfect and Progressive Aspects

In addition to constructions that relate to both progressive and perfective aspects outlined above, AAE has two other aspect forms. This illustrates that when compared to the aspectual system in sE, the AAE aspectual system is much richer and more complex. This, in turn, allows speakers to index meaning distinctions about a verb's action as it relates to time directly in the {VP}.

12.6.3.1 Habitual *be*

As always, we start with some data. Can you describe the pattern found in the {VPs}?

(128)　I *be listening* to the beats.[95]

(129)　And you *be running* up as fast as you can.[96]

(130)　She *be hollering* over there.[97]

(131)　He don't *be barking* at nobody.[98]

(132)　We Black folks *be knowin* we got some unique patterns of language …[99]

(133)　My parents *be correcting*, too.[100] (AAE)

(134)　Y'all *be wanting* to go somewhere.[101]

(135)　They *be hollering* over there.[102]

The {VPs} consist of *be + present participle*. This combination of auxiliary and main verb conveys that the verb's action occurs regularly or routinely. Because of this, it is called **habitual *be***. In sE, people can of course also indicate that an action happens habitually, repeatedly, generally. All that needs to happen is adding an adverbial of some kind as in *I listen to the beats all the time/a lot/generally*. The crucial difference is that in AAE, this meaning is encoded in the {VP} and an adverbial indicating this habitual nature of the verb's action is not required.

Habitual *be*

- *be* +present participle
- *be* on its own (when it is the main verb)

Habitual *be* is generally associated with AAE, but it is also common in ChE:[103]

(136)　The news *be showing* it too much.[104]

(137)　Me and my mom *be praying* in Spanish.[105]

Habitual *be* is spreading beyond the dialect community of AAE and ChE, and you'll likely have encountered it on social media and elsewhere by all kinds of dialect speakers. Even before this more recent development, it has been attested that some rural white SAE speakers also use habitual *be*.[106]

In addition to the construction of ***be* + present participle**, this habitual meaning can also be expressed without the present participle:

(138) She usually *be* home in the evening.[107]

(139) Your phone bill *be* high, don't it.[108]

(140) I *be* in my office.[109]

(141) Trash *be* everywhere.[110]

Many people who are unfamiliar with habitual *be* assume—wrongly—that it is interchangeable with sE progressive aspect. Compare these two sentences:

(128a) I *be listening* to the beats.[111] (AAE)

(128b) I *am listening* to the beats. (sE)

Example (128a) indicates that the action of *listening* happens regularly, habitually; (128b) indicates that the action of *listening* is happening right now. *Be* is thus **not** interchangeable with *am*. In many educational contexts, speakers who use habitual *be* are often told to replace *be* with *am/is/are*. Well, since they don't mean the same thing, it makes no sense to demand this change.

You already know about the addition of *steady* in the AAE progressive paradigm. *Steady* can also be added to habitual *be* constructions:

(142) Ricky Bell *be steady steppin'* in them number nines.[112]

(143) He *steady be tellin'* 'em how to run they lives.[113]

Adding *steady* again indicates that the action of the verb is especially intense and consistent, regardless of whether it is added to the progressive or habitual {VP}.

12.6.3.2 Remote Time BIN

This is our last type of aspect! Naturally, we'll start with some data taken from AAE. What's the auxiliary and main verb here?

(144) We *been married* almost twenty-six years.[114]

(145) And she *been started* conversating.[115]

(146) They just sent me this one, but I *BIN having* that one.[116]

(147) They ain't going bad, they *BIN* bad.[117]

(148) He *BIN* a preacher.[118]

All {VPs} include *been*, which is sometimes represented as *BIN*. There's some variation in terms of what follows *Been/BIN*:

- past tense form of the main verb (such as *married* and *started*);
- present participle of the main verb (such as *having*);
- {AdjP} as in *bad*; or
- {NP} as in *a preacher*.

What **remote-time BIN** communicates is that the action was started at some point in the past and is ongoing at the moment in which the sentence is said. While this form is called **remote time BIN**, the status of what qualifies as being "remote time" is relative. The action of the verb could have started fifty years or fifteen minutes ago, but what's crucial is that the time span from when the action started to the present is longer than expected.[119]

Remote time BIN

- *Been/BIN* +past tense form
- *Been/BIN* + present participle
- *Been/BIN* + adjective phrase
- *Been/BIN* + noun phrase

What's also interesting is that there is a form in sE that seems to be similar:

(149) Forget about the way you've *been brushing* your teeth.[120] (sE)

If we apply the meaning of remote time BIN[121] to this sentence, then this is the interpretation: *Forget about the way you've been brushing your teeth for a long time.*[122] It's more likely that the sentence is simply drawing a contrast between how you've brushed your teeth in the past and how you should be brushing them now, rather than it being about how you've brushed your teeth "for a long time."

Alright, this was the last construction related to verb aspect, which means our overview of tense and aspect is complete! It's important to note that our overview of AAE here is far from exhaustive. For that, you'd have to consult, for instance, Green's (2002) introduction to AAE. We hope that this book and this chapter, in particular, are showing you that dialect features are systematic, that they have patterns, and that by extension, speakers who use so-called non-sE dialect features are not making mistakes.

Exercise 6

What is each italicized feature called? Provide the name and then list the dialect(s) each feature is associated with.

a) You *be doing* a classwork in class.[123]

b) I *am after* cooking my dinner.[124]

c) The two-thousands *finna* be considered old.[125]

d) Them students *be steady trying* to make a buck.[126]

e) She *done told* me.[127]

f) They *been married*.[128]

g) They care about it now that you *done moved* everybody out.[129]

h) Ms. Helen *be correcting* us all the time.[130]

Foundations of Grammar

Terminology to Know

Term	Working definition	Example/Illustration
Tense		
Aspect		
Progressive aspect		
Perfective aspect		
Past participle		
Past tense form		
Simple present		
Simple past		
Simple future		
Present progressive		
Past progressive		
Future progressive		
Present perfect		
Past perfect		
Future perfect		
Present perfect progressive		
Past perfect progressive		
Future perfect progressive		
Complex {VP}		
Completive done		
Progressive aspect AAE		
a-prefixing		
After-perfect		
Habitual be		
Remote time Been		
Perfective had		

Chart 3 Key terminology Chapter 12

Notes

1. Bayley, 2012, p. 158.
2. Adapted from Wood, 2014.
3. Fought, 2003, p. 96.
4. Kendall, Quartey et al., 2018 Transcript ID DCB_se2_ag4_f_01_1.
5. Yerastov, 2010; cited in Wood, 2014.

6. Kendall, Quartey et al., 2018 Transcript ID DCB_se2_ag4_m_01_1.
7. T. McMurtry, personal communication, March 30, 2025.
8. Kendall, Fasold et al., 2018 Transcript ID DCA_se3_ag1_f_04_1.
9. Baker-Bell, 2020, p. 57.
10. University of South Carolina (n.d.).
11. Baker-Bell, 2020, p. 76.
12. Barrón and San Romón, n.d., pp. 30–1; cited in Bayley, 2012, p. 158.
13. T. McMurtry, personal communication, March 30, 2025.
14. Kaplan, 2015.
15. W. Beauregard, personal communication, August 29, 2024.
16. Corver, 2005; cited in Wood, 2012.
17. University of South Carolina (n.d.).
18. Barrón and San Romón, n.d., pp. 30–1; cited in Bayley, 2012, p. 162.
19. Kendall, Quartey et al., 2018 Transcript ID DCB_se3_ag3_m_02_1.
20. Wolfram and Christian, 1976, p. 69.
21. Baker-Bell, 2020, p. 43.
22. Green, 2002, p. 37ff.
23. Christian et al., 1988; cited in Matyiku, 2011a.
24. Mishoe and Montgomery, 1994; cited in Huang, 2011.
25. Baker-Bell, 2020, p. 74.
26. King et al., 2020 Transcript ID ROC_se0_ag1_m_02_1.
27. Fought, 2003, p. 94.
28. Fought, 2003, p. 94.
29. Ibid., p. 96.
30. Quartey et al., 2020 Transcript ID VLD_se0_ag3_m_01_2.
31. Green, 2002, p. 95.
32. Bayley and Santa Ana, 2004, p. 378.
33. Kendall, Quartey et al., 2018 Transcript ID DCB_se1_ag2_m_01_1.
34. Adapted from Huang, 2011.
35. Whitman, 2010; cited in Maher and Wood, 2011.
36. Di Paolo, 1989; cited in Huang, 2011.
37. Becker et al., 2021 Transcript ID LES_se0_ag2_f_02_1.
38. Bayley, 2012, p. 160.
39. Kendall, Quartey et al., 2018 Transcript ID DCB_se1_ag4_m_01_1.
40. University of South Carolina (n.d.).
41. Sentences created with the assistance of OpenAI, 2024.
42. Kendall, Fasold et al., 2018 Transcript ID DCA_se1_ag4_m_02_1.
43. Kendall, Quartey et al., 2018 Transcript ID DCB_se1_ag3_m_03_1.
44. Ibid., Transcript ID DCB_se3_ag3_f_02_1.
45. Farrington et al., 2020 Transcript ID ATL_se0_ag1_f_03_1.

46. Kendall, Quartey et al., 2018 Transcript ID DCB_se1_ag1_f_02_1.
47. Kendall, Fasold et al., 2018 Transcript ID DCA_se2_ag1_m_01_1.
48. Farrington et al., 2020 Transcript ID ATL_se0_ag2_m_01_1.
49. Kendall, Quartey et al., 2018 Transcript ID DCB_se3_ag3_m_02_1.
50. Ibid., Transcript ID DCB_se1_ag1_m_02_1.
51. Ibid., Transcript ID DCB_se1_ag2_m_03_1.
52. Ibid., Transcript ID DCB_se1_ag3_m_01_1.
53. King et al., 2020 Transcript ID ROC_se0_ag3_f_02_1.
54. Kendall, Quartey et al., 2018 Transcript ID DCB_se1_ag1_m_02_1.
55. Ibid., Transcript ID DCB_se2_ag3_m_01_1.
56. Farrington et al., 2020 Transcript ID ATL_se0_ag1_m_03_1.
57. Based on Green, 2002, p. 37.
58. Cf. Green, 2002, pp. 37 and 68.
59. Baugh, 1984, p. 4; Martin, 2018b.
60. Green, 2002, p. 72.
61. Ibid., p. 23.
62. Kendall, Quartey et al., 2018 Transcript ID DCB_se1_ag2_f_03_1.
63. Ibid., Transcript ID DCB_se3_ag1_m_01_1.
64. Farrington et al., 2020 Transcript ID ATL_se0_ag1_m_05_1.
65. Young, 2019, p. 4.
66. Ibid.
67. Ibid.
68. Matyiku, 2011a.
69. Wolfram and Christian, 1976, p. 69.
70. Matyiku, 2011a.
71. Wolfram, 1976; cited in Matyiku, 2011a.
72. See Reaser and Wolfram, 2007, pp. 7–9, for more details.
73. Staub and Zentz, 2017.
74. Kendall, Fasold et al., 2018 Transcript ID DCA_se1_ag1_m_03_1.
75. Farrington et al., 2020 Transcript ID ATL_se0_ag1_f_01_1.
76. Myers, 2014, p. 56; cited in Staub and Zentz, 2017.
77. Ching, 1987; cited in Staub and Zentz, 2017.
78. Staub and Zentz, 2017.
79. Reaser et al., 2017a.
80. Kendall, Quartey et al., 2018 Transcript ID DCB_se2_ag4_m_01_1.
81. Kendall, Fasold et al., 2018 Transcript ID DCA_se1_ag1_f_02_1.
82. Martin, 2018a.
83. Farrington et al., 2020 Transcript ID ATL_se0_ag1_m_03_1.
84. Kendall, Quartey et al., 2018 Transcript ID DCB_se1_ag4_f_01_1.

85. Martin, 2018a; for more information, refer to Dayton, 1996; Edwards, 1991; Green, 2002, 2011; and Terry, 2010.
86. Fruehwald and Myler, 2015; cited in Wood, 2014.
87. Wood, 2014.
88. Ibid.
89. Ibid.
90. Ibid.
91. Bismark, 2008, p. 104; cited in Martinez, 2018.
92. Ibid.
93. Martinez, 2018.
94. Ibid.
95. Farrington et al., 2020 Transcript ID ATL_se0_ag1_f_01_1.
96. Kendall, Fasold et al., 2018 Transcript ID DCA_se2_ag1_m_03_1.
97. Ibid., Transcript ID DCA_se2_ag1_f_07_1.
98. T. McMurtry, personal communication, March 30, 2025.
99. Smitherman, 2006, p. 2.
100. McMurtry, 2022, p. 42.
101. Kendall, Quartey et al., 2018 Transcript ID DCB_se1_ag2_f_03_1.
102. Kendall, Fasold et al., 2018 Transcript ID DCA_se2_ag1_f_07_1.
103. Fought, 2003.
104. Ibid., p. 96.
105. Ibid.
106. Reaser et al., 2017a.
107. Ibid., p. 280.
108. Green, 2002, p. 48.
109. Ibid.
110. McMurtry, 2022, p. 47.
111. Farrington et al., 2020 Transcript ID ATL_se0_ag1_f_01_1.
112. Baugh, 1984, p. 4.
113. Ibid.
114. Kendall, Quartey et al., 2018 Transcript ID DCB_se2_ag4_m_01_1.
115. Kendall, Fasold et al., 2018 Transcript ID DCA_se2_ag1_f_07_1.
116. Green, 2002, p. 56.
117. Ibid.
118. Ibid.
119. Ibid., p. 55.
120. Ibid.
121. This particular feature has been researched quite a bit (see Green, 2002 for an overview), and Reaser et al., 2017a. Note that it is dying out in some AAE dialects.
122. Green, 2002, p. 55.

123. Bayley, 2012, p. 163.
124. Martinez, 2018.
125. Farrington et al., 2020 Transcript ID ATL_se0_ag1_f_01_1.
126. Green, 2002, p. 72.
127. Rowe et al., 2018 Transcript ID PRV_se0_ag3_f_04_3.
128. Ibid.
129. Kendall, Quartey et al., 2018 Transcript ID DCB_se2_ag4_f_01_1.
130. Baker-Bell, 2020, p. 52.

CHAPTER 13
ARE YOU TALKIN' TO ME? MOOD AND VOICE

Overview

We're not quite done with {VPs}! This chapter will add to your knowledge about {VPs} by outlining **mood**, **voice**, and **finiteness**. See—we told you that the {VP} is a powerhouse! Our objectives are as follows. You'll be able to

- identify the mood of a given sentence;
- identify active voice and passive voice; and
- identify {VPs} as either finite or non-finite.

Pre-reading tasks

1. In any way you wish, describe how the sentence pairs below express different perspectives? How is this accomplished? No observation is too small!
   (1a) The dog and cat played.
   (1b) What game did the dog and cat play?
   (2a) The dog chased the cat around the table.
   (2b) The cat was chased around the table.
   (3a) I wish the cat and dog would play nicely together.
   (3b) The dog and cat do play nicely together.
   (4a) The veterinarian recommended the dog run for thirty minutes per day.
   (4b) The cat ran for an hour!

2. Many guidebooks argue against using passive voice. What do you make of the following statements? Have you heard similar statements from your teachers/educators?

   - "If energy has occurred in the work, unnatural passive voice saps the energy and leaves dead words on the pages"[1]
   - "Needlessly passive verbs slow your writing"[2]
   - Passive voice is "less bold, and less concise"[3]
   - "Never use the passive when you can use the active"[4]
   - Active voice is more "vigorous" and "straightforward"[5]

13.1 The Three Moods of English: Introduction

In addition to person, number, tense, and aspect, the {VP} can also express **mood**. The term "mood" might strike you as odd given that this is a grammar book, but this term has a highly specialized meaning within grammar that differs drastically from its everyday uses. Grammatical mood—unlike human emotional mood—allows speakers or writers to characterize their perspective about the situation expressed in the sentence. **Mood** is the intersection between verbal choice and the events being conveyed in the sentence. While languages have a wide array of methods for showing this quality, English mood is syntactically transparent: we can see or hear mood in the verb form choices and grammatical structures. What do the following sentences in each group have in common?

(1) Denzel teaches linguistics courses. (sE)
(2) [T]here were wicked fast teams.[6] (NEE)
(3) John was a-talkin' so loud my eardrums hurt.[7] (AE)
(4) How could you might do that?[8] (SAE)
(5) Sit down. (sE)
(6) Heat the solution to 125 degrees Fahrenheit. (sE)
(7) So speak up—speak out—even if yo voice shakes.[9] (AAE)
(8) [C]heck out at least one of dem dere sessions I spotlighted.[10] (AAE)
(9) [A]nd if power don't listen, it will hear us nonetheless.[11] (AAE)
(10) If he'd be here right now, he'd make me laugh.[12] (ChE)
(11) I'm going fishin if it don't be raining.[13] (AAE)
(12) If you give me thirty minutes, I mighta coulda thought of some names.[14] (AE)

The **indicative** includes statements and questions as in (1)–(4), **imperatives** are orders/commands as in (5)–(8), and **subjunctive** includes hypotheticals of some kind as in (9)–(12). We'll describe each of these three moods in turn next.

13.1.1 Indicative Mood

Many, if not most, English sentences are in **indicative mood**. Indicative mood includes **declaratives** (i.e., statements), **interrogatives** (i.e., questions), and **exclamatives**. These indicative mood constructions allow us to simply state, question, or exclaim a state of affairs. Look at the two example sets below. We start with declaratives, we then morph that declarative into an exclamation, and finally we show an interrogative version:

(13) Denzel teaches linguistics courses. (sE)
(13a) Denzel teaches linguistics courses! (sE)
(13b) Does Denzel teach linguistics courses? (sE)
(13c) Where does Denzel teach linguistics courses? (sE)

(14)   I was wicked jealous.[15] (NEE)

(14a) I was wicked jealous! (NEE)

(14b) Was I wicked jealous? (NEE)

(14c) Why was I wicked jealous? (NEE)

With declaratives, we simply express something about a certain state of affairs. Declaratives feature basic SVO word order. The exclamations might sound a bit more convincing with an added adverbial such as *finally* as in *I'm finally teaching linguistics courses!* but they feature the same basic word order as declaratives. With exclamations, we express—generally—some kind of emotion, and no special syntactic operation or verb form is required. In written form, we simply add the exclamation point; in spoken form, our intonation can convey that meaning, and in signed language, expression and manual movement indicate that something is an exclamation. With interrogatives, we can pose questions about a given state of affairs. Interrogatives are a bit more interesting, because the basic word order of SVO changes depending on whether the interrogative is a polar, yes/no-question as in (13b), or a *wh-*question as in (14c).

For **yes/no-questions**, a few different ways of forming the interrogative exist:

(15)   *Are* we almost home? (sE)

(16)   *Could* you *might go* to the store for me?[16] (SAE)

(17)   *Is* Bob *gon' leave*?[17] (AAE)

(18)   *Did* Hassan *eat* all the cake? (sE)

When the main verb of a sentence is a form of *be*, that verb moves to the beginning to form interrogatives (see (15) and (17)). Similarly, if the sentence has at least one auxiliary verb as in (16), then that auxiliary can move to the front of the sentence to form an interrogative (recall the superpowers of auxiliaries from Chapter 7!). If there is no auxiliary and the main form is something other than a form of *be*, *dummy do* is added (see (18)).

In addition to syntactic marking such as moving an auxiliary to the beginning of the sentence, many (if not all) dialects of American English have additional ways of formulating polar questions, such as using intonation to mark something as a question:

(19)   You teach linguistics classes? (sE)

(20)   He sleeping in the car?[18] (AAE)

Rather than performing a syntactic operation, each sentence ends with final rising intonation to convey that the sentence is a question (we represent final rising intonation with the question mark here). This way of formulating questions has been documented for many dialects, including AAE.[19] Note, however, that researchers have documented that even declaratives with final falling intonation can function as questions in conversations.[20] It's one of those things where we, as language users, don't always make our language use conform to what's written in grammar books!

Wh-word questions (also called content-seeking questions) are formed a little differently. They must be fronted with the appropriate question word: *who/whom, which,*

Foundations of Grammar

what, *where*, *when*, *why*, or *how*. Additional syntactic operations are necessary in some cases, as the declarative-interrogative pairs below illustrate. We start with examples that feature {VPs} that consist of just the main verb.

who

(21) I *heard* him a-fussin' about taxes.[21] (AE)

(21a) Who *heard* him a-fussin' about taxes?

whom

(22) We *took* our friends to the movies. (sE)

(22a) Whom *did* you *take* to the movies?

what

(23) Pantyhose *are* so expensive anymore.[22] (ME)

(23a) What *is* so expensive anymore?

which

(24) The ad *displays* the product features. (sE)

(24a) Which ad *displays* the product features?

where

(25) I *put* this wicked good recipe on top of the recipe book.

(25a) Where *did* I *put* that wicked good recipe?[23] (NEE)

when

(26) You *was* pretty weak by the tenth day.[24] (AE)

(26a) When *was* you pretty weak?

why

(27) My voice *get* shaky because …

(27a) Why your voice *get* shaky?[25] (AAE)

how

(28) The cake *turned out* fine. (sE)

(28a) How *did* the cake *turn out*?

If the main verb in the declarative is a form of *be*, then that verb moves up to immediately after the *wh*-word in the interrogative. This should be familiar from the subject–verb inversion test! In most examples, if the main verb is **not** a form of *be*, then our old friend, *dummy do*, makes an appearance. Remember that when *dummy do* does occur, it carries tense. In dialects such as AAE, we can see that this *dummy do* isn't required (see (27a)). In sE, *dummy do* isn't required in two instances either: In *who*-questions, because *who* both functions as and targets the subject, *who* is immediately followed by the verb. Similarly, in *which*-questions that target a component of the subject, no *do* is required.

How about declaratives that feature an auxiliary in the {VP} already? Well, given the superpowers of the auxiliary, we suspect that this auxiliary might do some heavy lifting once again. The next data set shows if/how the word order changes in *wh*-word interrogatives that feature one or multiple auxiliaries in the {VP}.

who

(29) She *was a-goin'* to the show.[26] (AE)

(29a) Who *was a-goin'* to the show?

whom

(30) I *am taking* Latoya to the movies. (sE)

(30a) Whom *are* you *taking* to the movies?

what

(31) Fatima *is studying* electrical engineering. (sE)

(31a) What *is* Fatima *studying*?

which

(32) The new client *is going* to the experience lawyer Carlos. (sE)

(32a) Which client *is going* to the experienced lawyer Carlos?

where

(33) I *am going* home. (sE)

(33a) Where *are* you *going*?

when

(34) Jean and Mary *have left* for vacation last night already. (sE)

(34a) When *had* Jean and Mary *left* for vacation?

why

(35) I'm looking like this because I'm ready to leave.[27] (AAE)

(35a) *Why* you *looking* like that?[28] (AAE)

how

(36) How *could* you *might do* that?[29] (SAE)

(36a) I *might could do* it over night.

Our data show that for most dialects, the first auxiliary switches place with the subject. For dialects such as AAE, auxiliary-verb inversion isn't required, in part, because the auxiliary form of *be* is not always required in declaratives either (*you looking* vs. *you are looking*). The fronting of the *wh*-word itself is sufficient in forming most of the *wh*-word questions in AAE.

There is only one exception in sE dialects: *wh*-word questions that target the subject or components of the subject. For *who*-questions and *which*-questions that target the subject, no subject–verb inversion is necessary. If a *which*-question targets a component

Foundations of Grammar

of the direct object, auxiliary-subject inversion happens (*which lawyer is the new client going to?*). To systematically review which constituent can be targeted by which *wh-* word, and for an opportunity to flex your sentence-pattern knowledge from Chapter 11, check out the companion website!

Exercise 1

Indicative mood. Practice turning declaratives into interrogatives and vice versa. If a declarative is provided, turn it into an interrogative that targets the italicized portion of the declarative. If an interrogative is provided, turn it into a declarative.

a) Ainsley is the *oldest* player on the team. (sE)
b) Now *I'm* wicked tired and I am going to go to bed.[30] (NEE)
c) *The soul* needs fed by creative, multi-dimensional teaching.[31] (ME)
d) I baked *them* banana bread. (sE)
e) We brushed the cats regularly *to keep their coats healthy*. (sE)
f) Did he yell at John for fixin' to change the plan?[32] (SAE/AAE)
g) Was she right on time? (sE)
h) Had they been reviewing the materials regularly? (sE)

13.1.2 Imperative Mood

Imperative mood is used to issue a command. In the data set below, where are the verbs located in the sentence? What form of the verb is being used? What/who is the subject in each?

(37) *Shut* the window. (sE)
(38) *Heat* the solution to 125 degrees Fahrenheit. (sE)
(39) Just *eat* them big black cherries.[33] (AAE)
(40) [C]*heck out* at least one of dem dere sessions I spotlighted.[34] (AAE)

The verb occurs in sentence-initial position (or right after an adverb such as *just* in (39)). The verb is in its base form (no tense marking). The implied subject is whomever is being addressed: singular *you* if you're addressing just one person or plural *you* if you're addressing more than one person.

If you want to tell someone **not** to do something, you need to add a negative element. Because the verb is in its base form, an auxiliary is necessary. Enter *dummy do* once more:

(37a) *Don't shut* the window. (sE)
(39a) Just *don't eat* them big black cherries.[35] (AAE)

Imperatives may strike you as direct, even rude, and yet they are very common and often not treated as rude at all, especially when something needs to be done quickly, such as a surgeon saying, "Hand me the scalpel." Plus, adding a *please*, for instance, as in *Please don't shut the window* makes any command more polite.

13.1.3 Subjunctive Mood

Subjunctive mood allows us to express hypotheticals, desires, wishes, predictions, and speculations about the past, present, or future. Subjunctive mood is also called the mood of irrealis—events that are not real.

13.1.3.1 Regular Subjunctive
Are the following sentences about factual events? What time frame is being referenced? And how would you describe the two events expressed in each sentence?

(41) If Sam *is* late, we *will start* without them. (sE)
(42) [A]nd if power *don't listen*, it *will hear* us nonetheless.[36] (AAE)
(43) I *will buy* pizza if you *come over*. (sE)
(44) If you *give* me thirty minutes, I *mighta coulda thought* of some names.[37] (AE)

None of these sentences expresses a factual event. The **regular subjunctive** mood allows us to express what will happen in the future if a condition is met. The sentence structure is of the *if-then* kind: an *if*-clause is dependent on a main clause. Note that generally, a comma is expected prior to the main clause if the *if*-clause begins the sentence as in (41), (42), and (44) (see Chapter 15 for more about punctuation).

How about the next data set?

(45) If we *had played* the lottery, we *would have won*. (sE)
(46) If we *had* more money, we *would go* on a vacation. (sE)
(47) If it *ain't making* dollars in they eyes, it just *don't make* sense.[38] (AAE)
(48) If she *were* president, she *would pass* the bill right away. (sE)
(49) If he'*d be* here right now, he'*d make* me laugh.[39] (ChE)

In (45), a hypothetical event in the past didn't take place because some condition (*lottery*) wasn't met. The subjunctive mood also allows us to express a current hypothetical that would lead to either a desired event in the future ((46)) or a desired event in the present ((47)–(49)). Note that *would* generally doesn't occur in an *if*-clause in sE, but this is possible in ChE (see (49)). If an *if*-clause contains a form of *be*, it occurs as *were* for all subjects, including first-person singular *I* (i.e., *If I were rich, ...*) and third-person singular *she/he/it/they* (i.e., *If she were president ...* (48)). This form of the subjunctive is also called **were-subjunctive**. This *were*-subjunctive can occur without an *if*-clause as well:

(50) I wish I *were* home. (sE)

Foundations of Grammar

The change in verb form from *I was* to *I were* signals that the sentence is employing subjunctive mood. The statement is not about a real event; it is about a possibility, a wish, or a desire.

13.1.3.2 Mandative Subjunctive

The **mandative subjunctive** mood uses a particular noun, adjective, or verbal construction that conveys speakers'/writers' authority, placing an obligation to comply on the recipient. The label "mandative subjunctive" may have given this authoritative function away, since "mandative" is related to "mandate" (i.e., an official order or law). Many professions actively use the mandative subjunctive: think law enforcers or law makers, teachers, administrators, health care workers, and, truly, bosses (or parents and caretakers, really!) of any sort.

What do you notice about the constructions in the next data set and the italicized portions in each?

(51)   The *recommendation* is that the sick child *stay* at home. (sE)

(52)   The *request* is the parents *seek* medical treatment for her. (sE)

(53)   Tammy *demanded* the best physician in the clinic *treat* her. (sE)

(54)   We *suggest* the best physician *get* a second opinion, too. (sE)

(55)   It is *vital* that the course of treatment *match* the diagnosis. (sE)

(56)   It is *imperative* that the child *get* sufficient rest. (sE)

The italicized nouns in (51) and (52), the verbs in (53) and (54), and the adjectives in (55) and (56) that occur early in the sentence are semantically all related to "mandating" something in some way, and the subjunctive verb later in the sentence is in its **bare infinitive form**. This is what makes the mandative subjunctive stand out.

Exercise 2

Subjunctive mood. Fill in each {VP} in the following subjunctive mood sentences (all sE examples).[40]

a) If you study hard, you _____ the exam. (verb = pass)

b) If she _____ her work, she will join us for dinner. (verb = finish)

c) If they had left earlier, they _____ the train. (verb = catch)

d) We will stay inside, if it _____. (verb = rain)

e) If she _____, she would reach across the aisle. (verb = elected)

f) The teacher insists that they _____ all assignments on time. (verb = complete)

g) It is essential that they _____ to vote. (verb = register)

h) They suggested that the proposal _____ by the board. (verb = review)

> **Exercise 3**
>
> Label each sentence (all sE) as indicative mood (Ind.M), imperative mood (Imp.M), or subjunctive mood (SM). For indicative mood, also specify if the sentence is a declarative (D), yes/no-question (y/n), *wh*-word question (wh), or exclamation (E).[41]
>
> a) The sun had just risen over the quiet village.
>
> b) Did you see the way the sunlight reflected off the lake this morning?
>
> c) Just look at that sunrise!
>
> d) If only their kitten were with them now.
>
> e) Where was their kitten?
>
> f) Take a look inside the barn.
>
> g) Was that a shadow moving in the corner?
>
> h) Don't be afraid!

13.2 What Is Grammatical Voice?

Grammatical voice allows a speaker or writer to present the facts of a sentence from two different perspectives. Compare the following sentences:

(57)   The associate composed the briefing. (sE)

(57a) The briefing was composed by the associate. (sE)

(57b) The briefings were composed. (sE)

You can see that (57) presents the agent/doer of the action in the subject slot; this is an example of **active voice**. In contrast, (57a) presents the affected party—*the briefing*—in the subject slot; this is an example of **passive voice**. Passive voice sentences can completely gloss over the doer of the action by omitting the agent as in (57b), thereby expressing a certain perspective about the facts of a sentence.

Grammatically speaking, turning an active sentence into a passive sentence requires a few steps. We illustrate those next.

(58)   [Casey] [cooked] [the casserole]. (sE)
          S   V   DO

(58a) [The casserole] [was cooked] [by Casey]. (sE)
             S   V   A

The doer is in the subject slot in (58), which has an S-V-DO sentence pattern. The DO slot is occupied by the affected party (*the casserole*). Note that the active voice verb *cooked* is in simple past tense. To turn this sentence into passive voice, we must do the following syntactic operations:

Foundations of Grammar

- turn the DO into the S (mandatory)
- modify the {VP} while keeping tense stable (mandatory)
- move the S into a *by-phrase* (optional)

In our example, the {VP} changes from *cooked* to *was cooked*. We need a form of *be* as our auxiliary, which carries tense (*was* is past tense). Now, is *cooked* a past-tense verb or a past participle? Let's look at this pairing to make sure:

(59)　[The artist] [drew] [the landscape]. (sE)
　　　　 S　　　 V　　　 DO

(59a)　[The landscape] [was drawn] [by the artist]. (sE)
　　　　　 S　　　　　 V　　　　 A

> **Passive**: Agent/'doer' omitted or included in *by*-phrase.

Once again, we have the DO move into the S slot and the S of the active sentence move to the *by-phrase* in the passive sentence. The {VP} consists of a form of *be* and a main verb *drawn*. *Drawn* is the past participle, *drew* is the past tense form for *draw*. We have now discovered the form our main verb must be in for passive voice: past participle. This is essentially the rule for how to form a **passive voice {VP}: form of *be* + *past participle*.**

What if an active sentence has two objects, both an IO and a DO? Let's try it out:

(60)　[Casey] [gave] [Sam] [a casserole]. (sE)
　　　　 S　　 V　　 IO　　 DO

(60a)　Sam was given a casserole by Casey. (sE)

(60b)　A casserole was given (to) Sam by Casey. (sE)

Either of the objects can be moved to the subject slot, but you can see that if the IO stays in its original slot in (60b), it might sound better to you with the addition of the preposition *to*.

In our examples so far, we've always included the *by-phrase* to make visible where the subject of the active sentence goes when we transform an active sentence into a passive one. A passive sentence that includes the *by-phrase* is often called a **full passive**. However, this *by-phrase* is not required; a passive sentence is perfectly grammatical without the *by-phrase* and often called a **truncated passive**:

(60c)　The casserole was cooked by Casey. (sE)

(61)　Every time I am asked by you not to hum, I'll hum more louder.[42] (AE/AAE)

(62)　That custom is still used by them anymore.[43] (ME)

(63)　A wicked amount of money was spent by her.[44] (NEE)

(64)　I ain't saying that these frameworks have not been discussed by these linguists.[45] (AAE)

When you encounter a sentence without a *by-phrase*, and you're not sure if it is in passive or active voice, adding a *by-phrase* to see if the sentence can accommodate it is a great way to test for passive voice. Some of our students prefer using *by zombies* rather than the more boring *by people* or *by someone/something*. For our examples here, we could add *by zombies* as in *Our dog was bitten **by zombies*** or *The casserole was baked **by zombies***.

If you want to gloss over who is responsible for an action (maybe you don't want to blame zombies all the time!), then omitting the *by-phrase* is a convenient choice. The infamous *Mistakes were made* is a case in point and seems to be a popular expression for US presidents ranging from Nixon and Reagan to Clinton. Of course, adding the *by-phrase* as in *Mistakes were made by me* or *Mistakes were made by my administration* would end up highlighting the agent's role in those mistakes even more so than the active equivalent of *I made mistakes* or *My administration made mistakes*.

Let's compare a few active-passive sentence pairs. Which ones do you like better?

(65) My dad *baked* cookies. (sE)

(65a) Cookies *were baked* by my dad. (sE)

(63a) She *spent* a wicked amount of money.[46] (NEE)

(63b) A wicked amount of money *was spent* by her.[47] (NEE)

(64a) I ain't saying that these linguists *have not discussed* these frameworks.[48] (AAE)

(64b) I ain't saying that these frameworks *have not been discussed* by these linguists.[49] (AAE)

Some of these sentences might strike you as odd; maybe you stumbled over some of them as you were reading. We think that *a wicked amount of money was spent by her* definitely just doesn't roll off the tongue as easily as *she spent a wicked amount of money*. However, *these frameworks have not been discussed by linguists* sounds just as "good" as *linguistics have not discussed these frameworks*. You may prefer either active or passive voice for some or all the examples above. This shows you that using active or passive voice really is a choice that we as language users can make. Granted, sometimes, passive voice really isn't the best choice, but sometimes, it is the best choice! Keep that in mind when folks tell you that you should avoid passive voice. Remember those statements from the prereading task? In fact, this oft-repeated guidance to avoid passive voice has been taken to heart by so many teachers, writers, and editors that rather awkward situations result: Dr. Alan Rubin, author of *Diabetes for Dummies* (2015) said,

> Sometimes I'll write something like 'the patient was comatose and was given thyroid hormone,' and they'll [editors] change that to 'the patient was comatose and took thyroid hormone .... I have to tell them these are extremely sick patients, [*sic*] they can't take care of themselves.'

Regardless of how you feel about passive and active voice personally, both voices are equally grammatical as syntactic structures.

In some dialects, slightly different passive constructions are possible:

(66) The soul *needs fed* by creative, multi-dimensional teaching.⁵⁰ (ME)

(67) The dog sure does *like petted*.⁵¹ (ME)

In this **needs washed**-feature (that's the actual name of this grammatical construction!), the auxiliary *be* is replaced by *need, like,* or *want* to form passive voice. Another variation that has to do with passive voice occurs in Philadelphia and other East Coast regions:

(68) I'*m done* my homework.⁵² (ECE)

(69) I'*m started* the project.⁵³ (ECE)

(70) I'*m finished* my fries.⁵⁴ (ECE)

In each case, the passive auxiliary of *be* precedes the past participle of either *do, finish,* or *start*. This construction requires an {NP} next, such as *my homework*. While this construction uses the same {VP} components a passive voice {VP} requires (form of *be* + past participle), it is notably different from the other passive voice examples, and still, it is perfectly grammatical.

Across really **all dialects** of American English, there is yet another passive voice variation: the ***get*-passive,** where a form of *get* is combined with a past participle:⁵⁵

(71) The cat *got jabbed* by the vet.

(72) The vet *got promoted* by their boss.

(73) The flowers *got smashed* by the storm.

(74) Jean *has gotten fired* the other day.

Now, in addition to active and passive voice, there is a third voice: **middle voice**. How is (75) different from the active (60d) and passive (60e) sentences about Casey and the casserole?

(60d) [Casey] [cooked] [the casserole]. (sE)
        S   V   DO

(60e) [The casserole] [was cooked] [by Casey]. (sE)
        S   V   A

(75) [The casserole] [cooked] [in the oven]. (sE)
        S   V   A

The subject in (75) is *the casserole*, but we have no agent/doer (no Casey in sight!). Since we can leave off the agent in passive voices, you may be tempted to think that this is passive voice, but we don't have a {VP} that is marked for passive voice (no auxiliary *be* and no past participle!), so it's not passive voice. The casserole seems to be doing double duty: it's doing the cooking **and** it's being cooked simultaneously (what!?). This is what **middle voice** is. Since some topics are for the true grammar warriors among us, we focus on active and passive voice in the remainder of this chapter.

With the basics about active/passive in place, let's add tense and aspect to the mix. Our {VPs} will get pretty complex right about now, so prepare yourself. What if we wanted to convey both perfective and progressive aspects in a passive voice sentence? Recall the following components for aspect and voice:

- progressive: form of *be* + *-ing* verb
- perfective: form of *have* + past participle of verb
- passive voice: form of *be* + past participle of verb

Here's what a {VP} that combines progressive and perfective aspect looks like:

(76) Aisha *has been swearing* an oath. (sE)

- progressive: form of *be* = *been*; *-ing*-form = *swearing*
- perfective: form of *have* = *has*; past participle of verb = *been*

Now, let's look at what that {VP} looks like when we add passive voice to it:

(77) An oath *has been being sworn*. (sE)

- progressive: form of *be* = *been*; *-ing*-verb = *being*
- perfective: form of *have* = *has*; past participle of verb = *been*
- passive: form of *be* = *being*; past participle of the verb = *sworn*

The auxiliaries can clearly do double duty: *been* serves as the required *be* for progressive aspect, and at the same time as the required past participle for perfective; and *being* serves as the required *-ing* verb for progressive and as the form of *be* for passive. Chart 1 below provides an overview of all possible combinations!

Tense	Active voice	Passive voice
Simple present	(78) Aisha *swears* an oath. (sE) (79) Every time you *ask* me not to hum, I'll hum more louder.[56] (AE/AAE)	(78a) An oath *is sworn*. (sE) (79a) Every time I *am asked* not to hum, I'll hum more louder.[57] (AE/AAE)
Simple past	(80) Aisha *swore* an oath. (sE) (81) She *spent* a wicked amount of money.[58] (NEE)	(80a) An oath *was sworn*. (sE) (81a) A wicked amount of money *was spent*.[59] (NEE)
Present perfect	(82) Aisha *has sworn* an oath. (sE) (83) I ain't saying that these linguists *have not discussed* these frameworks.[60] (AAE)	(82a) An oath *has been sworn*. (sE) (83a) I ain't saying that these frameworks *have not been discussed*.[61] (AAE)
Past perfect	(84) Aisha *had sworn* an oath. (sE) (85) She *had spent* a wicked amount of money.[62] (NEE)	(84a) An oath *had been sworn*. (sE) (85a) A wicked amount of money *had been spent*.[63] (NEE)
Present progressive	(86) Aisha *is swearing* an oath. (sE) (87) He*'s putting* a towel in his head.[64] (ChE)	(86a) An oath *is being sworn*. (sE) (87a) A towel *is being put* in his head.[65] (ChE)

Foundations of Grammar

Tense	Active voice	Passive voice
Past progressive	(88) Aisha *was swearing* an oath. (sE) (89) The vets *were examining* the cats. (sE)	(88a) An oath *was being sworn*. (sE) (89a) The cats *were being examined*. (sE)
Present perfective + progressive	(90) Aisha *has been swearing* an oath. (sE) (91) People *have been planning* this for the last fifteen to twenty year.[66] (AAE)	(90a) An oath *has been being sworn*. (sE) (91a) This *has been being planned* for the last fifteen to twenty year.[67] (AAE)
Past perfective + progressive	(92) Aisha *had been swearing* an oath. (sE) (93) The vets *had been examining* the cats. (sE)	(92a) An oath *had been being sworn*. (sE) (93a) The cats *had been being examined*. (sE)
Modal	(94) Aisha *may swear* an oath. (sE) (95) Sometimes, you know, people *would kill* a beef or a sheep.[68] (AE)	(94a) An oath *may be sworn*. (sE) (95a) Sometimes, you know, a beef or sheep *would be killed*.[69] (AE)
Modal + perfective	(96) Aisha *may have sworn* an oath. (sE) (97) We *must have driven* the cats to the vet already. (sE)	(96a) An oath *may have been sworn*. (sE) (97a) The cats *must have been driven* to the vet already. (sE)
Modal + progressive	(98) Aisha *may be swearing* an oath. (sE) (99) The vet *may be examining* the cats already. (sE)	(98a) An oath *may be being sworn*. (sE) (99a) The cats *may be being examined* already. (sE)
Modal + perfective + progressive	(100) Aisha *may have been swearing* an oath. (sE) (101) They *should have been writing* the report last night. (sE)	(100a) An oath *may have been being sworn*. (sE) (101a) The report *should have been being written* last night. (sE)

Chart 1 Active and passive voice combinations—Examples

Whew! That is a lot of different and increasingly complex {VPs}! Chart 2 summarizes the patterns by providing just the {VPs} themselves—we'll use just the sE paradigm here:

Tense and aspect	Active voice	Passive voice
simple present	swears	is sworn
simple past	swore	was sworn
present perfect	has sworn	has been sworn
past perfect	had sworn	had been sworn
present progressive	is swearing	is being sworn
past progressive	was swearing	was being sworn
present perfective + progressive	has been swearing	has been being sworn

Tense and aspect	Active voice	Passive voice
past perfective + progressive	*had been swearing*	*had been being sworn*
modal	*may swear*	*may be sworn*
modal + perfective	*may have sworn*	*may have been sworn*
modal + progressive	*may be swearing*	*may be being sworn*
modal + perfective + progressive	*may have been swearing*	*may have been being sworn*

Chart 2 Active and passive voice combinations across tense, aspect, and modal verbs

Just like dialects of a language can have different ways of forming passive voice, so do the world's languages. Some languages use inflection—adding an affix to one of the words in the sentence (e.g., Latin, Japanese) or a designated word (e.g., Iroquoian), and some require a different word order or a different sentence pattern (e.g., Vietnamese that employs a serial verb construction), and some form the passive through a combination of morphological and word order changes (e.g., English). Some languages have what is called the **antipassive voice** (e.g., Basque, Mayan) which deletes the overt object and marks it on the verb form, with the agent occurring in a by phrase, and, as such functions like passive voice. To find differences—like the presence or absence of passive voice—The World Atlas of World Languages Online is a terrific resource (https://wals.info).[70]

> **Exercise 4**
>
> Label the italicized {VPs} as either active (A) or passive (P) voice.
> a) Three cats *were rescued* the other day. (sE)
> b) The DVD recorder *was being repaired* when I walked into the store. (sE)
> c) The cats *are* hungry all the time. (sE)
> d) Its origins *need traced*.[71] (ME)
> e) Your brain *needs fed* to work out.[72] (ME)
> f) The glass *got shattered* by me. (sE/non-sE)
> g) Pies *can be* yummy. (sE)
> h) I've been so involved with her life since the day she *was born* that she was my kid before my kids was my kids.[73] (AAE)

Foundations of Grammar

Exercise 5

Formulate your own sentences based on the provided components below. You can choose either active or passive voice. Explain your reasoning for either choice!

Sentence components	Sentence	Voice	Reasoning
the child, broke, vase			
the thief, stole, jewels,			
virus, people, infected			
the dog, the cat, the fish, ate			
Bob, fired, the company			
Your choice			

13.3 Finiteness

Individual verbs and {VPs} overall can be either **finite** (i.e., bear tense) or **non-finite** (i.e., not bear tense). The term **finiteness** may seem like a mysterious, or, at least, unusual term. You'll see, however, that it's not all that complicated, especially since we've stealthily trained you for this moment throughout this book. We'll build on this knowledge in the next chapter when we get to finite and non-finite clauses.

13.3.1 Finite Verbs and Finite {VPs}

When a verb is **finite**, it means that it is marked for tense (either present or past). Given that you've been knee-deep in tense and aspect in Chapter 12, we hope that it is not too difficult to figure out which of the individual verbs in the following examples are marked for tense and which ones are not.

(102) Juan *walked* three miles this morning. (sE)
walked: past tense marked via morphological *-ed* marker

(103) My friend *drinks* a lot of coffee. (sE)
drinks: present tense marked via morphological *-s* marker

(104) Alls I *want* to do is have fun.[74] (ME)
want: present tense—no overt morphological marker

(105) They *is making* stuff up.[75] (AAE)
is: present tense is marked via present tense form of *be* (*is* is present tense of *be*)
making: **not** marked for tense

(106) He's *smiling* to the cat.[76] (ChE)

's: present tense is marked via present tense form of *be* (*'s* is contracted form of *is*, which is present tense of *be*)
smiling: **not** marked for tense

(107) Sarah *has* just *written* an essay for publication. (sE)
has: present tense is marked via present tense form of *have* (*has* is present tense form of *have*)
written: **not** marked for tense

Now that we know which of these verbs are marked for tense, we can label them as either **finite (F)** or **non-finite (NF)**. These two labels (F/NF) really are just a shorthand to avoid having to spell out "is marked for tense via … /is not marked for tense." Here we go:

- *walked* = **F**
- *drinks* = **F**
- *want* = **F**
- *is* = **F**
- *making* = **NF**
- *'s* = **F**
- *smiling* = **NF**
- *has* = **F**
- *written* = **NF**

In addition to individual verbs being able to occur in finite or non-finite forms, {VPs} overall can also be finite or non-finite. Each {VP} in (102)–(104) consists of only a finite verb, so the {VPs} overall are finite. What if the {VP} consists of a finite verb **and** a non-finite verb, as in *is making*? As long as one of the individual verbs in a {VP} is finite, the overall {VP} will be finite as well:

- *was* (F) + *walking* (NF) = finite {VP} "*was walking*"
- *is* (F) + *making* (NF) = finite {VP} "*is making*"
- *'s* (F) + *smiling* (NF) = finite {VP} "*'s smiling*"
- *had* (F) + *glanced* (NF) = finite {VP} "*had glanced*"
- *has* (F) + *written* (NF) = finite {VP} "*has written*"

In fact, this demonstrates a key point: in a finite {VP}, **one** and only **one** verb can be finite, and it is the **first** verb that is finite. If there is only **one** verb in a **finite** {VP} (as in *walked*), that verb will be finite, as it will be in either past or present tense. In all our examples of two-word {VPs} above, the first verb is the finite auxiliary, which is followed by the non-finite main verb. Those main verbs so far were in either the present participle form or the past participle form. Present participle and past participle, on their own, don't tell you if the {VP} is in present or past tense, and as such, don't bear tense. You have to combine those two forms with an auxiliary in either present or past tense to know if the action of *walking* or *making* is in present or past tense: a *was* or *were* would mean past tense, an *is*, *am*, *are* would mean present tense (remember that *was smiling* is past progressive, *am smiling* is present progressive!). In a nutshell, our participle forms **don't indicate** tense, the auxiliary does! Again, nomenclature is a bit confusing because the grammarian gods have decided to call a verb form that is **not tensed** by a name that includes the words "present" or "past;" we know, it can be confusing.

Because the terminology can be a bit confusing, let's clarify this one more time by looking at two sets of **finite {VPs}**:

(108) They *are* jogging. (sE)

(108a) They *were* jogging. (sE)

(109) We *have* baked cookies already. (sE)

(109a) We *had* baked cookies before we ate dinner. (sE)

All {VPs} here consist again of two verbs: the **finite** (i.e., tensed) auxiliary (*are/were* and *have/had*) and the **non-finite** (i.e., non-tensed) present participle *jogging* or the **non-finite** (i.e., non-tensed) past participle *baked*. Only because of the finite auxiliary verb do you know when the action of jogging and when the action of baking happened. So, all four examples feature {VPs} that are **finite {VPs}** because of our tensed auxiliary.

In addition to primary auxiliaries, **modal auxiliaries** can be finite as well (the modals are italicized and underlined):

(110) Hunter *might* arrive on time. (sE)

(111) This *will* be particularly important once you're done with the tattoo …[77] (ECE)

(112) You still *can* play many game.[78] (SAE/ChE/AAE/others)

(113) He *could* talk smart … He's like a straight-A student.[79] (ChE)

(114) The new set still *needs* washed to kill germs.[80] (ME)

Grammatically speaking (not semantically), *could* is considered the past tense form (as is *might* and *would*) while *can* is the present tense form (as is *may* and *will*).

13.3.2 Non-finite {VPs}

If there are {VPs} overall that are finite, are there {VPs} that are non-finite, you might ask. Yes, yes, there are! Let's look at some examples.

(115) *Sleeping* all morning was relaxing for Chiara. (sE)

(116) I ain't really thinking about *getting* with J. or any other guy.[81] (ChE)

(117) She tell me *to go* to bed earlier tomorrow.[82] (AAE)

(118) Bob was walking last night when I called *to talk* to him. (sE)

(119) Alls I want *to do* is have fun.[83] (ME)

(120) *Written* in an engaging style, the scientific book sold lots of copies. (sE)

Did the actions expressed by the present participles *sleeping* in (115), *getting* in (116) as well as the past participle *written* in (120) happen in past time or present time? Did the actions expressed by the infinitive forms *to go* in (117), *to talk* in (118), and *to do* in (119) happen in the past or present? None of these verbs reveals this information on their own. We can of course infer from context of the sentences, but these particular {VPs} on their own are devoid of tense-marking. Because these verbs lack tense-marking, and because the respective {VPs} consist of just these **non-finite** verb forms, the entire {VPs} are non-finite, i.e., not tensed.

For the infinitive, there's an easy way to remember that it is, in fact, non-finite because this information is contained in the term *infinitive* itself! Using our morphological knowledge to decode the term *infinitive* underscores this:

- *in-*: prefix, means "not"
- finite: the base of the word
- *-ive*: derivational suffix ADJ marker

Since you know that *finite* means "marked for tense," adding the prefix *-in* reverses that, indicating the opposite of *finite*, i.e., *not finite*. So, the term for the base form of a verb—infinitive—already indicates that it will be non-finite! To recap, there are only **three verb forms** that are non-finite, that do not show tense:

- present participle
- past participle
- infinitive

Just remember, if the present or past participle is part of a larger {VP} and is preceded by a finite auxiliary, then the entire {VP} will be finite; if not, then it's non-finite. Compare these two pairs of {VPs}:

(115a) *Sleeping* all morning was relaxing for Chiara. (sE)

(115b) Chiara *was sleeping* all morning, which was relaxing for her. (sE)

(120a) *Written* in an engaging style, the scientific book sold lots of copies. (sE)

(120b) The scientific book *was written* in an engaging style, and as such sold lots of copies. (sE)

In (115a), the {VP} is just *sleeping*; in (115b), the {VP} consists of *was sleeping*. The entire {VP} *sleeping* in (115a) is non-finite, whereas the entire {VP} *was sleeping* in (115b) is finite, and within this entire finite {VP}, there is a finite auxiliary verb *was* and a non-finite verb *sleeping*. This means that for (120a), *written* again is a non-finite {VP} whereas the {VP} *was written* in (120b) is finite. Here's the difference in more general terms:

Foundations of Grammar

- non-finite verb on its own = non-finite {VP}
- finite auxiliary + non-finite verb = finite {VP}

Exercise 6

Finite/non-finite. Label each of the verbs within the italicized {VPs} as either finite (F) or non-finite (NF).

a) *Adopting* cats makes me *feel* warm and fuzzy. (sE)
b) *Having prepared* for the client meeting all day, Moesha *rocked* the presentation. (sE)
c) She *was a-goin'* to the show.[84] (AE/OE)
d) He *could talk* smart.[85] (ChE)
e) I *had came* out of it.[86] (ChE)
f) Or they *might have* their own song that they created theirself.[87] (AAE)
g) Martin *is done* his bass tracks and we are ready to start vocals.[88] (ECE)
h) I*'ve call* her my sister.[89] (AAE)

Exercise 7

Finite/non-finite {VPs}. Label the entire {VPs} that are italicized as either finite (F) or non-finite (NF).

a) *Adopting* cats makes me *feel* warm and fuzzy. (sE)
b) *Having prepared* for the client meeting all day, Moesha *rocked* the presentation. (sE)
c) She *was a-goin'* to the show.[90] (AE/OE)
d) He *could talk* smart.[91] (ChE)
e) I *had came* out of it.[92] (ChE)
f) We *is* here![93] (AAE)
g) Martin *is done* his bass tracks and we *are* ready to start vocals.[94] (ECE)
h) I*'ve call* her my sister.[95] (AAE)

Terminology to Know

Term	Working definition	Example/Illustration
Indicative mood		
Imperative mood		
Subjunctive mood		
Mandative subjunctive		
Passive voice		
Active voice		
Finite verb		
Non-finite verb		

Chart 3 Key terminology Chapter 13

Notes

1. Alley, 1996, p. 106.
2. Ibid.
3. Strunk and White, 2000, p. 18.
4. Orwell, 1946.
5. Iida, 2020.
6. Wood, 2024.
7. Wolfram, 1976; cited in Matyiku, 2011a.
8. Hasty, 2011; cited in Huang, 2011.
9. Young, 2019, p. 4.
10. Ibid.
11. Ibid.
12. Bayley, 2012, p. 158.
13. Green, 2002, p. 53.
14. University of South Carolina (n.d.).
15. W. Beauregard, personal communication, August 29, 2024.
16. Hasty, 2011; cited in Huang, 2011.
17. Green, 2002, p. 42.
18. Green, 2011, p. 84.
19. Among others, Green, 2002.
20. Couper-Kuhlen, 2012.
21. Matyiku, 2011a.
22. Murray, 1993; cited in Maher and McCoy, 2011.
23. W. Beauregard, personal communication, August 31, 2024.
24. Wolfram and Christian, 1976, p. 71.

25. Kendall, Quartey et al., 2018 Transcript ID DCB_se1_ag1_f_03_1.
26. Matyiku, 2011a.
27. T. McMurtry, personal communication, November 27, 2024.
28. Green, 2011, p. 85.
29. Hasty, 2011; cited in Huang, 2011.
30. W. Beauregard, personal communication, August 29, 2024.
31. Maher and Wood, 2011.
32. Slightly modified from Staub and Zentz, 2017.
33. Rowe et al., 2018 Transcript ID PRV_se0_ag3_m_01_1.
34. Young, 2019, p. 4.
35. Slightly modified from Rowe et al., 2018 Transcript ID PRV_se0_ag3_m_01_1.
36. Young, 2019, p. 4.
37. University of South Carolina (n.d.).
38. Farrington et al., 2020 Transcript ID ATL_se0_ag1_m_05_1.
39. Bayley, 2012, p. 158.
40. Based on sentences produced by OpenAI, 2024.
41. Ibid.
42. Slightly modified from Corver, 2005; cited in Wood, 2012.
43. Modified from Eitner, 1949, p. 311; cited in Maher and McCoy, 2011.
44. Modified from W. Beauregard, personal communication, August 29, 2024.
45. Modified from Baker-Bell, 2020, p. 15.
46. W. Beauregard, personal communication, August 29, 2024.
47. Modified from Ibid.
48. Baker-Bell, 2020, p. 15.
49. Modified from Ibid.
50. Maher and Wood, 2011.
51. Murray and Simon, 2002; cited in Maher and Wood, 2011.
52. Fruehwald and Myler, 2015.
53. Ibid.
54. Ibid.
55. Cambridge University Press, 2021.
56. Corver, 2005; cited in Wood, 2012.
57. Slightly modified from Corver, 2005; cited in Wood, 2012.
58. W. Beauregard, personal communication, August 29, 2024.
59. Modified from Ibid.
60. Baker-Bell, 2020, p. 15.
61. Modified from Ibid.
62. W. Beauregard, personal communication, August 29, 2024.
63. Modified from Ibid.
64. Bayley, 2012, p. 162.

65. Modified from Ibid.
66. Becker et al., 2021 Transcript ID LES_se0_ag2_f_02_1.
67. Modified from Becker et al., 2021 Transcript ID LES_se0_ag2_f_02_1.
68. University of South Carolina (n.d.).
69. Modified from Ibid.
70. Dryer and Haspelmath, 2013.
71. Stabley, 1959; cited in Maher and Wood, 2011.
72. Wood, 2014.
73. Farrington et al., 2020 Transcript ID ATL_se0_ag1_f_02.
74. Putnam and van Koppen, 2011; cited in Wood, 2013.
75. Kendall, Fasold et al., 2018 Transcript ID DCA_se1_ag4_m_02_1.
76. Barrón and San Romón, n.d., pp. 30–1; cited in Bayley, 2012, p. 162.
77. Adapted from Wood, 2014.
78. Reaser et al., 2017b.
79. Fought, 2003, p. 100.
80. Edelstein, 2014; cited in Maher and Wood, 2011.
81. Bayley, 2012, p. 163.
82. Kendall, Fasold et al., 2018 Transcript ID DCA_se1_ag1_m_07_1.
83. Putnam and van Koppen, 2011; cited in Wood, 2013.
84. Christian et al., 1988; cited in Matyiku, 2011a.
85. Adapted from Fought, 2003, p. 108.
86. Based on Ibid., p. 94.
87. Kendall, Quartey et al., 2018 Transcript ID DCB_se1_ag2_m_02_3.
88. Wood, 2014.
89. Farrington et al., 2020 Transcript ID ATL_se0_ag1_f_01_1.
90. Christian et al., 1988; cited in Matyiku, 2011a.
91. Adapted from Fought, 2003, p. 108.
92. Based on Ibid., p. 94.
93. Young, 2019, p. 4.
94. Wood, 2014.
95. Farrington et al., 2020 Transcript ID ATL_se0_ag1_f_01_1.

CHAPTER 14
TO BE OR NOT TO BE: COORDINATION/ SUBORDINATION

Overview

So far, we have mainly focused on simple sentences: one subject paired with one {VP}. Most of the time, we don't speak or write just in simple sentences comprised of one subject and one {VP}. Rather, we often combine clauses in different ways, resulting in compound and complex sentences. In this chapter, we examine in detail the different types of **coordination** and **subordination**. Our objectives are as follows. You'll be able to

- test clauses for their dependence or independence;
- identify and label subordinate clause types; and
- identify the functions of various clauses.

Pre-reading tasks

1. Split each of the following sentences into two sentences:

    a) Alejandra and Sam, *who work together*, run together each morning. (sE)

    b) *When I don't have hockey and I'm done my homework*, I go there and skate.[1] (ECE)

    c) We learned our grammar from our caretakers and those around us, *attesting to how we learn languages through interacting with others*. (sE)

2. Try to create a really, really, really long sentence that includes several clauses. How long is your sentence: how many words? how many clauses? Would YOU want to read this sentence?

3. Below is a text produced by ChatGPT in response to the question "What makes a good language learner?" We also asked ChatGPT to produce a text to simulate a novice writer. How would you revise this paragraph for a formal, written academic assignment? Why would you make the changes you're suggesting?

    > A good language learner, well, they're not just someone who memorizes vocabulary and grammar rules, you know? It's more about having this insatiable curiosity, like constantly wanting to explore and understand how a language works, diving deep into its nuances, and embracing its quirks

> and idiosyncrasies. They're the ones who aren't afraid to make mistakes, because they see them as opportunities to learn and improve. They're persistent, always seeking out new challenges and pushing themselves out of their comfort zones. And oh, let's not forget about being open-minded and culturally sensitive, because language learning is as much about understanding different cultures as it is about mastering words and phrases. So yeah, a good language learner is a bit of an adventurer, a risk-taker, and a perpetual student all rolled into one.[2]

14.1 Introduction

The sentence *The CEO who works all day is very successful* features an {NP} as its subject. That {NP} includes a POST (*who works all day*) that is an embedded clause: it has its own {VP} (*works*) and its own subject (*who*)! Below are a few more examples of sentences that consist of more than one clause:

(1) *Although we business professional*, our goal is to work with underprivileged youth.[3] (AAE)

(2) *When I exercise at night*, I push myself. (sE)

(3) Sam talks non-stop, *which can be annoying*. (sE)

(4) Alls Greg and Marsha want to do is kiss each other *when no one else is around*.[4] (ME)

One of each of the sentences' clauses (the italicized portions) cannot stand on its own because each is a **dependent**, or **subordinate**, clause:

(1a) *Although we business professional. (AAE)

(2a) *When I exercise at night. (sE)

(3a) *Which can be annoying. (sE)

(4a) *When no one else is around. (ME)

However, the other clause in each sentence can stand alone because each is an **independent**, or **main**, clause:

(1b) Our goal is to work with underprivileged youth.[5] (AAE)

(2b) I push myself. (sE)

(3b) Sam talks non-stop. (sE)

(4b) Alls Greg and Marsha want to do is kiss each other.[6] (ME)

Put together, each independent and dependent clause forms a **complex sentence**. They contrast with **compound sentences**, which consist of two independent, or **simple**, clauses, such as the ones below:

(5) Our professor is very tired, *and she wants to go home early*. (sE)

(6) I know he was a-tellin' the truth, *but I was a-comin' home*.[7] (AE)

Exercise 1

Identify each sentence below as complex, compound, or simple.

a) Casey ordered pad thai. (sE)
b) I ordered a steak, and Casey ordered pad thai. (sE)
c) While I ordered a steak, Casey ordered pad thai. (sE)
d) Casey, who loves pad thai, is my best friend. (sE)
e) Each kiddo gets a piece of candy that needs unwrapped.[8] (ME)
f) I was wicked stuffed, but it was well worth it.[9] (NEE)
g) This will be particularly important once you're done the tattoo.[10] (ME)
h) Maybe it is what he like or even all he know.[11] (AAE)

14.2 Coordination

A **coordinating conjunction** (CC) joins two or more independent clauses of equal weight. Think of the CC as the fulcrum of a scale that connects two equal items:

(7) Casey and Hassan cooked the casserole  they invited Sam for dinner. (sE)

By choosing to combine two independent clauses via a CC, the author places equal weight on each clause. You already know the mnemonic *FANBOYS* to remember CCs, each of which is illustrated below. Notice that with *nor* as the CC, the order of subject and verb changes (*was he* versus *he was*):

(8) Sam went to Casey's house, *for* they knew that Hassan was an excellent cook. (sE)

(9) Now I'm wicked tired, *and* I am going to go to bed.[12] (NEE)

(10) Jessie wasn't Sam's friend, *nor* was he Alex's friend. (sE)

(11) They done tore it down, *but* the building is still there.[13] (AAE)

(12) Sam could have helped, *or* they could have at least tried. (sE)

(13) Farah tore a muscle, *yet* she finished in second place. (sE)

(14) She hear my grandmama call her, *so* she would jump out of that car ....[14] (AAE)

297

In addition to connecting entire clauses, CCs can also connect smaller units such as phrases and words, including {NPs} such as in (15) and (16), {AdjPs} such as (17) and (18), and prepositions such as (19) and (20). Refer to Chapter 9 for a full list and examples of such smaller connected units.

(15)   Denzel *and* Trevor ate dinner together. (sE)

(16)   Me *and* my mom be praying in Spanish.[15] (ChE)

(17)   I picked her because she nice *and* calm.[16] (AAE)

(18)   The pie came out dry *yet* delicious. (sE)

(19)   So you was in *and* out of DC.[17] (AAE)

(20)   The student was prepared above *and* beyond expectations. (sE)

Notice that CCs connect like constituents: {NPs} and {NPs}, {AdjPs} and {AdjPs}, prepositions and prepositions, and so on. The connected words or phrases function as one unit at the sentence level. Can you identify the basic sentence patterns for the following sentences? Go back to Chapter 11 if you need a quick refresher.

(21)   Latoya and Nazira ate dinner together. (sE)

(22)   Me and my mom be praying in Spanish.[18] (ChE)

(23)   They flipping and flopping.[19] (AAE)

(24)   Casey and Hassan cooked the casserole, and they invited Sam for dinner. (sE)

Here's how they each break down:

(21a)   [Latoya and Nazira] [ate] [dinner] [together]. (sE)
              S   V   DO   A

(22a) [Me and my mom] [be praying] [in Spanish].[20] (ChE)
           S   V   A

(23a) [They] [flipping and flopping].[21] (AAE)
        S   V

(24a)   [They] [cooked] [the casserole], and [they] [invited] [Sam] [for dinner]. (sE)
         S   V   DO   S   V   DO   A
      (independent clause)   +   (independent clause)

Coordinated phrases, thus, function together at the sentence level. When two clauses are coordinated (as in (24a)), each clause will feature the syntactic patterns you already know as sentence patterns. This means that sentences *and* clauses follow the sentence patterns you already know. After all, sentences are independent clauses. In a way, our sentence patterns really are clause patterns!

Exercise 2

Create your own example sentences for each of the FANBOYS conjunctions.

14.3 Subordination

Next, let's contrast what we know about coordination with subordination. Many different subordinating conjunctions, or subordinators, exist. So, more important than memorizing an exhaustive list is understanding what they do. The **subordinator** tips the scale in favor of the independent clause—the main clause—and makes the clause to which it is attached to dependent upon that main clause. Because the dependent clause can't stand on its own, it carries less weight on the clause scale. Now, the scales are tipped contingent upon the positioning of the dependent clauses:

(25)   *When I exercise at night,*

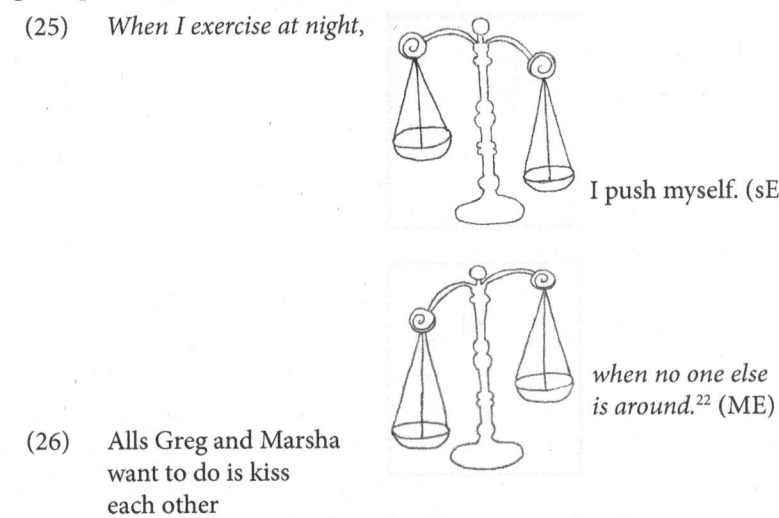

I push myself. (sE)

when no one else is around.[22] (ME)

(26)   Alls Greg and Marsha want to do is kiss each other

Structurally, a subordinate clause is formed by adding a subordinator to an independent clause, making it dependent. A subordinate clause will then function as its own sentence-level constituent:

(27)   [When I exercise at night], [I] [push] [myself]. (sE)
            A   S   V   DO

How do you know that the subordinate clause in (27) functions as one sentence-level constituent? Question-test! The question *When do I push myself?* isolates *When I exercise at night* as the answer, demonstrating that this entire clause performs a syntactic function. To further illustrate this point, compare this to a slightly different sentence:

(28)   [At night], [I] [push] [myself]. (sE)
            A   S   V   DO

We're pretty sure that you would have been able to identify *at night* as the adverbial here. Crucially, the form of the adverbial is a {PP} in (28), whereas the form of the adverbial in (27) is an entire clause. Because these types of subordinate clauses have their own subject and {VP}, we can identify sentence patterns for the clauses; we label the subordinator as SUB for our purposes here:

(27a)   [When] [I] [exercise] [at night] … (sE)
             SUB S   V   A

Foundations of Grammar

(27b) [I] [push] [myself]. (sE)
     S   V   DO

For complex sentences, you'll want to identify an overall sentence pattern first (as we did in (27)), which includes figuring out which syntactic function the subordinate clause plays at the sentence level. Then, you can look inside the subordinate clause and determine the syntactic pattern within that clause (i.e., S-V, S-V-SC, S-V-IO-DO, etc.).

14.3.1 Adverbial Clauses

Adverbial clauses, as the name suggests, give us information about when, where, how, and why something happened, which is what adverbials in general do:

(29) Sam visited Juan nightly *since he was a cook*. (sE)

(30) *Because Sam visited Juan every night*, they brought Juan a gift. (sE)

(31) *Although we business professional*, our goal is to work with underprivileged youth.[23] (AAE)

(32) *When I don't have hockey and I'm done my homework*, I go there and skate.[24] (ECE)

In each example, a subordinating conjunction introduces the adverbial clause. In all instances, the adverbial clause functions as the adverbial at the sentence level. As an adverbial, an adverbial clause can be (i) moved elsewhere in the sentence (from sentence-initial position to sentence-final, for example), and (ii) deleted and what's left will still be grammatically complete. Remember that "adverbial clause" refers to the **form** of a constituent, and "adverbial" refers to the **function** of the constituent.

Exercise 3

Identify the adverbial clauses in each sentence below.

a) These sentences are much better than normal because I have copied and pasted them from random online sources. (sE)

b) Hunter and Ainsley left before the party even started. (sE)

c) Some example sentences are okay, even though I came up with them myself. (sE)

d) While we attended the Tigers game, we received an important call. (sE)

e) As I welcome you to Pittsburgh and to 4C19, let me be real wit y'all right from jump.[25] (AAE)

f) [A]nd if power don't listen, it will hear us nonetheless.[26] (AAE)

g) When you're coming down thataway, they ain't many places to stop.[27] (AE)

h) This will be particularly important once you're done the tattoo and need to leave the shop.[28] (ECE)

> **Exercise 4**
>
> Practice creating complex sentences with adverbial clauses by completing each sentence below. For a)-c), add a main clause, for d)-f), add a subordinate adverbial clause.
>
> a) When I arrive home
>
> b) After I complete the homework
>
> c) Because the class was cancelled
>
> d) The grammar test was delayed
>
> e) Students participated in the grammar game
>
> f) My mentor helped me develop the game
>
> Bonus: Can you identify all the phrases and their functions in the sentences you created?

14.3.2 That-clauses

In *that*-clauses, a *that* introduces the subordinate clause (at least some or most of the time):

(33) *That Quinn crunches ice* annoys me. (sE)

(34) Nobody believes *that you could fix anything.*[29] (ChE)

(35) The problem is *that they read junk.* (sE)

(36) I ain't saying *that these linguists have not discussed these frameworks.*[30] (AAE)

In contrast to adverbial clauses, *that*-clauses are necessary for a sentence to be grammatically complete. The *that*-clause cannot be deleted without either drastically changing the meaning or resulting in a grammatically incomplete structure:

(33a) *~~That Quinn crunches ice~~ annoys me. (sE)

(34a) ~Nobody believes ~~that you could fix anything~~. (ChE)

(35a) *The problem is ~~that they read junk~~. (sE)

(36a) *I ain't saying ~~that these linguists have not discussed these frameworks~~. (AAE)

Clearly, except for (34a), the structures that result when we delete the *that*-clause are incomplete. You may be able to envision someone stating something like "Nobody believes!" in sort of an aggravated way in response to some sad state of affairs … but that's not what the original sentence was about. Subordinate clauses that are essential for a sentence (i.e., can't be deleted) are also called **embedded clauses**.

Now, we said earlier that the word *that* introduces a *that*-clause some or most of the time. Surprise! Sometimes, the *that* can be left out, but the structure is still a *that*-clause. We put *that* in parentheses to represent that this word is optional, even in a clause named after it!

(37) Grandma and grandpa decided (*that*) *y'all was coming to DC.*[31] (AAE)

(38) Jimena knew (*that*) *something terrific had happened.* (sE)

(39) I don't think (*that*) *he deserves fired.*[32] (ME)

(40) I reckon (*that*) *I might should better try to get me a little bit more sleep.*[33] (SAE)

Like adverbial clauses, *that*-clauses play a syntactic role at the sentence level. Before you read on, see if you can identify the syntactic function of the *that*-clauses in (33)–(36) above.

(33b) [*That Quinn crunches ice*] [annoys] [me]. (sE)
        S   V   DO

(34b) [Nobody] [believes] [*that you could fix anything*].[34] (ChE)
      S   V   DO

(35b) [The problem] [is] [*that they read junk*]. (sE)
      S   V   SC

(36b) [I] [ain't saying] [*that these linguists have not discussed these frameworks*].[35] (AAE)
      S   V   DO

How do you know that the entire *that*-clause functions at the sentence level? Applying one of our tests (we're really getting a lot of mileage out of those tests!):

(35c) [The problem] [is] [*that they read junk*]. (sE)
           [*something/it*]

(34c) Nobody believes *that you could fix anything*.[36] (ChE)

Q&A: What does nobody believe?—*that you could fix anything.*

Note that a *that*-clause can also function as a POST within an {AdjP}. As POSTs, each *that*-clause further specifies the headword (bolded below):

(41) It was **clear** *that we had to leave.* (sE)

(42) The cats were **sure** *that they'd get more food later.* (sE)

(43) And it's **sad** *that you got five managers that's from the outside driving to that store.*[37] (AAE)

Exercise 5

Identify the syntactic function that each italicized *that*-clause plays at the sentence level.

a) *That every meeting requires in-depth preparation* is a well-known fact. (sE)
b) I think *that's what they need to invest they money in.*[38] (AAE)
c) You know *that baby coming here.*[39] (AAE)
d) It seems *that they've done left.*[40] (AE)
e) I don't think *I have any grants you might could apply for.*[41] (SAE)
f) It's drug on for so long *that I've got sick of it.*[42] (AE)
g) They were saying *that they had a lot of problems at Garner.*[43] (ChE)
h) I wasn't sure *that nothing wasn't gonna come up t'all.*[44] (AE)

Exercise 6

Create your own example sentences that feature a *that*-clause as DO, subject, SC, and POST in an {AdjP}.

14.3.3 Relative Clauses

Relative clauses are usually embedded in the middle of a sentence, not at the beginning or end. They are introduced by a relative pronoun and they always refer back to something in the sentence (the **antecedent**). Can you identify the antecedent for the italicized relative clauses below?

(44) Not to mention those *who be sayin ain no such thang as Black Language!*[45] (AAE)
(45) The candidate, *whom the committee interviewed first*, was impressive. (sE)
(46) Those were the most people *that I hanged around with.*[46] (ChE)
(47) This chapter, *which features multiple examples*, is a bit lengthy. (sE)
(48) And I have a friend *whose son went to University of Michigan.*[47] (AAE)
(49) And it's sad that you got five managers *that's from the outside* driving to that store.[48] (AAE)

A limited number of **relative pronouns** introduce the relative clause: *who, whom, that, which, whose,* and the dialect version *that's* (see (49)), which younger people rate as grammatical more than older people do.[49] Prescriptive rules about relative pronouns demand *who* be used for humans and *that* for inanimate objects. Yet, in reality, speakers commonly use *that* for people, not just for objects, and *who* is often used for animals, especially pets.

In each example, the relative pronoun refers to another {NP}. For instance, in (45), *whom the committee interviewed first* refers to *the candidate*, and in (49), *that's from the outside*, refers to *five managers*. **Relative clauses** thus get their name because they relate to (i.e., modify) a noun in the sentence. That noun is called an **antecedent**.

14.3.3.1 Relative Clauses as Postmodifiers in {NPs}
Because relative clauses add information about an antecedent, they always function at the phrase-level, specifically as POSTs within {NPs}.

(50) [I] [gave] [the cats *whom the neighbor adopted*] [their food]. (sE)
       S   V   IO   DO

(51) [We] [was discussing] [the initiative *that Obama curated*].[50] (AAE)
       S   V   DO

How do we know that the relative clauses belong within the larger {NP}? Well, six words: "question test" and "one-word replacement test":

(50a) [I] [gave] [the cats *whom the neighbor adopted*] [their food]. (sE)

Q: Whom did I give their food?—A: *The cats whom the neighbor adopted.*

(51a) [We] [was discussing] [the initiative *that Obama curated*].[51] (AAE)

[We] [was discussing] [it   ].

Because they function as POSTs within larger {NPs}, relative clauses are, grammatically speaking, not required for a sentence to be grammatically complete, just like any other POST.

14.3.3.2 Restrictive vs. Non-restrictive Relative Clauses
All relative clauses are, grammatically speaking, optional. Semantically speaking, some relative clauses are more important than others. Relative clauses that are essential to readers' understanding are called **restrictive relative clauses.** As the name suggests, they restrict the meaning of a noun in definite ways and, thereby, define exactly how a noun is supposed to be understood. In contrast, those relative clauses that are not essential to readers' understanding are called **non-restrictive**. In some cases, the "essentialness" is crystal clear and sometimes the "essentialness" is a judgment made by the writer as the writer knows or estimates what the reader already knows or needs to know. Restrictive relative clauses cannot be separated from their antecedents. Because they're so, so closely related, nothing can come in between them! Non-restrictive relative clauses are usually set off from the main clause by commas. But remember, the essentialness does often depend on the writer's (and the reader's) perspective. Compare (52) and (52a):

(52)   My father, who owns a sheep farm, gave me a wool blanket. (sE)

(52a)   My neighbor *who owns a sheep farm* gave me a wool blanket. (sE)

In (52), the relative clause *who owns a sheep farm* is **non-restrictive**, i.e., non-essential. While it provides interesting information about my father, it is not necessary either for the sentence to be grammatically complete or for an understanding of the main clause. Because of this, commas are used to separate this additional information from the rest of the sentence. In (52a), the relative clause *who owns a sheep farm* is **restrictive**. It narrows *neighbor* down to the sheep-farm-owning neighbor, as opposed to the neighboring plumber or doctor. Because the antecedent and this necessary relative clause are so closely related, no commas can separate the two.

How about (53)? Is the relative clause restrictive or non-restrictive?

(53)   The report *which identifies the chemical compound* is on my desk. (sE)

We suggest that it is restrictive. The relative clause provides essential information for identifying the report in question. Note though that if a sentence prior to this had identified the report in question beyond a doubt, then this example could be read as a non-restrictive relative clause! Interpreting a relative clause as either restrictive or non-restrictive really does often depend on the writer's or the reader's perspective.

14.3.3.3 *Who* vs. *Whom*

Now, when to use *whom* and when to use *who*? The answer lies in the pronoun's syntactic function. Compare (54) to (55):

(54)   We invited Rose, **who** *baked banana bread*, to the party. (sE)

(55)   We invited Rose, **whom** *you met last night*, to the party. (sE)

Turning the relative clause into its own independent clause and replacing the constituent with a pronoun illustrates the point here nicely:

(54a)   [*Rose*] [baked] [banana bread].

       [*She*]

        S   V   DO

(55a)   [You] [met] [*Rose*] [last night].

                 [*her*]

       S   V   DO   A

In (54a), *Rose* functions as the subject, and as such is replaced with the subject form of the personal pronoun *she*. In (55a), however, *Rose* functions as the DO, and as such is replaced with the object form of the personal pronoun *her*. If we turn these two sentences into echo-questions (where *who* and *whom* now function as interrogative pronouns!), this is what we get:

(54b) [*Who*] [baked] [banana bread]?
           S   V   DO

(55b) [You] [met] [*whom*] [last night]?
           S   V   DO   A

Who and *whom* are relative pronouns we can use to introduce relative clauses. Return to the independent clauses in (54a) and (55a), replace *Rose* with *who* and *whom*, respectively, and then place the pronouns at the beginning of each clause. Finally, we merge each newly-created relative clause with the original main clause *We invited Rose to the party*:

(54c) We invited Rose, [*who*] [baked] [banana bread], to the party. (sE)
                           S   V   DO

(55c) We invited Rose, [*whom*] [you] [met] [last night], to the party. (sE)
                           DO   S   V   A

This shows that when the relative pronoun functions as the DO within its relative clause, our normal S-V-DO word order is flipped so that the DO comes before the subject!

What if the relative pronoun functions as the IO or the object of the preposition? Here's how those work:

(56) We invited Rose, *whom* Casey gave the banana bread, to the party. (sE)

(57) We invited Rose, for *whom* we made a cocktail, to the party. (sE)

Let's once again isolate the relative clauses as independent clauses and replace the constituents in question with pronouns:

(56a) [Casey] [gave] [*Rose*] [the banana bread].
                          [*her*]
          S   V   IO   DO

(57a) [We] [made] [a cocktail] [for *Rose*].
                             [for *her*]
          S   V   DO   A

When an independent clause such as *Casey gave Rose the banana bread* is embedded as a **relative clause** inside another independent clause, *Rose* is replaced with the relative pronoun *whom* (not *who*) because *Rose* functions as the IO. The relative pronoun must then move to the beginning of the relative clause when we embed it in the main clause. This is how we end up with the original sentences (56) and (57). In (56), *whom* functions as the IO within the relative clause, and in (57), *whom* functions as the object of the preposition within the {PP} *for whom*. In short, when the relative pronoun functions as the IO, DO, or object of the preposition, *whom* will be its form, just like *her* (not *she*!) replaces *Rose* in (56a) and (57a).

Now, *who* is becoming more common no matter which syntactic slot it occupies, and *whom* is becoming less so because people are merging the two. In fact, it's not hard to find examples such as these:

(58) Every time we talk about people *who we interview* ....[52] (sE)

(59) These people *who we elect* are going to be making decisions about things ....[53] (sE)

When we isolate those relative clauses, we end up with this:

(58a) [We] [interview] [*people*].
                         [them]
           S   V   DO

(59a) [We] [elect] [*these people*].
                    [them]
           S   V   DO

Once again, our relative pronoun stands in for a constituent of the original clause that functioned as the DO, and as such, technically (or prescriptively!), it should be *whom*, and yet, *who* is used instead. In short, this is a language change we are observing in real time, which is fascinating! We predict that eventually, *who* will win and *whom* will simply go out of style. But, you never know. The prescriptivists can be strong, and so *whom* may stick around longer than we are expecting!

14.3.3.4 *That* versus *That*

When relative clauses are introduced by the relative pronoun *that*, how do you know that it is indeed a relative clause and not a *that*-clause? It's actually pretty easy! If you can replace *that* with *which*, you're looking at a relative clause. If you **cannot** replace *that* with *which*, then you're looking at a *that*-clause:

(60) The cat **that** *I adopted* has an extra thumb. (sE)

(60a) The cat **which** *I adopted* has an extra thumb. (sE)

(61) Or they might have their own song **that** *they created theirself*.[54] (AAE)

(61a) Or they might have their own song **which** *they created theirself*. (AAE)

(62) You know **that** *I love cats*. (sE)

(62a) *You know **which** *I love cats*. (sE)

In (60) and (61), we can use *which* to replace *that*. We can be sure that *that I adopted* and *that they created theirself* are both relative clauses. In (62), we cannot replace *that* with *which* (*which I love cats* is clearly ungrammatical!), and that means that *that I love cats* is a *that*-clause.

> **Exercise 7**
>
> Identify the italicized clauses below as either relative clauses or *that*-clauses.
>
> a) Our favorite restaurant *that opened last year* is right down the road from us. (sE)
>
> b) I make sure *that they aks their parents*.[55] (AAE)

> c) I told my friends *that I would be late.* (sE)
>
> d) John was a-talkin' so loud *[that] my eardrums hurt.*[56] (AE)
>
> e) It was in the apple *that the witch had gave Snow White* that wasn't poisonous.[57] (ChE)
>
> f) I could hear in your voice *that you were unhappy.* (sE)
>
> g) We bought the two rugs *that we thought were the prettiest.* (sE)
>
> h) The decision *that was made by the committee* was breaking news. (sE)

14.3.3.5 Reduced Relative Clauses

In some relative clauses, the relative pronoun is optional, which is why we included it in the data set below in parentheses—even without them, the relative clauses are grammatical:

> (63) The cat *(that) Juan was brushing* started to purr. (sE)
>
> (64) That was the very first area *(that) we was asked to evacuate.*[58] (AAE)
>
> (65) The gift *(that) Moesha unwrapped right away* was beautiful. (sE)
>
> (66) There's some guys *(that) I can't stand.*[59] (ChE)

Compare those relative clauses to this one:

> (67) The cat *that was purring* was cute. (sE)
>
> (67a) *The cat ~~that~~ *was purring* was cute. (sE)

Leaving out *that* in (67) results in an ungrammatical sentence (67a). Can you determine the underlying pattern for when a relative pronoun is optional and when it is required? Hint: What is the relative pronoun's syntactic function? Compare (67) from above to (68) below:

> (68) The cat *(that) I was brushing* curled up on the couch. (sE)

The relative clause in (68)—*(that) I was brushing*—is based on this independent clause:

> (69) [I] [was brushing] [the cat]. (sE)
>   S   V   DO

When this clause is combined with the main clause *That cat curled up on the couch*, the relative pronoun *that* replaces *the cat* in (69), moves to clause-initial position, and becomes optional (see (68)). Now, in (67), the relative clause *that was purring* is based on this independent clause:

> (70) [The cat] [was purring]. (sE)
>   S   V

When this clause is combined with the main clause *The cat was cute*, the relative pronoun *that* replaces *the cat* in (70) and remains in sentence-initial position.

The crucial difference between (67) and (68) is that the relative pronoun replaces constituents that played different roles in the underlying independent clauses: that of subject in (67) and that of DO in (68). This shows that when the relative pronoun functions as the DO in a relative clause, it is optional. Those relative clauses are called **reduced relative clauses**. When the relative pronoun functions as the subject, it is required (at least for sE dialects). Compare this pattern to the attested and grammatical AAE and ChE pattern:

(71) You the one *be telling me*.[60] (AAE)

(72) I guess it's always gon be some folk *don't believe fat meat is greasy*.[61] (AAE)

(73) Because there's a lot of people Ø *do need help*.[62] (ChE)

(74) Since my grandmother is the only one Ø *has a Nintendo* ....[63] (ChE)

In each example, the relative clause is introduced by a **zero relative pronoun**.[64] You can see that the relative pronoun *who* could be added in each example, but it is not necessary in AAE or ChE. You might also have noticed that the relative clause in each example above is part of a {NP} that itself functions as the SC (remember that in AAE, the copula verb in SVSC sentences isn't required!), so the implied subject in the relative clause is the same as the subject for the overall sentence. The data once again shows what is grammatically possible in a dialect and what isn't.

14.3.4 A Note about Appositives

This next construction isn't exactly a clause, but we include it here because it adds information about another noun in a sentence. Plus, when asked to create relative clauses, many people will form a structure such as this:

(75) My father, *a nurse*, made everyone feel welcome. (sE)

Compare that to our relative clause example from earlier:

(75a) My father, *who is a nurse*, made everyone feel welcome. (sE)

Semantically, the {NP} *a nurse* conveys information that is very similar to the information in the relative clause *who is a nurse*, but grammatically speaking, the two constructions are not similar at all. One is a phrase; one is a clause that has its own {VP}. An {NP} that renames another {NP} is called an **appositive** or an **apposition**. Appositions are usually separated via commas or parentheses. Here are a few more examples:

(76) Dr. Smith, *my favorite professor*, introduced me to linguistics. (sE)

(77) [H]e got a performing arts center *(the August Wilson Center)* in his name just steps from dis here convention center.[65] (AAE)

(78) My neighbor, *a sheep farmer*, is teaching me how to play the guitar. (sE)

(79) This here's the old residenter bear hunter, *Fonze Cable*.[66] (AE)

For most appositives, you could switch the first {NP} with the apposition:

(76a) My favorite professor, *Dr. Smith*, introduced me to linguistics. (sE)

(79a) This here's Fonze Cable, *the old residenter bear hunter*.[67] (AE)

Because appositions appear *after* a noun within an {NP}, you may be tempted to think that they're POSTs. And yet, a POST such as the one in (76b) can't switch places with the preceding noun in the same way an apposition can:

(76b)   Dr. Smith, *who is my favorite professor*, introduced me to linguistics. (sE)

(76c)   *Who is my favorite professor, *Dr. Smith*, introduced me to linguistics. (sE)

In terms of sentence structure, the appositive functions together with the larger {NP} and it can occur in various syntactic slots:

(77a)   [He] [got] [a performing arts center *(the August Wilson Center)*] ....[68] (AAE)

        S   V   DO

(78a)   [My neighbor, *a sheep farmer*,] [is teaching] [me] [how to play ...]. (sE)

                S   V   IO   DO

(79b)   [This here] ['s] [the old residenter bear hunter, *Fonze Cable*].[69] (AE)

        S   V   SC

Exercise 8

Create four sentences that each contain one appositive (or maybe you can double up on appositives in one sentence!). Each {NP} that contains the appositive should function differently in the sentence (as S, IO, DO, and SC).

Exercise 9

Using the pieces provided below, create your own sentences that correspond to the specific construction:

a) restrictive relative clauses:
   i. *Pat, who, sells, farm, my neighbor*
   ii. *black cat, nine lives, that, own*

b) non-restrictive relative clauses:
   i. *Quinn, my brother, owns, from Chicago, who*
   ii. *car, which, my aunt, purchased, yellow*

c) an appositive: *Dr. Smith, wrote, favorite teacher, best-selling novel*

14.3.5 Nominal Relative Clauses

Another subordinate clause type is called **nominal relative clause**. They are introduced by the pronouns *what, whatever, whoever, where, how*. Notice that in AE, the pronoun can be followed by *that* as in *how that* in (83). These clauses express something **noun-y**, something **nominal** (hence the name), which we illustrate via the rephrased version underneath each example below:

(80) It done changed so many times to *what it is now*.[70] (AAE)
     to the <u>thing</u> (that) it is now.

(81) *Whoever gets to the bowl first* gets the most food. (sE)
     <u>The cat</u> that gets to the bowl first ….

(82) I don't know *where all he sold it at*.[71] (AE)
     the <u>place</u> where all he sold it at.

(83) Tell us *how that you would find and get the sheep in*.[72] (AE)
     the <u>way</u> (that) you would find and get the sheep in.

Some of the **syntactic functions** that nominal relative clauses can take on are the following:

(84) [*What you need*] [is] [some cat cuddly time]. (sE)
         S   V   SC

(85) [He] [get] [*what you mean*].[73] (AAE)
      S   V   DO

(86) [I] [don't know] [*where all he sold it at*]. (AE)
     S   V   DO

(87) [Tell] [us] [*how that you would find and get the sheep in.*] (AE)
     V   IO   DO

Note that we have an example of the imperative mood in (87): the entire sentence starts with the base form of the verb *tell*, and there's no overt subject!

Exercise 10

Identify all nominal relative clauses in the sentences below.

a) What I like best is soccer. (sE)
b) She be teachin bout dem necessary feminist rhetorics and showin us how rhetorical silence is just as important as talk. ….[74] (AAE)
c) The prize will go to whoever submits the best cat picture. (sE)
d) My daughter is teaching me how to use email. (sE)

e) I can remember what all happened.⁷⁵ (AE)
f) It's where people gathers up and shucks corn in the fall.⁷⁶ (AE)
g) This is where Maya Angelou was born. (sE)
h) He asked me where did I live.⁷⁷ (ChE)

14.4 Non-finite Clauses

So far, our clauses had their own subject and their own **finite** {VP}. Recall that a **finite verb** is marked for tense and a **non-finite** verb is not. We now turn to **non-finite clauses** which are built around non-finite {VPs}:

(88) Tricia wanted *to draw trees*. (sE)
(89) *Drawing trees* is easy. (sE)
(90) The trees looked beautiful *covered in snow*. (sE)

The non-finite {VPs} *to draw*, *drawing*, and *covered* each introduce their own non-finite clause. As clauses, these structures can, for instance, add additional sentence constituents such as DOs and IOs. Many times, there won't be an overt subject, but there can be:

(91)   [Kori] [made] [*Ahmed draw ten trees*]. (sE)
         S   V   DO

In (91), at the sentence level, the non-finite clause *Ahmed draw ten trees* functions as the DO. This non-finite clause itself consists of constituents that play syntactic roles at the clause-level, and as such, this non-finite clause has its own sentence pattern:

(91a)   [Ahmed] [draw] [ten trees].
          S   V   DO

We'll get into the details of the three types of non-finite clauses in English next: *to*-clauses, *-ing*-clauses, and *past participle clauses*.

14.4.1 To-clauses

To-clauses are formed using the infinitive form of the verb; this is why they are often also called **infinitival clauses**. Both full infinitives (i.e., those marked with *to*, hence the name *to*-**clause**) and bare infinitives (without a *to*) can occupy the {VP} in *to*-clauses. Just like phrases and other clauses, *to*-clauses can take on syntactic functions, such as DO in (91) above. We outline various functions next.

14.4.1.1 Functions of *To*-clauses

***to*-clauses as Subjects**:

(92)   [*To decorate the house for the holiday season*] [is] [imperative] … (sE)
(93)   [*To shovel all the snow*   ] [was] [impossible] … (sE)
                      S   V   SC

To Be or Not To Be: Coordination/Subordination

to-clauses as Subject Complements:

    (94)   [The best excuse] [is] [*to say that you have an exam tomorrow*].⁷⁸ (sE)

    (95)   [The best time ever] [is] [*to cuddle with all cats at the same time*]. (sE)
                  S   V   SC

to-clauses as Direct Objects:

    (96)   [I] [like] [*to be by my own self*   ].⁷⁹ (ChE)

    (97)   [We] [want] [*the experts to teach us linguistics*]. (sE)
                  S   V   DO

to-clauses as Adverbials:

    (98)   [We] [brought] [the cats] [to the vet] [*to get a second opinion*]. (sE)
              S   V   DO   A   A

    (99)   [He] [was] [a good hand] [*to break a oxen*].⁸⁰ (AE)
              S   V   SC   A

to-clauses as POST in {NP}:

    (100)   A job *to help pay the bills* is necessary. (sE)

Here's how the {NP} breaks down:

DET	PRE	HEAD	POST
A		job	to help pay the bills

This entire {NP} that has the *to*-clause embedded within it functions as the subject in the overall sentence:

    (100a) [A job *to help pay the bills*] [is] [necessary]. (sE)
                S   V   SC

to-clauses as POST in {AdjPs}:

    (101)   Martin is done his bass tracks and we are ready *to start vocals*.⁸¹ (ECE)

    (102)   Fifi was happy for *to go*.⁸² (OE/AE/SAE)

Here's how the {AdjPs} break down:

PRE	HEAD	POST
	ready	to start vocals
	happy	for to go

And the entire {AdjPs} function as the SC in the overall sentences:

    (101a) … and [we] [are] [ready *to start vocals*].⁸³ (ECE)
                       S   V   SC

    (102a) [Fifi] [was] [happy for *to go*].⁸⁴ (OE/AE/SAE)
                 S   V   SC

Foundations of Grammar

This last example is yet another dialect feature which allows for *for* and *to* to double up, resulting in *for to go*. In sE dialects, this would be similar to *Fifi was happy to go*.

14.4.1.2 Internal Structure of *To*-clauses

Because we are looking at clausal structures, these *to*-clauses exhibit syntactic patterns that follow the sentence pattern structures you already know (i.e., S-V, S-V-DO, etc.). We provide the entire sentence the *to*-clause is embedded in but only provide the syntactic pattern for the *to*-clause:

(103) My colleague expected [*Casey*] [*to visit*]. (sE)
                                S   V

(104) We want [*the experts*] [*to teach*] [*us*] [*linguistics*]. (sE)
                     S   V   IO   DO

(105) Julissa wants [*me*] [*to label*] [*Fluffy*] [*a fiend*]. (sE)
                       S   V   DO   OC

(106) My job requires [*us*] [*to be*] [*pleasant*]. (sE)
                         S   V   SC

(107) They want [*to do*] [*they own thing*].[85] (AAE)
                     V   DO

(108) [*To decorate*] [*the house*] [*for the holiday season*] is imperative. (sE)
             V   DO   A

Some *to*-clauses feature their own overt subject, while some feature what's called an **implied subject** (see (107) and (108)), which is usually inferable. In (107), *to do they own thing* is embedded in *They want to do they own thing*, for instance. The subject in the overall sentence is *they*, and that's the implied subject for the *to*-clause, too.

When *to*-clauses have an overt subject, it comes prior to the non-finite {VP}, i.e., prior to the infinitive. In (105) and (106), the pronouns *me* and *us* are in the overt slot at the clause level. You may be wondering: Wait a second, *me* and *us* are object forms of the pronouns *I* and *we*. How can the object form function in the subject slot? Well, you may also have noticed that each of those *to*-clauses in their entirety functions as the DO at the sentence-level, and that overall DO-function of the entire *to*-clause at the sentence level determines the form of the pronoun. This is how we end up with a *me* and *us* in subject position within the clause!

A caveat is in order: *To*-clauses can be short and sweet and consist just of the {VP}:

(109) [Our students] [like] [*to study*]. (sE)

(110) [We   ] [was asked] [*to evacuate*].[86] (AAE)

(111) [I   ] [asked   ] [*to go*].[87] (sE)
              S   V   DO

(112) [*To stop*] [would be] [*premature*]. (sE)
             S   V   SC

To Be or Not To Be: Coordination/Subordination

Now, just like with *to*-clauses that are more fully fledged out, these very short *to*-clauses can function at the overall sentence level in different ways. In (109)–(111), the *to*-clause functions as the DO, and in (112), it functions as the subject. Now, different grammar books treat these structures differently, with some labeling them simply non-finite {VPs}, which means those grammars propose that a {VP} can function as a DO or S, for instance. We follow Quirk et al. (1985) and treat such {VPs} as *to*-clauses.

> **Exercise 11**
>
> Identify all *to*-clauses in the sentences below. Then, label their function in the overall sentence, or phrase (if embedded in a phrase).
>
> a) Our only solution to the budget shortfall is to recruit more clients. (sE)
> b) This will be particularly important once you're done the tattoo and need to leave the shop.[88] (ECE)
> c) To surrender seemed disgraceful. (sE)
> d) Our mind tricks us to think that we going to sleep ....[89] (AAE)
> e) Alejandra asked to be included in the preparations. (sE)
> f) Y'all be wanting to go somewhere.[90] (AAE)
> g) The table to sit at is over there. (sE)
> h) My grandmother always told me to choose wisely. (sE)

14.4.2 -*ing*-clauses

-*ing*-clauses are another type of non-finite clause, this time introduced by the present participle. Just like *to*-clauses, -*ing*-clauses can consist of just the verb:

(113) [Sleeping] [is] [imperative for people's health]. (sE)
 [It]
  S   V   SC

(114) [Everybody] [start] [hollering].[91] (AAE)
               [it]
   S   V   DO

The pronoun replacement test provides evidence that the -*ing*-verb forms *sleeping* and *hollering* function in a noun-y sentence slot: Subject and DO. As you know, pronouns replace nouns, and so these one-word -*ing*-clauses do behave in ways similar to nouns. This is why they are often differentiated from other, longer -*ing*-clauses, and labeled **gerunds**. The gerund sits in between a noun and a verb—it has features of both depending on the context. Different grammarians have different takes on this distinction. Since

Foundations of Grammar

these *-ing-*verbs forms are easily expandable into longer *-ing-*clauses (as in *Sleeping all night long is imperative* where an adverbial *all night long* is added to form a longer *-ing-*clause), we treat even one-word instances like (113) and (114) as *-ing-*clauses rather than gerunds. Just like *to-*clauses, *-ing-*clauses can take on various functions.

14.4.2.1 Functions of *-ing*-clauses

-*ing*-clauses as Subjects

(115) *Racing my younger sibling* was a terrible idea. (sE)

(116) *Working retail* has made me hate the human race all the more.[92] (ME/SAE)

-*ing*-clauses as Subject Complements

(117) My favorite activity has been *lifting weights.* (sE)

(118) I reckon most of the deal in getting your license (i.e., a marriage license) is *having the three dollars it takes to pay.*[93] (AE)

-*ing*-clauses as Direct Objects

(119) I had start *believing in myself.*[94] (AAE)

(120) They love *watching their favorite shows at night.* (sE)

-*ing*-clauses as Adverbials

(121) I grew up *going over to my father house maybe a couple times.*[95] (AAE)

(122) *Having prepared for the client meeting,* Moesha rocked the presentation. (sE)

-*ing*-clauses as Object of the Preposition

(123) Just before *taking the test,* it is crucial to review the content. (sE)

(124) But special thanks go to the tireless work that Marlene Knight do in *securing the convention sites.*[96] (AAE)

Here is how the {PPs} break down:

PRE	HEAD	Object of the Preposition
just	before	*taking the test*
	in	*securing the convention sites*

-*ing*-clauses as POST in {NP}

(125) The photo *hanging in the center* was bought immediately. (sE)

(126) We got some real special ones, like the double session *featuring the inimitable Dr. Geneva Smitherman.*[97] (AAE)

DET	PRE	HEAD	POST
The		photo	hanging in the center
the	double	session	featuring the inimitable Dr. Geneva Smitherman

-ing-clauses as POST in {AdjP}

(127) They are busy *preparing a barbecue*.[98] (sE)

(128) My grandpa is extremely nervous *handling the hot grill*. (sE)

PRE	HEAD	POST
	busy	preparing a barbecue
extremely	nervous	handling the hot grill

14.4.2.2 Internal Structure of -*ing*-clauses

-*ing*-clauses internally are organized like the general sentence patterns you're very familiar with by now. We illustrate some of them here, but this is not an exhaustive list. Note that we label the -*ing*-clauses' internal syntactic patterns only, not the pattern for the overall sentence that contains the -*ing*-clause.

(115a) [*Racing*] [*my younger sibling*] was a terrible idea. (sE)
          V   DO

(118a) I reckon most of the deal in getting your license (i.e., a marriage license) is
       [*having*] [*the three dollars it takes to pay*].[99] (AE)
          V   DO

(119a) I had start [*believing*] [*in myself*].[100] (AAE)
                      V   A

(122a) [*Having prepared*] [*for the client meeting*], Moesha rocked it. (sE)
              V   A

(124a) But special thanks go to the tireless work that Marlene Knight do in
       [*securing*] [*the convention sites*].[101] (AAE)
           V   DO

Most -*ing*-clauses start with the -*ing*-verb form itself, without an overt subject. However, overt subjects are possible, as illustrated by these sentences:

(129) [*Her aunt*] [*having left*] [*the room*], I asked Ann for help.[102] (sE)
          S   V   DO

(130) I didn't know about [*the weather*] [*being*] [*so awful in this area*].[103] (sE)
                                S   V   SC

Exercise 12

Identify all -*ing*-clauses in the sentences below. Identify their function at the sentence or phrase level.

a) Their hobby is collecting cat pictures. (sE)
b) Dancing after a long day can be helpful in reducing stress. (sE)
c) I ain't really thinking about getting with J. or any other guy.[104] (ChE)
d) Also, in the da house is past C's chairs Keith Gilyard and Adam Banks, laying it down bout black rhetoric.[105] (AAE)
e) Having the before picture taken makes this diet seem all the more real.[106] (ME/SAE)
f) My friends are complaining a lot about being so far away. (sE)
g) Having a new bike made the commute much easier. (sE)

14.4.3 Past Participle Clauses

The last non-finite clause type is the **past participle clause**. Since you know that the past participle is a non-finite verb form, you can guess that this type of clause will be introduced by that very verb form. Sometimes, this type of class is also called an -*ed*-clause:

(131) *Considered works of art*, they were admitted into the country.[107] (sE)

(132) Most dogs *raised in loving homes* are wonderful. (sE)

(133) *Given insufficient time*, the prosecutor asked for a recess. (sE)

14.4.3.1 Functions of Past Participle Clauses

Very often, the past participle clause provides more information about a noun in a sentence. Because past participle clauses often provide additional information, their most common functions are that of adverbial at the sentence level and that of POST at the phrase level.

Past participial clauses as Adverbials:

(131a) [*Considered works of art*], [they] [were admitted] [into the country].[108] (sE)
                   A   S   V   A

(134) [*Written in passive voice*], [the apology] [missed] [its mark]. (sE)
           A   S   V   DO

(135) [*Adopted by their new owners*], [the three cats] [felt] [happy]. (sE)
           A   S   V   SC

The classification of these clauses as adverbial relies on an interpretation of the clause as giving us information about *why* something happened. In other words, we could rephrase them as *because*-clauses: (134) could turn into *Because it was written in passive voice, the apology* ....

Past participle clauses as POSTs:
First, let's look at the examples where the past participle clauses occupy the slot after a noun. Just like other non-finite clauses, past participle clauses can expand an {NP}, where it will occupy the POST slot:

(132a) Most dogs *raised in loving homes* are wonderful. (sE)

(136) Tasty sweets *eaten at night* don't count. (sE)

DET	PRE	HEAD	POST
Most		dogs	*raised in loving homes*
	tasty	sweets	*eaten at night*

In each of these examples, the entire {NP} functions as the subject in the overall sentence. Now, we could do the following to our sentences from earlier, where we proposed the function of adverbial for the past participle clause. Bear with us!

(134a) *Written in passive voice*, the apology missed its mark. (sE)

(134b) The apology, *written in passive voice*, missed its mark.

(135a) *Adopted by their new owners*, the three cats felt happy. (sE)

(135b) The three cats, *adopted by their new owners*, felt happy. (sE)

In (134b) and (135b), we have made it clear that the past participle clause has to be read as a modification of the noun; we've taken away the possibility of interpreting the clause as an answer to *why* (i.e., as an adverbial). The syntactic position—moving the clause to immediately after the {NP}-head—means that when written in this way, the past participle clause will function as a POST:

DET	PRE	HEAD	POST
the		apology	*written in passive voice*
the three		cats	*adopted by their new owners*

So, context and how someone utilizes past participle clauses determine their syntactic functions.

14.4.3.2 Internal Structure of Past Participle Clauses

In terms of their internal structure, past participle clauses are a bit more limited in how we can expand them and which types of constituents we can add. The most common structure is V-A, but V-DO and V-SC are possible as well.

(131b) [Considered] [*works of art*], they were admitted into the country.[109] (sE)
      V   SC

Foundations of Grammar

(133a) [*Given*] [*insufficient time*], the prosecutor asked for a recess. (sE)
        V   DO

(134c) [*Written*] [*in passive voice*], the apology missed its mark. (sE)
        V   A

(136a) Tasty sweets [*eaten*] [*at night*] don't count. (sE)
                V   A

No overt subjects are included in the examples above. For each clause, an implied subject matches the subject of the overall sentence.

Exercise 13

Identify all past participle clauses and identify their functions.

a) Most of the toys made in this factory are exported to other countries. (sE)
b) Taylor showed me many drawings painted by their aunt. (sE)
c) The treasure stolen during a recent break-in was never recovered. (sE)
d) I have met many pets raised in wonderful homes. (sE)
e) Done with ease, the magic trick stunned the audience. (sE)
f) Kept inside the house, the cats weren't at risk of being hit by cars. (sE)
g) Exhausted from the long day, my friend fell asleep immediately. (sE)
h) We finally located the missing sets of tests, hidden under a stack of books. (sE)

14.5 When Embedded Clauses Violate Grammar

As you saw earlier, some clauses are movable within the sentence. In written language use, it's important to clarify what in the sentence is being modified via placement of the modifier. If not, you may be constructing sentences that feature **dangling modifiers** or **dangling participles.** These occur when the writer doesn't place an embedded clause that modifies an {NP} next to that {NP}, which results in the sentence becoming nonsensical or, at least, ambiguous. Can you spot the dangling participles and dangling modifiers below?

(137) Running down the street, the house was on fire. (sE)
(138) Lying in a heap on the floor, she found the clothes. (sE)
(139) The waiter brought the waffles to the table drenched in maple syrup. (sE)

We're confident that you've been able to spot the ambiguity in each of these! In (137), the -*ing*-clause conveys an action we attribute to a person or animal—something animate—

but there is no actual "human" or animate object in this sentence. In fact, the nearest {NP} is *the house*. It makes it sound as if the house, which was on fire, was running down the street! Note, though, that the structure *Running down the street* itself is perfectly grammatical. It doesn't have an overt subject, so it is prone to ambiguity if it isn't matched with the overt subject of the main clause. Because the *-ing*-clause isn't "attached" to the overt subject of the main clause, it sort of, literally, dangles!

In (138), we have another dangling participle. The *-ing*-clause is placed next to the pronoun *she*, creating the impression that she is lying in a heap on the floor. However, we can probably recognize that it's *the clothes* that are *lying in a heap on the floor*. Moving the *-ing*-clause to after the {NP} *the clothes* resolves that ambiguity, and the dangling participle becomes a regular POST-modifier:

(138a) She found the clothes lying in a heap on the floor. (sE)

In (139), *drenched in maple syrup* can potentially modify any of these {NPs}: *the waiter, the waffles, the table*. It is placed closest to the {NP} *the table*, and—granted—the table could be drenched in maple syrup, although we find that pretty gross and unappetizing. We'd hope the waiter would bring some clean-up supplies and not the waffles! Now, *the waiter* itself could be drenched in maple syrup, too. Again, not something that inspires a lot of confidence in the establishment and its cleanliness standards. So, most likely, it's *the waffles* that are drenched in maple syrup, as they should be for a proper breakfast.

The fix for this ambiguity, for this dangling modifier, is again rearranging the pieces in the sentence (as in (139a)) or by expanding the past participle clause into a fully-fledged relative clause (as in (139b)):

(139a) The waiter brought the waffles, *drenched in maple syrup*, to the table. (sE)

(139b) The waiter brought the waffles, which were drenched in maple syrup, to the table. (sE)

Dangling modifiers are quite common and happen to the best of us. Case in point: Can you find the dangling modifier in Shakespeare's Hamlet passage?

GHOST:
Now, Hamlet, hear.
'Tis given out that, sleeping in my orchard,
A serpent stung me; so the whole ear of Denmark
Is by a forged process of my death
Rankly abus'd; but know, thou noble youth,
The serpent that did sting thy father's life
Now wears his crown.
—*The Tragedy of Hamlet, Prince of Denmark*
Act I, Scene V

Did you find it?
GHOST:
Now, Hamlet, hear.

'Tis given out that, *sleeping in my orchard,*
A serpent stung me; so the whole ear of Denmark
.....

What is the {NP} being modified by the embedded clause *sleeping in my orchard*? Hamlet's father, the King, who is now the Ghost? The serpent? Hamlet? Well, the way it is written, *sleeping in my orchard* must refer to the serpent and not the King (who is now a ghost), but, really, the Ghost means "When I was sleeping in my orchard, a serpent stung me."

Many dangling modifiers are quite comedic, and if nothing else, you'll get a laugh out of them. All joking aside, if you want to avoid such ambiguity in your writing, you'll want to double-check these kinds of constructions.

Exercise 14

Putting it all together. Take a moment to contemplate how much information you now know about English sentences and clauses. For each sentence below (all sE), do the following:

- Identify the overall sentence pattern first (e.g., S-V, S-V-DO) by bracketing each component and labeling it.
- Name the type of verb for each sentence (e.g., transitive, intransitive, ditransitive).
- Identify any and all clauses. That means you have to label them correctly (e.g., adverbial clause, relative clause, *that*-clause, nominal relative clause, *to*-clause, *ing*-clause, past participle clause).
- Identify the function of each of those clauses (either at the sentence level or the phrase level, depending on where it occurs).

Here are your sentences:

a) The awesome store on main street in Midland sold the pretty bag that I mentioned yesterday.
b) This cry for help was the last warning.
c) The player who scored the most touchdowns secured the biggest endorsement deal.
d) Armstrong was the first man to walk on the moon.
e) I cuddled with all the cats, while Fatima cleaned the litter boxes in the basement without knowing what he was missing.
f) The students said that the cats are so annoying.
g) Our cat Fluffy senses whenever tension is in the room.
h) Although he has a thumb, Mr. Kitty can't hold a spoon.

Terminology to Know

Term	Working definition	Example/Illustration
Simple sentence		
Compound sentence		
Complex sentence		
Coordinator		
Independent clause		
Dependent clause		
Main clause		
that-clause		
Relative clause		
Zero relative pronoun		
Adverbial clause		
Nominal relative clause		
Restrictive relative clause		
Non-restrictive relative clause		
Non-finite clauses		
to-clauses		
apposition		
-ing-clause		
Past participle clause		

Chart 1 Key terminology Chapter 14

Notes

1. Wood, 2014.
2. OpenAI, 2024.
3. Kendall, Quartey et al., 2018 Transcript ID DCB_se2_ag2_f_01_1.
4. Putnam and van Koppen, 2011; cited in Wood, 2013.
5. Kendall, Quartey et al., 2018 Transcript ID DCB_se2_ag2_f_01_1.
6. Putnam and van Koppen, 2011; cited in Wood, 2013.
7. Wolfram, 1976; cited in Matyiku, 2011a.
8. Maher and Wood, 2011.
9. W. Beauregard, personal communication, August 29, 2024.
10. Hinnell, 2012, p. 4; cited in Wood, 2014.
11. Baker-Bell, 2020, p. 45.

Foundations of Grammar

12. W. Beauregard, personal communication, August 29, 2024.
13. Kendall, Quartey et al., 2018 Transcript ID DCB_se1_ag4_f_01_1.
14. Rowe et al., 2018 Transcript ID PRV_se0_ag3_f_02_1.
15. Fought, 2003, p. 96.
16. Baker-Bell, 2020, p. 76.
17. Kendall, Quartey et al., 2018 Transcript ID DCB_se1_ag3_m_03_1.
18. Fought, 2003, p. 96.
19. Kendall, Quartey et al., 2018 Transcript ID DCB_se2_ag4_f_04_1.
20. Fought, 2003, p. 96.
21. Kendall, Quartey et al., 2018 Transcript ID DCB_se2_ag4_f_04_1.
22. Putnam and van Koppen, 2011; cited in Wood, 2013.
23. Kendall, Quartey et al., 2018 Transcript ID DCB_se2_ag2_f_01_1.
24. Wood, 2014.
25. Young, 2019, p. 4.
26. Ibid.
27. University of South Carolina (n.d.).
28. Wood, 2014.
29. Fought, 2003, p. 100.
30. Baker-Bell, 2020, p. 15.
31. Kendall, Quartey et al., 2018 Transcript ID DCB_se2_ag3_m_01_1.
32. Maher and Wood, 2011.
33. Mishoe and Montgomery, 1994; cited in Huang, 2011.
34. Fought, 2003, p. 100.
35. Baker-Bell, 2020, p. 15.
36. Fought, 2003, p. 100.
37. Quartey et al., 2020 Transcript ID VLD_se0_ag3_m_03_1.
38. Becker et al., 2021 Transcript ID LES_se0_ag3_m_01_2.
39. Kendall, Quartey et al., 2018 Transcript ID DCB_se2_ag4_f_05_1.
40. Wolfram and Christian, 1976, p. 82.
41. Di Paolo, 1989; cited in Huang, 2011.
42. Wolfram and Christian, 1976, p. 87.
43. Bayley, 2012, p. 163.
44. Wolfram and Christian, 1976, p. 107.
45. Smitherman, 2006, p. 3.
46. Fought, 2003, p. 94.
47. Roger et al., 2023 Transcript ID DTA_se3_ag3_f_02_1.
48. Quartey et al., 2020 Transcript ID VLD_se0_ag3_m_03_1.
49. Martinez and Wood, 2023.
50. Kendall, Quartey et al., 2018 Transcript ID DCB_se1_ag1_m_02_1.
51. Ibid.

52. Davis, 2008.
53. Ibid.
54. Kendall, Quartey et al., 2018 Transcript ID DCB_se1_ag2_m_02_3.
55. King et al., 2020 Transcript ID ROC_se0_ag1_m_03_1.
56. Slightly modified; Wolfram, 1976; cited in Matyiku, 2011a.
57. Bayley and Santa Ana, 2004, p. 378.
58. Rowe et al., 2018 Transcript ID PRV_se0_ag2_m_02_1.
59. Bayley, 2012, p. 159.
60. Green, 2002, p. 90.
61. Smitherman, 2006, p. 3.
62. Bayley, 2012, p. 161.
63. Ibid.
64. Green, 2002, p. 90.
65. Young, 2019, p. 4.
66. University of South Carolina (n.d.).
67. Word order switched, taken from Ibid.
68. Young, 2019, p. 4.
69. University of South Carolina (n.d.).
70. Rowe et al., 2018 Transcript ID PRV_se0_ag2_m_01_1.
71. University of South Carolina (n.d.).
72. Ibid.
73. Kendall, Fasold et al., 2018 Transcript ID DCA_se2_ag2_m_02.
74. Young, 2019, p. 5.
75. University of South Carolina (n.d.).
76. Ibid.
77. Bayley, 2012, p. 164.
78. Quirk et al., 1985, p. 1061.
79. Bayley, 2012, p. 157.
80. University of South Carolina (n.d.).
81. Hinnell, 2012, p. 4; cited in Wood, 2014.
82. Carroll, 1983; cited in Kaplan, Scruton, and Wood, 2017.
83. Hinnell, 2012, p. 4; cited in Wood, 2014.
84. Carroll, 1983; cited in Kaplan, Scruton, and Wood, 2017.
85. Green, 2002, p. 103.
86. Shortened from Rowe et al., 2018 Transcript PRV_se0_ag2_m_02_1.
87. Quirk et al., 1985, p. 995.
88. Hinnell, 2012, p. 4; cited in Wood, 2014.
89. Farrington et al., 2020 Transcript ID ATL_se0_ag2_m_01_1.
90. Kendall, Quartey et al., 2018 Transcript ID DCB_se1_ag2_f_03_1.
91. Kendall, Fasold et al., 2018 Transcript ID DCA_se2_ag2_m_02_1.

92. McCoy, 2016a.
93. University of South Carolina (n.d.).
94. Rowe et al., 2018 Transcript ID PRV_se0_ag2_f_01_1.
95. Kendall, Quartey et al., 2018 Transcript ID DCB_se1_ag1_m_02_1.
96. Young, 2019, p. 6.
97. Ibid., p. 4.
98. Quirk et al., 1985, p. 1063.
99. University of South Carolina (n.d.).
100. Rowe et al., 2018 Transcript ID PRV_se0_ag2_f_01_1.
101. Young, 2019, p. 6.
102. Adapted from Quirk et al., 1985, p. 993.
103. Ibid., p. 1065.
104. Bayley, 2012, p. 163.
105. Young, 2019, p. 5.
106. McCoy, 2016a.
107. Quirk et al., 1985, p. 995.
108. Ibid.
109. Ibid.

CHAPTER 15
STOP, PAUSE, CONSIDER: THE ROLE OF PUNCTUATION

Overview

Our motivation for ending this textbook with a chapter on **punctuation** is simple: now that you have a solid understanding of American English grammar(s), understanding the roles of different punctuation marks will help you select the most appropriate punctuation to help your readers. Our objectives are as follows. You'll be able to

- differentiate end punctuation marks;
- apply four basic rules of the comma;
- apply three basic rules of the semicolon; and
- apply one basic rule of the colon.

> **Pre-reading tasks**
>
> In the following sentences, the punctuation marks in bold font are used correctly. Can you develop a rule for their use based on the data provided? Make as many observations as possible.
>
> 1. End punctuation
>   a) The cat jumped over the little dog to get to the hamster.
>   b) The hamster screamed!
>   c) What do you think was the result?
>   **Rule:**
>
> 2. Commas
>   a) We bought our new pets food, bowls, beds, and collars.
>   b) When we brought them home, they seemed happy.
>   c) We were happy, of course, to add them to our family.
>   d) The animals played for hours, and they promptly fell asleep in their beds afterwards.

Foundations of Grammar

> **Rules:**
> 3. Semicolons
>   a) Our veterinarian examined each animal; all were declared healthy.
>   b) The cat did need some special supplements; however, the others did not.
> **Rules:**
> 4. Colons
>   a) We currently have the following animals as pets: three dogs, two cats, a hamster, a parrot, and three goldfish.
>   b) We must agree with Anatole France's statement on the benefits of pets to humans: "Until one has loved an animal, a part of one's soul remains unawakened."
>   c) According to Forbes Advisor, pet ownership is on the rise: in 2024, 66 percent of US citizens own a pet, which is up from 58 percent in 1988.[1]
> **Rule:**

15.1 Introduction

Punctuation is a contrived system developed in ancient Rome to help orators (and others) read a text aloud in the manner the writer intended.[2] The "rule" to put a comma where you would take a pause when speaking comes from this. However, the system we outline here is syntactic punctuation, a system that was developed in the seventeenth century that is designed to work with the grammar of a written text to clarify meaning and reduce ambiguity for readers.[3] This system of punctuation was developed for standardized American English writing, but it works just as well for writing in non-standardized American English dialects, as the examples will illustrate. Because there is still a dearth of published (academic) work that is written in non-sE dialects, the dialects represented in this chapter are limited to AAE and Hawaiian Pidgin English (HPE).

Punctuation is often thought to be central to grammar. In fact, both spelling and punctuation are routinely named as examples of "good grammar." We want to emphasize, however, that punctuation actually isn't part of "grammar" as it was defined in Chapter 1: "Words must be combined into larger units, and grammar encompasses the complex set of rules specifying such combinations."[4] Thus, grammar is all about the possible structures we can form based on underlying rules that members of a linguistic community share. Throughout this book, you've seen many, many examples of the grammatical structures and grammar rules of various American English dialects. Crucially, these grammar rules are descriptive in nature. We don't prescribe that you use one structure (such as sE final *-ed* ending or AAE/ChE's optional use of final *-ed* on regular verbs for past tense); we have simply described the various possible and grammatically correct structures within a variety of American English dialects.

These descriptive kinds of grammar rules—not punctuation rules—are what children learn when they acquire a dialect of a language (and remember that sE is still just another dialect of American English!). We learn spelling and punctuation rules in educational settings, in schools, via explicit instruction! As such, punctuation rules are the kinds of rules that we, as a society, impose on the written version of our language; they are agreed on by the members of a society—well, not by all the members of a given society, but by certain groups of people including teachers, editors, lexicographers, usage guide writers, and so on. And generally, people who produce written work are expected to follow these established rules. By nature, punctuation rules are prescriptive: they prescribe where and when and which punctuation mark to use. Even though they are not organic to language, or an inherent feature of language (in the way being able to form a comparative of an adjective is, for example!), they are still important because they help reduce ambiguity and help clarify exactly what we hope to get across in our writing.

Like all aspects of language, these rules have changed and will continue to change over time. So, when you read a document written in an earlier century of American English, the uses of commas, semicolons, or colons may be different from how they're used today. And even within current punctuation rules, variation exists! Not all writers and editors, not even all usage guides, agree on all punctuation rules. For instance, some resources suggest that a comma can be skipped in shorter compound sentences connected with *and* such as *You pitch and I'll catch*. Writers can—and do—use punctuation for reasons other than the basic punctuation rules we introduce here, and there may be differences in how writers punctuate their texts. Punctuation marks often are stylistic choices, and writers have some leeway in how to use those stylistic devices. Additionally, we are not aware of systematic differences between punctuation usage in sE texts versus non-sE texts. For this reason, we limit our examples from non-sE texts to those that use the basic conventions we introduce here.

For written language use, including creative works—poems, novels, short stories—a language community generally agrees to stick to a set of punctuation and spelling rules. When they do not, the reader will likely notice and wonder what the artist might be attempting by circumventing the standardized rules. Perhaps the most well-known poet who manipulates our expectations of such rules is e. e. cummings (1913–62). Take, for example, the lower-case spelling of his name and the first line of "Sonnets: Realities III" in his collection entitled *&* (1925):[5]

i have loved, let us see if that's all.

We could spend much time and print discussing the effects cummings creates by playing with such rules (and literary critics have!). What's your interpretation for his use of the lower-case "i" and the comma between two independent clauses (otherwise known as a comma splice)?

While most guidebooks break down the rules to be extremely specific, we have intentionally simplified our coverage to one basic end punctuation rule, four comma rules, three semicolon rules, and one colon rule. These overarching principles will help ensure your readers glean the meaning of your sentences as you intend it.

15.2 End Punctuation

As soon as we learn how to write a sentence, we are taught to put some form of punctuation at the end. While our concept of a sentence further develops over time, children recognize early that a series of words which have a subject and an action (i.e., verb) form something "complete." As you know by now, an English sentence must, minimally, consist of a subject and a verb, and so children's early recognition of what makes something complete is not surprising, since they've acquired this basic grammar feature (not the punctuation rule!) of what a sentence is as part of the language acquisition process. Most of us become proficient in using the following three end punctuation marks quickly with minimal errors.

15.2.1 *The Period (.)*

It may seem too simple of a term to define and illustrate, but the common period designates to the reader that the clause is complete—syntactically and semantically:

(1) The dog chased the cat. (sE)
(2) The kind of humility that made you feel like you was swimmin instead of walkin.[6] (AAE)

Easy, right? When a misuse of the period occurs, it usually happens when a complicated clause is not truly an independent clause:

(3) *While we traveled a long distance to find the lost puppy, an adorable yellow lab, a suitable home. (sE)

The subordinator *while* makes (3) a dependent clause. Even though it consists of a subject and predicate, it is incomplete.

15.2.2 *The Question Mark (?)*

Question formation, although a complex syntactic operation, is acquired early in first language development (*Yes-No* questions by about two and a half years of age; *Wh*-questions at two to four years[7]). In terms of learning the correlated punctuation rule, all a child must do is remember to use the correct symbol (?) for both yes/no questions and *wh*-word questions:

(4) *Is* ice cream available? (sE)
(5) [Y]ou *comin* to that ain't you?[8] (AAE)
(6) *Where is* Fatima *going*? (sE)

(7) So *what* we gon do?⁹ (AAE)

(8) *When did* Bob *eat* ice cream? (sE)

15.2.3 The Exclamation Point (!)

Even young writers understand that the exclamation point signals to the reader that their written sentence ending in an exclamation point expresses intense emotion.¹⁰

(9) The angry parrot yelled at the dog, "Go outside!" (sE)

(10) Not to mention those who be sayin ain no such thang as Black Language!¹¹(AAE)

15.3 Commas (,)

An internet search for English comma rules turns up counts of four to sixteen or more rules, reflecting different emphases and details. The four basic rules we present encapsulate general principles of comma usage, and can be summarized via the acronym LIES (which we did not invent and are not sure who did):

- **Lists** = Place a comma between the items in a series.
- **Introductions** = Place a comma before elements that precede the main, independent clause.
- **Extra information** = Surround extra information with commas on each side.
- **Sentence** = Place a comma before a coordinating conjunction that joins two independent clauses (i.e., sentences).

15.3.1 "L" Is for Lists

The comma separates three or more syntactically identical items in a series. These items may be words, phrases, or clauses.

Words

(11) I bought *ice cream, bananas, macaroni, and cheese.* (sE)

(12) Thank god you is here *members, colleagues, honored guests, and newcomers!*¹² (AAE)

Phrases

(13) Amir looked for my keys *on the table, behind the couch, and in the garbage.* (sE)

(14) At this conference we be steeped in the practice of rhetoric—*all kinds, all modes, for all reasons*—personal, public, professional, and whateva else.¹³ (AAE)

Clauses

(15) Carlos and Julissa knew *that the cat was scared, the dog was angry, and the parrot was worried about our trip.* (sE)

Such lists don't have to be placed only at the end of a sentence. In (14), two {NPs} and one {PP} are connected in the middle of a sentence. Connecting a {PP} to an {NP} is another one of those examples of how punctuation and conventions are stylistic choices: the choice of using a different phrase type is a stylistic choice.

One variation across and between Englishes and for other languages exists for the rule governing the serial comma. We have adopted what is called the **Oxford Comma** (or serial comma). According to this convention, a comma is placed after the penultimate item (the one before the last) and before the coordinator (*and*, *or*). Writers who do not use the Oxford comma simply won't put a comma before the coordinator. Style guides vary as to whether they demand this comma; the Associated Press (AP) doesn't require it and simply says writers should be consistent in their comma usage.

Proponents of the Oxford comma generally argue that it makes clear exactly how many items are in a list:

(11a) I bought ice cream, bananas, macaroni, and cheese. (sE)
          1   2   3   4

If the author were writing this sentence for a UK publisher and some US publishers, then the Oxford comma would not be required (the reasoning being that the conjunction *and* does the job of the comma):

(11b) I bought ice cream, bananas, macaroni and cheese. (sE)

Do you see a possible ambiguity in this construction? Is the writer buying four items, like in (11a), or only three items?

(11c) I bought ice cream, bananas, macaroni and cheese. (sE)
          1   2   3

If we interpret the sentence as being about three items, then *macaroni and cheese* as item three would be something like an instant mac and cheese in a box rather than a box of pasta and a block of cheese.

If the writer meant that we only bought three items with the last being the box of instant macaroni and cheese, moving this coordinated item higher in the list would both clarify this and separate the two *ands* that are used in the sentence:

(11d) I bought macaroni and cheese, ice cream, and bananas. (sE)
              1   2   3

So, the Oxford comma can prevent ambiguity—if you have a genuine list. Consider the next example:

(16) I adopted two cats, Fluffy and Daisy. (sE)

This sentence clearly uses apposition, where the {NP} *two cats* is renamed with the pet names *Fluffy and Daisy*, thereby conveying that two cats in total were adopted. It is not a list. If you insert a comma after *Fluffy*, the sentence becomes ambiguous. The revised sentence could be awkwardly naming two cats that you adopted, or it might indicate that you adopted two unnamed cats along with Fluffy and Daisy. The apposition in (16) makes clear there is no list, so the Oxford comma does not apply. Sometimes, tongue-in-cheek examples are provided as knockout evidence for why the Oxford comma is necessary:

(17)   I love my parents, Taylor Swift and Humpty Dumpty. (sE)

Given what you know about grammar, this is clearly an apposition, right? Grammatically speaking, it is, but the absurdity argues against that reading. Honestly, to us, such examples seem a bit overly dramatic. Who really thinks that Taylor Swift and Humpty Dumpty are someone's actual parents? Be that as it may, we do concede that this version of the sentence, with the Oxford comma, removes all doubt (and with it, the apposition interpretation) as to what the sentence means:

(17a)   I love my parents, Taylor Swift, and Humpty Dumpty. (sE)

In most instances, context clarifies that a list of three is, indeed, a list of three—even without the Oxford comma:

(18)   Like, if you a sociolinguist and write pages and pages on *multiple negation, invariant be and copula deletion*, ain no way in the world you can tell a teacher it ain somethin important.[14] (AAE)

Clearly, *invariant be* and *copula deletion* are not the same as *multiple negation*; hence, we know that these three {NPs} are a list of three. In the end, you'll want to follow the style guide you're using and take into consideration whether there's potential for ambiguity; if there is, an Oxford comma will help remove it.

When we are interpreting a series of phrases and clauses, the ambiguity can intensify. In fact, there have been contractual lawsuits over whether items joined by a coordinator without the Oxford comma refer to one item or two items (see Chapter 1). Similarly, poets often construct their lines strategically by using or omitting the Oxford comma. In Robert Frost's poem "Stopping by Woods on a Snowy Evening," the poet uses the absence of the Oxford comma in the last stanza to create an important meaning in lines 13–16.[15] Why does Frost group the adjectives *dark* and *deep* as one unit after the adjective *lovely*? What is your hypothesis?

> The woods are *lovely, dark and deep*,
> But I have promises to keep,
> And miles to go before I sleep,
> And miles to go before I sleep.

Foundations of Grammar

> **Exercise 1**
>
> Oxford comma. Create three (or more) sentences that include lists of three that could be interpreted as lists of two, similar to what Frost does in his poem.

15.3.2 "I" Is for Introductory Elements

In Chapter 14, we observed that if the dependent clause was positioned at the beginning of the complex sentence, a comma was needed to separate an introductory clause from the independent clause. We can see in (19) that this applies to introductory phrases, too:

(19) *In that forest*, I found a small cottage. (sE)

(20) *Running quickly*, I escaped the witch. (sE)

(21) *When the last bus finally pulled up to the stadium*, madd people rushed out.[16] (AAE)

Notice that the introductory phrase in (19) and the introductory clauses in (20) and (21) function as adverbials at the sentence level. They help move the story along by connecting the main clauses and adding details such as when, where, how, or why. The commas ensure the reader sees each as connective tissue and does not confuse them with the main clause.

Now, let's turn the order around. What if those same phrases/clauses were not serving to introduce information before the independent clause but were just added details?

(19a) I found a small cottage *in that forest*. (sE)

(20a) *I escaped the witch *running quickly*. (sE)

(21a) Madd people rushed out *when the last bus finally pulled up to the stadium*.[17] (AAE)

Moving the clause *running quickly* in (20a) to the end of the sentence changes the function of the clause: it now is very close to the noun *witch*, and we may be tempted to interpret *running quickly* as modifying *the witch*, which makes it a dangling modifier! In the other examples, moving the adverbial to the end of the sentence works just fine. Is a comma needed? Well, that depends. Moving either of these phrases/clauses to the end of their respective sentences allows the reader to process the main clause first, preventing any confusion as to the main grammatical element in the sentence and making a comma unnecessary. The writer might, however, have rhetorical reasons for adding a comma after the last word of the main clause. Consider (19b):

(19b) I found a small cottage, *in that forest*. (sE)

Because the adverbial in (19b) is a simple {PP}, and because that {PP} and the sentence overall are short, the comma isn't grammatically necessary and could be deleted. However, if the writer is interested in more than just providing information—perhaps, for instance, by shifting emphasis slightly to the forest or inserting a brief pause in the flow—then she might opt for an otherwise "unnecessary" comma.

15.3.3 "E" Is for Extra Information

Let's continue our makeshift fairy tale and see how writers use commas to either integrate material with the main clause or set it off as supplementary. Compare (22) to (22a):

(22)   The witch, *who was hideous*, chased me. (sE)

(22a) The witch *who was hideous* chased me. (sE)

Do you remember our discussion in Chapter 14 about restrictive and non-restrictive relative clauses and the sheep-farm-owning neighbor? In (22), we again see a non-restrictive clause that, while grammatically unnecessary, provides additional information about the subject. Deleting the commas does not make the sentence ungrammatical—it changes the meaning entirely. The hideous witch in (22a) who is doing the chasing is integral to the sentence; the restrictive clause identifies her in opposition to other less-than-hideous witches who might give chase. Be aware: if you prefer "that" over "who," most style guides treat it as restrictive only, with no commas allowed.

A writer can put almost any phrase or clause, including appositives, into a sentence, surround it by commas, and by doing so, deem it as supplemental:

(23)   Salim, *my best friend*, saved me from the witch! (sE)

(24)   I had one student, *Frazier we go call 'em*, who wo ....[18] (HPE)

(25)   We can, *via the use of commas*, show that some material is extra. (sE)

(26)   *In today's enlightened times*, I would've hoped dat people's attitudes toward Pidgin would be way bettah now.[19] (HPE)

(27)   Then, *outta nowhere*, the afternoon thunder rolled in ...[20] (AAE)

When a writer includes material in a sentence beyond that in the main clause, there is a hierarchy of punctuation strategies. If writers choose the comma structure, then the message sent to the reader is "while this is not essential, I still expect you to read it for its other effects." If writers choose parentheses (), then they are saying, in essence, that the material is a bit less important than information separated from the main clause by commas. On the other hand, writers may use dash(es) to emphasize additional material —in fact, we have done that quite often in this text! If, however, writers choose to add

Foundations of Grammar

information as footnotes or endnotes, it signals that here is something for those who want to geek out on the subject. The key is to choose punctuation that not only works with the grammar of a sentence but achieves the desired rhetorical effect.

15.3.4 "S" is for Sentences

When two independent clauses are joined with a coordinating conjunction (CC), a comma is placed before the CC, unless the two clauses are very short.[21]

(28) I ate lunch and I left. (sE)

(29) I found the river, *and* I saw a beautiful cottage. (sE)

(30) No one answered the door, *nor* did anyone come outside. (sE)

(31) The house was warm, *yet* I saw no person. (sE)

Here are two longer sentences where the comma is necessary prior to the CC (italicized below) to combine independent clauses:

(32) The "done my homework" construction is a widespread characteristic of Canadian English, *and* it is also found in the United States among speakers in the Philadelphia area, southern New Jersey, Delaware, Maryland, and the northern part of New England.[22] (sE)

(33) In English, the past participle and passive participle of a verb look identical, *but* we label them differently because they have different functions.[23] (sE)

Now, as long as the words after the CCs form an independent clause (i.e., one that can stand on its own), then the comma is required before the CCs. If, however, the words following the CCs share the subject with the first clause and, thus, cannot stand on their own as independent clauses, then the writer cannot place a comma before the CC:

(34) She be teachin bout dem necessary feminist rhetorics *and* showin us how rhetorical silence is just as important as talk.[24] (AAE)

(35) Quinn introduced phrases first *and* covered clauses next. (sE)

In (34), the verbs *teachin* and *showin* share the subject *she*, and so we don't place a comma prior to *and*. In (35), *introduced* and *covered* share the subject *we*, which is why there's no comma prior to the conjunction *and*.

Exercise 2

Remove the subject in the second clause. Which, if any, alterations do you have to make for the resulting sentences to be grammatical?

a) I went to the forest, *for* I wanted to see the river. (sE)

b) I found the river, *and* I saw a beautiful cottage. (sE)

c) No one answered the door, *nor* did anyone come outside. (sE)

d) I wanted to go inside, *but* I was afraid. (sE)

e) I thought I could just peak, *or* I could go in for a minute. (sE)

f) The house was warm, *yet* I saw no person. (sE)

g) No one was home, *so* I thought I was safe. (sE)

Now, for subordinate clauses, generally, a comma is required when the clause opens the sentence (as in (36)). If the subordinate clause follows the main clause, there's usually no comma (as in (37)).

(36) Thus *if we all commenced to speak naturally and supported each other in this effort*, nothin disastrous would happen ….[25] (AAE)

(37) We label them differently *because they have different functions*.[26] (sE)

If we switched the order of the two clauses in (37), we'd add a comma:

(37a) *Because they have different functions*, we label them differently. (sE)

15.4 Semicolons (;)

Students often say they were advised not to use semicolons—that they are too complicated. Since semicolons are such a convenient punctuation tool, let's remedy this situation and empower you to start using them!

15.4.1 Between Sentences

A semicolon can connect independent clauses much in the same way a CC can. The semicolon, in a way, replaces the conjunction. Why do (38) and (39) work, but (38a) and (39a) seem off?

(38) The budget was cut significantly; we will lose programs. (sE)

(39) I received a bonus this year; I am planning a vacation. (sE)

(38a) *We will lose programs; the budget was cut significantly.

(39a) *I am planning a vacation; I received a bonus this year.

Notice that in (38) and (39), the second independent clause follows logically from the first: because A, then B ("Because traffic is terrible, we'll be late," and so on) while (38a) and (39a) do not. So, this is one underlying rule for using the semicolon to connect two independent clauses (i.e., sentences): The semicolon allows you to make a claim, then follow it up with the result. If you use a period rather than a semicolon, this causal

Foundations of Grammar

connection between the clauses will not be conveyed as forcefully. This makes the semicolon powerful in an argumentative paper.

15.4.2 Sentences Joined with Conjunctive Adverbs

The semicolon together with a **conjunctive adverb** (italicized below) can also join two independent clauses. Can you explain the relationship between the two clauses?

(40)   I did not receive a bonus this year; *consequently*, I am not planning a vacation. (sE)

(41)   She figure it got to be; *otherwise*, why the complicated linguistic symbology and lengthy presentation?[27] (AAE)

In each case, the two clauses that are joined by the semicolon + conjunctive adverb are closely connected in thought. You could separate them with a period, but choosing the semicolon shows that close connection between the two clauses. Why are there commas after the conjunctive adverbs? Well, since we are connecting the conjunctive adverb to the beginning of the second clause, it both connects two independent clauses and serves as an introductory piece to clause number two. How many conjunctive adverbs are there? A lot! They can be grouped into six broad semantic categories:

- cause and effect: *hence, therefore,* ...
- contrast: *however, nonetheless,* ...
- illustration: *namely, specifically,* ...
- summation: *finally, in conclusion,* ...
- addition: *moreover, additionally,* ...
- comparison: *likewise, contrastively,* ...

Exercise 3

Create your own sentences that use the semicolon and a conjunctive adverb of your choice (ideally, a different one from the ones provided above!) for each of those six categories.

a) cause and effect:

b) contrast:

c) illustration:

d) summation:

e) addition:

f) comparison:

15.4.3 Semicolons Separate Items That Have Internal Commas

Finally, the semicolon can disambiguate complex lists of items. When a list has internal commas after modifiers, the reader needs some help identifying the main items. So, after each item, instead of a comma that will get mixed up with all the other commas, we use a semicolon to separate them. Compare (42) to (42a):

(42)   I bought ice cream, bananas, and wine. (sE)

(42a) I bought sugar-free chocolate ice cream, over-ripe, organic bananas, and inexpensive, red Italian wine. (sE)

With all these commas, we just made a confusing mess for our readers. So, to ease the reading process, we place semicolons between each {NP}:

(42b) I bought sugar-free chocolate ice cream; over-ripe, organic bananas; and inexpensive, red Italian wine. (sE)

Now the main items are clearly delineated. Lists can get complex quickly, so let's look at a couple more examples where the semicolon is a great tool to separate out each item in the list:

(43)   Our gray cat, Fluffy; our orange cat, Daisy May; and our black cat, Norma Jean had appointments at the vet at the same time. (sE)

(44)   So on this same topic is Elizabeth West, Af Am lit specialist; Donja Thomas, literacy scholar; Jeffrey McCune, performance studies brotha; Vorris Nunley, hush harbor rhetoric genius; and Gwen Pough, feminist, novelist ....[28] (AAE)

15.5 Colons (:)

The colon can be used to introduce evidence, which means that the word(s), phrase(s), or clause(s) after the colon provide support for the claim made prior to the colon. Now, it's important to remember that the colon must be placed at the end of an independent clause. This is why (45) below doesn't work: the colon separates the DO from the verb. You could eliminate the colon entirely; or, if you want to emphasize the number of items in your list, use (46).

(45)   *We will buy: chocolate, whipped cream, and strawberries. (sE)

(46)   We will buy three items: chocolate, whipped cream, and strawberries. (sE)

Thus, the colon is best used when what comes after it supports what came before:

(47)   The data shows the intervention is working: 87 percent of students demonstrated improved test scores. (sE)

(48)   The steps to making a good Mai Tai are simple: choose a really good rum, add some juice, and shake with ice. (sE)

Foundations of Grammar

(49) But peep this: the LWC [Language of Wider Communication] ain decreed by the Divine One from on High.[29] (AAE)

15.6 Bonus: A Note on the Em-dash

Em-dashes are used to denote sudden changes in sentence structure. They are also used to set off an explanation, and to add emphasis. They have the opposite effect from commas. Think of the em-dash as the neon light of punctuation: it draws attention to something the writer wants the reader to notice.

(50) So speak up—speak out—even if yo voice shakes.[30] (AAE)

(51) That is, they need the kind of instruction that reflects and centers the cultural beauty or—aesthetic—in Black literature.[31] (sE)

(52) For the uninformed, since everybody and they momma seem so interested in my background, I not only done taught "disadvantaged" black students, I done lived "disadvantaged," havin been brought up in Detroit's Black Bottom, and havin been forced, as a freshman at Wayne State, to take speech therapy cause of my "regional"—nowadays they just say "black"—dialect.[32] (AAE)

Exercise 4

Supply the punctuation needed for each sentence below; briefly explain why you added which punctuation mark.

a) I wrote my paper however I forgot to include the supporting data.
b) When signing up for a student group make sure to consult your class schedule.
c) Bob studied diligently therefore he passed the exam.
d) Susan didn't study she failed the exam.
e) I walked to the store bought food for our group and went to the study session.
f) The professor recommended the following steps 1) review the chapter questions 2) write out full responses 3) partner with a fellow student to quiz each other.
g) The teacher asked "Who is ready to submit the final paper"
h) I wondered if anyone had completed the project so soon

Exercise 5

In the following passages from various authors, examine the use of the highlighted punctuation and discuss its role in helping ensure the writer's meaning is conveyed. Are there any uses of punctuation that you would change? Why?

1. **The Unparalleled Adventure of One Hans Pfaall (1835), Edgar Allan Poe**

    His feet, of course, could not be seen at all. His hands were enormously large. His hair was gray, and collected into a queue behind. His nose was prodigiously long, crooked, and inflammatory; his eyes full, brilliant, and acute; his chin and cheeks, although wrinkled with age were broad, puffy, and double; but of ears of any kind there was not a semblance to be discovered upon any portion of his head.

2. **A Jelly-Fish (1909), Marianne Moore**

    Visible, invisible,
    A fluctuating charm,
    An amber-colored amethyst
    Inhabits it; your arm
    Approaches, and
    It opens and
    It closes;
    You have meant
    To catch it,
    And it shrivels;
    You abandon
    Your intent—
    It opens, and it
    Closes and you
    Reach for it—
    The blue
    Surrounding it
    Grows cloudy, and
    It floats away
    From you.

3. **'Twas the Night Before Christmas (1823*/1837**), Clement Clarke Moore**
    But I heard him exclaim, ere he drove out of sight—
    "Happy Christmas to all, and to all a good night!"
    *published anonymously; **published with author identified

4. **Smitherman, G. (1974). Response to Hunt, Meyers, et al.** *College English,* **35,** 729–32.

> But what I done seen convinces me all the more that we black folk is definitely caught in the cross. Like, bout the time somebody who doesn't even know me runs down a thang bout a new prescriptivist wearing an Afro (actually I wear a gelee most of the time); and somebody else tells me how I might more profitably use my time (presumably runnin down how language is a tool of oppression ain useful); and still another somebody tells me that every important point I made was in standard English (which only points out what that person deems important)—I mean bout this time, I bees wantin to agree with the Brother who quipped: "Ain no hope for dese white folks." (p. 730)

Terminology to Know

Term	Working definition	Example/Illustration
Period		
Question mark		
Exclamation point		
Comma, lists		
Comma, introductory		
Comma, extra material		
Comma, sentences		
Semicolon, sentences		
Semicolon, with conjunctive		
em dash		
Semicolon, lists		
Colon		

Chart 1 Key terminology Chapter 15

Notes

1. Megna, 2024.
2. Brown, 2024.
3. Ibid.
4. Quirk et al., 1985, p. 12.
5. Cummings, n.d.
6. Alim and Smitherman, 2012, p. 1.
7. O'Grady and Cho, 2001.
8. Young, 2019, p. 5.

9. Smitherman, 2006, p. 135.
10. Burrell and Beard, 2024.
11. Smitherman, 2006, p. 3.
12. Young, 2019, p. 4.
13. Ibid., p. 6.
14. Smitherman, 1974, p. 730.
15. Frost, 1923.
16. Alim and Smitherman, 2012, p. 1.
17. Based on Alim and Smitherman, 2012, p. 1.
18. Tonouchi, 2004, p. 76.
19. Ibid., p. 77.
20. Alim and Smitherman, 2012, p. 1.
21. https://writing.wisc.edu/handbook/coordconj/.
22. Wood, 2014.
23. Maher and Wood, 2011.
24. Young, 2019, p. 5.
25. Smitherman, 2006, p. 731.
26. Maher and Wood, 2011.
27. Smitherman, 1974, p. 730.
28. Young, 2019, p. 5.
29. Smitherman, 2006, p. 6.
30. Young, 2019, p. 4.
31. McMurtry, 2023, p. 2.
32. Smitherman, 1974, p. 730.

GLOSSARY

Acronym—a new word formed by using the first letters of the individual words in a phrase (e.g., *UN, IQ, USA*)

Adjective—the lexical category for words that describe nouns and as such are optional components of noun phrases; many are gradable, able to form the comparative and superlative forms

Adjective phrase—a grouping of words (i.e., phrase) with an adjective as its headword; typically functions as premodifier in a noun phrase or subject complement/object complement in a sentence

Adverb—the lexical category for words that describe verbs or verbal clauses, adjectives, or other adverbs; many are gradable, able to form the comparative and superlative forms

Adverbial—a sentence-level constituent that is optional and generally provides information about time, place, manner, location, etc.

Adverbial complement—a required sentence-level constituent that generally provides information about time, place, manner, location, etc.

Adverb phrase—a grouping of words (i.e., phrase) with an adverb as its headword; typically functions as a premodifier in an adjective phrase, adverb phrase, or adverbial in a sentence

Affix—an additional element placed at the beginning, end, middle of a root, stem of a word to modify its meaning

African American English (AAE)—an American English dialect with its own linguistic patterns and structures. It is generally not limited to just one geographic area and instead is used, chiefly, by African American speakers in the United States. As with any dialect, variation among speakers exists and no single term or list of features can capture that variety.

Agreement—a word changes form depending on the other words to which it relates. This is usually an instance of inflection in which the change makes the value of some grammatical category such as gender, number, or person "agree" between two words or parts of a sentence (e.g., *I **walk** to the store. She **walks** to the store.*)

Analytic processes (see also periphrastic)—to use additional words to form meaning rather than particles to create meaning (e.g., use of *more* or *most* to form comparative and superlative forms rather than **synthetic** processes such as adding *-er* and *-est* suffixes)

Appalachian English (AE)—a dialect with its own linguistic patterns and structures. It is found in the southern region of the United States which stretches from West Virginia and Ohio to Georgia, as well as parts of southwest New York and northeastern Mississippi. This variety is associated with speakers of Scots-Irish, German, and English who migrated south, beginning in the 1730s, and whose communities did and may remain isolated. As with any dialect, variation among speakers exists and no single term or list of features can capture that variety.

Apposition—a grammatical construction in which two elements, normally noun phrases, are placed next to each other in which the second identifies the first in a different way (e.g., *Shonda, **my neighbor**, drives a truck.*)

Attributive position—the syntactic placement before another lexical category (e.g., adjective placement in relation to nouns as in *the **orange** cat*)

Auxiliary verb—a verb that adds functional or grammatical meaning to the clause, such as tense, aspect, modality (*Bob **has** eaten.*); also referred to as helping verbs

Chicano English (ChE)—a dialect with its own linguistics patterns and structure. It is influenced by Spanish and used by monolingual English speakers and bilingual speakers mostly but not exclusively in Southwestern regions of the United States. As with any dialect, variation among speakers exists and no single term or list of features can capture that variety.

Circumfix—a pair of affixes in which one is added to the beginning of the word and the other is added to the end of the word (e.g., **em**bol**den**)

Clause—a group of words that contains a verb and in most cases a subject; non-finite clauses often lack an overt subject.

Closed class (for contrast, see Open class)—the category of words which is stable and to which words are infrequently added

Colon—punctuation mark that introduces an explanation or evidence supporting the claim in the independent clause that comes before it. Thus, the colon is placed at the end of a clause that can stand alone (i.e., the colon goes where end punctuation can be placed). The evidence can be in the form of a clause, phrase, or a series of either: a quotation, a list, numeric data, or image.

Comma—punctuation mark that has four primary roles: 1) separates items in a list; 2) sets off introductory material; 3) sets off extraneous or extra material; and 4) joins two independent clauses that are joined by a coordinator (i.e., conjunction).

Comparative—a gradability process for many adjectives and adverbs (*-er* inflectional suffix or by adding the adverb *more*); see related term **Superlative**

Complement—a word or group of words that helps complete the meaning of another noun or noun phrase within a sentence

Constituent—a unit of words (a chunk) that works together in a sentence, sometimes called component

Copula verb—a verb that connects the subject to its subject complement; required in sE and optional in some non-sE dialects; the verb *be* is the most common copula; also referred to as linking verb

Dependent clause—a clause that cannot stand alone

Derivation—the process of making a new word by adding an affix; the change can maintain the lexical category (*happy > unhappy*) or change the lexical category (*construct > construction*)

Descriptivist/Descriptivist Grammar—the study of how language is actually used, grounded in how language is rather than what it should be (contrast with prescriptive grammar)

Determiner—a functional word that introduces a noun (e.g., *the cat*), to clarify what or whom a noun belongs to (e.g., *your cat*), to indicate quantity or number (e.g., *four cats*), to point to which noun (e.g., *that cat*).

Dialect (see also Variety)—a neutral term used for any variety of a language

Dialect continuum—intra-dialect differences; variations within a given dialect

Direct object—a sentence-level constituent that takes the form of a noun phrase or clause that directly receives the action of the main verb

Do support—the insertion of the auxiliary verb *do* for emphasis or for question formation; followed by a bare infinitive verb, also called **dummy do** or **dummy operator**

Exclamation mark—an end punctuation mark often used to convey emotional affect

Form—the structure of a given unit, such as word class, phrase, or clause

Function—the syntactic slot a word, phrase, or clause (i.e., a given **form**) is filling within a sentence

Function words—words that have a grammatical purpose, such as pronouns, prepositions, determiners, conjunctions, auxiliary verbs

Gradable—the linguistic concept of adding inflection or periphrasis to increase or to decrease the strength of the word

Glossary

Grammar—the rules for how we can combine words into phrases, clauses, and sentences
Grammatical class—the lexical category or word class of a word (e.g., noun, verb)
Grammatical hierarchy—the ordering of grammatical units like words and phrases
Independent clause—a clause that can stand on its own
Indirect object—a sentence-level constituent in the form of a noun phrase that is the beneficiary or recipient of the direct object
Infinitive—the base form of a verb
    Bare—the base form of the verb (e.g., *walk*)
    Full—the base form of the verb with the *to* infinitive marker (e.g., *to walk*)
Infix—an affix that is placed in the middle of a word
Inflection/Inflectional Morphology—change in form of a word to mark such distinctions as tense, person, number, gender, mood, voice, and case using affixes; the available changes are governed by the word's lexical category and such changes always maintain the original lexical category (e.g., nouns can add pluralness; verbs change tense)
Interjection—lexical items which express a speaker's current mental state, attitude, or reaction toward a situation, and which do not enter into the syntax of the clause
Inversion test—a process that involves manipulating the normal word order of a sentence to determine how different elements of a language behave and interact. This allows for the identification of specific grammatical properties, specifically to help understand the underlying rules of syntax within a language (e.g., inverting the subject and verb in question formation).
Language Acquisition Device (LAD)—a hypothetical faculty used to explain a child's ability to acquire language. The early model was proposed by US linguist Benjamin Lee Whorf (1897–1941). The LAD was revitalized in Noam Chomsky's theory of Universal Grammar in which he proposed that the LAD contains significant innate syntactic knowledge that actively interprets linguistic input that serves to explain how a highly abstract competence in language results from a relatively limited input.
Lexical category (see also Grammatical class)—the grammatical category or word class a word belongs to (e.g., noun, verb)
Midwest English (ME)—the US dialect with its own linguistics patterns and structure; associated with the middle of the United States—a vast area from central Ohio to Nebraska and Oklahoma and sometimes including bordering areas such as Illinois, Iowa, Indiana, as well as other states. This dialect is considered to have the most features associated with standard English dialect and is often thought to have flattened phonological and syntactic features that do not stand out. Features particular to the dialect or to regional speakers of the dialect are, however, patterned, and noticeable. As with any dialect, variation among speakers exists and no single term or list of features can capture that variety.
Modal auxiliary—a type of auxiliary verb within the verb phrase to express epistemic or deontic stance
Mood—a feature of verbs that allows the speaker or writer to express various relationships to reality or truth
    Indicative mood—most English sentences are in indicative mood; includes declaratives (i.e., statements), interrogatives (i.e., questions), and exclamatives
    Imperative mood—expresses a command; sentence is marked with zero manifestation of a subject that is understood to be the subject you (e.g., *Go do your homework!*)
    Subjunctive mood—expresses a hypothetical or irrealis circumstance (e.g., *If I were the teacher, I would make quizzes optional.*) or expresses the expertise/authority of the speaker/writer (*I recommend Sami study every night.*) (this is also called the mandative subjunctive)

Morpheme—the smallest meaningful unit of a language that cannot be further divided (e.g., *un-*, *re-*)

Morphology—the rules of a language that dictate internal composition of words, including word formation processes

Movement test—a method used to identify a group of words, a constituency, within a sentence by checking whether the group can be moved to a different position and allow the sentence to maintain grammatical correctness (e.g., moving a prepositional phrase)

Multiple negation—using more than one negator or negation marker within the same phrase (*He does **not** have **no** cash.*)

Negation—using a word that will change a word, a phrase, or the entire clause from positive to negative polarity (*three cats > no cats; run > do not run*)

Nonstandard English—the term which refers to any dialect of English other than the standardized form; often used disapprovingly by non-linguists to describe usages that are deemed "bad" or "incorrect"

Noun—the lexical category that includes words which refer to people, places, things, ideas, or concepts; can endure plural marking and possessive marking

    Count—a noun that can be modified by a quantity and that occurs in both singular and plural forms, and that can co-occur with quantificational determiners like every, each, several, etc. (e.g., *cat*, two *cats*)

    Non-count—nouns that cannot be counted or pluralized directly (e.g., *honesty*)

Noun phrase—a word or a grouping of words (i.e., phrase) with a noun as its headword; can function as a premodifier in a noun phrase as well as any of the following at the sentence-level: subjects, direct object, indirect object, subject complement, object complement, object of the preposition

Null morpheme (see also Zero morpheme)—a morpheme that has no phonetic (or orthographic) form (e.g., no overt plural *-s* in *one sheep > two sheep*)

Object complement—a sentence-level constituent typically in the form of a noun phrase or adjective phrase; appears immediately after the direct object in a sentence and completes the meaning of the sentence's direct object

Object of the preposition—a noun phrase that appears within the prepositional phrase (e.g., *on the table*)

Open class (see also Closed class)—the class of words to which others are routinely and frequently added

Orthography—a language's spelling system

Paradigmatic evidence—using a word of a known lexical category (e.g., a noun, a verb) to substitute for and determine a word of an unknown lexical category

Past participle—a inflected verb form that has the *-ed* (or comparable, e.g., *-en*) inflectional affix (e.g., *walked* or *broken*)

Period—the punctuation mark that is placed at the end of an independent, declarative clause

Phonetics—the study of speech sounds of languages; includes how sounds are formed via articulatory organs such as lips, tongue, teeth, etc., how sounds are transmitted, and how sounds are received.

Phonology—the study of sound combinations, patterns, and rules that are possible within a language

Plurality—the process by which a noun is changed from expressing singularity (one item: *cat*) to more than one (*two, three, or one hundred cats*)

Present participle—a verb form that has the *-ing* inflectional suffix (e.g., *breaking*)

Predicate—one of the two required parts of a sentence (the other being the subject); the predicate must contain a verb, and the verb requires or permits other elements to complete the predicate

Glossary

Predicative adjectives—adjectives that occur in the predicate, in contrast to attributive adjectives that occur before the nouns they modify; predicative adjectives function as the subject complement, e.g., *The dog is **happy**.*)

Prefix—an affix added to the beginning of a word

Premodifier—a word or group of words that describes the headword in a phrase and is placed prior to the headword

Preposition—a word used before a noun phrase to show direction, time, place, location, spatial relationships in relation to another noun phrase, adjective phrase, or verb phrase

Prepositional complement—a noun phrase that appears within the prepositional phrase (e.g., *on the table*); see also: **Object of the preposition**

Prepositional phrase—a grouping of words (i.e., phrase) with a preposition as its headword; often functions as postmodifier in a phrase or adverbial at the sentence level

Prescriptivist/Prescriptivist Grammar—a perspective on language that stipulates a clear right and wrong and prescribes how language should be used; prescriptive rules are often externally imposed onto a language (contrast with descriptive grammar)

Primary auxiliary—the set of *be*, *have*, and *do* verb forms when they are used within the verb phrase to express aspect, tense, passive voice, emphasis, and question-formation; also referred to as regular auxiliaries

Pronoun—a word that stands in for a noun phrase and can function by itself as a noun phrase

    Demonstrative—a type of pronoun that stands in for a noun phrase and points to a specific reference (e.g., *I like **that**)*

    Interrogative—a type of pronoun that stands in for a noun phrase within a question (e.g., ***What*** *did you buy?*)

    Personal—a type of pronoun that stands in for a noun phrase that represents a person; they match the person in gender and number and now include non-binary selections (e.g., *he, she, ze, singular they*)

    Possessive—a type of pronoun that stands in for a noun phrase that indicates possession; they match person and number and often function as determiners (e.g., *his/her/their shoes*)

    Quantifying—a type of pronoun that stands in for a noun phrase that indicates the quantity of that noun phrase; these can be countable or uncountable (e.g., *both, all, many*)

    Reflexive—a type of pronoun that refers back to the noun phrase it stands in for (e.g., *yourself, myself*)

    Relative—a type of pronoun that introduces a relative clause (e.g., *that, who, which*)

Punctuation—a system of symbols (e.g., colon, comma, semicolon, period) arbitrarily prescribed meaning that work within the grammar of a clause to clarify meaning for the reader

Question mark—the end punctuation that completes an independent clause in interrogative mood

Question test (see also stand-alone test)—a method used to identify whether a group of words can stand alone as an answer to a question. If so, the group of words functions as a single unit (i.e., a constituent)

Raciolinguistics—a theory that seeks to understand how language and race interact in constructing race, and how views about race impact how we use and see language

Regional dialect—a variation of a language associated with a geographic area (e.g., Appalachian English)

Root—the part of a word that has lexical meaning; roots can be free, existing independently without affixes within a sentence (e.g., *cat*) or bound, which can only exist with added affixes within a sentence (e.g., *electr*)

Semantics/Semantician—a sub-discipline of linguistics which focuses on the study of meaning; one who studies the ways meaning is made within a language

Semicolon—a punctuation mark that has three main roles: (1) joins two independent clauses in which the second clause is the logical result of the first clause; (2) joins two independent clauses that are joined by a conjunctive adverb that make explicit the relationship between the clauses; and (3) to set off items in a list that have internal commas.

Sentence—a set of words that is complete in itself; typically and minimally containing a subject and predicate

Social dialect—a variation of a language associated with a social feature, including ethnicity/race, class, gender, socioeconomic status, and identity (e.g., Chicano English)

Southern American English (SAE)—a dialect with its own linguistics patterns and structure; associated with Southern areas in the United States that stretch at least as far north as southern Maryland and Kentucky, as west as Texas and New Mexico, but excluding southern Florida. SAE shares many features with AAE. As with any dialect, variation among speakers exists and no single term or list of features can capture that variety.

Stand-alone test (see also question test)—a method used to identify whether a group of words can stand alone as an answer to a question. If so, the group of words functions as a single unit (i.e., a constituent)

Standard English (SE)—a language variety that people believe is devoid of regional/social accents, regional/social words, or regional/social grammatical features. Scientific linguistic research, however, has shown that such a "Standard English" does not really exist. It is an abstract idea rather than reality.

standardized English (sE)—a term that highlights the fact that so-called standard forms do not exist neutrally and objectively as "the standard;" rather, they are continually (re-)constructed as "standard"

Standard Language Ideology—A belief that there is only one correct form of English–Standard English–which is thought to be superior to other dialects of English

Subject—a sentence-level constituent that is one of the two main parts of a sentence (the other being the predicate)

Subject complement—a sentence-level constituent in the form of a noun phrase or adjective phrase that completes the meaning of the subject

Suffix—an affix added to the end of the word

Superlative—a gradability process for many adjectives or adverbs (*-est* inflectional suffix or by adding the adverb *most*); see related term **Comparative**

Syntagmatic evidence—using the words that are collocated or associated with a lexical category to determine a word of unknown lexical category (e.g., a single count noun can take a determiner)

Syntax—the rules that govern the ways in which words combine to form phrases, clauses, and sentences for a given language; the study of the syntactic properties of a language

Synthetic processes—the reliance on adding morphemes to form meaning rather than extra words to create meaning (e.g., use of *-er* and *-est* to form comparative and superlative forms, respectively, rather than **analytical or periphrastic** processes such as adding the words *most* or *more*)

Tag test—a method used to identify the subject of a sentence whereby a tag such as *isn't it* or *is it* is added to a statement; the pronoun in the tag refers back to the subject of the sentence

Universal Grammar—the theory proposed by Noam Chomsky that humans possess innate faculties related to the acquisition of language

Variety (see also Dialect)—a neutral term for any dialect of a language

Glossary

Verb—the lexical category for words that typically signal events, actions, state of being; required in the predicate of a well-formed sentence; can endure tense marking

Verb forms—the pattern of verbs used in grammar to help convey different aspects of time and action, including full/bare infinitive and present/past participle, present/past forms

Verb phrase—a word or grouping of words (i.e., phrase); the phrase may contain a main verb, alone, or a main verb plus any modal and/or auxiliary verbs

Word—the smallest independent grammatical unit that has meaning

Zero copula—the absence of the copula verb in variations of English in contrast to the copula's presence in standardized English (sE)

Zero morpheme (see also Null morpheme)—morpheme that has no phonetic (or orthographic) form (e.g., *one sheep > two sheep*)

BIBLIOGRAPHY

Abrams, K. D., and T. Stickle (2017), "Discovering DARE: Linguistic Lessons from the Dictionary of American Regional English," *Teacher Manual, Student Workbook, and Accompanying Digital Materials*, UW-Madison: Dictionary of American Regional English. https://dare.wisc.edu/.

Adams, M. (2001), "Infixing and Interposing in English: A New Direction," *American Speech*, 76 (3): 327–31.

Alaka, A. M. (2010), "The Grammar Wars Come to Law School," *Journal of Legal Education*, 59 (3): 343–56.

Alim, H. S., and G. Smitherman (2012), *Articulate while Black: Barack Obama, Language, and Race in the U.S*, Oxford: Oxford University Press.

Alim, H. S., J. R. Rickford, and A. F. Ball (2016), *Raciolinguistics: How Language Shapes Our Ideas about Race*, Oxford: Oxford University Press.

Alley, M. (1996), *The Craft of Scientific Writing*, 3rd edn, Princeton, NJ: Springer.

Anderson, H. C. (1839), *The Garden of Paradise*, Urbana, IL: Project Gutenberg. https://www.gutenberg.org/files/17860/17860-h/17860-h.htm.

Anttila, A., M. Adams, and M. Speriosu (2010), "The Role of Prosody in the English Dative Alternation," *Language and Cognitive Processes*, 25 (7–9): 946–81.

Baker-Bell, A. (2020), *Linguistic Justice: Black Language, Literacy, Identity and Pedagogy*, New York: Routledge.

Barnes, R. (2015), "Justices Uphold Robber's Sentencing in Case That Hinged on the Meaning of 'Accompany,'" January 13. https://www.washingtonpost.com/politics/courts_law/justices-uphold-robbers-sentencing-in-case-that-hinged-on-the-meaning-of-accompany/2015/01/13/b981dd1e-9b51-11e4-a7ee-526210d665b4_story.html.

Baron, D. (2022), *You Can't Always Say What You Want*, Cambridge: Cambridge University Press.

Baugh, J. (1984), "Steady: Progressive Aspect in Black Vernacular English," *American Speech*, 59 (1): 3–12.

Baugh, J. (2018), *Linguistics in Pursuit of Justice*, Cambridge: Cambridge University Press.

Bayley, R. (2012), "Chicano English," In B. Kortmann, and K. Lunkenheimer (eds), *The Mouton World Atlas of Variation in English*, 156–65, Berlin: De Gruyter Mouton.

Bayley, R., and O. Santa Ana (2004), "Chicano English: Morphology and Syntax," In B. Kortmann, E. Schneider, K. Burridge, R. Mesthrie, and C. Upton (eds), *A Handbook of Varieties of English*, vol. 2, 374–90, Berlin/New York: Mouton de Gruyter.

BBC.com (2018), "The Commas that Cost Companies Millions." https://www.bbc.com/worklife/article/20180723-the-commas-that-cost-companies-millions.

Becker, K., C. Farrington, T. Kendall, C. Tacata, and J. McLean (2021), T*he Corpus of Regional African American Language: LES* (Lower East Side, NY 2008). Version 2021.07, Eugene, OR: The Online Resources for African American Language Project.

Bresnan, J., A. Cueni, T. Nikitina, and R. H. Baayen (2007), "Predicting the Dative Alteration," In G. Bouma, I. Kramer, and J. Zwarts (eds), *Cognitive Foundations of Interpretation*, 69–94, Chicago, IL: University of Chicago.

Brown, R. (1973), *A First Language: The Early Stages*, Boston, MA: Harvard University Press.

Bibliography

Brown, T. J. (2024), "*Punctuation,*" Encyclopedia Britannica, May 1. https://www.britannica.com/topic/punctuation.

Burrell, A., and R. Beard (2024), "Playful Punctuation in Primary Children's Narrative Writing," *Research Papers in Education*, 39 (2): 249–76.

Bybee, J. (2010), *Language, Usage and Cognition*, Cambridge: Cambridge University Press.

Callahan, E. (2017), "Interlanguage and Cross-generational Assimilation: Past Tense Unmarking in Hispanicized English," *Journal of English Linguistics*, 45 (2): 103–29. DOI: 10.1177/0075424217702948.

Cambridge University Press (2021), "*Get* Passive," Dictionary Cambridge.org. https://dictionary.cambridge.org/us/grammar/british-grammar/get-passive.

Chambers, J. K., and P. Trudgill (2004), *Dialectology*, 2nd edn, Cambridge: Cambridge University Press.

Chomsky, N. (1965), *Aspects of the Theory of Syntax*, Boston, MA: The MIT Press.

Chomsky, N. (1975), *Reflections on Language*, New York: Pantheon Books.

Chomsky, N. (1981), *Lectures on Government and Binding*. Dordrecht: Foris.

Chomsky, N. (1986), *Knowledge of Language: Its Nature, Origin and Use*, Westport: Praeger.

Coles, F. (2001), "The Authenticity of Yat: A real New Orleans dialect," *Southern Journal of Linguistics*, 25: 74–86.

College Board (2004), "Writing: A Ticket to Work … or a Ticket Out." http://www.collegeboard.com/prod_downloads/writingcom/writing-ticket-to-work.pdf.

Conrod, K. (2022), "Variation in English Gendered Pronouns: Analysis and Recommendations for Ethics in Linguistics," *Journal of Language & Sexuality*, 11 (2): 141–64. https://doi.org/10.1075/jls.20026.con.

Couper-Kuhlen, E. (2012), "Some Truths and Untruths about Final Intonation in Conversational Questions." In J. P. de Ruiter (ed), *Questions: Formal, Functional and Interactional Perspectives*, 123–45, Cambridge: Cambridge University Press. https://doi.org/10.1017/CBO9781139045414.009/.

Crain, S., and P. Pietroski (2001), "Nature, Nurture and Universal Grammar," *Linguistics and Philosophy*, 24 (2): 139–86.

Cummings, E. E. (n.d.), "E. E. Cummings Free Poetry Archive. Sonnets—Actualities: III. I Have Loved, Let Us See If That's All." (Available online at https://cummings.ee/book/and/poem/sonnets-actualities-iii/).

Curzan, A. (2003), *Gender Shifts in the History of English*, Cambridge: Cambridge University Press. https://doi.org/10.1017/CBO9780511486913.

Curzan, A., and M. Adams (2012), *How English Works: A Linguistic Introduction*, London: Pearson.

Cushing, I., and A. Carter (2022), "Using Young Adult Fiction to Interrogate Raciolinguistic Ideologies in Schools," *Literacy*, 56 (2): 106–19.

D'Annunzio, P. J. (2021), "Nearly $250K in Legal Fees in Trade Secret Case Hinged on Just 1 Word," July 13. https://www.law.com/thelegalintelligencer/2021/07/13/nearly-250k-in-legal-fees-in-trade-secret-case-hinged-on-just-1-word/.

Davies, M. (2018), *The iWeb Corpus*. (Available online at https://www.english-corpora.org/iWeb/).

Dayton, E. (1996), *Grammatical Categories of the Verb in African-American Vernacular English*, Ph.D. Thesis, University of Pennsylvania.

Delaney, R. (2000), *Dialect Map of American English*, Roberts Page. (Available online at http://robertspage.com/dialects.html).

Diessel, H. (2013), "Grammar and First Language Acquisition," In T. Hoffman, and G. Trousdale (eds), *The Oxford Handbook of Construction Grammar*, 347–64, Oxford: Oxford University Press.

Dryer, M. S., and M. Haspelmath (eds) (2013), *The World Atlas of Language Structures Online*, Leipzig: Max Planck Institute for Evolutionary Anthropology. (Available online at http://wals.info, Accessed on 2021-11-29).

Bibliography

Edwards, W. F. (1991), "A Comparative Description of Guyanese Creole and Black English Preverbal Aspect Marker Don," In W. F. Edwards, and D. Winford (eds), *Verb Phrase Patterns in Black English and Creole*, 240–55, Detroit, MI: Wayne State University Press.

Farrington, C., T. Kendall, P. S. Brooks, L. Jenson, C. Tacata, and J. McLean (2020), *The Corpus of Regional African American Language: ATL (Atlanta, GA 2017)*. Version 2020.05, The Online Resources for African American Language Project. https://oraal.github.io/coraal.

Figueroa, M., and A. Gerken (2019), "Experience with Morphosyntactic Paradigms Allows Toddlers to Tacitly Anticipate Overregularized Verb Forms Months before They Produce Them," *Cognition*, 191: 1–10.

Flores, N., and J. Rosa (2015), "Undoing Appropriateness: Raciolinguistic Ideologies and Language Diversity in Education," *Harvard Educational Review*, 85 (2): 149–71.

Fought, C. (2003), *Chicano English in Context*, London: Palgrave Macmillan.

Fought, C. (2006), *Language and Ethnicity*, Cambridge: Cambridge University Press.

Frost, R. (1923), "Stopping by Woods on a Snowy Evening," In E. C. Lathem (ed), *The Poetry of Robert Frost* Poetry Foundation. Henry Holt and Company, Inc. (Available online at https://www.poetryfoundation.org/poems/42891/stopping-by-woods-on-a-snowy-evening).

Fruehwald, J., and N. Myler (2015), "I'm Done My Homework. Case Assignment in a Stative Passive," *Linguistic Variation*, 15 (2): 141–68. DOI: https://doi.org/10.1075/lv.15.2.01fru.

Garner, B. (1995), *A Dictionary of Modern Legal Usage*, 2nd edn, Oxford: Oxford University Press.

Gaston, P. (2011), "Drama SO," *Yale Grammatical Diversity Project: English in North America*. (Available online at http://ygdp.yale.edu/phenomena/drama-so. Accessed on 2020-11-07). Updated by Tom McCoy (2015) and Katie Martin (2018).

Gonzalez, C. (2020), "Tryna," *Yale Grammatical Diversity Project: English in North America*. (Available online at http://ygdp.yale.edu/phenomena/tryna. Accessed on 2024-10-03).

Green, L. (2002), *African American English: A Linguistic Introduction*, Cambridge: Cambridge University Press.

Green, L. (2011), *Language and the African American Child*, Cambridge: Cambridge University Press.

Harmon, M. R., and M. J. Wilson (2006), *Beyond Grammar: Language, Power, and the Classroom*, New York: Routledge.

Harris, A., and J. Wood (2013), "Stressed BIN," *Yale Grammatical Diversity Project: English in North America*. (Available online at http://ygdp.yale.edu/phenomena/stressed-bin. Accessed on 2023-09-21). Updated by Tom McCoy (2015) and Katie Martin (2018).

Henner, J., C. L. Caldwell-Harris, R. Novogrodsky, and R. Hoffmeister (2016), "American Sign Language Syntax and Analogical Reasoning Skills are Influenced by Early Acquisition and Age of Entry to Signing Schools for the Deaf," *Frontiers in Psychology*, 7: 1–14.

Henner, J., R. Novogrodsky, C. L. Caldwell-Harris, and R. Hoffmeister (2019), "The Development of American Sign Language-Based Analogical Reasoning in Signing Deaf Children," *Journal of Speech, Language & Hearing Research*, 62 (1): 93–105.

Hoffmann, T., and G. Trousdale (2013), *The Oxford Handbook of Construction Grammar*, Oxford: Oxford University Press.

Huang, N. (2011), "Multiple Modals," *Yale Grammatical Diversity Project: English in North America*. (Available online at http://ygdp.yale.edu/phenomena/multiple-modals. Accessed on 2024-02-23). Updated by Tom McCoy (2015) and Katie Martin (2018).

Huang, N., and T. McCoy (2015), "Personal Datives," *Yale Grammatical Diversity Project: English in North America*. (Available online at http://ygdp.yale.edu/phenomena/personal-datives. Accessed on 2021-12-22). Updated by Katie Martin (2018).

Iida, P. (2020), *The Concise APA Handbook: APA*, 7th edn, Charlotte, NC: Information Age Publishing.

Bibliography

Johnstone, B. (2013), *Speaking Pittsburghese: The Story of a Dialect*, Oxford: Oxford University Press.

Jones, T., J. R. Kalbfeld, R. Hancock, and R. Clark (2019), "Testifying while Black: An Experimental Study of Court Reporter Accuracy in Transcription of African American English," *Language*, 95 (2): e216–e252.

Kaplan, A. (2015), "Come With," *Yale Grammatical Diversity Project: English in North America*. (Available online at http://ygdp.yale.edu/phenomena/come-with. Accessed on 2024-03-22). Updated by Tom McCoy (2015) and Katie Martin (2018).

Kaplan, A., E. Scruton, and J. Wood (2017), "For to Infinitives," *Yale Grammatical Diversity Project: English in North America*. (Available online at http://ygdp.yale.edu/phenomena/for-to-infinitives. Accessed on 2024-09-15). Updated by Katie Martin (2018).

Kendall, T., and C. Farrington (2023), *The Corpus of Regional African American Language*. Version 2023.06. Eugene, OR: The Online Resources for African American Language Project. http://doi.org/10.7264/1ad5-6t35.

Kendall, T., M. Quartey, C. Farrington, J. McLarty, S. Arnson, and B. Josler (2018), *The Corpus of Regional African American Language: DCB (Washington, DC 2016)*. Version 2018.10.6, Eugene, OR: The Online Resources for African American Language Project. http://oraal.uoregon.edu/coraal.

Kendall, T., R. Fasold, C. Farrington, J. McLarty, S. Arnson, and B. Josler (2018), *The Corpus of Regional African American Language: DCA (Washington, DC 1968)*. Version 2018.10.06, Eugene, OR: The Online Resources for African American Language Project. http://oraal.uoregon.edu/coraal.

King, S., C. Farrington, T. Kendall, E. Mullen, S. Arnson, and L. Jenson (2020), *The Corpus of Regional African American Language: ROC (Rochester, NY 2016)*. Version 2020.05, Eugene, OR: The Online Resources for African American Language Project. http://oraal.uoregon.edu/coraal.

Kohn, M., W. Wolfram, C. Farrington, J. Renn, and J. Van Hofwegen (2020), *African American Language: Language Development from Infancy to Adulthood*, Cambridge: Cambridge University Press. DOI: 10.1017/9781108869607.

LGBTQ+ Resource Center, UW-Milwaukee (2021), *Gender Pronouns*, University Wisconsin-Milwaukee. (Available online at https://uwm.edu/lgbtrc/support/gender-pronouns/).

Lindemann, L. (2018), "What All," *Yale Grammatical Diversity Project: English in North America*. (Available online at http://ygdp.yale.edu/phenomena/what-all. Accessed on 2021-02-19). Updated by Katie Martin (2018).

Lippi-Green, R. (2012), *English with an Accent: Language, Ideology and Discrimination in the United States*, 2nd edn, New York: Routledge.

Loosen, S., and T. McMurtry (2019), "Extending the Conversation: Two Teachers' Response to Linguists." In M. D. Devereaux, and C.C. Palmer (eds), *Teaching Language Variation in the Classroom: Strategies and Models from Teachers and Linguists*, 120–5, London: Routledge.

MacWhinney, B., and E. Bates (1989), *The Crosslinguistic Study of Sentence Processing*, Cambridge: Cambridge University Press.

MacWhinney, B., and W. O'Grady (2015), *The Handbook of Language Emergence*, Hoboken, NJ: John Wiley & Sons.

Maher, Z., and J. Wood (2011), "Needs Washed," *Yale Grammatical Diversity Project: English in North America*. (Available online at http://ygdp.yale.edu/phenomena/needs-washed. Accessed on 2023-04-14). Updated by Tom McCoy (2015) and Katie Martin (2018).

Maher, Z., and T. McCoy (2011), "Positive Anymore," *Yale Grammatical Diversity Project: English in North America*. (Available online at http://ygdp.yale.edu/phenomena/positive-anymore. Accessed on 2024-02-23). Updated by Katie Martin (2018).

Mallinson, C., A. C. Charity Hudley, L. R. Strickling, and M. Figa (2011), "A Conceptual Framework for Promoting Linguistic and Educational Change," *Language and Linguistics Compass*, 5 (7): 441–53. DOI:10.1111/j.1749-818X.2011.00289.x.

Martin, K. (2018a), "Perfective Done," *Yale Grammatical Diversity Project: English in North America*. (Available online at http://ygdp.yale.edu/phenomena/perfective-done. Accessed on 2021-06-21).

Martin, K. (2018b), "Steady," *Yale Grammatical Diversity Project: English in North America*. (Available online at http://ygdp.yale.edu/phenomena/steady. Accessed on 2021-06-21).

Martinez, R. (2018), "After-Perfects," *Yale Grammatical Diversity Project: English in North America*. (Available online at http://ygdp.yale.edu/phenomena/after-perfects. Accessed on 2021-06-21). Updated by Oliver Shoulson (2020).

Martinez, R., and J. Wood (2023), "Relative Possessive *That's*," *Yale Grammatical Diversity Project: English in North America*. (Available online at http://ygdp.yale.edu/phenomena/. Accessed on 2024-09-12).

Matyiku, S. (2011a), "A-prefixing," *Yale Grammatical Diversity Project: English in North America*. (Available online at http://ygdp.yale.edu/phenomena/a-prefixing. Accessed on 2024-02-24). Updated by Tom McCoy (2015) and Katie Martin (2018).

Matyiku, S. (2011b), "Negative Concord," *Yale Grammatical Diversity Project: English in North America*. (Available online at http://ygdp.yale.edu/phenomena/negative-concord. Accessed on 2024-02-24). Updated by Tom McCoy (2015) and Katie Martin (2018).

McCoy, T. (2016a), "All the Further," *Yale Grammatical Diversity Project: English in North America*. (Available online at http://ygdp.yale.edu/phenomena/all-the-further. Accessed on 2020-11-07). Updated by Katie Martin (2018) and Oliver Shoulson (2020).

McCoy, T. (2016b), "Subject Contact Relatives," *Yale Grammatical Diversity Project: English in North America*. (Available online at http://ygdp.yale.edu/phenomena/subject-contact-relatives. Accessed on 2024-03-06). Updated by Katie Martin (2018) and Oliver Shoulson (2020).

McMillan, J. B. (1980), "Infixing and Interposing in English," *American Speech*, 55 (3): 163–83.

McMurtry, T. (2022), "Prioritizing Black Language: Teacher Reflection Plus Action," *English Journal*, 111 (5): 41–9.

McMurtry, T. (2023), "'Changing the Course of the Stream': A Retrospective Analysis of Artful Language Learning Opportunities," *Journal of Adolescent & Adult Literacy*, 67 (2): 74–84.

McWhorter, J. (2000), *Spreading the Word: Language & Dialect in America*, Portsmouth, VI: Heinemann.

Megna, M. (2024), "Pet Ownership Statistics 2024," *Forbes Advisor*, January 25. (Available online at https://www.forbes.com/advisor/pet-insurance/pet-ownership-statistics/#:~:text=Pet%20ownership%20in%20the%20U.S.,part%20of%20their%20owners'%20lives).

Merriam-Webster (n.d.), "Can vs. May." (Available online at https://www.merriam-webster.com/grammar/when-to-use-can-and-may).

Millemann, M. A., and S. D. Schwinn (2006), "Teaching Legal Research and Writing with Actual Legal Work: Extending Clinical Education into the First Year," *Clinical Law Review*, 12: 441–99.

Mills, B. (2022), Do All Adverbs End in "-Ly"? What Are Flat Adverbs and What Makes Them Special? *Quick and Dirty Tips: Do Things Better*, April 28. https://www.quickanddirtytips.com/articles/do-all-adverbs-end-in-ly/.

Mitchell, K. M. (2018), "Constructing Writing Practices in Nursing," *Journal of Nursing Education*, 57 (7): 399–407.

Mufwene, S. S., J. R. Rickford, G. Bailey, and J. Baugh (1998), *African-American English: Structure, History, and Use*. New York: Routledge.

Mustanoja, T. F. (1960), *A Middle English Syntax*. (Mémoires de la Société Néophilologique de Helsinki xxiii.), Helsinki: Société Néophilologiq.

Bibliography

O'Grady, W., and S. W. Cho (2001), "First Language Acquisition," In W. O'Grady, J. Archibald, M. Aronoff, and J. Rees-Miller (eds), *Contemporary Linguistics: An Introduction*, 409–48, Bedford: St. Martin's.

OpenAI (2024), *ChatGPT* (3.5 version) [Large Language Model]. https://chat.openai.com/chat.

ORAAL (2021), Online Resources for African American Language. Glossary of Terms. https://oraal.uoregon.edu/glossary.

Orwell, G. (1946), "Politics and the English Language," *Literary Cavalcade*, 54 (5): 20–6.

Parsard, K. (2016), "Null Copula," *Yale Grammatical Diversity Project: English in North America*. (Available online at http://ygdp.yale.edu/phenomena/null-copula. Accessed on 2024-07-13). Updated by Jim Wood (2017) and Katie Martin (2018).

Practical Law Commercial (2013), "NAD: Superlative Adjectives in Comparative Ad Claims are Not Puffery," August 16. (Available online at https://content.next.westlaw.com/5-538-1025?__lrTS=20200721130640396&transitionType=Default&contextData=(sc.Default)&firstPage=true).

Quartey, M., C. Farrington, T. Kendall, L. Jenson, C. Tacata, and J. McLean (2020), *The Corpus of Regional African American Language: VLD (Valdosta, GA 2017)*. Version 2021.07, Eugene, OR: The Online Resources for African American Language Project.

Quirk, R., S. Greenbaum, G. Leech, and J. Svartvik (1985), *A Comprehensive Grammar of the English Language*, New York: Longman.

Reaser, J., and W. Wolfram (2007). *Voices of North Carolina: From the Atlantic to Appalachia –Teacher's manual*. Raleigh, NC: Languages and Life Project at NC State. https://cdn.chass.ncsu.edu/sites/linguistics.chass.ncsu.edu/documents/teacher_hi-res.pdf

Reaser, J., C. T. Adger, W. Wolfram, and D. Christian (2017a), *Dialects at School: Education Linguistically Diverse Students*, New York: Routledge.

Reaser, J., C. T. Adger, W. Wolfram, and D. Christian (2017b), *Instructor and Student Resource Website – Chapter 1: An Introduction to Language Variation in America*. https://routledgetextbooks.com/textbooks/9781138777453/chapters.php.

Rickford, J. R., and S. King (2016), "Language and Linguistics on Trial: Hearing Rachel Jeantel (And Other Vernacular Speakers) in the Courtroom and beyond," *Language*, 92 (4): 948–88.

Roger, S., W. Wolfram, C. Farrington, T. Kendall, J. McLean, and C. Tacata (2023), *The Corpus of Regional African American Language: DTA (Detroit, MI 1966)*. Version 2023.06, Eugene, OR: The Online Resources for African American Language Project.

Rosa, J., and N. Flores (2017), "Unsettling Race and Language: Toward a Raciolinguistic Perspective," *Language in Society*, 46 (5): 621–47.

Rowe, R., W. Wolfram, T. Kendall, C. Farrington, and B. Josler (2018), *The Corpus of Regional African American Language: PRV (Princeville, NC 2004)*. Version 2018.10.06, Eugene, OR: The Online Resources for African American Language.

Rubin, A. (2015), *Diabetes for Dummies*, 5th edn, Hoboken, NJ: Wiley.

Ruffing, K. (2012), "Liketa," *Yale Grammatical Diversity Project: English in North America*. (Available online at http://ygdp.yale.edu/phenomena/liketa. Accessed on 2021-03-31). Updated by Tom McCoy (2015) and Katie Martin (2018).

Smitherman, G. (1974), "Response to Hunt, Meyers, et al.," *College English*, 35 (6), 729–32. https://doi.org/10.2307/375269.

Smitherman, G. (2006), *Word from the Mother: Language and African Americans*, New York: Routledge.

Staub, P., and J. Zentz (2017), "Fixin' To," *Yale Grammatical Diversity Project: English in North America*. (Available online at http://ygdp.yale.edu/phenomena/fixin-to. Accessed on 2024-03-07). Updated by Katie Martin (2018).

Strunk, W., and E. B. White (2000), *The Elements of Style*, 4th edn, Oxford: Allyn and Bacon.

Tenny, C. (1998), "Psych Verbs and Verbal Passives in Pittsburghese," *Linguistics*, 36 (3): 591–8.

Terry, J. M. (2010), "Variation in the Interpretation and Use of the African American English Preverbal Done Construction," *American Speech*, 85 (1): 3–32.

Tomasello, M. (2003), *Constructing a Language: A Usage-Based Theory of Language Acquisition*, Boston, MA: Harvard University Press.

Tonouchi, L. A. (2004), "Da State of Pidgin Address," *College English*, 67 (1): 75–82. https://doi.org/10.2307/4140726.

University of South Carolina (n.d.), Grammar and Syntax of Smoky Mountain English (SME). (Available online at https://appalachian-english.library.sc.edu/node/796.html).

Vygotsky, L. (1978), "Interaction between Learning and Development," In M. Gauvain, and G. M. Cole (eds), *Readings on the Development of Children*, 34–40, New York: Scientific American Books.

Warburton, T., and B. Dorough (1973), *SCHOOLHOUSE ROCK!*, USA. https://www.loc.gov/item/jots.200022677.

Weber, D. (2012), "English Prepositions: A Historical Survey," Unpublished Thesis Submitted to the Faculty of Arts. University of Masaryk.

Wolfram, W., and D. Christian (1976), *Appalachian Speech*, Arlington, TX: Center for Applied Linguistics.

Wolfram W., and N. Schilling-Estes (2000), *American English: Dialects and Variation*, Oxford: Blackwell.

Wood, J. (2012), "Double Comparatives," *Yale Grammatical Diversity Project: English in North America*. (Available online at http://ygdp.yale.edu/phenomena/double-comparatives. Accessed on 2020-11-07). Updated by Tom McCoy (2015) and Katie Martin (2018).

Wood, J. (2013), "The Alls Construction," *Yale Grammatical Diversity Project: English in North America*. (Available online at http://ygdp.yale.edu/phenomena/alls-construction. Accessed on 2021-2-19). Updated by Tom McCoy (2015), Katie Martin (2018), and Oliver Shoulson (2020).

Wood, J. (2014), "Done My Homework," *Yale Grammatical Diversity Project: English in North America*. (Available online at http://ygdp.yale.edu/phenomena/done-my-homework. Accessed on 2023-04-14). Updated by Tom McCoy (2015), Katie Martin (2018), and Oliver Shoulson (2020).

Wood, J. (2015), "Dative Presentatives," *Yale Grammatical Diversity Project: English in North America*. (Available online at http://ygdp.yale.edu/phenomena/dative-presentatives. Accessed on 2023-09-21). Updated by Katie Martin (2018), Jim Wood (2019).

Wood, J. (2024), "Wicked," *Yale Grammatical Diversity Project: English in North America*. (Available online at http://ygdp.yale.edu/phenomena/wicked. Accessed on 2024-08-29).

Yale Grammatical Diversity Project: English in North America (2021). https://ygdp.yale.edu/.

Young, V. A. (2019), "Greetings from the 2019 Program Chair," In *Program for Seventieth Annual Convention Conference on College Composition and Communication*, 4–6, Urbana, IL: National Council of Teachers of English.

Zanuttini, R., and K. Martin (2017), "Invariant Be," *Yale Grammatical Diversity Project: English in North America*. (Available online at http://ygdp.yale.edu/phenomena/invariant-be. Accessed on 2021-12-21).

INDEX

A

AAE (*see also* African American English)
  be verb 82
  completive done 261
  dependent possessives 158
  double comparative 71
  double modals 137
  double negation 142
  dummy do 140
  features 16–19
  habitual be 263–4
  multiple negation 142
  negative concord 142
  null copula 131
  past perfect marking 254
  past tense marking 108, 115–16, 248
  plural marking 53–5, 57–8
  possession 55
  possessive determiner 170
  progressive aspect 258–9
  pronunciation 113
  remote time Bin 264–5
  Smitherman 4
  social dialect 4
  stigmatized 5
  systematic 5
  third person singular 114
  variety 5, 8
  zero copula 131, 230–1
AC (*see also* adverbial complement) 199–200, 235, 237–8
adjective 16, 28, 67
  attributive 1–2, 11, 34, 68, 78–9, 106
  comparative and superlative 3, 70–7, 183
  morphology of 29–33, 68–75, 125
  number and order of 80
  predicative 78–84
  premodifiers 81, 189, 192
  vs. determiner 12, 173
  vs. noun 63
adjective phrase (*see also* AdjP) 2, 34, 187, 189, 200
AdjP (*see also* adjective phrase) 2, 34, 187, 189, 200, 202
adverb 16, 87–8, 204
  comparative and superlative 71, 94–6, 102
  degree 91, 93
  flat 91–2
  morphology of 29–33, 93–4, 96–7, 124
  of manner (*see also* manner adverb) 90
  of place (*see also* place adverb) 90
  of stance (*see also* stance adverb) 91
  of time (*see also* time adverb) 90
  placement 34, 79–80, 83, 98–9, 184
  premodifiers 99–100
adverb phrase (*see also* AdvP) 34–5, 203
adverbial 100, 199
  clause 300–2
  complement 199, 235–6, 300
AdvP (*see also* adverb phrase) 34–5, 203–7
AE (*see also* Appalachian English) 4, 260
affix 29–31, 250, 256, 285
African American English (*see also* AAE)
  features 16–19
  social dialect 4
ain't 142, 144–5
alls construction 17, 162
American Sign Language (ASL) 3, 22
analytic construction (*see also* periphrastic construction) 74
antecedent 163, 304
Appalachian English (*see also* AE) 4, 153, 260
apposition 309–10, 333
appositive 309–10
a-prefixing 18, 260
article 12, 59, 170, 172
  definite and indefinite 28, 170, 174
aspect 109, 245–7, 249, 255–6, 258, 272, 283–6
  after-perfect 18, 262
  a-prefixing 261
  completive done 261
  continuous (*see also* progressive) 248
  done my homework 261
  fixing to do/finna 260–1
  future perfect 254–5
  future perfect progressive 257–8
  future progressive 250–1
  habitual *be* 263–4
  past perfect progressive 256–8
  perfect 261–2
  perfective 213, 262
  perfective aspect 131–2, 213, 261
  present perfect progressive 256
  progressive 18, 109, 130
  remote time Bin 264–5
aspectual system 258, 263
attributive position 78–80

Index

auxiliary *be* 130
    future-ness 251
auxiliary verb (*see also* helping verb) 28, 118, 122, 128–45

B
barely, in ChE 16, 35, 90
be absence (*see also* copula absence, null copula, zero copula) 18

C
cardinal numeral 181
case ending 153
central modal 133–6
ChE (*see also* Chicano English) 5
    features 16–18
    social dialect 16
    stigmatized 7
Chicano English (*see also* ChE) 5
    social dialect 16
Chomsky, Noam 13
    Language Acquisition Device (LAD) 13
    Universal Grammar 13
Christian (Donna) 4
clause 36–7, 42–5
    dependent 44, 179–80, 220, 296, 299, 330, 334
    embedded 296, 301, 320
    finite 286
    gerund 106, 315–16
    independent 43–4, 178–80, 200, 220, 297–9, 305–8, 330–1, 338–9
    infinitival 312
    -ing clause 312, 316–17, 321
    main 181, 277, 299, 304
    nominal relative 311
    non-finite 312, 315, 318–19
    non-restrictive relative 304–5, 335
    participle 318–19
    reduced relative 308–9
    relative 163–4, 303–7
    restrictive relative 304–5, 335
    simple 296
    subordinate 181, 298–301, 311, 337
    that-clause 301–2, 307
    to-clause 312–16
closed-class words (*see also* open-class words) 28, 129, 150, 158, 169, 178, 183
colon 339
come *with* 17
comma 178, 180–1, 277, 331–7
    Oxford 332–4
comma splice 329
command (*see also* imperative) 276–7
complement 61
completive *done* 18, 261

complex transitive 119, 122, 233, 237
conjunction 28, 169, 177–8, 183–4, 297–300, 331–2, 336–7
conjunctive adverb 338
constituent 25, 36–40, 42
    AdjP 201
    AdvP 211
    noun phrase 189
    PP 208
    required 119
    tests 221, 227, 236
constructivist approaches 14
coordinating conjunction 178, 297, 331, 336
coordination 295, 297–8
coordinators 169, 177–8
    coordinating conjunction 178, 297, 331, 336
    FANBOYS 178
    subordinating conjunction 179, 299–301
copula absence (*see also be* absence, null copula, zero copula) 19, 230
copula verb (*see also* linking verb) 19, 61, 79, 82, 121–2
    subject complement 202, 230
co-reference 155–6
cummings, e. e. 151, 329
    "Sonnets: Realities III" 329

D
dangling modifier (*see also* dangling participle) 320–1, 324
dangling participle (*see also* dandling modifier) 320
dative presentative 19, 229
degree adverb 16, 91–2
deletion test 190, 195
deontic meaning 136
dependent possessive 157–8
dependent quantifier 162
derivation 29, 31–2, 50, 56, 68, 74, 93, 96, 113
derivational morphology 56
derivational suffix 29–30, 124
    adjectives 68–70, 75–7, 289
    adverbs 93–4, 96–7
    nouns 50–1, 56–7
    verbs 107, 113–14
descriptive grammar 9, 11
descriptive rule 9, 42
determiner 9, 26, 170–1
    adjective vs. determiner 173–4
    central 172
    demonstrative 161, 170–2
    interrogative 165
    possessive 55–6
    post-determiner 173–4
    pre-determiner 174
    pronoun vs. determiner 150, 161, 163–4

Index

quantifying 171–2
singular and plural agreement 171–2
with nouns 34, 59–60, 172
dialect continuum 4–5
direct object (*see also* DO) 9, 19, 36–7, 61
   direct object absence 229
   ditransitive verb 121
   ing-clauses 316
   monotransitive verb 120
   nouns as 198–
   sentence patterns 224, 226, 233
   to-clauses 313
DO (*see also* direct object) 9, 61–2, 120–2
   dative presentative 229
   direct object absence 229
   sentence patterns 224–7, 229–31, 233–4, 237
   testing 227, 234
do-support (*see also* dummy do, dummy operator) 140, 274, 276
double comparative 71–2, 74, 77, 88
double modal 18, 213
double negative(s) (*see also* multiple negation, negative concord) 9, 142
Drama so/Drama SO 16, 92
dummy do 140, 274, 276
dummy operator 140, 274, 276

E

East Coast English (ECE) 2, 5, 261
echo question 305, 306
embedded clause 239, 296, 301
   dangling modifiers 320, 322
   dangling participles 320, 322
   relative clause 303, 306
   to-clause 313–14
em-dash 340
end punctuation 330
epistemic meaning 136
exclamation point 40, 182, 273, 331
exclamatives 272

F

finite verb 286–7, 312
finiteness 245
finna/fixing to 18, 260
flat adverb 91–2
for/to-rephrasing test 227
Frost, Robert 333
   "Stopping by Woods on a Snowy Evening" 333
function words 28, 169–70, 176

G

gender-neutral pronoun 28, 158–9
gerund 106, 315–16
Global Englishes 2

going-to future 250–1
grammar (*see also* syntax) 3–5, 8–15
grammatical hierarchy 44–5, 206
grammatical voice 279
   active 9, 131, 271, 279, 281–5
   antipassive 285
   middle voice 282
   passive 18, 130–1, 279–85
      full 280
      get- 282
      truncated 280
grammaticality 2, 16, 98

H

habitual *be* 18, 263–4
Hawaiian Pidgin English (HPE) (*see* Hawaiian Creole English, HCE) 328
head word 190
helping verb (*see also* auxiliary verb) 121, 130, 135

I

imperative (*see also* command) 118, 224
imperative mood 224, 276–8, 311
indicative mood 272
   declarative 139–40, 272–5
   exclamatives 272
   interrogative 139–40
indirect object (*see also* IO) 9, 19, 61
   nouns as 198–9
   pronouns as 153
   selection of ditransitive verb 120
   sentence patterns 226, 233
infinitive 9, 109, 253, 289, 312
   bare 134, 246, 248, 250, 257, 278
   base 10, 108, 112, 255, 276, 289, 311
   full 10, 108, 135, 246
   marker 10
   post modal 137
   split 10
   to-clauses 312, 314
infix 31
inflection 29, 31–2, 51
   adjectives 70, 75
   adverbs 94, 96
   nouns 56
   passive voice 285
   verbs 107, 113, 246
inflectional morphology 70, 107, 113–14, 124
inflectional suffix 30, 32, 51–2, 54, 56–8, 72, 74–7, 83, 108–9, 114–15, 124, 246, 249
interjection(s) 169, 181–3
internal commas 339
intonation 182, 273
intransitive 119–21, 223, 237
inversion test 221–2, 274

Index

IO (*see also* indirect object) 9, 61, 120–2, 226–9, 233, 238, 280
    test 234

L

Language Acquisition Device (LAD) 13
Latin 10, 31, 150, 252, 285
lexical category
    defined 33
lexical verb 63, 118–19, 130
liketa 18, 134–5, 137
linguistic discrimination 2, 8, 15–16
linguistic prejudice 15
linking verb (*see also* copula verb) 19, 61, 79, 82, 121–2
    subject complement 202, 230
-*ly* suffix 91–4, 96–7, 101, 124

M

main verb 181, 277, 299, 304
Mainstream American English (MAE) 6
mandative subjunctive 278
Midwestern English (ME) 4–5, 135
    come *with* 17
modal auxiliary 18, 133, 136–8, 212–13, 257
    central 133–5
    marginal 133–5
modal verb (*see also* modal auxiliary) 134, 136
mood 271
    imperative 118, 224, 272, 276–7
    indicative 272
    mandative 278
    regular 277
    subjunctive 272, 277
    were- 277
Moore, Clement Clarke 341
    Twas the Night Before Christmas 341
Moore, Marianne 341
    "A Jelly-Fish" 341
morpheme 29, 31
    bound roots 31
    free roots 29, 50–1
    null 52–3, 57
    zero 52–3, 57
morphological criteria
    adjectives 67
    adverbs 31, 93–6
    nouns 49
    verbs 105
morphological evidence
    adjective 63, 75–7
    adverbs 96
    nouns 56–8
    object 152
    subject 152
    verbs 106, 113

morphology 3, 25, 27, 29, 33
movement test 39–40
    adverbs 88
    prepositional phrases 208
multiple negation (*see also* double negative, negative concord) 19, 142–4

N

nativist theories 13
needs washed 2, 4, 18, 135, 282
negation 19, 141–4
    multiple negation 19, 142–4
    single negation 143
negative concord (*see also* double negative, multiple negation) 142
nominal relative clause 311
non-finite 286–90
    clauses 312
    -*ing* clauses 315
    past participle clauses 318
    POSTs 319
non-standard 7, 112–13
non-standard dialects 27, 33, 55, 108, 111–12, 116–17, 135, 140, 153
    dependent possessives 158
    negation 142
    present aspect 252
    reflexive pronouns 155
non-standardized English (non-sE) 7–8, 15–16, 27, 53, 91
non-stigmatized 6, 7
noun
    abstract 171–2
    concrete 172
    count 34, 59, 174
    non-count 54
    possessive 171
noun phrase (*see also* NP) 149, 184, 187, 189, 198, 265
NP (*see also* noun phrase) 34–6, 62, 78, 187, 189–90
    antecedent 163
    apposition 309–10
    appositive 309
    commas 332–3
    dangling modifiers 320
    dangling participles 320
    demonstrative pronouns 160
    dependent demonstratives 161
    dependent possessives 158
    determiners 170, 173–4
    DO 234
    embedding 205
    functions 198–9
    independent quantifying pronouns 161
    ing-clauses 316
    intransitive verbs 119

Index

monotransitive verbs 120
object of the preposition 198
OC 235
one-word replacement test 150, 201
plural test 196
predicates 118
premodifiers 190–5, 202–3
prepositional complement 207
prepositional phrases 149, 176, 209–10
POSTs 210, 214, 225, 319
postmodifiers 192–4
relative clause 309
SC 232
semicolons 339
S-V-IO-DO 228
to-clauses 313
null copula (*see also* be absence, copula absence, zero copula) 19, 131, 230
number agreement 172–3
numeral
   cardinal 181–2
   ordinal 181–2

O
object complement (*see also* OC) 122, 198–9, 202–3, 233
object form 153, 158–9, 305, 314
object of the preposition (*see also* preposition complement) 27, 35, 62, 152, 198, 207, 306, 316
object slot 131, 152
OC (*see also* object complement) 122, 203, 210–11, 236
   adjective 82–3
   nouns 61–2
   sentence patterns 233, 235, 237
   test for 234
one-word replacement test (*see also* pronoun replacement test) 36
OP (*see also* object of the preposition, preposition complement) 207
open-class words (*see also* closed-class words) 28, 83, 124, 129, 181, 183
orthography 26–7, 113
Oxford comma 332–3

P
paradigmatic evidence 49, 60, 64, 67, 82, 87, 101, 105, 123, 173–4
participial adjective 69, 106
past participle 17, 109
   irregular verbs 110, 117
   leveling 17
   passive 131
PC (*see also* prepositional object, object of the preposition) 62, 207–8

period 40, 180, 330, 337–8
periphrastic construction (*see also* analytic construction) 74, 76–7, 83, 94, 96–7
person 108–9, 111–12, 114–15, 123–4, 135, 153–4, 156–7, 259
personal dative 17, 155–6
phrase 33, 35, 43, 189
   deletion test 190, 195, 200
   embedded 202–3, 205, 207, 210–11
   head 190
   movement test 39
   phrase vs. constituent 35
   types 187
phrase structure 79, 181
Pittsburghese 8
plural –*s* 16, 30, 32–3, 52–3, 55–8, 196
plural test 196
pluralization 50–5
Poe, Edgar Allan 341
   The Unparalleled Adventure of One Hans Pfaall 341
positive anymore 19, 144
possessive '*s* 55
POST (*see also* postmodifier) 172, 192, 197, 209, 211, 225, 296, 302, 304, 313, 316–17, 377
postmodifier (*see also* POST) 192–4, 200–1, 207
poverty of stimulus 13
PP (*see also* prepositional phrase) 35, 62, 187, 198, 207–9
   adverbial 228–9
   POST 209–11
   relative clause 308
PRE (*see also* premodifier) 172–4, 191–8, 313
   adjective 200–2
   adverb 203–7
   derivational prefix 31
   -*ing* clause 316–17
   noun phrase 198, 225
   past participle 319
   prepositional phrase 208
   verb phrase 212
predicate 42–3, 49
   simple and complex sentences 177–8
   transitivity 118–22
predicative adjective 79–80, 82–3
prefix 29, 31, 121, 289
premodifier (*see also* PRE) 81, 191–4, 197, 201, 208
   to adverbs and adjectives 99
   to prepositions 100
   pronoun replacement test (*see also* one-word replacement test) 36
preposition 175
   locative 175
   variation 17
prepositional complement (*see also* PC, OP) 62, 207

362

Index

prepositional phrase 35, 207
prepositional phrase (*see also* PP) 176, 207, 209
prescriptive grammar 8–9
present participle 109, 114–15, 124, 130–1, 134, 249–50, 253, 255–7, 262–5, 287–9, 315
primary auxiliary 130–3, 137
pronoun 149–66
    demonstrative 160–1
    dependent possessive 158
    freestanding possessive 157
    gender-neutral 28, 108, 111, 158–9
    indefinite 161
    independent quantifying 161
    personal 17, 152–6
    possessive 17, 156–9
    pronoun variation 17
    quantifying 161–2
    reflexive 17, 156–9
    relative 17, 19, 163–4, 303–9
    resumptive 17
    zero subject 224
    zero-relative 309
pronoun replacement test (*see also* one-word replacement test 36, 150, 226, 315
punctuation 3, 40, 180, 327–40

Q

question
    formation 139–40
    mark 40, 273, 330
    test 40, 42, 108, 120, 201, 203, 208, 210, 221, 236, 299, 301
    wh- 211, 273–6
    yes/no 273, 330
question test 38–40

R

raciolinguistic ideologies 7
regional dialect 4, 21
regularized agreement 17
relative clause 163–4, 303, 305–9, 311, 321
remote time bin (been) 18, 264–5
reverse test 150
root
    bound 131
    free 29, 51, 53, 76, 94–5, 107

S

SAE (*see also* Southern American English) 4, 7–8, 14, 16–19, 52, 137, 142, 155
    a-prefixing 18
    be absence 18
    completive done 18, 158
    dative presentatives 19
    dialect labels 8
    double modals 18, 213
    fixing to do / *finna* 18
    habitual *be* 263
    liketa 18
    personal datives 17, 229
    present progressives 258
    subject contact relatives 19
SC (*see also* subject complement) 61, 82, 121
Schilling-Estes (Natalie) 4
Schoolhouse Rock 50, 89
sE (*see also* standardized English) 6–8, 16–17, 19, 27, 34
    aspect 263
    auxiliary verbs 213
    comparative and superlative 74
    dative presentative 229
    determiners 34, 173
    dependent possessives 158
    DO 229
    do support 140
    double comparative 72
    freestanding possessive pronouns 157
    IO 228
    modals 136–8
    negation 142
    OC 202
    past participle 119, 252, 254
    person 111
    plural 51–3, 196
    possessive 55
    present 113
    progressive 264
    pronouns 153
    reflexive pronoun 155
    relative pronoun 309
    SC 61, 202
    sentence patterns 237
    simple past tense 108, 113, 116
    subordination 180–1, 295, 297, 299
    SV 224
    third-person singular 108, 112, 135
    voice 283
    were subjunctive 277
    wh-words 275
second-person plural 17
semantics
    concept 26–7, 62, 90
    criteria 50
    evidence 62–4
semicolon 327, 330, 337–9
sentence patterns 132, 199, 203, 219–20, 223, 229, 236–7, 239, 300
sentence type(s)
    complex 44, 177, 179–80, 239, 295–6, 300, 334
    compound 177
    simple 177
serial comma 332

Index

Shakespeare 71, 321
   Hamlet 321
singular they 108, 199
Smitherman, Geneva 4, 341
   Response to Hunt Meyers et al, College English, 1974 341
social dialect 5, 135
Southern American English (SAE) 4, 52
split infinitive(s) 10
stance adverb 89–91, 94
Standard English 3, 6–7, 25
Standard Language Ideology 7
standardized English (sE) 2, 6–7
subject 41–3, 61, 118–20
   implied 224, 276, 309, 314, 320
   passive voice 131
subject-auxiliary inversion 276
subject complement (*see also* SC) 27, 36, 92, 121, 153, 198–9, 202–3, 207, 230–1
subject contact relatives 19
subject form 153–4, 159, 305
subject slot 29, 61, 131, 152, 224, 279–80, 314
subjunctive mood
   mandative 278
   regular 277
   were-subjunctive 277
subordination 180–1, 295, 299
subordinator 180, 299, 330
suffix 29–31
   adjective 68–9, 75–7, 289
   adverb 93–4, 96–7
   comparative 70, 74
      derivation 50–1
      double comparative 71–2
   inflection 51, 113, 124
   nouns 33, 57–8
   plural 51–5
   progressive 256
   reflexive 155
   -self/-selves 155
   superlative 71, 74, 76–7
   tense 246, 248–50
   third person singular 108
   verb 56–7, 107–9, 112–16
   zero morpheme 110–11
syntactic environment 28
   adjectives 78
   adverbs 98–9
   nouns 58
   verbs 117–18, 123
syntactic evidence 49–50, 62, 64, 67, 87
syntactic position (*see also* syntactic placement) 78, 87, 98, 105, 117, 319
syntactic punctuation 328

syntagmatic evidence 59, 63, 78–80
syntax (*see also* grammar) 3, 8, 19, 25, 27, 182, 224, 228
synthetic construction 74

T

tag 42
   tag-test/tag question 42, 61, 106, 221
tense
   future-tense-ness 246
   simple future 246, 248
   simple past 17, 108, 246, 248, 253, 261, 283–4
   simple present 246–8, 283
third person singular 108–9, 124, 227
time adverb 90
transitivity (*see also* verb type) 105, 121–2, 219

U

usage-based approaches 14

V

verb 9, 11, 18, 28, 105–28
   clause 220
   complement 61
   derivational suffixes 29, 32, 107, 113
   forms 246
   full 108
   infinitive 108
   inflectional suffixes 30, 32, 107, 113
   inversion test 222–3
   irregular 109–10, 116, 121, 253
   linking 79, 82
   location 42
   main vs. auxiliary 132
   modification of 88–9
   morphology 56, 58, 113
   participial adjectives 69
   predicate 42
   regular 109–10, 112–13, 116, 253
   replacement 60, 63
   strong 110
   subject verb order 41
   SVO 42
   syntactic position 78
   tense forms 108
   weak 110
verb phrase (*see also* VP) 19, 34, 42, 63, 212, 245
verb type (*see also* transitivity) 105, 119, 121–2
   complex 119, 122, 233
   copula (*see also* linking verb)
   ditransitive 119–22, 226, 237
   intransitive 119–22, 223, 237
   monotransitive 119–22, 125, 224, 237

Index

VP (*see also* verb phrase) 212–13
   auxiliary 130
   clauses 43, 106
   located in 118, 130
   multiple 177
   phrase types 35
   predicate choices 118
   types 119
Vygotsky, Lev 14

W
wh-question 211, 273, 330
wicked 16, 79, 88, 91
Wolfram (Walt) 4

Z
zero copula (*see also* be absence, absent copula, null copula) 113, 140, 230–1
zero-morpheme 110